Modernism and Copyright

Modernist Literature and Culture

Kevin J. H. Dettmar and Mark Wollaeger, Series Editors

Modernism and Copyright

Edited by

Paul K. Saint-Amour

OXFORD
UNIVERSITY PRESS

2011

OXFORD
UNIVERSITY PRESS

Oxford University Press, Inc., publishes works that further
Oxford University's objective of excellence
in research, scholarship, and education.

Oxford   New York
Auckland   Cape Town   Dar es Salaam   Hong Kong   Karachi
Kuala Lumpur   Madrid   Melbourne   Mexico   City Nairobi
New Delhi   Shanghai   Taipei Toronto

With offices in
Argentina   Austria   Brazil   Chile   Czech Republic   France   Greece
Guatemala   Hungary   Italy   Japan   Poland   Portugal   Singapore
South Korea   Switzerland   Thailand   Turkey   Ukraine   Vietnam

Published by Oxford University Press, Inc.
198 Madison Avenue, New York, New York 10016

www.oup.com

Oxford is a registered trademark of Oxford University Press.

Library of Congress Cataloging-in-Publication Data
Modernism & copyright / edited by Paul K. Saint-Amour.
    p. cm. — (Modernist literature & culture)
    Includes bibliographical references and index.
    ISBN 978-0-19-973153-4 (cloth : alk. paper)   ISBN 978-0-19-973154-1 (pbk. : alk. paper)
1. Copyright.   2. Copyright—Great Britain.   3. Modernism (Literature)
4. Law and literature.   I. Saint-Amour, Paul K.   II. Title: Modernism and copyright.
K1420.5.M63 2011
346.04'82—dc22   2010009509

1 3 5 7 9 8 6 4 2

Printed in the United States of America
on acid-free paper

For David Foster Wallace

Contents

Series Editors' Foreword

Choosing the first essay collection to appear in the Modernist Literature and Culture series felt like a big decision: a big decision that, ultimately, was no decision at all. Scholarly presses are rightly wary of taking a risk on collections, which often don't sell as well as monographs; in kicking off the series, Mark and I had an agreement with our editor, Shannon McLachlan, that we'd establish MLC exclusively with monographs. But we also knew that there would be room, when the time was right, for just the right collection.

And then at just the right moment, Paul Saint-Amour brought it to us: *Modernism and Copyright.* A collection "by many hands," in that quaint old publishing phrase, can prove its worth by doing one of two things. The first is to bring together ten or twelve luminaries to polish up a topic that has started to lose its luster. A mixture of established and younger scholars, for instance, on the current status of "the death of the Author" (still dead?), or *New Directions in [Your Problematic Here].* Such a volume serves to establish the state-of-the-discipline, or state-of-the-discourse: it might venture one or two forward-looking pieces, but its primary project is consolidation, as it attempts to master all it surveys.

Modernism and Copyright is not in the business of rehabbing well-worn ground. Rather, it earns its spot on the Modernist Literature & Culture list by giving shape to a field that has, to date, remained largely inchoate: the field so simply denominated in its title. This is the second great service that an edited volume can perform for the profession or the discipline: to focus, to galvanize, a scholarly conversation; to draw together the various threads in a conversation hitherto only dimly recognized *as* a conversation. In short, the most powerful collections of this kind help to establish a field of inquiry, and to provide it with a theoretical and methodological basis, where before one heard only individual voices crying in the scholarly wilderness. Before the intervention of this kind of collection, we know there's something happening but we don't know what it is: the volume comes along and gives it a name, and an intellectual center.

Writing for the first type of collection is a chore, something of a scholarly obligation (unless one happens to be the new kid in the volume); when writing for the second type, one has the sense of redrawing the boundaries of disciplinary inquiry, being part of something big.

We're very pleased with the wide range of essays in what might, to the uninitiated, sound like a somewhat narrow project; Paul Saint-Amour must be commended not just for this range, which he had the foresight to seek out, but for the very clear organization of paired essays on topics ranging from "Portraits of the Modernist as Copywright" to "The Fall and Rise of Remix Culture" to "Modernism after Modernism after Modernism." If this is the ideal first collection for the MLC series, Paul is ideally positioned at the center of this intellectual welter. His first book, *The Copywrights: Intellectual Property and the Literary Imagination* effectively put issues of intellectual property on the radar of modernist studies, and his years of working on these questions, in both very theoretical and highly practical terms, pay a great dividend here. "Modernism and the Lives of Copyright," Paul's introduction to the collection, goes far beyond the typical remit of a collection introduction, adumbrating at least two important new matrices for understanding the volume's titular interaction: his novel application of Foucaultian biopolitics to questions of copyright maximalism, on the one hand, and his deft deployment of counterfactual narratives, on the other. At the other end of the volume, *Modernism and Copyright* adapts an eminently practical FAQ for modernist scholars on questions of copyright, the public domain, fair use, and permissions, initially prepared by a group of scholars chaired by Saint-Amour at the behest of the International James Joyce Foundation.

In between these rich bookends, a wealth of information and provocation on modernism's vexed relationship with evolving international copyright systems and with adjacent regimes of privacy, publicity, and attribution: laws that modernist works provoked and contested, decried and celebrated.

We feel confident now in saying that modernism's interpellation within questions of intellectual property—and the inseparability of copyright law itself from the intellectual and juridical structures of modernism—has achieved the status of an important subfield within modernist studies. *Modernism and Copyright* is something like its establishing text; we're proud to have played a role in bringing the book to light.

Kevin J. H. Dettmar and Mark Wollaeger

Acknowledgments

Gravity and levity met often in the making of this book. My collaborators at Oxford University Press and its Modernist Literature and Culture series have been a delight to work with. I am grateful to Shannon McLachlan for encouraging me to undertake this project in the first place and for leavening the years of its assembly with her curiosity, enthusiasm, and commitment to scholarly access. Kevin Dettmar and Mark Wollaeger befriended the book early on, guiding its editor with their signature mix of wit, precision, and generosity. Amid his whiplash-quick responses to my queries, Brendan O'Neill made a strong case for faux chinchilla outerwear, even if he remained unaccountably skeptical about the magnificent Prefab Sprout. And two anonymous readers for the press gave the book a strong push toward its current shape.

Modernism and Copyright's contributors are an exceptional, and exceptionally patient, group of writers; each of them has my gratitude and admiration. I would like to single out Robert Spoo for particular thanks: he not only contributed the book's opening essay but also served as the project's unofficial legal advisor. Bob's friendship and good will were nothing less than this book's enabling conditions. My research assistant, Beth Blum, was dauntless in pursuit of documents, alive to serendipities, and a terrific interlocutor. Jed Esty helped me to sharpen my introduction, and Hilary Schor, Caroline Levine, and Richard Begam supplied crucial hints and correctives. The vigilant Merryl Sloane copyedited the manuscript, saving us from innumerable lapses.

Karen Green, thank you for haiku, machines, and your marvelous cover art. Alison, Claire, and Julia, thank you for bringing me back to earth, eternally and ever Aspen Street.

Modernism and Copyright

Introduction

Modernism and the Lives of Copyright

Paul K. Saint-Amour

No one listening to the hit records "I Got You Babe" or "The Beat Goes On" in the 1960s would have singled out their writer, Sonny Bono, as the future patron saint of perpetual copyright. It wasn't until the mustachioed songster had spent four years as mayor of Palm Springs and gone on to the U.S. House of Representatives that he became a public advocate of longer copyright terms, thanks in part to his involvement with the rights-heavy and litigious Church of Scientology. After Congressman Bono's 1998 death in a skiing accident, his widow and political successor, Mary Bono, took up the copyright cause as a way of commemorating her husband. "He was active on intellectual property issues," she told the House during its deliberations, "because he truly understood the goals of [the] Framers of the Constitution: that by maximizing the incentives for original creation, we help expand the public store-house of art, films, music, books, and now, also, software.... Actually, Sonny wanted copyright to last forever." If the framers of the Constitution had indeed wanted to *maximize* incentives, they had also created an impediment to that aim by empowering Congress to confer exclusive rights only "for limited Times" upon authors and inventors.[1] As an eventual remedy for this oversight, Mary Bono suggested, her colleagues might work toward a copyright

---

1. The U.S. Constitution (art. I, § 8) empowers Congress "[t]o promote the Progress of Science and useful Arts, by securing for limited Times to Authors and Inventors the exclusive Right to their respective Writings and Discoveries."

term that lasted "forever less 1 day." For the present, though, a substantial increase in the length of protection would serve as "a very fitting memorial for Sonny."[2] Even if it fell vastly short of the eternal term he had wanted, the new law would be another pulse in copyright's steady prolongation, and thus a legal complement to the late congressman's epitaph: "And the Beat Goes On."

When the Sonny Bono Copyright Term Extension Act was passed on October 27, 1998, it introduced a change of enormous consequence to scholars of modernism, adding twenty years to the duration of copyright in published and unpublished works. As a result of the Bono Act, works published between January 1, 1923, and December 31, 1977, are now copyrighted for ninety-five years from their first publication, while works created after that period enjoy protection for the author's life plus seventy years. Copyrights in unpublished works created before January 1, 1978, and not theretofore in the public domain or copyrighted now subsist for the author's life plus seventy years.[3] A wide range of people—scholars, teachers, adapters, publishers, performers, preservation groups—had timed their projects to the 1976 Copyright Act's shorter terms. After the Bono Act, many of them had to alter, shelve, or abandon their ventures. Because the threshold between property and the public domain had frozen for twenty years at the end of 1922, U.S. copyright reform had effectively cut modernism in half at its wonder year, partitioning it into a freely accessible early modernism and a heavily protected late one.[4] The Proust shelves of libraries and bookstores in the United States exhibit this cut with stark clarity. In 1995, Penguin announced a new English translation of *À la recherche du temps perdu* (1913–1927), but the Bono Act intervened: although the four volumes originally published before Proust's death in 1922 have appeared under the Penguin imprint, the 1998 act extended Random House's right in the classic Moncrieff-Kilmartin translation of the final three volumes. Until 2019 at the earliest, the new translations of *The Prisoner, The Fugitive,* and *Time Regained* will sit in the same suspended state as compositions by Ravel, Bartok, and Strauss; orphaned films awaiting restoration; and countless other post-1922 works whose

---

2. Statement of Mary Bono (R-CA), *Congressional Record, House* 144 (1998), 9952, 9951.

3. Under 17 U.S.C. § 303, as amended by the Bono Act, any such works (i.e., unpublished before January 1, 1978, and not theretofore in the public domain or copyright) that were subsequently published before January 1, 2003, enjoy a bonus copyright protection through December 31, 2047. This amendment added twenty years to the corresponding bonus protection (through Dec. 31, 2027) put in place by the Copyright Act of 1976.

4. Another reason that 1922 is the *annus mirabilis* of modernism: until 2019, it is the last year whose works are all in the public domain in the United States.

entry into the public domain and thus into a new phase of accessibility and circulation has been deferred.[5]

The fortification of U.S. copyright during the 1990s was not an eccentric domestic move but was spurred by developments across the Atlantic, most immediately by a 1993 EU directive calling for member states to harmonize their copyright terms at seventy years *post-mortem auctoris (p.m.a.)*.[6] Although this was the same term that the United States would shortly adopt, it was implemented differently in Europe. To begin with, term extensions in the European Union did not completely halt the advance of the public domain for twenty years as the Bono Act subsequently did. Instead, they delayed public-domain status on an author-by-author basis, according to the date of a given author's death.[7] More spectacularly, the EU directive differed from Bono by reviving copyrights in works that had fallen into the public domain during the previous twenty years.[8] Works by authors who died on or between January 1, 1925, and December 31, 1944—works that had already entered the public domain under the old term of fifty years *p.m.a.*—went back into copyright for the remainder of the new seventy-year postmortem term. In much of Europe, for instance, works of Virginia Woolf and James Joyce that

5. Peter Brooks, "The Shape of Time," *New York Times* (Jan. 25, 2004). For a partial list of publishing, performance, and restoration projects delayed by the Bono Act, see *Eldred v. Ashcroft* (01–618), 537 U.S. 186 (2003), 239 F.3d 372, *aff'd*, especially "Brief for Petitioners," 3–7.

6. This was EU Copyright Directive 93/98/EEC, passed in 1993 and implemented in 1995 by various statutory instruments.

7. Until the 1976 act implemented a fifty-year postmortem term, U.S. law had granted copyright for a set term from the date of a work's publication. Works that appeared under that earlier regime continue to have their copyrights measured from their publication date, with the result that extensions to their copyright terms freeze the moving wall of the public domain for the duration of the extension. Under Bono, nothing new will enter the public domain in the United States until 2019, when the ninety-five-year copyright in works published during 1923 expires. Because most European countries have been measuring copyright from the date of the author's death since the 1886 Berne Convention for the Protection of Literary and Artistic Works, if not before, term extensions in Europe delay public-domain status on an author-by-author basis rather than halting the advance of the public domain altogether. In 1996, when the EU directive took effect in the United Kingdom, the works of authors who died in 1946 (J. M. Keynes, Gertrude Stein, H. G. Wells) were a year away from entering the public domain under the old fifty-year p.m.*a.* term and gained protection under the new one until 2017. Copyright in the works of authors who died in 1965 (Winston Churchill, T. S. Eliot, Somerset Maugham) was extended from 2016 to 2036.

8. Although the Bono Act did not revive already-expired copyrights in the United States, the 1994 Uruguay Round Agreements Act did revive the U.S. copyright in a foreign work when that copyright had been prematurely forfeited due to the rights-holder's earlier noncompliance with the U.S. law.

were published during the authors' lifetimes had entered the public domain at the end of 1991, fifty years after both writers died in 1941. Under the 1995 harmonization, their copyrights were revived until the end of 2011, alongside those of many other modernist writers and their contemporaries.[9] The EU directive also reactivated protection in works by some of the longer-lived late Victorians.[10] To pore over a list of authors who died between 1924 and 1945 and were therefore subjected to revived copyrights is to confront odd facts about both mortality and property.[11] It reminds us that Arthur Conan Doyle and D. H. Lawrence, writers whose best-known contributions were separated by about thirty years, both died in 1930, and that because of Lawrence's early death his copyrights would lapse nine years *before* those of W. B. Yeats, a writer twenty years his senior. Such a list exhibits the more arbitrary effects of pinning a copyright's duration to the date of a writer's biological death. And it opens territory to which we will return—that of actuarial tables, demographic calculations, average life expectancies, and generational lengths, all of which bear with surprising force on copyright law.

Modernism and Copyright was written in the wake of the European directive, the Sonny Bono Act, and the Digital Millennium Copyright Act.[12] In the wake, too, of *Eldred v. Ashcroft*, the 2003 U.S. Supreme Court case that upheld the constitutionality of Bono. The *Eldred* decision, said a *New York Times* editorial, "makes it likely that we are seeing the beginning of the end of [the] public domain and the birth of copyright perpetuity."[13] Determined not to see this likelihood become fact, several of this book's contributors have been involved in efforts to mitigate the recent legislation's chilling effects on teaching and scholarship

9. E.g., Arnold Bennett (d. 1931); John Galsworthy (d. 1933); G. K. Chesterton and Federico García Lorca (d. 1936); Ford Madox Ford (d. 1939); F. Scott Fitzgerald (d. 1940); and Robert Musil (d. 1942).

10. E.g., Thomas Hardy (d. 1928); Arthur Conan Doyle (d. 1930); Rudyard Kipling (d. 1936); and Arthur Rackham (d. 1939).

11. For one version of such a list, see Clive Reynard, "The Impact of the European Directive on Inexpensive Reprint Editions," in *Textual Monopolies: Literary Copyright and the Public Domain*, ed. Patrick Parrinder and Warren Chernaik (London: Office for Humanities Communication, 1997), 49–54. Reynard, a company secretary and chief editor at the bargain classics publisher Wordsworth Editions, provides two useful tables: one of leading authors whose works were revived by the EU directive and one of authors whose works would, in the absence of the directive, have entered the public domain during the next twenty years.

12. Passed in October 1998 and signed into law on the same day as the Bono Act, the DMCA increased penalties for internet infringement and criminalized technological attempts to circumvent measures to control access to protected works.

13. "The Coming of Copyright Perpetuity," *New York Times* (Jan. 16, 2003).

generally and, in some cases, on modernist studies specifically. In that respect, *Modernism and Copyright* precipitates directly out of the advocacy and activism provoked by the last wave of copyright extensions and thus testifies to the invigorating effects that overreaching legislation can have on scholarly communities. For those of us who must reproduce protected material in the course of our work, this book is planted crucially in the twenty-first-century present with an eye to our prospects in the coming decades. In theoretical, practical, and polemical terms, it addresses how, under current laws and coming reforms, we are to do what we do.

At the same time, however, *Modernism and Copyright* seeks to extend the conversation about its keywords beyond present-day concerns with term extension, scholarly practice, and digital rights, as important as those concerns are. Delving back into late nineteenth- and early twentieth-century legal debates and reforms, it brings to light how significantly copyright has shaped the composition, publication, reception, and institutionalization of modernisms in a range of media. In the process, the book's contributors revisit and deepen some of the central currents in modernist studies past and present. While scholars have long recognized in modernism a "radical intertextuality"—a drive to excerpt, adapt, quote, appropriate, translate, and recombine earlier expressive works—we think about how these moves traverse, disrupt, and replenish fields of propertized expression.[14] Where recent work has taken modernism's portrait of the artist as a lone insurgent and repopulated it with collaborators, coteries, patronage networks, and canny commercial ventures, we place *this* broadened portrait, in turn, amid decades when corporations became authors and personality began to look like a property right.[15] As current scholarship works at theorizing a modernist Atlantic, we consider how transatlantic exchange was skewed by disparities among

14. See, for example, Jennifer Schiffer Levine, "Originality and Repetition in *Finnegans Wake* and *Ulysses*," *PMLA* 94 (1979): 106–120; Perry Meisel, *The Myth of the Modern: A Study in British Literature and Criticism after 1850* (New Haven, CT: Yale University Press, 1987).

15. See, for example, Jennifer A. Wicke, *Advertising Fictions: Literature, Advertising, and Social Reading* (New York: Columbia University Press, 1988); Kevin J. H. Dettmar and Stephen Myers Watt, eds., *Marketing Modernisms: Self-Promotion, Canonization, Rereading* (Ann Arbor: University of Michigan Press, 1996); Joyce Piell Wexler, *Who Paid for Modernism? Art, Money, and the Fiction of Conrad, Joyce, and Lawrence* (Fayetteville: University of Arkansas Press, 1997); Lawrence Rainey, *Institutions of Modernism: Literary Elites and Public Culture* (New Haven, CT: Yale University Press, 1998); Catherine Turner, *Marketing Modernism between the Two World Wars* (Amherst: University of Massachusetts Press, 2003); Aaron Jaffe, *Modernism and the Culture of Celebrity* (Cambridge: Cambridge University Press, 2005).

national copyright regimes.[16] And as modernist studies becomes more interested in its own disciplinary history, *Modernism and Copyright* explores how the law shapes what is published, studied, and canonized, and how "copying" has come to signify differently in postcolonial societies versus former and current imperial centers.

But for all that law shapes works of culture, it is itself, quintessentially, a work *shaped;* indeed, one could say that nothing is more "made" than law. So during a period when copyright was vastly expanding what could be protected as "writing," thereby exhibiting its own capacity to be rewritten, we should not be surprised to find modernists engaging vigorously with the law as a made, rather than a given, thing. Some—predominantly writers and composers—became conversant enough with intellectual property law to circumvent or design around its constraints on their creativity. Others attempted through legal actions to enlist copyright, along with neighboring regimes such as unfair competition and the nascent right of publicity, in safeguarding the integrity of their works and maximizing those works' status and profitability.

There have been vociferous objections to the law, too. In one of international modernism's first public moments of canon formation—the 1927 protest against Samuel Roth's unauthorized serialization of Joyce's *Ulysses* (1922)—162 prominent writers signed their names both to deplore the book's exclusion from U.S. copyright and, so they hoped, to spur the reform of the copyright laws that had made Joyce's novel vulnerable to piracy.[17] And as Robert Spoo shows in this volume's opening chapter, at least one prominent modernist—Ezra Pound, who refused to sign the 1927 protest because he thought its opposition to "the infamous state of the American law" too oblique—went so far as to propose an alternative U.S.

16. See, for example, the Modernist Atlantic Conference organized by the Modernist Magazines Project and held in July 2007 at De Montfort University, Leicester, United Kingdom.

17. For the text and signatories of the protest, see James Joyce, *Letters of James Joyce*, ed. Richard Ellmann (New York: Viking, 1966), 3:151–153. Joyce described the protest to his brother Stanislaus as intended "to make [the case against Roth] a test case for the reform of U.S. law" (ibid., 149). Sylvia Beach, Joyce's publisher and agent and one of the protest's orchestrators, dictated the following in a letter to George Bernard Shaw: "The suit we have entered against Roth may not be successful under existing Am[erican] law but a repeal of that law is what is ultimately aimed at and the more comprehensive the protest is the firmer will be the basis for a vigorous international movement of writers in that direction" (Sylvia Beach to G. B. Shaw, 1927, Sylvia Beach Papers, box 194, folder 6, Princeton University Library). Beach hoped (in vain, as it turned out) that Shaw would sign the protest.

copyright statute that would harmonize national regimes and enable living authors to compete more favorably with the dead.[18]

Because a number of the essays in this book are rooted in early twentieth-century law, it is worth surveying the copyright regimes and the influential reforms that were roughly contemporary with modernism. During most of the nineteenth century, copyright systems from one country to the next differed widely. Where works by foreign authors enjoyed any protection, it was through a patchy array of trade courtesy practices and bilateral agreements.[19] Transnational piracy was rampant, and countries whose domestic intellectual property had not yet, as David Saunders puts it, "acquired importance as an exportable product and as a source of cultural legitimacy" had little incentive to enter into reciprocal relations with net exporters of such works.[20] But as more and more European nations began to see themselves as net exporters of copyrightable works, and therefore as victims rather than as beneficiaries of piracy, the way opened for what was called "universal" copyright. In 1886, the signing of the Berne Convention for the Protection of Literary and Artistic Works established the first multilateral system of reciprocal copyright privileges. Among Berne signatories, a work originating in one country enjoyed the same rights and privileges in other countries as works by their nationals did, though for a term not to exceed the term of copyright in the work's country of origin. What's more, these rights and privileges subsisted from the moment a work was created and therefore applied to unpublished as well as to published works. The new arrangement created an impetus for member states to harmonize their domestic copyright systems, particularly the term of copyright, so that countries with shorter terms did not put their authors at a disadvantage abroad. The Berne Convention's inaugural signatories were Belgium, Haiti, Italy, Liberia, Switzerland, and Tunis, and four major colonial powers: France, Germany, Great Britain, and Spain. Because these acceded to the convention on behalf of their territories, colonies, and protectorates, Berne had a sizable jurisdiction from the start.

18. "The minor peccadillo of Mr. Roth," Pound concluded, "is dwarfed by the major infamy of the law." Ezra Pound, *Pound/Joyce: The Letters of Ezra Pound to James Joyce, with Pound's Essays on Joyce*, ed. Forrest Read (New York: New Directions, 1967), 226.

19. At the time of the first Berne Convention, two European countries, France and Belgium, unilaterally protected works published abroad.

20. David Saunders, *Authorship and Copyright* (London: Routledge, 1992), 171. The asymmetries among national copyright regimes during the nineteenth century—some of which persist today—would have been major contributors to the geoliterary rivalries described by Pascale Casanova in *The World Republic of Letters*, trans. M. B. DeBevoise (Cambridge, MA: Harvard University Press, 2004).

Its extension to its adherents' colonies and overseas possessions had the effect of securing a vast captive market for the copyright export nations whose interests the convention principally served.[21]

The United States, with its entrenched copyright exceptionalism and its industrial view of literary production, would not become a party to the Berne Convention until 1989.[22] As a result, the epochal developments in U.S. copyright during the modernist decades were unilateral ones, yet with immense repercussions for other nations. The Chace Act of 1891 extended copyright to foreign-origin works, provided they were published on U.S. soil simultaneously with or prior to publication in their country of origin. But these arrangements were "reciprocal" in name only, owing both to the difficult requirement of simultaneous or prior publication and to U.S. copyright's comparatively short term. Of the United States, one can say that on or about July 1, 1909, the character of cultural production changed.[23] The Copyright Act that took effect on that date fundamentally altered the contours of the law, from the scope of protectable works to the very definition of authorship. On the question of copyright's duration, the act seemed to make only a modest change, doubling the optional fourteen-year renewal term that could follow the initial twenty-eight-year term. But while the new maximum of fifty-six years meant that a work's copyright

21. For a discussion of Berne's impact on former colonies and industrializing nations, see Peter Dranos with John Braithwaite, *Informational Feudalism: Who Owns the Knowledge Economy?* (New York: Norton, 2003), esp. ch. 5.

22. The U.S. response to the 1884 Berne Conference testifies to a non-author-centered view of literary production:

> Differences in tariffs, and the fact that, apart from the author or artist, several industries have an interest in the production or the reproduction of a book or a work of art should be taken into account when considering whether to accord to the author of a work the right to have it reproduced or to prevent its reproduction in all countries. There is a distinction between the painter or the sculptor, whose work is saleable as made by his hands, and the literary author, to whose work the paper manufacturer, the type-setter, the printer, the bookbinder and many other persons in commerce contribute.

Quoted in Samuel Ricketson, *The Berne Convention for the Protection of Literary and Artistic Works: 1886–1986* (London: Centre for Commercial Law Studies, Queen Mary College and Kluwer, 1987), 56. This view of literary production interlocked with the requirement that works bear a copyright notice, be deposited, and be registered in order to obtain U.S. copyright protection and enforceability.

23. As I set to work on this introduction, a group of scholars in the San Francisco Bay area were celebrating the centenary of the 1909 Copyright Act, which for many copyright aficionados was vastly preferable to the 1976 act that eventually superseded it. In fact, the question "1909 or 1976?" is something like the Great Schism among students of U.S. copyright law.

would likely outlive its author, the act pointedly refused to adopt an explicitly postmortem term, much less the fifty-year *p.m.a.* term that had just become the new standard for Berne signatories. This recommitment to U.S. exceptionalism was underscored by the act's consolidation of certain "manufacturing requirements," which protected domestic artisans by requiring that foreign-origin works in English be deposited in the U.S. Copyright Office within thirty days and printed by U.S. printers within thirty days of their foreign publication.[24] Imported works that failed to clear these hurdles, moreover, could be seized by customs or the U.S. Post Office and subjected to forfeiture proceedings in federal courts.[25] When coupled with anti-obscenity statutes that deterred U.S. artisans from printing "immoral" works, the provisions in the 1909 act would cast some of international Anglophone modernism's more transgressive works, including Joyce's *Ulysses* and Lawrence's *Lady Chatterley's Lover* (1928), directly into the public domain.

The act's innovations were just as dramatic when it came to U.S.–origin works. In music, it responded to the rise of new recording technologies by introducing two provisions: a right of mechanical reproduction, which gave composers and lyricists the exclusive right to make the first phonographic recording or player piano roll of a work; and a compulsory license system that allowed anyone to produce a new recording of a work, in the wake of its authorized premiere, simply by paying a statutory royalty. Even more important, the act created a new copyright sector through the work-for-hire doctrine. This was based in a single expanded definition: "the word 'author' shall include the employer in the case of works made for hire."[26] Under the new doctrine, employees relinquished their authorship status to their employer, the corporate "author," not just for the first twenty-eight years of copyright but for the full fifty-six: unlike authors who temporarily assigned their copyrights to publishers, employees did not recapture their rights upon commencement of the renewal term.[27] Finally, the act introduced a change whose

---

24. The time periods of the manufacturing clause were later extended. Under a 1919 amendment, English-language works of foreign origin had to be deposited in the U.S. Copyright Office within sixty days and printed by U.S. printers within four months of their foreign publication; a 1949 amendment extended these periods to six months and five years, respectively. For a detailed discussion of the manufacturing requirements, see Robert Spoo's "Copyright Protectionism and Its Discontents: The Case of James Joyce's *Ulysses* in America," *Yale Law Journal* 108 (1998): 633–667.

25. Act of Mar. 4, 1909, ch. 320, §§ 31–33, 25 Stat. 1075.

26. Ibid., § 62.

27. On the work-for-hire doctrine, see Catherine L. Fisk, *Working Knowledge: Employee Innovation and the Rise of Corporate Intellectual Property, 1800–1930* (Chapel Hill: University of North Carolina Press, 2009).

importance would only later become clear: copyright owners were empowered not just to print, reprint, publish, and vend their works but also to *copy* them.[28] In that one emendation lay a world of course-packet and file-sharing legal actions to come. The 1909 act opened the way to these millennial conflicts because it initiated the long goodbye to a less extensive system. In the terms of one influential analysis, it marked the beginning of a shift from the *regulatory* model prevalent during the nineteenth century to the *proprietary* one that would become dominant later in the twentieth.[29] Put another way, U.S. copyright began in 1909 to be imagined less as a limited bundle of rights and more as an absolute entitlement.

Britain's act of 1911 was momentous as well, designed to harmonize with the Berne Convention where its U.S. counterpart declared an ongoing independence from Berne. Since 1842, copyright in Great Britain had subsisted for forty-two years from publication or seven years *p.m.a.*, whichever was longer. Now, for the first time, it was fixed at a definitively (rather than a de facto) postmortem term of fifty years, although during the second half of that term anyone could reprint an already-published work by paying a 10 percent royalty. The 1911 act also codified *fair dealing* (the related U.S. doctrine of *fair use* would not be articulated in statute until the 1909 act was reformed in 1976) as non-infringing copying "for purposes of private study, research, criticism, review, or newspaper summary."[30] Emerging media left their mark on the UK act not only in a compulsory license system for sound recordings but also in giving authors the right to authorize or prohibit phonographic, pianola, and cinematographic recordings of literary, dramatic, and musical works. Work-for-hire provisions reminiscent of those in the U.S. act appeared. And the new legislation—technically, an imperial act—released all self-governing dominions (Canada and Australia, plus the newly proclaimed New Zealand, Newfoundland, and South Africa) to

---

28. Act of Mar. 4, 1909, ch. 320, § 1(a). L. Ray Patterson was the first to parse the new significance of "copy" in the 1909 act (versus earlier statutes' references to "copies" of non-publishable objects); see his "Free Speech, Copyright, and Fair Use," *Vanderbilt Law Review* 40 (1987): 40–43. For an engaging discussion titled "Decriminalizing the Copy," see Lawrence Lessig, *Remix: Making Art and Commerce Thrive in the Hybrid Economy* (New York: Penguin, 2008), 268–271.

29. L. Ray Patterson and Stanley W. Lindberg, *The Nature of Copyright: A Law of Users' Rights* (Athens: University of Georgia Press, 1991), 77. Patterson and Lindberg put it as a matter of proportion, while sounding an admonitory note: "The 1909 act marks the beginning of a change from the nineteenth-century view that copyright was more regulatory than proprietary to the contemporary consensus—whether or not sound—that copyright is more proprietary than regulatory."

30. Copyright Act, 1911, 1 and 2 Geo. 5, ch. 46, § 2 (Eng.).

adopt or reject the act's provisions, as well as those of the Berne Convention, as they saw fit.

Copyright reform around the turn of the twentieth century fashioned a series of legal components that would be assembled into a more uniformly global system in the 1990s. By then, the benefits of international harmonization were largely treated as self-evident. Studying the world copyright system's first stirrings from the 1880s onward allows us to rediscover both the complex origins of this harmonization imperative and its effaced connections to modernism. N. N. Feltes writes provocatively that the pressure for a universal law of copyright "arose less out of a desire for juridical consistency than from the material contradictions of time and place for which 'modernism' was the resolution elsewhere on the ideological level."[31] These contradictions clustered around the acceleration of bodies, information, and capital, and they included the spatial oxymorons of national, transnational, imperial, and global "localities" and the temporal enigma, in cultural production, of the instant classic. Both contradictions, we should notice, involve the imperative of simultaneity, which, as Benedict Anderson and others have argued, is a key element of the "homogeneous, empty time" in which the modern nation-state constitutes itself.[32] The difference here is that we are no longer dealing with the nation-state alone but with larger transnational and imperial formations. The Berne Convention, for instance, asserted a simultaneity among member states by starting the international copyright clock at the moment of a work's creation and stopping it at the end of the same calendar year both abroad and at home. The U.S. manufacturing clause made simultaneous (and, after 1909, near-simultaneous) publication in the United States the price certain foreign works had to pay in order to gain copyright there. And, as I have shown elsewhere, one of the chief engines of late nineteenth-century British copyright reform was the desire to minimize the lag time between expensive first editions for elite readers and cheap editions for working-class and colonial markets.[33] In all three instances, simultaneity both ensured the widest dissemination of what was current and acted as the portal to long copyright terms designed to reward the descendants of those who had written for posterity. That *posterity* function had been a part of copyright's self-conception for at least a century. But the law's *punctuality* function—its

31. N. N. Feltes, "International Copyright: Structuring 'the Condition of Modernity' in British Publishing," *Cardozo Arts and Entertainment Law Journal* 10 (1991–1992): 535.

32. Benedict Anderson, *Imagined Communities*, rev. ed. (London: Verso, 1991), 26.

33. See Saint-Amour, *The Copywrights: Intellectual Property and the Literary Imagination* (Ithaca, NY: Cornell University Press, 2003), ch. 2.

imperative against belatedness—may have been where turn-of-the-century copyright most registered the accelerating world.

For Feltes, international copyright and modernism offered differing "resolutions" to the material contradictions of time and place. We might object that, far from resolving anything, both copyright and modernism are sites where such contradictions become sharply legible. By the same token, we might require a more flexible definition of *modernism* than the one Feltes provides ("the general ideological level of the capitalist social formation").[34] Nonetheless, the suggestion that modernism and copyright might share certain homologous relationships to modernity is a compelling place for us to begin, and in respect to domestic no less than international regimes. We have already seen above that copyright's shift toward the propertization of expressive works was accomplished through its grappling with new media, evolving notions of corporate personhood, and asymmetries in transnational cultural and commercial flows—some of the same pressures scholars currently recognize as constitutive of modernism. One overview of the new modernist studies identifies two particularly vital areas of debate in the field: transnational exchange and media in an age of mass persuasion.[35] Many of the essays in this book participate in one or both of these debates while insisting that we attend to one of their key points of convergence: intellectual property law. Witness, for example, Joseph R. Slaughter's bold proposal that we date international modernism's beginning to the twin property grabs of the 1880s: the Berlin Convention that divided Africa among European powers, and the Berne Convention that established international copyright to the advantage of the global North. In thus exploring modernism's relation to copyright, the essays in this book implicitly question the *and* in its title. If copyright heaps its inconsistencies and contingencies behind the myth of an integral law; if it responds, always belatedly, to the rise of new media through sometimes violent recursions to form; if it downplays its entanglement with questions of territory, sovereignty, and race—then it might have made more sense, after all, to speak of the modernism *of* copyright.

To return to our own moment, *Modernism and Copyright* addresses what is often portrayed as a deadlock between the gatekeepers of modernist intellectual properties (estates, heirs, beneficiaries, and executors), on one hand, and the scholars, performers, and adapters of modernist works, on the other. Because of the legal chronologies I described earlier, those who engage academically or crea-

34. Feltes, "International Copyright," 538.
35. Douglas Mao and Rebecca L. Walkowitz, "The New Modernist Studies," *PMLA* 123 (2008): 737–748.

tively with modernism are often embroiled in combustible interactions with rights-holders. Some of these clashes have, in turn, been widely reported in the mainstream press. Given the media's attraction to contretemps, user/rights-holder discord is, more and more, what nonspecialists know about modernism. How many who have never opened *Ulysses* have nonetheless read, in the *New Yorker* and uncountable newspaper articles, of attempts by the author's grandson and sole literary beneficiary, Stephen James Joyce, to obstruct Joyce scholarship?[36] Or, without having seen *Waiting for Godot*, know of Samuel Beckett's and his estate's history of bringing legal action against performances of the play that made unauthorized use of female leads, racially mixed casts, or incidental music?[37] How many chuckled at the news that John Cage's publishers have not only collected royalties on the composer's silent piece *4'33"* but also threatened performers of other soundless pieces, of both longer and shorter duration, for infringing Cage's silence?[38] Or on reading about the Picasso estate's refusal to allow his paintings to appear in the 1996 film *Surviving Picasso?*[39] This book attends seriously to several disputes that have been described in the past along familiar lines: as pitting advocates of free

36. See D. T. Max, "The Injustice Collector: Is James Joyce's Grandson Suppressing Scholarship?" *New Yorker* (June 19, 2006): 34–43. On *Shloss v. Sweeney and the Estate of James Joyce*, see, for example, Leslie Simmons, "James Joyce Copyright Case Settled in California," *Washington Post* (Mar. 24, 2007); and Andrea L. Foster, "James Joyce Scholar, in Deal with Author's Estate, Wins Right to Use Copyrighted Works," *Chronicle of Higher Education* (Mar. 26, 2007).

37. On Beckett's prohibitions and legal actions regarding his plays, see James Knowlson, *Damned to Fame: The Life of Samuel Beckett* (London: Bloomsbury, 1996), 501–503, 607–611. On the Beckett estate's prescriptive handling of the dramatic work, see Mel Gussow, "A Reading Upsets Beckett's Estate," *New York Times* (Sept. 24, 1994); and Matthew Rimmer, "Damned to Fame: The Moral Rights of the Beckett Estate," *Australian Library and Information Association* (May 2003), http://www.alia.org.au/publishing/incite/2003/05/beckett.html (accessed Aug. 3, 2009).

38. See Ben Greenman, "Silence Is Beholden," *New Yorker* (Sept. 30, 2002). Mike Batt of the crossover classical ensemble the Planets received notice from the Mechanical-Copyright Protection Society that he owed Cage's publisher, Peters Edition, royalties beginning at £400 for his recording "A One Minute Silence." (The piece was attributed to Batt/Cage, where "Cage" was Clint Cage, one of Batt's registered pseudonyms.) As Batt quipped, "[M]y silence was a copyright infringement on Cage's silence." After defiantly releasing the piece as a single, Batt registered hundreds of other silent pieces of various durations: "If there's ever a Cage performance where they come in a second shorter or longer, then it's mine." See also Dennis Kurzon, "*Peters Edition v. Batt:* The Intertextuality of Silence," *International Journal for the Semiotics of Law* 20 (2007): 285–303.

39. See Anthony Haden-Guest, "The Talk of the Town: Picasso Pic Has Heirs Seeing Red!" *New Yorker* (Aug. 21, 1995): 53.

speech, fresh creation, and scholarly access against rights-holders concerned to defend the integrity of works and the privacy of families. Paying a different, perhaps reparative kind of attention to such disputes means thinking about copyright's externalities—the costs, benefits, and functions that attach to the law but are typically excluded from the economic calculations and legislative processes that determine the law's parameters. I have in mind not the "congestion externalities" that economic theorists of copyright like to talk about, but another kind of consideration: nebulous but powerful factors such as copyright's frequent enlistment in preserving personal and cultural memory, its calendrical relationship to the work of mourning, and its role in constructing the boundary between the living and the dead.

In the hope of fostering productive, mutually beneficial relationships between the users and the gatekeepers of modernist intellectual properties, this book does something unprecedented: it places work by legal professionals and by scholars from a range of disciplines beside contributions from two individuals closely tied to major modernist estates. These are Mary de Rachewiltz, the daughter, translator, and literary beneficiary of Ezra Pound and curator of the Pound Archive at Yale; and Stanford G. Gann Jr., the literary executor of Gertrude Stein. Their views are, of course, particular to them and should not be taken as representative of beneficiaries or executors generally. In addition, the reader should bear in mind the selection bias that accompanies their contributions to this volume: de Rachewiltz's and Gann's willingness to participate accords with their generally receptive approach to permissions requests from scholars and adapters. Thanks to the same selection bias, the views of less receptive heirs and estates, which might be of equal interest to readers, are unrepresented here.[40] Yet, despite the fact that de Rachewiltz and Gann express highly specific points of view, they look out on the same broad prospect of legacy, privacy, responsibility, access, and futurity, inviting their readers imaginatively to occupy different positions within that prospect. It is hoped that their participation in this volume will give new visibility to the generative conversations that can and do take place between rights-holders and permissions-seekers but that have so far been eclipsed by reportage on modernism's more embattled legatees.

---

40. Though for a forceful privileging of privacy and integrity considerations over scholarly access, one could do worse than to consult Stephen James Joyce, "The Private Lives of Writers," *New York Times* (Dec. 31, 1989); and Catherine Bédarida, "Stephen James Joyce, petit-fils de l'écrivain: 'Il existe une véritable industrie James Joyce,'" *Le Monde* (Mar. 22, 1995): 26. For another, more recent example, see Paul Zukofsky, "Copyright Notice by PZ," *Z-site: A Companion to the Works of Louis Zukofsky*, http://www.z-site.net/copyright-notice-by-pz (accessed Oct. 22, 2009).

Each of this book's seven parts consists of a pair of essays sharing some premise, theme, or central question. Part I peers through the aperture of copyright at the attitudes and practices of two canonical literary modernists. Robert Spoo's "Ezra Pound, Legislator" gives us a Pound we have only seen glancingly before: the "passionate copyright polemicist" and would-be lawmaker who, in 1918, published his suggestions for a reformed U.S. copyright law. In a detailed reading of Pound's statute, Spoo shows us how much more was at stake for the poet than ending the American "booklegging" of foreign works. For Pound, the current system stood in the way of Anglo-American cultural reciprocity; it hurt U.S. writers in their home market by giving cheap, pirated English-language works of foreign origin a competitive advantage; and it gave dead, public-domain authors a similar advantage over living ones. As Spoo reads it, Pound's proposed remedy—perpetual copyright ventilated by a compulsory license system to permit inexpensive reprints of successful works—innovatively fused strong protection for authors with an even stronger provision for the public interest. "Pound's legislative energies," writes Spoo, "were stirred by the prospect of unchecked dissemination of books and art, not by economic stimulus packages for creators." Celia Marshik's "Thinking Back through Copyright" reads Virginia Woolf's major works of nonfiction by the light of literary property and citationality. For Marshik, the possessive individualism seemingly encoded in the title of *A Room of One's Own* (1929) is belied by "the radically *collective* implications of both the book's argument and its intertextual practices." Copyright might appear to typify the lone room that one hopes to own, but in Marshik's discussion of *Room* and *Three Guineas* (1938), it emerges as something more complex, at once a haven for the individual writer and a passage for the collective energies that course through her work. Marshik demonstrates how critical the balance between these functions was for women writers of Woolf's generation: copyright had to be robust enough to support the individual writer's material autonomy but not so strong as to hinder her from thinking and writing back through her predecessors.

Part II, "Melodic Properties of the Culture System," shifts the discussion from literature to music, an especially thorny territory for copyright during the last hundred years. One major difficulty has been music's uneasy relationship with the idea/expression dichotomy, which evolved under a literary conception of protected works. As Mark Osteen shows in "Rhythm Changes: Contrafacts, Copyright, and Jazz Modernism," U.S. courts have tended to solve this difficulty by treating melody as (protectable) expression and harmony as (nonprotectable) idea. This distinction has meant that even *de minimis* copying of protected melodies risks infringement. But it also makes the chord changes of a song, no matter how popular and recognizable, freely available for reuse. Among the liveliest "design-around" forms begotten by this distinction is the jazz "contrafact," a staple sub-genre of 1940s and '50s bebop whose practitioners wrote and improvised new melodies over established songs' chord changes, thereby avoiding having to pay royalties under the compulsory licensing system. According to Osteen, contrafacts link jazz to circumventive modernist hybrids in other media while also epito-mizing "the improvisatory, rebellious spirit of jazz as an African-American art form that 'signifies' upon established orthodoxies." Although Theodor Adorno wrote disparagingly about jazz, the Frankfurt School critic shared bebop's impa-tience with how melody was fetishized as the primary locus of originality (and thus of ownership) in musical works. Joanna Demers's "Melody, Theft, and High Culture" connects Adorno's critique of this fetishization to the rise in Western art music of the "work concept," which envisioned classical music compositions as unified, inspired, autonomous, and permanent works. From the vantage of the work concept, derivative works that looted classical compositions for their melodic hooks and cultural prestige were guilty not just of vulgarizing the original but of destroying it; as Adorno wrote, "The man who in the subway triumphantly whis-tles loudly the theme of the finale of Brahms's First is already primarily involved with its debris." In Adorno's view, modernist atonal music sought to avoid this ter-rible domestication by forgoing tuneful, detachable melodies and preemptively commodifying its musical materials. But, as Demers points out, the work concept would find a more durable and widespread defense in the sound-recording copy-right introduced by the 1976 act. By propertizing the full range of recorded sound, from melody and harmony to timbre and sound world, corporate-rights-holder-driven legislation, says Demers, "has succeeded in doing what the modernist com-posers, with their dedication to the work concept, could only dream of."

The two essays that comprise part III, "The Fall and Rise of Remix Culture," illustrate how key developments in early twentieth-century U.S. law both antici-pated and helped to shape the digital present. Peter Decherney's "Gag Orders: Comedy, Chaplin, and Copyright" begins by asking: if we are now witnessing the *resurgence* of copying, collage, and recombination, how did that remix culture become marginalized to begin with? Decherney reads our mashup moment as the second coming of Hollywood's early years, when filmmakers borrowed liberally from vaudeville acts and produced shot-for-shot remakes of one another's films. But as the industry's profits rose, so did the incentive to safeguard them through intellectual property law. Charlie Chaplin, one of the period's most lauded, influ-ential, and widely copied figures, initiated a pair of lawsuits against imitators in the hope of securing copyright in his character, the Tramp. The initial and appellate decisions in *Chaplin v. Amador* (1925, 1928), says Decherney, "transformed comic authorship for the age of mass media and finally broke with the imitative cultures of vaudeville and the early film industry." Decherney's piece gives us a new way to link Chaplin's modernism to that of radically intertextual writers of his generation: both aimed to propertize works whose components—or, in Chaplin's case, characters whose traits—had been appropriated from the cultural commons. For W. Ron Gard and Elizabeth Townsend Gard, contrastingly, modernism is not a set of cultural or legal practices but something more fundamental: an economic period characterized by "high industrialist metaphysics." The 1909 Copyright Act in the United States was, as their title puts it, "marked by modernism" because it was founded on a materialist conception of the protected work as a tangible, saleable good. Because the 1976 act largely clung to this conception of the work, they argue, our current system is ill adapted to the era of user-generated digital content. But to avoid a brutal presentism in our reforms, they add, we need to think simultaneously about today's cultural practices and the "traditional contours of copyright protection," an emerging doctrine that measures legislative change against copyright's basic emplotment of a work's progress from creation to protection to the public domain.

Part IV, "Regimes of Attribution and Publicity," presupposes that the story of copyright remains incomplete until we study its neighboring regimes, several of which were introduced or consolidated during the modernist decades. Catherine L. Fisk's "The Modern Author at Work on Madison Avenue" shifts our focus from a scarce number of elite works produced by individual creators—the default case for modernism—to the vast array of bureaucratic and mass-cultural works produced under the 1909 and 1911 acts' new work-for-hire provisions. In corporate contexts where workers signed away their legal authorship as a condition of employment, laws and internal codes involving attribution replaced copyright as a site of incentive and reward. Through her study of attribution and the employment relation in the Arts and Crafts movement, the Tiffany Studio, and the J. Walter Thompson Company, Fisk argues that modernist and corporate authorship were not discrete antitypes so much as secret sharers, linked by mimicry, parasitism, and even homage. Fisk's tandem reading of modernism and Madison Avenue produces a compound portrait of authorship, one in which origination, ownership, recognition, employment, and persona are separable operations governed by distinct areas of law. Oliver Gerland's "Modernism and the Emergence of the Right of Publicity" is also concerned with the development of an exclusive right to control and benefit from the commercial use of one's identity. Whereas Fisk describes the publicity right's postwar elaborations, Gerland narrates its differentiation from the right of privacy around the turn of the twentieth century. Two figures help him plot this trajectory: the protagonist of Ibsen's *Hedda Gabler* (1890) and Lucy, Lady Duff-Gordon, Hedda Tesman's real-world contemporary and the fashion designer who invented the "personality dress" and the runway show. As Gerland reads it, Hedda's suicide is both the ultimate defense of her privacy and an act whose inscrutability implies the presence of a public audience to bear witness to it. Lucy, for whom publicity was an economic tool rather than a means to seclusion, reappointed Ibsen's private interiors as a stage for commerce and was the defendant in a lawsuit that helped to establish a person's (alienable) property in the indices of her identity. The indecipherable stylist and the canny self-brander, Hedda and Lucy incarnate two strategies, both of them recognizably modernist, for facing publicity's abyss.

Although it was conceived as an inducement to publish expressive works, copyright has become an effective tool for safeguarding the privacy of authors, their families, and their circles. Part V investigates copyright's deepening entanglement with privacy in respect to the heavily contested genre of literary biography. Mark A. Fowler's "'The Quick in Pursuit of the Dead'" uses the touchstone figure of Ian Hamilton, whose biography of J. D. Salinger was found to have infringed the novelist's copyright in letters that Hamilton quoted and paraphrased. Tracing the judicial aftermath of the biographer's clash with Salinger, Fowler provides an overview of recent decisions and legislation with an eye toward helping scholars of modernism utilize the fullest possible extent of fair use without putting themselves in legal peril. Carol Loeb Shloss's "Privacy and the Misuse of Copyright" picks up, in a sense, where Fowler leaves off by reflecting on her 2007 suit against the estate of James Joyce to obtain a declaratory judgment that her biography of Joyce's daughter, Lucia, was non-infringing. Despite having been settled rather than fully adjudicated, Shloss's suit illustrates that the doctrine of "unclean hands" and the related equitable defense of "copyright misuse" are emerging as legal recourses for scholars when rights-holders attempt to abuse their copyright privileges. In her chapter, however, Shloss is less concerned to rehearse the particulars of her case than to explore its background in earlier skirmishes and, more distantly, in evolving ideas about privacy and privilege. The heir's favored battle cry of "family privacy," she argues, relies on a bourgeois model of seclusion that was unavailable to a poor, nomadic, urban family like the young James Joyce's. When that same edifice of "family privacy" is reinforced by copyright holdings, Shloss contends, it can immure uncelebrated family members, particularly women and people with mental health difficulties, behind a virtually impenetrable private censorship.

Stanford G. Gann Jr. opens part VI with a brief but forceful meditation based on his experience as Gertrude Stein's literary executor. He proposes that executors faced with a request to perform, adapt, reprint, or quote from a protected work might retrace the work's itinerary, starting with the life, character, and stated preferences of the author and moving outward to consider the interests of the heirs, the users, and the work itself. Gann is instructed by Stein's modernism in a way that scholars should find heartening: "Gertrude Stein's avant-garde lifestyle and tastes," he writes, "should expand rather than contract the range of her work's permissible uses." After the author's death, he adds, considerations of her privacy should decline and the interests of the living—including the living work—take precedence. The work's passage from generation to dissemination resonates with the part's title, "Calving the Wind," an allusion to two lines in Pound's Canto IV—"No wind is the king's wind. / Let every cow keep her calf." In her essay, "*Mens Sine Affectu*," Mary de Rachewiltz reads these two lines as indexing competing views on copyright within Pound's work. For however much he was, in her words, "dead against all forms of monopoly," the mandate "Let every cow keep her calf" fuses monopoly, filiation, and literary property in a manner that must elicit both passion and caution in a writer's child.[41] Equal parts annotation, reminiscence, and polemic, de Rachewiltz's chapter defies simple paraphrase. But it may well be the most complex, evocative piece yet written on the responsibilities of literary inheritance, curation, and rereading.

The book's seventh and final part turns from matters of permission and inheritance to another aspect of modernism's afterlife—the question of how its appropriative, self-reflexive practices have been both resources and problems for subsequent generations of writers and critics. In " 'It's Good to Be Primitive,' " Joseph R. Slaughter takes up Malian novelist Yambo Ouologuem's *Le Devoir de violence* (1968), which was initially hailed as "the first truly African novel" only to be stripped of its laurels three years later when readers found passages from a number of Western works embedded, unacknowledged, in the text. Thanks to the "intertextual color line" that divided European modernism from its ostensibly primitive source cultures, "*l'affaire* Ouologuem" stigmatized the novel as a clumsy, incoherent plagiarism. But for Slaughter, *Le Devoir de violence* is something else entirely: a slippery rejoinder to Western primitivism and a study in the arbitrary but highly consequential distinction between plagiarism and allusion—a

41. For the link between "Let every cow keep her calf" and ancient Irish copyright, see Robert Spoo's brief discussion of "*Mens sine affectu*" in his contribution to this volume. Spoo's and de Rachewiltz's pieces are powerfully complementary.

distinction Slaughter connects to copyright's idea/expression dichotomy and thence to the color lines threaded throughout the world's intellectual property system. Ouologuem's novel also detonates the notion of a unitary African identity kept pristine until the moment of its Western appropriation. It reminds us, writes Slaughter, "that everything is already touched, miscegenated, contaminated, counterfeited, and compromised by the institutional power structures that *originated* it and the abstraction processes that *authenticated* it." Eric Hayot and Edward Wesp's "Solomon's Bluff: Virtual Property and the Aesthetics of Modern Worldmaking" uses early twenty-first-century digital online worlds as an extreme case from which we may apprehend a general rule: "[t]he history of modern aesthetics, particularly narrative aesthetics, is at least partly a history of orientation toward the question of the world." Whether the fictional world in question is *Don Quijote, Ulysses,* or *EverQuest,* its claims to represent an independent, self-enclosed world are vexed by its status as intellectual property in the world we call real—all the more so when, as in multi-user online worlds, the game creator's intellectual property is the ontological matrix out of which players create virtual property they may sell to other players for real-world money. Whereas these virtual worlds let conventional economic relations persist beneath fanciful content, Hayot and Wesp argue that certain modernisms—the nested ontologies of Borges, the heteronyms of Pessoa— offer us views of worldmaking and of intellectual property that are at once more critical and more imaginative. At the same time, Hayot and Wesp suggest, our increasingly virtual orientation to the question of the world lets us see in the most familiar works of modernism a set of provocations we have never seen before or needed to see.

An appendix, "Copyright Protection and Users' Rights: Frequently Asked Questions," follows *Modernism and Copyright*'s body chapters. Redacted from a more detailed FAQ on James Joyce's copyrights that I prepared with Michael Groden, Carol Loeb Shloss, and Robert Spoo for the International James Joyce Foundation, the appendix aims to familiarize scholars, teachers, performers, and adapters of protected works with the basic parameters of copyright law in the United States, the European Union, the United Kingdom, the Republic of Ireland, Canada, and Australia. In pursuing these pragmatic aims, the document testifies to the significant disparities that persist among national jurisdictions despite the international harmonization efforts of the 1990s. It illustrates, as well, the degree to which twenty-first-century copyright law continues to be shaped by the legislative reforms of the modernist decades.

The remainder of this introduction proposes two new ways of traversing the space limned by modernism and copyright: the biopolitical and the counterfactual. Neither of them is explicitly discussed in the essays that follow, but both are implied or entailed at key moments in a number of contributions— moments where the focus shifts to copyright's collective ramifications, its regulatory functions within and among states, its penchant for imitating the parameters of organic life, and its tendency to provoke both creative circumvention and alternate-historical thinking. Hayot and Wesp understand copyright as part of the integument in which our fictional and virtual worlds are encased—as the membrane separating the bounded infinity of such worlds from their status as an intellectual property in this one. My suggestions here are similarly organic, if you will: that copyright in the modernist decades exceeds the limited incentive-making function in which it originated and becomes crucially entangled in the management of lives and even in the question of what a life *is*. As a consequence, intellectual property law comes to participate in questions to which it was once a stranger. What is it to live? What rights accrue to the living? What lives accrue to the dead? And what other lives are entrained and even negated in the unfolding of this one?

Biopolitics

Michel Foucault's influence on the study of authorship and copyright has been enormous, the result largely of his celebrated 1969 article "What Is an Author?" Indeed, it is difficult to imagine the subsequent copyright scholarship in both law and the humanities having developed as it did without the following sentence— fascinatingly, one in which the essay maps a road it then declines to follow:

> Certainly it would be worth examining how the author became individualized in a culture like ours, what status he has been given, at what moment studies of authenticity and attribution began, in what kind of system of valorization the author was involved, at what point we began to recount the lives of authors rather than of heroes, and how this fundamental category of "the-man-and-his-work criticism" began.[42]

In its call to investigate "how the author became individualized," "What Is an Author?" engendered crucial work on the rise and persistence of a possessive-individualist model of authorship, on that model's co-emergence with the romantic figure of "original genius," and on what is lost when the individualist model prevails over

42. Michel Foucault, "Qu'est-ce qu'un auteur?" (1969), trans. Josué V. Harari as "What Is an Author?" in *The Foucault Reader*, ed. Paul Rabinow (New York: Pantheon, 1984), 101.

collaborative modes of innovation, expressive freedom, and the public domain.[43] These same studies necessarily focused on copyright's individualist dimensions in the course of historicizing and critiquing them. As the beneficiaries of that work, we are now in a position to attend to the stones that it left unturned. Chief among them is the fact that copyright, for all the individualist formations it has come to support, has also been intimately, and increasingly, linked to the masses and particularly to questions of population, generation, and mortality. To pursue this insight is to turn the conversation toward a different Foucault, the Foucault of biopolitics.

Foucault defined biopolitics in contrast to two modalities of state power that he held to have emerged earlier: sovereignty and discipline. Grounded in the right to put subjects to death, classical theories of sovereignty were less concerned with the conditions of those subjects' survival. One might even say that the sovereign ignored living subjects until they needed to be compelled or punished through death or the threat of execution. But in the seventeenth century, Foucault held, states began to take an interest in the life conditions they had previously ignored. The sovereign's "right to take life or let live" began, in Foucault's compact formulation, to be superseded by the state's "power to 'make' live and 'let' die."[44] This new "task of administering life" took two forms: first, the disciplinary technologies of the seventeenth and eighteenth centuries, and second, the biopolitical technologies that arose in the late eighteenth and nineteenth centuries.[45] Although they

43. This body of scholarship is too extensive to cover thoroughly here, but important titles from its first fifteen years include Martha Woodmansee, "The Genius and the Copyright: Economic and Legal Conditions of the Emergence of the 'Author,'" *Eighteenth-century Studies* 17 (1984): 425–448; Mark Rose, *Authors and Owners: The Invention of Copyright* (Cambridge, MA: Harvard University Press, 1993); Peter Jaszi, "Toward a Theory of Copyright: The Metamorphoses of 'Authorship,'" *Duke Law Journal* (1991): 455–502; Jaszi, "On the Author Effect: Contemporary Copyright and Collective Creativity," in *The Construction of Authorship: Textual Appropriation in Law and Literature*, ed. Martha Woodmansee and Peter Jaszi (Durham, NC: Duke University Press, 1994); James D. A. Boyle, *Shamans, Software, and Spleens: Law and the Construction of the Information Society* (Cambridge, MA: Harvard University Press, 1996); and Rosemary J. Coombe, *The Cultural Life of Intellectual Properties: Authorship, Appropriation, and the Law* (Durham, NC: Duke University Press, 1998). For a critique of the use of the term *romantic* to designate a possessive-individualist model of authorship, see Tilar J. Mazzeo, *Plagiarism and Literary Property in the Romantic Period* (Philadelphia: University of Pennsylvania Press, 2006).

44. Michel Foucault, *"Society Must Be Defended": Lectures at the Collège de France, 1975–1976*, ed. Mauro Bertani and Alessandro Fontana, trans. David Macey (New York: Picador, 2003), 241.

45. Michel Foucault, "Right of Death and Power over Life," in *The History of Sexuality*, vol. 1: *An Introduction*, trans. Robert Hurley (New York: Vintage, 1990), 139.

often worked in tandem, these two regimes were importantly distinct. Whereas the disciplinary mode isolated individual bodies the better to train, inspect, and punish them, the biopolitical mode sought to manage the lives of whole populations, a project aided by the concurrent rise of sciences such as demography, epidemiology, and statistics. Instead of threatening individuals with bodily punishment or isolating them in order to cultivate their habits of self-surveillance, biopower regulated masses of citizens by compelling the parameters and conditions of their living, adjusting a citizenry's aggregate natality, fertility, and mortality toward some best-possible equipoise.[46] Death itself was resignified in this shift to state-controlled biology: no longer the transfer of power from earthly to heavenly sovereign, death became the thing that lay beyond power's grasp: "Power no longer recognizes death. Power literally ignores death." Thus, if the subject's death is biopower's unpassable limit, the state can maintain its hold in two ways: by prolonging life and "by keeping individuals alive after they are dead," whether by medical, technological, legal, or informational means.[47] Of course, for all that biopower is concerned to "make live" rather than to "take life," the biopolitical state is prepared to take the lives of others—and in the era of genocidal weapons, of other *populations*—in order to ensure the security of its own. But where the sovereign is prepared to expend lives in defeating political adversaries, the biopolitical state can justify the taking of life only "in the elimination of the biological threat to and the improvement of the species or race" whose collective life processes the state secures and regulates.[48] And this, for Foucault, is the function of racism, which turns the adversary, whether external or internal, into a biological other whose life can be taken, effaced, or nakedly compelled in the name of making a better, purer life for a citizenry.

So far, Foucault's discussion of biopolitics has informed intellectual property studies exclusively in the area of patents. This shouldn't surprise us. After several millennia of treating individual animals as private property—indeed, of being able to imagine our legal relationship to animals exclusively through property law—we are now living at a time when bacterial strains, seed lines, and genetically engineered life forms have become patentable. This "bioproperty," as it is known, differs from the private ownership of animals and plants in several ways. What it

---

46. Questions of population, fertility, and birth control converge intriguingly with copyright law in *Ulysses*' "Oxen of the Sun" episode, which may well be literary modernism's most extended meditation on the biopolitics of intellectual property.

47. Foucault, *"Society Must Be Defended,"* 248.

48. Ibid., 256.

confers upon the patent-holder is not ownership in a particular living entity but exclusive rights in a life form, as it were—in a reproducible genetic code that, when activated, produces a particular strain or species of life. Unlike, say, my ownership of a particular pig, DuPont's property in the OncoMouse did not terminate with the death of a particular transgenic organism but rather with the expiration, after seventeen years, of its patent in that type of transgenic mouse. DuPont, that is, did not own *a life* but rather the power to *make live*. As with the transition from sovereign to biopolitical power, the pig owner's sovereign right to take the life of the pig is being succeeded (if not superseded) by the bioproperty owner's generative power to make OncoMice and to exclude others from making them.

If patent law's creation of bioproperty has initiated a new phase in the propertization of life, we might say that copyright has enacted, over the course of its history, the reverse: the biologization of property. At British copyright's inception in 1710, the fourteen-year term granted by the law derived from the existing patent term of that length, which in turn had been computed as twice the seven-year statutory term of trade apprenticeships. Measured by analogy with apprenticeship, and from publication rather than from the author's death, copyright at that point resembled organic forms only in its temporariness, a feature that distinguished it from most other property forms. Although the first U.S. Copyright Act also adopted a term of fourteen years (with the option of a fourteen-year renewal term if the author was still living), Thomas Jefferson had initially suggested a term of nineteen years, one he calculated by consulting mortality tables compiled by the Comte de Buffon.[49] Jefferson's actuarial reasoning seems not to have persuaded the congressmen who, in their deliberations on the 1790 act, simply replicated the British term with minor modifications. But as U.S., UK, and European terms grew over the course of the nineteenth century and eventually came to be calculated from the author's death, the demographic approach to determining copyright's duration gained wide acceptance. One thing, however, sets Jefferson crucially apart from those who have

49. Buffon's statistics on 23,994 deaths put the average (French) life expectancy at fifty-five years. Assuming an adult population distributed evenly between age twenty-one and its oldest members, Jefferson calculated the average remaining life expectancy for that population was eighteen years, eight months, of adulthood. Rounding up, he set the median adult generational length, and thus the term of copyright, at nineteen years. See Thomas Jefferson to Richard Gem, undated [Sept. 1789], rpt. in *The Writings of Thomas Jefferson: Memorial Edition*, vol. 7 (Washington, DC: Thomas Jefferson Memorial Association of the United States, 1903), 462–463. According to the same letter, the nineteen-year term would have applied to "Every constitution...and every law," which Jefferson took to expire at the end of a generation's ascendancy. "If it be enforced longer, it is an act of force, not of right" (ibid., 459).

lately advocated term extensions based on growing life expectancies. Whereas the latter group deploys its life tables to argue for longer postmortem terms, Jefferson's figuring proceeded from a premise he supposed "to be self-evident, that the *earth belongs in usufruct to the living;* that the dead have neither powers nor rights over it." No generation, he maintained, had "the right to bind another"; each generation must receive the earth "clear of the debts and encumbrances" of its forerunners.[50] Jefferson turned to mortality tables as a way of ensuring that no generation held sway from beyond the grave—as a way of ensuring, in effect, that copyright did *not* extend postmortem.

If we want to see the present-day ascendancy of the demographic logic Jefferson so presciently used—though, again, to different ends—we need look no further than the 1990s debates over term extension. The EU commission on copyright made two main arguments in favor of "harmonizing upward" from the Berne standard term of fifty years *p.m.a.* to the German and Austrian term of seventy years *p.m.a.* Both arguments had to do with generations and mortality. First, the commission surmised that postmortem copyright was "intended to provide for the author and the first two generations of his descendants," and that because the average life span in the European Union had grown, the Berne term adopted in 1908 was no longer sufficient to fulfill that intention. (Significantly, the chief counterargument to this claim—that the commission should consider changes not in longevity but in the shifting average age of childbearing—was also demographic.) Second, the commission favored term extension because it would "offset the effects of the world wars on the exploitation of authors' works."[51] The unusually long German and Austrian terms that other countries would adopt resulted not from long-standing legal traditions but from 1960s *années de guerre* measures designed to compensate literary estates in those countries for the premature deaths and lost productivity caused by the world wars.[52] Reluctant to diminish rights already enjoyed by its member states, the European Union has tended to generalize the

50. Thomas Jefferson to James Madison, Sept. 6, 1789, rpt. in *The Writings of Thomas Jefferson*, vol. 7, 454–456.

51. European Union Directive 93/98/EEC on Copyright Term of Protection, recitals 5 and 6, qtd. in Brad Sherman and Lionel Bently, "Balance and Harmony in the Duration of Copyright: The European Directive and Its Consequences," in *Textual Monopolies: Literary Copyright and the Public Domain*, ed. Patrick Parrinder and Warren Chernaik (London: Office for Humanities Publication, 1997), 24–25.

52. Belgium and France had made similar, albeit slightly shorter, compensations for the war years. See Julian Barnes, "Letter from Paris," *Times Literary Supplement* (Dec. 21, 2001) 13.

most comprehensive national rights to all member states. For that reason, a copyright term that stemmed from two nations' temporary postwar compensations became the permanent Euro-American standard, and is now well on its way to becoming the global one; copyright is, in effect, conscripting the world to a perennialized mourning for two generations of German and Austrian war dead. At the same time, corporate work-for-hire copyright terms also gained twenty years even though the demographic rationales invoked on behalf of individual creators were irrelevant to corporate "authors," who have neither the incentive of heirs nor the need to be compensated for lost productivity in wars. Even setting aside the work-for-hire extensions, corporate rights-holders were the primary beneficiaries of the EU directive and the Bono Act. Creative individuals and their descendants, on whose behalf the arguments about life expectancy and generation are ostensibly made in the first place, often sell their copyrights to media corporations when they prove valuable. The result is that corporate owners reap the benefits of longer terms that were instituted as individual incentives.

Copyright is clearly entangled in what Foucault called biopolitical techniques, as witnessed by the fact that even opponents of the 1990s term extensions did not reject the relevance of demographic arguments as such. What's more, copyright's entanglement in these techniques intensified both during and as a result of the modernist decades—in the internationalization of postmortem terms, in the subsumption of a working population's legal authorship under new corporate work-for-hire doctrines, and in the massive death events that would later prompt legal compensations.

But to what extent can we really call copyright biopolitical in its function? Is literary property law a technology of state bioregulation? Here, let me contrast copyright to the state censorship regime from which it both precipitated and differentiated itself. Like the disciplinary regime of which it is a part, censorship individuates, subjecting to a visible discipline the bodies of both the transgressive work (by expurgation, impounding, burning) and the transgressive author (by negative publicity and incarceration). Censorship either lets live or makes die. Early copyright may have served a censorship function by making attribution a precondition of the monopoly right.[53] But as it becomes more actuarial, copyright

---

53. Indeed, Foucault implied as much, and with particular emphasis on the compensatory relationship between literary property and transgressive *literature*:

> Texts, books, and discourses really began to have authors...to the extent that authors became subject to punishment, that is, to the extent that discourses could be transgressive.... Once a system of ownership for texts came into being, once strict rules concerning author's rights, author-publisher relations, rights of

participates in what Foucault called "a second seizure of power that is not individualizing but, if you like, massifying, that is directed not at man-as-body but at man-as-species"; it becomes a device not for singling out anomalies but for managing the balance, at the level of population, between innovation and legacy, access and incentive, public good and private monopoly, even natality and mortality.[54] The subject imagined by copyright is a biopolitical subject, one that can be compelled to live and create in particular ways through the regulation of the fields and systems it shares with its population. And if the *subject* that copyright comes to imagine is a biopolitical one, the *work* that copyright protects is, oddly, its doppelgänger—a property form endowed with the lineaments of a life form. By regulating the conditions of an intellectual property's creation and vitality, copyright makes property live; by making regulation coterminous with that vitality, copyright lets property die. And the death into which the work dies is, like the death into which its author retreats, an escape into a "privacy" where power ceases to recognize it, a privacy from power called, only a little paradoxically, the public domain. What clearer illustration of Foucault's thesis do we need than the fact that copyright law, in the age of biopolitics, can only imagine propertizing a work by first constructing it as a life?

Of course, like the disciplinary and biopolitical regimes to which I have linked them, censorship and copyright are not mutually exclusive but have coexisted—not least during the modernist period, when anti-obscenity statutes and copyright laws were both vigorously exertive, producing a variety of interference and amplification effects. Returning for a moment to the 1927 protest over the unauthorized *Ulysses*, we might see Joyce's and Pound's reactions as responding to the disciplinary and the biopolitical aspects, respectively, of the censorship-copyright system. Singled out and rendered visible by censorship, Joyce sought an individualist remedy through the protest, with its insistence on the particulars of his injury and its conscription of other great names to his cause. Contrastingly, Pound refused to add his own name because he saw U.S. copyright as the worse problem, insofar as it failed in its biopolitical regulatory function by creating what were, in

---

reproduction, and related matters were enacted…the possibility of transgression attached to the act of writing took on, more and more, the form of an imperative peculiar to literature. It is as if the author, beginning with the moment at which he was placed in the system of property that characterizes our society, compensated for the status that he thus acquired by rediscovering the old bipolar field of discourse, systematically practicing transgression and thereby restoring danger to a writing which was now guaranteed the benefits of ownership. (Foucault, "What Is an Author?" 108–109)

54. Foucault, *"Society Must Be Defended,"* 243.

effect, trade imbalances between populations (European versus U.S. writers) and generations (the dead versus the living). Strangely, this contrast remains legible in how the estates of Joyce and Pound—two writers whose intertextual practices, at least, were similarly radical—have come to present themselves: one as a ferocious defender of individual genius, reputation, privacy, memory, and taste; the other as a mediator between filiative and disseminative models of artistic meaning, that is, between calf and wind. Although we should expect no straight lines to connect artist, oeuvre, and estate, we can observe that the ethos of an estate is nearly always a *reading* of the work and its creator. We are beginning to learn to read those readings—to read estates not just as coming after what they protect but also as transmitting something decipherable about it. And in the case of modernism, the copyright-censorship system will be part of what we read, even as it has shaped the means by which we come to read it.

The conflation of intellectual property estates with an artist's legacy, privacy, and integrity may seem to issue from copyright's encounter with romantic individualism, but it belongs equally to the law's more recent shift to the biopolitical. We speak readily of "revived" or "zombie" copyrights and "orphan" works because intellectual properties whose duration is measured from the author's death are envisioned in the eerily organic ways I have been discussing. At the same time, the more that postmortem copyright acts as a surrogate for the authorial organism, the more intellectual property becomes a receptacle for fantasies of transcending that organism's mortal condition. Because copyright likes to linger in the graveyard, it entertains a dream fostered by that place: the dream of eternal life, or at least of an eternally visited tomb. The crucial point here is that one of copyright's most powerful affective externalities—its quasi-religious role of protecting, commemorating, and even conferring a kind of immortality upon creative individuals—is not incidental to the law's regulatory and demographic logic but is the result of that logic. We may visit the tombs of the great at such places as Westminster Abbey, Père Lachaise, San Michele, and Fluntern, but postmortem copyright raises the lone revenant of the artist from a mass grave.

Following copyright's biopolitical turn opens related aspects of the law to critique, not least from the perspectives of gender and sexuality studies. For, in addition to being a creature of mortality tables, the subject of postmortem copyright is also emphatically reproductive, sitting at the threshold where sexual individuals produce (or fail or refuse to produce) regulable populations. In debates preceding the 1976 U.S. act, the proponents of an explicitly postmortem term argued that authors were motivated primarily by the desire to bequeath a patrimony to their children and grandchildren, and that a longer term would accommodate that incentive. Long before he was appointed to the Supreme Court, Stephen Breyer named this the "child-caring father" argument in the course of dismissing it as unconvincing.[55] But the majority of lawmakers have not shared Breyer's skepticism: the child-caring father argument, with its presumptively reproductive model of authorial incentive, prevailed in the term extensions of 1976 and 1998. Nor was this the first time that copyright had built its statutes around the portrait of a married, progenerative male author. The U.S. act of 1831 vested ownership of the fourteen-year renewal term exclusively in the author's "widow, or child, or children, either or all then living" if the author died during the first term.[56] (Previously, works whose author died during the first term entered the public domain at the end of that term even if he had heirs.)[57] Of course, copyright does not now compel authors to bequeath their literary estates to their children. But the rhetoric of heritable intellectual property estates invariably points to the biological descendant as the primary beneficiary.[58] Insofar as its incentives presuppose biological heirs, copyright exhibits what Lee Edelman has called "reproductive futurism"—the inability "to conceive of a future without the figure of the Child," that fantasy figure who "has come to embody for us the telos of the social order and come to be seen as the one for whom that order is held in perpetual trust."[59] On finding this heteronormative model of futurity deeply embedded in our legal incentives for innovation and expression, we need to pursue a series of questions. What people and incentives fall beyond the pale of a copyright law whose universal subject is the child-caring father? What political orientations toward time and what modes of cultural dissemination does such a law disserve? What else, conversely, would be changed if we were to shift copyright's incentives away from its current reproductivist bases? Given that the rhetoric of futurity has been such an effective tool of both rights-holder sovereignty and regressive conceptions of gender and sexuality, we are likely to find compelling reasons to rebalance the law in favor of living subjects and present freedoms.

---

55. Stephen Breyer, "The Uneasy Case for Copyright: A Study of Copyright in Books, Photocopies, and Computer Programs," *Harvard Law Review* 84 (1970): 324.

56. Act of Feb. 3, 1831, 21st Cong., 2nd sess., 4 Stat. 436, § 2.

57. William F. Patry, *Copyright Law and Practice* (Washington, DC: Bureau of National Affairs, 1994), ch. 1, n. 116. See http://digital-law-online.info/patry/index.html (accessed Sept. 4, 2009).

58. The locus classicus of this argument in verse is William Wordsworth's "A Poet to His Grandchild" (1838), a sonnet that conscripts its titular figures to the cause of perpetual copyright.

59. Lee Edelman, *No Future: Queer Theory and the Death Drive* (Durham, NC: Duke University Press, 2004), 11.

Clearly, copyright's biopolitical logic should become an object of critique. But it might also become a critical tool, one that equips us to question legal maximalism in terms that its advocates have already embraced. What populations, we might ask, do long postmortem copyright laws most extensively protect and thereby more effectively make live? To the extent that longevity is correlated with socioeconomic status, copyright gives the greatest "incentive" to those who will tend to need it least—i.e., highly educated, economically secure people living in politically and environmentally stable communities. If growing life expectancy has driven copyright term extension in developed nations, should countries where life expectancy is shorter (say, Yambo Ouologuem's native Mali, where the average life expectancy as of 2009 is 50.35 years, versus 78.11 years in the United States) have commensurately shorter copyright terms?[60] If not, what does it mean that copyright terms in the industrializing world are driven by life expectancies in industrialized countries? Should one lament or celebrate the fact that intellectual property's long duration in Mali results from the greater life expectancies in nations whose development was fueled, in many cases, by explicitly racist, often genocidal, imperialist projects during the modernist decades followed by a postindustrial phase of net intellectual property export? To what extent has the hemispheric (and concomitantly racial) imbalance in intellectual property fields—one of imperialism's most durable legacies—been underwritten by a demographic logic that, starting from different, more Jeffersonian premises, might have secured the resources of the global South for the usufruct of the global South?

Counterfactual

Might have been otherwise. It's a gesture we recognize from counterfactual fiction and allo-historical narratives: imagining the outcome of some mutation in history's course. A world in which President-elect Franklin Delano Roosevelt was assassinated in 1933, or in which the Confederacy won the U.S. Civil War—such thought experiments can be powerful ways to describe historical contingency and incite in us either a homesickness for our own time stream or a longing for some better one. But why do we find so much late twentieth- and early twenty-first-century scholarship on intellectual property and culture, including several essays in this

---

60. These life expectancies at birth, for both men and women together, are taken from U.S. Central Intelligence Agency, *The World Factbook 2009* (Washington, DC: U.S. Central Intelligence Agency, 2009). See https://www.cia.gov/library/publications/the-world-factbook/fields/2102.html (accessed Sept. 5, 2009).

book, performing similar moves? Neil Netanel's study of the tension between copyright and free speech, for example, is rife with "downward" counterfactual scenarios that imagine the obstacles that thicker copyright regimes would have posed to modernism. "T. S. Eliot might today run afoul of copyright," Netanel postulates, "were not *The Waste Land* a pastiche of centuries-old material." Elsewhere, he observes, "Yeats [borrowed] from Shelley; Kafka from Kleist and Dickens; Joyce from Homer; and T. S. Eliot from Shakespeare, Whitman, and Baudelaire, all in ways that would infringe today's bloated copyright."[61] The authors of a microeconomic analysis of intellectual property law cite many of the same examples in remarking that "the echo of the literature of the past has been a common device of modernist literature; one is not just talking about a vanished era of literary conventions." Contemporary writers, they add, are prevented by extensive copyright laws from engaging in "noble plagiarisms" like those of Chaucer, Shakespeare, and Milton; in order to avoid infringement suits, they must either restrict their literary borrowing to public-domain works or engage in parody, paraphrase, or minimal quotation that is clearly within the bounds of fair use.[62] My book *The Copywrights* imagines how Joyce's *Ulysses* might have fared had it been published under a post-Bono copyright regime and concludes that the private censorship underwritten by long postmortem terms would have impeded the novel's publication and circulation at least as much as 1920s state censorship did in fact. In all these examples, modernism is invoked as the last flourishing of neoclassical practices (i.e., those that rely heavily on extant models, sometimes to the point of verbatim copying) before copyright made such practices legally dangerous. But, again, why do these invocations take place in a counterfactual mode?

One answer to this question has to do with the difficulty of assessing the numbers and quality of new works that strong copyright law has prevented people from publishing, completing, or even undertaking. As James Surowiecki puts it, "[T]he effects of underuse created by too much ownership are often invisible. They're mainly things that don't happen."[63] Mark Fowler's chapter in the present volume concurs: "There is no means of determining the number of projects that have been scuttled or drastically re-engineered in the face of opposition from copyright owners. The accounts of censorship or self-censorship are mostly

61. Neil Weinstock Netanel, *Copyright's Paradox* (New York: Oxford University Press, 2008), 60, 22.

62. William M. Landes and Richard A. Posner, *The Economic Structure of Intellectual Property Law* (Cambridge, MA: Belknap, 2003), 59, 61.

63. James Surowiecki, "The Permission Problem," *New Yorker* (Aug. 11, 2008), 34.

anecdotal." At least one particularly aggressive estate not only has shut down projects it dislikes but also—in a kind of second-order private censorship—has issued a variety of threats in order to prevent would-be users from discussing those scuttled projects. Laws that constrain our expressive powers put us in the strange position of having to *imagine* the works—the unmade film, the unwritten play, the unpublished novel—whose real legal preclusion we deplore. And it is a short distance from that act of imagination to envisaging a legal order in which the creative works we *do* possess were themselves altered, hindered, or prohibited. We should recognize some of these dynamics from the work of mourning, in which we rue the loss not only of the beloved and of our years together but also of the years there would have been had death come less soon. But where such mourning occurs only partly through an imagined "otherwise," any attempt to measure or lament the works foreclosed by the law must take place solely in the counterfactual mode. It's a little like mourning the unborn.

Attempting to travel roads untaken by history is a mark of the literary imagination, as Celia Marshik reminds us when she quotes Virginia Woolf catching herself "play[ing] for a moment with the thought of what might have happened if Charlotte Brontë had possessed say three hundred a year—but the foolish woman sold the copyright of her novels outright for fifteen hundred pounds."[64] Still, for all that such musings attest to literature's power and its material dependencies, the counterfactual turn may be even more endogenous to the legal imagination than to the literary one, which tends to alter many variables in its worldmaking rather than cleave to the single-variable logic of *ceteris paribus* ("all the rest being equal").[65] We find the latter more strictly counterfactual logic not only in courtroom imputations of causality from evidence but also in judicial decisions and legal statutes, particularly those with remedial or reparative agendas. As Catherine Gallagher has shown, the U.S. Supreme Court decision in *Milliken v. Bradley* (1977), a key desegregation case, affirmed that equitable remedies (in this instance, for de jure segregation) "must be designed as nearly as possible 'to restore the

---

64. See Marshik's chapter in the present volume. Woolf goes on to imagine the life forgone in that sale—how by parting with her copyrights, Brontë denied herself "more knowledge of the busy world, and towns and regions full of life; more practical experience, and intercourse with her kind and acquaintance with a variety of character." Virginia Woolf, *A Room of One's Own* (New York: Harcourt Brace Jovanovich, 1981), 70.

65. There is a rich literature about the nature, role, and limits of counterfactual reasoning in legal argumentation, standards of evidence, and philosophical investigations of causality. A good place to begin is Peter Murphy, ed., *Evidence, Proof, and Facts: A Book of Sources* (New York: Oxford University Press, 2003).

victims of discriminatory conduct to the position they would have occupied in the absence of such conduct.'"[66] Copyright statutes, for their part, contain a number of allo-historical gestures seeking to remediate past asymmetries among national regimes or to compensate for geopolitical disruptions of culture making. The 1994 Uruguay Round Agreements Act restored U.S. copyright in foreign-origin works when their protection had been prematurely lost through failure to comply with thorny U.S. legal formalities or through the absence of a treaty between the United States and the work's country of origin. The act's delineation of the restored term, now embedded in the U.S. copyright code, is counterfactual: the revived copyright subsists "for the remainder of the term of copyright that the work would have otherwise been granted in the United States if the work [had] never entered the public domain in the United States."[67] And we have already seen that the seventy-year postmortem copyright term stemmed from *années de guerre* provisions that sought (to adapt the language of the *Milliken* decisions) as nearly as possible to restore the victims of the world wars, or their heirs or assignees, to the position they would have occupied in the absence of those wars. In such cases, the law does more than use a counterfactual logic; it becomes, itself, a counterfactual sanctuary. In the virtual world of our copyright laws, it is as if the United States had signed the Berne Convention in 1886 and two world wars had never happened.

I observed earlier that substantial postmortem copyright terms in the age of biopolitics confer a kind of second life on artists through the surrogate body of their intellectual property estates. In fact, if we were looking for a single term to capture the functionality of postmortem copyright, we could do worse than "second life." That this name belongs to an online virtual world should alert us to a certain proximity between additional lives and alternate ones, both kinds of life sharing a logic of surrogacy, sharing, even more essentially, the structure of a life: if copyright often moves its critics to acts of counterfactual imagination, this is partly because the law grants intellectual property a life span and thus a life, which are the preconditions of imagining other lives. Already a second life in itself, postmortem copyright cannot help but pose, in turn, the question of alternate second lives—lives in which *copyright* is otherwise. To find that very counterfactual mode within the law itself is to discover a new tool for advocating copyright reduction—a tool, as I argued about demographic logic, that copyright maximalists

---

66. Catherine Gallagher, "Undoing," in *Time and the Literary*, ed. Karen Newman, Jay Clayton, and Marianne Hirsch (New York: Routledge, 2002), 22, quoting *Milliken v. Bradley*, 433 U.S. 267, 280 (1977), quoting *Milliken v. Bradley* 418 U.S. 717, 746 (1974).

67. 17 U.S.C. § 104A(a)(1)(B).

already accept as legitimate and have therefore left ready-to-hand for other purposes. The counterfactual energies of equitable remedy, in other words, may become a mode not just for measuring loss but also for proposing remediation. Of course, demanding equitable remedy on the part of a public domain victimized by excessive legal protections would require us to upend the dominant portrait of that public domain. We would need to think of it as a space where memory is not annihilated but crucially regenerated; as equivalent not to the radical privacy of the dead but to the making of life for those living; as a wronged entity in itself rather than as the place where entities dissolve. But if corporate authors may benefit from equitable remedies supposedly dispensed to compensate wronged individual authors, why should the collective space of the public domain not benefit from a similar dispensation? The equitable remedy for decades of excessive copyright would seek as nearly as possible to restore the victims of that excess to the position they would have occupied in its absence.

Copyright is stranger than we knew, and its strangeness becomes more visible as modernism draws near. It is the strangeness of a legal regime that anoints the individual, reasons through populations, and swears fealty to the corporate rightsholder; a regime that both provokes and accommodates an astonishing amount of counterfactual thinking despite being rooted in the facts of this world. At the same time, intellectual property law has begun to make our understanding of modernism strange to itself. This owes partly to the ways in which copyright's late twentieth-century fortification separates us from modernism, measuring the intervening decades in legal reforms that have delayed and perhaps dissipated certain aspects of modernism's reception. But just as copyright and modernism should not be treated simply as homologous responses to modernity, it would be a mistake to see some essential antipathy between the law and modernism tout court—to imagine, say, that copyright, as a thing constitutively opposed to modernism, could provide us with a unified-field theory of modernism as literary antiproperty. This book insists in many registers that modernism and copyright cannot be disentangled along such starkly oppositional lines. Rather, copyright's productive influence was knit into its power to compel; whether it abets state censorship, holds out the prospect of fair competition between nations and generations, or strikes some of its practitioners and students as "communistic,"[68] it does so as both a coercive force and an enabling condition of expression. Copyright has been an

---

68. Thomas Scrutton, *The Laws of Copyright: An Examination into the Principles Which Should Regulate Literary and Artistic Property in England and Other Countries* (London: John Murray, 1883), 290.

important factor in making modernism live, and in ways we are just beginning to understand.

Even less well understood is copyright's equally complex influence on modernist studies. Here, I refer not just to the fact that scholars are themselves copyright owners but also to the role that legal impediments play in shaping scholarly communities and the canonical status of certain works and authors. Scholarship has unquestionably been chilled by the actions of some rights-holders endowed with long postmortem copyrights—just ask those senior Joyceans who have discouraged graduate students from working on Joyce because of the history of adversarial encounters between scholars and the author's estate.[69] Yet the fact that there is still a field called "Joyce studies" that is well populated with "Joyceans" also owes something to this same antagonism. The Joyce community may feel its work to be jeopardized by the legal pugnacity of the Joyce estate, but much of that community has been galvanized, too, by the sense of having a shared adversary. One also imagines that the media attention generated by several copyright-related clashes has, on balance, reinforced rather than injured Joyce's reputation and canonical status. Scholars of modernism might well celebrate the fact that copyright can accommodate such strength-through-adversity narratives. But we must also turn our attention to how the law participates in the feedback loop of canonicity and the ossified portrait of modernism it tends to reproduce. By this I mean, the self-perpetuating cycle by which the most valuable properties are the most contested, the most contested are the most publicized, and the most publicized are again the most valued. If modernism is not just something that "happened" but also a contemporary problem space—a shifting totality of askable questions and

69. Irish literature scholar David Pierce, for example, told the *New York Times*, "The copyright issue is so crucial, so difficult, that Joyce research is not something I would recommend." Dinitia Smith, "A Portrait of the Artist's Troubled Daughter," *New York Times* (Nov. 22, 2003). Pierce edited the Cork University Press anthology *Irish Writing in the Twentieth Century: A Reader* (2000), whose Joyce section consists of twenty-two blank pages following the notice: "Pages 323–346 have been removed due to a dispute in relation to copyright." (The dispute had culminated in the Joyce estate's obtaining a preliminary injunction against the press's reprinting excerpts from a putatively public-domain *Ulysses*, a plan the press had made in attempting to avoid paying the prohibitively high permissions fee initially demanded by the estate.) I had occasion to hear many more such testimonies from senior Joyceans in 2004–2006, when I chaired a panel initiated by the International James Joyce Foundation to study the permissions criteria, practices, and history of the estate of James Joyce. My fellow panelists—Robert Spoo, Michael Groden, and Carol Loeb Shloss—and I encountered a number of scholars who had given this advice but were reluctant to go on record as having done so for fear of further antagonizing the estate.

comprehensible answers about modernism—then its vitality depends on the flexibility and mutability of that space. We need to attend to copyright's role not only in modernism's dynamic, embattled making but also in its ongoing circuits of institutionalization and consecration.

Perhaps the strangest place to which modernism and copyright jointly lead us is the graveyard. We revisit the grave of a celebrated modernist author as his grandson consults him about which copyright permissions to grant and which to deny; we look for the headstone of a congressman who has come to symbolize the hope of eternal life through perpetual copyright.[70] We return to the tombs of the French writers and composers killed in action during the world wars, creators whose thirty-year copyright bonus bears an official designation—*Mort pour la France*—that insists on intellectual property's links to nation, mortality, and population. Even our jokes about modernism and copyright take us to, and sometimes across, the threshold between the living and the dead, as in the case of the Theater Oobleck/neofuturist spoof *The Complete Lost Works of Samuel Beckett as Found in an Envelope (Partially Burned) in a Dustbin in Paris Labeled "Never to Be Performed. Never. Ever. EVER! Or I'll Sue! I'LL SUE FROM THE GRAVE!"*[71] And yet, the more extensively postmortem it becomes, the more emphatically copyright declares its connections to life: to the life terms and expectancies of authors and heirs, to the surrogate life of the copyright itself, and to the citizens' collective life process that each national regime exists to encourage, curb, and compel. The law's bid to grant authors a second life through copyright arises less from its fascination with last things than from its need to give the form of a life—and concomitantly the form of an afterlife or an alternate life—to what it regulates. Even in calling for less extensive regimes to secure the usufruct of earth and culture to the living rather than to the dead, critics of strong copyrights must come to recognize intellectual property law's penetration of life conditions and its sway over the vitality of the living. In the midst of life, we are in copyright.

70. For references to these graveside consultations, see Bédarida, "Stephen James Joyce, petit-fils de l'écrivain," 26; and Iain S. Bruce, "Joyce Grandson Fury over Fringe Musical Filth," *Sunday Herald* (July 30, 2000).

71. See Rimmer, "Damned to Fame." The spoof was first performed at the 2000 New York Fringe Festival and, says Rimmer, "made light of [the] ongoing conflict between the Beckett estate and artistic directors.... The plot concerned a fight between three producers and the Beckett estate."

PART ONE

Portraits of the Modernist as Copywright

1 Ezra Pound, Legislator

Perpetual Copyright and Unfair Competition with the Dead

Robert Spoo

In the midst of copyright, we are in death. Copyrights—those legal monopolies that confer, for "limited Times," the power to control the use of creative works—are mortal creatures of statute.[1] Their terms are tightly bound to the lives and deaths of authors. In many countries today, copyrights endure for fifty or seventy years *post-mortem auctoris*, persisting as a sort of afterimage of the author, a prolongation of legal and economic consequences after the incandescence of living creativity has been quenched. The very thought of these time-bound monopolies calls forth a lugubrious poetry of last things. We speak of copyrights "expiring," of works "lapsing" or "falling" into the public domain. Copyright maximalists clamor for "perpetual rights" or for protection that will last "forever less 1 day."[2] Public-domain advocates retort that legislators are already granting "perpetual copyright

A longer, substantially different version of this essay appeared as "Ezra Pound's Copyright Statute: Perpetual Rights and the Problem of Heirs," *UCLA Law Review* 56 (2009): 1775–1834.

1. The phrase "limited Times" is used in the U.S. Constitution, art. I, § 8, to admonish that, in the United States, copyrights and patents may not be granted for indefinite periods.

2. Statement of Congresswoman Mary Bono in support of the Sonny Bono Copyright Term Extension Act, 105th Cong., 2nd sess., *Congressional Record* 144 (Oct. 7, 1998): 9951–9952.

on the installment plan."[3] Unlike most forms of property, but like the religious doctrines of death and resurrection, copyrights inspire rhetorical and conceptual extremism, a vivid eschatology of "property talk."[4]

Ezra Pound was a passionate copyright polemicist who believed that intellectual property played an important role in culture. For Pound, an indispensable condition of creativity was the artist's ability to move about freely in time and space. Writing to the English poet F. S. Flint in 1912, he defended his preoccupation with medieval poetry by explaining, "I have not been penned up within the borders of one country and I am not minded to be penned into any set period of years."[5] Just as he had "escaped the limitations of place" through a restless expatriate wanderlust, so he resisted "the limitations of time" by making the works of long-dead poets—Dante, Guido Cavalcanti, the twelfth-century troubadours—central to his evolving métier.[6] But travel in time and space can occur only to the extent permitted by law. Pound denounced passport regulations, book tariffs, obscenity laws, and customs seizures as meddlesome interferences with the ability of writers and their works to gain free passage across national borders and exposure to new readers. Throughout the 1920s, he inveighed against "passport and visa stupidities, arbitrary injustice from customs officials;... Article 211 of the Penal Code [banning obscene materials from the mails], and all such muddle-headedness in any laws whatsoever."[7] Prominent on his list of legal abuses was "the thieving copyright law" of the United States.[8]

Pound recognized the power of copyright law to police the borders of geography and history. Backed by the state, a rights-holder could permit distribution

3. Testimony of Professor Peter Jaszi, "The Copyright Term Extension Act of 1995: Hearings on S483 before the Senate Judiciary Committee," 104th Cong., 1st sess. (Sept. 20, 1995), available in 1995 WL 10524355, at *6. Jaszi discusses the remark in "Caught in the Net of Copyright," *Oregon Law Review* 75 (1998): 303.

4. Carol M. Rose, "Canons of Property Talk, or, Blackstone's Anxiety," *Yale Law Journal* 108 (1998): 601–632. Paul K. Saint-Amour has cataloged the "memento mori rhetoric" used by proponents of copyright term extension and has observed that copyright, as it has evolved over time, "presides over last things, last wishes, and the possibility of a life, or legacy, at least, that outlasts death" (*The Copywrights: Intellectual Property and the Literary Imagination* [Ithaca, NY: Cornell University Press, 2003], 126, 129). See especially ch. 4, "The Reign of the Dead: Hauntologies of Postmortem Copyright," 121–158.

5. Ezra Pound to F. S. Flint, unpublished draft letter, ca. May 1912, in the Ezra Pound Collection at Yale University's Beinecke Library (YCAL MS 43, box 17, folder 743).

6. Ibid.

7. Ezra Pound, letter to the editor, *Nation* 125 (Dec. 14, 1927): 685, reprinted in *Ezra Pound's Poetry and Prose: Contributions to Periodicals*, ed. Lea Baechler et al. (New York: Garland, 1991), 4:393. This eleven-volume edition is hereafter cited in the notes as *Contributions to Periodicals*, followed by volume and page number.

8. Ibid.

of a copyrighted work in some countries and deny it in others. As with book tariffs, the supra-competitive pricing that copyrights allowed could discourage the importation and sale of new works. Throughout much of the twentieth century, protectionist features of U.S. law empowered customs officials to seize certain classes of imported books that had not been printed on American soil in accordance with "manufacturing" requirements inscribed into the copyright act.[9] If not complied with, these requirements of the "thieving copyright law" also withheld American copyright protection from certain foreign-origin works, thus encouraging legalized piracy within the United States. What was banned at the docks could thus reappear, sometimes in distorted forms, as knockoff copies issued from the shops of "bookleggers."[10]

Copyright law also plays a role in controlling access to the past. A copyright holder's failure or refusal to keep a work in print or to authorize translations slams shut one window on history. The length and scope of copyrights ensure that many letters, diaries, and other unpublished writings will not soon become part of the historical record and that "orphan works"—out-of-print texts whose copyright owners cannot be located—will play only a limited role in our understanding of the past.[11] A misused or neglected copyright can, Cerberus-like, bar the way to dialogue with the dead, denying living creators a valid passport for time-travel. Pound was aware of both the power of copyrights and the fallibility of copyright holders, and his attitudes toward intellectual property were accordingly more complex and more ambivalent than his tirades against literary piracy and wrongheaded laws would sometimes suggest.

Nowhere are Pound's views more fully revealed than in a copyright proposal he advanced toward the end of World War I. In 1918, he wrote in the British periodical the *New Age:*

> The present American copyright regulations tend to keep all English and Continental authors in a state of irritation with *something* American—they don't quite know what, but there is a reason for irritation. There is a

9. See Act of Mar. 4, 1909, ch. 320, § 31 (prohibiting importation of certain works not manufactured on American soil), § 32 (providing for seizure and forfeiture of such works), § 33 (empowering the secretary of the treasury and the postmaster general to make and enforce regulations to prevent the importation of such works in the U.S. mails).

10. *Booklegging* was a term used to refer to literary piracy and the trade in pornography. See Jay A. Gertzman, *Bookleggers and Smuthounds: The Trade in Erotica, 1920–1940* (Philadelphia: University of Pennsylvania Press, 1999), 15, 87.

11. In the United States, legislation has been proposed that would mitigate the problem of orphan works. See, for example, Orphan Works Act of 2008, H.R. 5889, 110th Cong. (2008).

continuous and needless bother about the prevention of literary piracy, a need for agents, and agents' vigilance, and the whole matter produces annoyance, and ultimately tends to fester public opinion.[12]

Insisting that even recent American victories on the Western Front were no lasting remedy for the strained relations between Britain and his native country, Pound called for a "cure" that only a new law of "reciprocal copyright" could bring about. "The cure must be effected *now*," he declared, "now while the two countries are feeling amiable" ("CT," 208, 209).

Pound envisioned an international copyright law that would provide authors fair remuneration for their intellectual labor but would not stand in the way of the wide dissemination of their works at affordable prices. He believed that, with America's entry into "Armageddon" in 1917, the need for cross-cultural communication among writers and thinkers was more urgent than ever, and he sought to eliminate the barriers raised by "the red tape and insecurity of the copyright regulations" and high American book tariffs.[13] Such "hindrance[s] to international communication [are] serious at any time," he wrote, "and doubly serious now when we are trying to understand France and England more intimately" ("TC," 348).

Pound believed that now and again a gifted author emerges as an unofficial communicator among nations, a sort of literary ambassador-interpreter with the ability to "translate" the meaning of one culture for the benefit of other cultures. A month or so before his copyright proposal appeared in the *New Age*, Pound edited a special issue of the New York literary magazine the *Little Review* devoted to Henry James. James's recurrent theme in *The American* (1877), *The Portrait of a Lady* (1881), *The Ambassadors* (1903), and other works of fiction was the moral and cultural implications of the encounter between Americans and Europeans, and the differences between the New World and the Old. Like Pound, James had lived as an American expatriate in England and had deplored the coming of the Great War.[14] In the *Little Review*, Pound wrote that James—who died in 1916—had spent a "life-time...in trying to make two continents understand each other, in trying...to make three nations [Britain, France, and the United States] intelligible one to

12. Pound, "Copyright and Tariff," *New Age* 23 (Oct. 3, 1918): 363, reprinted in *Contributions to Periodicals*, 3:208, emphasis in original. This article is hereafter cited in the text as "CT."

13. Pound, "Tariff and Copyright," *New Age* 23 (Sept. 26, 1918): 348, reprinted in *Contributions to Periodicals*, 3:190. This article is hereafter cited in the text as "TC."

14. See Jonathan Atkin, *A War of Individuals: Bloomsbury Attitudes to the Great War* (Manchester, UK: Manchester University Press, 2002), 79.

another."[15] James, Pound observed, was a "hater of tyranny" whose entire career had been a "labour of translation, of making America intelligible, of making it possible for individuals to meet across national borders."[16]

As Pound saw it, James had been a literary laborer for world peace. "Peace comes of communication," he observed in one of his essays on James. "The whole of great art is a struggle for communication. All things set against this are evil whether they be silly scoffing or obstructive tariffs."[17] Pound viewed his own efforts to reform copyright laws and book tariffs as consistent with James's attempts to remove cultural barriers through the creation of fictional worlds.[18] A reformed copyright law would serve as a legal counterpart to James's efforts to get nations to understand each other, even as it furthered Pound's vision of modern writing as the abolition of geographic and historical borders. As he put it in one of his *New Age* articles, forging an international copyright law would require "reciprocal intelligence and reciprocal action between England and America" ("TC," 190).

Pound was profoundly dissatisfied with the copyright law of the United States as it stood in the early part of the twentieth century. He considered its technicalities to be hindrances to authorship and its provisions regarding foreign works to be an open and cynical invitation to literary piracy,[19] or what earlier critics had called "bookaneering."[20] No true cultural bond could exist between Britain and the United States, he believed, until the copyright laws of the two nations were amended to provide better protection for foreign authors. Convinced that he could do a better job than the legislators, Pound used the pages of the *New Age* to "set down a sketch of what the copyright law ought to be, and what dangers should be guarded against" ("CT," 208).

15. Pound, "In Explanation," *Little Review* 4 (1918): 5, reprinted in *Contributions to Periodicals*, 3:143.

16. Ibid., 143–144. See also "Ezra Pound's American Scenes: Henry James and the Labour of Translation" (ch. 3), in Daniel Katz, *American Modernism's Expatriate Scene: The Labour of Translation* (Edinburgh: Edinburgh University Press, 2007), 53–70.

17. Pound, "In Explanation," 145.

18. Henry James also took an interest in international copyright law and probed American book piracy and cultural tariffs in a witty colloquy. See his "An Animated Conversation" (1889), in Henry James, *Essays in London and Elsewhere* (New York: Harper, 1893), 280–285.

19. For a discussion of Pound's criticisms of U.S. copyright law, see Robert Spoo, "Copyright Protectionism and Its Discontents: The Case of James Joyce's *Ulysses* in America," *Yale Law Journal* 108 (1998): 633–634, 641–642. For a useful treatment of Pound's interest in international copyright and in efforts to amend American copyright law, see E. P. Walkiewicz and Hugh Witemeyer, eds., *Ezra Pound and Senator Bronson Cutting: A Political Correspondence, 1930–1935* (Albuquerque: University of New Mexico Press, 1995), 28–29.

20. See, for example, Thomas Hood, "Copyright and Copywrong, Letter II," in *Prose and Verse*, vol. 2 (New York: Wiley and Putnam, 1845), 84.

This "sketch" was more than a poet's florid wish for a better world; it was a set of detailed prescriptions expressed in a statutory idiom, with separate provisions for entitlements, exceptions, and remedies. Although Pound did not specify a mechanism for giving his plan the force of law, he seems to have imagined it as a kind of self-executing treaty or a statute to be implemented by each nation on the basis of a bilateral protocol. Like William Wordsworth and Mark Twain, whose efforts to reform copyright law are much better known,[21] Pound's views on literary property were shaped by a particular conception of authorship and the role of art in society. Drafted at a critical moment in the development of modernism, his copyright statute reflects the complex legal and economic conditions that underlay literary production in the early twentieth century. Ambitiously, Pound sought to reform intellectual property laws that had created transatlantic asymmetries in the protection and circulation of works and that hobbled American authors by giving a competitive advantage within the U.S. market to European writers, living and dead. These inequities, Pound believed, only increased the burden of the past with which modern authors generally and American authors in particular already struggled. Torn between a desire for enhanced legal protection for authors and a commitment to the broad dissemination of affordable books, Pound sought in his copyright statute to reconcile, on one hand, his ideal of borderless access to past and present cultural achievements and, on the other, the rigorous control over those achievements that strong intellectual property rights confer.

American Book Piracy, Trade Courtesy, and the Manufacturing Clause

Pound made it clear that one of the chief purposes of his proposed statute was to render it "easier for an author to retain the rights to the work of his brain than for some scoundrel to steal them." The particular source of Pound's irritation was the "continuous and needless bother about the prevention of literary piracy" ("CT," 208). Legalized American book piracy was a theme he returned to again and again over the next decade. In 1927, he announced, "For next President I want no man

---

21. See Susan Eilenberg, "Mortal Pages: Wordsworth and the Reform of Copyright," *English Literary History* 56 (1989): 351–374; and Catherine Seville, "Authors as Copyright Campaigners: Mark Twain's Legacy," *Journal of the Copyright Society U.S.A.* 55 (2008): 283–359.

who is not lucidly and clearly and with no trace or shadow of ambiguity against...the thieving copyright law."[22] The "infamous state of the American law," he wrote to James Joyce, "not only tolerates robbery but encourages unscrupulous adventurers to rob authors living outside of the American borders."[23] At every opportunity, Pound heaped colorful invective on U.S. copyright law: "dishonest," "rascally," a "clot," a law "originally designed to favour the printing trade at the expense of the mental life of the country."[24]

Pound's anger had been shared by many who complained of "Yankee pirates" during the nineteenth century.[25] By the 1830s, the practice of reprinting British books and periodicals without permission had become widespread in the American book trade.[26] Although some American publishers made ex gratia payments to British authors, the U.S. copyright law, which withheld protection from foreign writers, did not impose any such duty, and other publishers in the highly competitive book trade capitalized on this legal vacuum by reprinting British works without authorization or courtesy payments.[27] In 1842, Charles Dickens denounced "the scoundrel-booksellers" who "grow rich [in the United States] from publishing books, the authors of which do not reap one farthing from their issue," along with the "vile, blackguard and detestable newspaper[s]" that also reprinted British writings without authorization or remuneration.[28] Even Walt Whitman, usually a lyrical advocate of the interests of American multitudes, lamented his compatriots' exploitation of the legal vulnerability of British authors:

22. Pound, letter to the editor, *Nation* 125 (Dec. 14, 1927): 685, reprinted in *Contributions to Periodicals*, 4:393.

23. Ezra Pound to James Joyce, Dec. 25, 1926, in *Pound/Joyce: The Letters of Ezra Pound to James Joyce, with Pound's Essays on Joyce*, ed. Forrest Read (New York: New Directions, 1967), 226.

24. Pound, "The Exile," *Exile* 3 (1928): 102, reprinted in *Contributions to Periodicals*, 5:17; "Ezra Pound and Will Irwin Denounce Copyright and Boston Censorship," *Chicago Tribune* (Paris; Mar. 9, 1928): 2, reprinted in *Contributions to Periodicals*, 5:27; "Newspapers, History, Etc.," *Hound and Horn* 3 (1930): 574, reprinted in *Contributions to Periodicals*, 5:229.

25. S. S. Conant, "International Copyright: An American View," *Macmillan's Magazine* (May–Oct. 1879): 159.

26. John Feather, *Publishing, Piracy, and Politics: An Historical Study of Copyright in Britain* (London: Mansell, 1994), 153. David Saunders observes that "such reprinting was not illegal, even though it might be deemed unethical" and discusses American publishers' ex gratia payments to British authors. *Authorship and Copyright* (London: Routledge, 1992), 155–156.

27. Feather, *Publishing, Piracy, and Politics*, 157–158. Some British publishers "were equally unscrupulous in reprinting American books without permission" in the nineteenth century. Ibid., 154.

28. Charles Dickens to Henry Austin, May 1, 1842, in *The Letters of Charles Dickens, 1842–1843*, ed. Madeline House et al. (Oxford: Clarendon, 1974), 230.

Do not our publishers fatten quicker and deeper? (helping themselves, under shelter of a delusive and sneaking law, or rather absence of law, to most of their forage, poetical, pictorial, historical, romantic, even comic, without money and without price—and fiercely resisting the timidest proposal to pay for it.)[29]

Efforts to establish a reciprocal Anglo-American copyright law repeatedly met with obstacles during the nineteenth century. British law granted copyrights to foreign authors, including Americans, on conditions roughly similar to those imposed on British authors,[30] but a comparable privilege did not exist for British authors in the United States. Although some American publishers observed what was called "courtesy of the trade"—a self-regulating system in which the first publisher to reprint a British work, after paying the author a sum, would enjoy "title" to the work that was generally respected by competitors in the American market—no formal protections existed for foreign writers.[31]

When Congress finally granted rights to foreign authors in the Chace International Copyright Act of 1891,[32] protection came at the price of large concessions to American book manufacturers. Chief among these was the express condition that a foreign work in any language could acquire copyright protection in the United States only if the work was printed from type set within the United States and if two copies of the American imprint were deposited in the Copyright Office on or before the date of first publication anywhere else.[33] Although resourceful or well-connected foreign authors might be able to satisfy this tricky requirement of first or simultaneous publication in the United States,[34] others could not.

The 1909 U.S. Copyright Act—the law in force when Pound proposed his copyright statute in 1918—modified the manufacturing conditions of the

29. Walt Whitman, *Democratic Vistas* (1871), reprinted in *The Complete Poetry and Prose of Walt Whitman*, ed. Malcolm Cowley (New York: Pellegrini and Cudahy, 1948), 2:242.

30. See Eaton S. Drone, *A Treatise on the Law of Property in Intellectual Productions in Great Britain and the United States* (Boston: Little, Brown, 1879), 230.

31. For discussions of American trade courtesy, see Feather, *Publishing, Piracy, and Politics*, 160; Saunders, *Authorship and Copyright*, 156–157; and Conant, "International Copyright," 157–159. See also John Tebbel, *A History of Book Publishing in the United States* (New York: Bowker, 1972), 1:208, 2:54–55. For an analysis of the courtesy copyright that was improvised for the edition of Joyce's *Ulysses* published in the United States in 1934, see Spoo, "Copyright Protectionism," 656–659.

32. Act of Mar. 3, 1891, ch. 565, 26 Stat. 1106.

33. Ibid., § 4956, 1107–1108.

34. Feather describes the deft negotiations by George Bernard Shaw's publisher for publication in New York of Shaw's *The Perfect Wagnerite* in 1898. Feather, *Publishing, Piracy, and Politics*, 169.

Chace Act but did not abolish them. First, the 1909 act granted automatic protection to foreign-language works of foreign origin by exempting them from the manufacturing requirements.[35] Second, although foreign-origin works *in English* still had to be printed in the United States to acquire an American copyright,[36] the 1909 act relaxed this requirement somewhat by providing a thirty-day "ad interim" copyright if a copy of the foreign edition was deposited in the U.S. Copyright Office within thirty days of its publication abroad.[37] Once a copy was deposited, the work then had to be reprinted on U.S. soil within the thirty-day ad interim window, in accordance with the 1909 act's manufacturing clause.[38] Failure to do so—and thus to give American artisans their due—would result in the loss of American copyright after ad interim protection had expired.[39]

Thus, when Pound assailed the U.S. copyright law as "originally designed to favour the printing trade at the expense of the mental life of the country,"[40] he had in mind a history of codified protectionism for domestic book manufacturers that, as one American observer put it in 1879, "has been the occasion of more bitter feelings between the two countries than many a war has engendered."[41] Although there were other, more altruistic reasons for withholding automatic protection from British works—such as the fear that inexpensive American reprints of British titles, which served a large and increasingly literate population, would be replaced by small, pricey British import editions[42]—there is no question that this protectionism rendered the United States an outcast from the international copyright community. The manufacturing requirements, together with other copyright formalities, prevented the United States from joining the Berne Convention for the Protection of Literary and Artistic Works for more than a hundred years after

35. Act of Mar. 4, 1909, ch. 320, § 15, 35 Stat. 1075, 1078–1079.

36. Ibid.

37. Ibid., §§ 15–16, 1079–1080.

38. Ibid., § 22, 1080. In recognition of the disruptions caused by the war, the ad interim and reprinting provisions were extended in 1919 to sixty days and four months, respectively. Act of Dec. 18, 1919, ch. 11, § 21, 41 Stat. 368, 369. Later, the time periods were lengthened again. For a discussion of the ad interim and manufacturing provisions and their impact on foreign authors, see Spoo, "Copyright Protectionism," 642–653.

39. Richard Bowker, who was close to the drafting of the 1909 U.S. Copyright Act, explained that failure to comply with the act's ad interim and manufacturing provisions "will forfeit the right to obtain copyright protection and throw the foreign work into the public domain." Richard Rogers Bowker, *Copyright: Its History and Its Law* (Boston: Houghton Mifflin, 1912), 147.

40. Pound, "Newspapers, History, Etc.," 229.

41. Conant, "International Copyright," 156.

42. Saunders, *Authorship and Copyright*, 156.

other major nations had signed it.[43] It was not until 1989, a few years after the last vestiges of the manufacturing clause had been repealed, that the United States finally became a member of Berne.[44]

In 1918, when Pound drafted his proposal, American copyright exceptionalism distorted the international publishing scene and encouraged legalized book piracy. A few years later, these distortions would result in Joyce's *Ulysses* being printed in the United States in expurgated forms and without authorization.[45] Although Pound knew well that piracy was one source of cheap books in the United States— and he did not deny this benefit—he was outraged by a law that protected some foreign-origin works but not others and that, by discouraging legitimate publication of the latter, abetted their dissemination at the hands of bookleggers. Paradoxically, because U.S. copyright law failed to protect numerous English-language works of foreign origin, those were the works that opportunistic publishers could produce most cheaply in the American market, adding new materials to an already vast public domain that, in Pound's view (as discussed below), unfairly competed with living authors whose copyrighted works were sold at higher prices.

The Text of Pound's Statute

In one of his *New Age* articles, after explaining the urgent need for an Anglo-American copyright law to "cure" American book piracy and the ill will it fostered, Pound settled down to the details of his proposed statute. He began by declaring that "[t]he copyright of any book printed anywhere should be and remain automatically the author's," and "[c]opyright from present date should be perpetual" ("CT," 208). Thus, under Pound's statute, copyright in a work published anywhere in the world would vest automatically and exclusively in the author and would last forever.[46] The statute's indifference to the country of publication would have tacitly repealed the manufacturing clause of the 1909 Copyright Act and would have

43. Feather, *Publishing, Piracy, and Politics*, 165, 168; Saunders, *Authorship and Copyright*, 166.
44. Public Law No. 100–568, 102 Stat. 2853 (1988). The version of the manufacturing clause that had survived into the 1976 Copyright Act expired on July 1, 1986. Public Law No. 97–215, 96 Stat. 178 (1982).
45. See Spoo, "Copyright Protectionism."
46. Other American authors have urged that copyrights be made perpetual. Samuel Clemens (Mark Twain) made such an argument in an unpublished manuscript, "The Great Republic's Peanut Stand," composed in 1898, and again before a select committee of the House of Lords in 1900. See Siva Vaidhyanathan, *Copyrights and Copywrongs: The Rise of Intellectual Property and How It Threatens Creativity* (New York: New York University Press,), 69–79.

brought U.S. law closer to the principles of the Berne Convention, which protected the rights of authors as long as their works were first published in any of the member countries.[47]

Two things are immediately striking about this first provision of Pound's statute. First, as might be expected of a poet and freelance journalist, Pound thought of authorship in traditional, individualistic terms, apart from any rights that an employer might acquire through work-for-hire principles.[48] He therefore made no provision for employer- or corporate-owned copyrights and did not address basic issues of joint authorship and copyright transfer. More startling, he blithely legislated a perpetual copyright, despite the fact that such an enactment would be unconstitutional in the United States, where the supreme law of the land empowers Congress to grant copyrights for "limited Times" only.[49] Pound was not the first or the last prominent American to argue that authors' rights should last for eternity, but his unconstitutional prescription is especially curious in light of his originalist insistence, later in his career, on the plain meaning of the textually proximate clause empowering Congress "[t]o coin Money [and] regulate the Value thereof."[50] Pound believed that the latter clause by its clear terms gave the power to regulate the value of money exclusively to the federal government, effectively prohibiting banks and other private interests from fixing usurious lending rates or otherwise "arrogat[ing] to themselves unwarranted responsibilities."[51]

In exchange for exclusive, perpetual rights, Pound's statute required the author to "place on file copies of his book at the National Library, Washington, and in the municipal libraries of the four largest American cities" ("CT," 208). This requirement reflected Pound's commitment to the preservation and accessibility of cultural products. The 1909 U.S. Copyright Act already required that domestic authors deposit two copies of the "best edition" of a copyrighted work in the Copyright Office and that foreign authors deposit one copy of the foreign edition in order to obtain an ad interim copyright.[52] Pound expanded the requirement to include libraries in the four largest American cities at the time—New York,

47. See Berne Convention, art. 2, § 1 (1886).

48. In her chapter in this volume, Catherine L. Fisk discusses work-for-hire copyrights and authorial attribution in the modern advertising agency and links these developments to the prestige of attribution in literary modernism.

49. U.S. Constitution, art. I, § 8, cl. 8.

50. Ibid., cl. 5.

51. "A Visiting Card," reprinted in Ezra Pound, *Selected Prose: 1909–1965*, ed. William Cookson (New York: New Directions, 1973), 326–327.

52. Act of Mar. 4, 1909, ch. 320, §§ 12, 21, 35 Stat. 1075, 1078, 1080.

Chicago, Philadelphia, and either St. Louis or Detroit[53]—apparently in emulation of the 1911 British Copyright Act's provision for the deposit of copies in the British Museum and, upon demand, libraries in Oxford, Cambridge, Edinburgh, Dublin, and Wales.[54]

The deposit requirement is the only copyright formality that Pound retained in his statute. All the other formalities that the 1909 U.S. Copyright Act included as mandatory—domestic manufacture, affixation of copyright notice, renewal of the copyright after the first twenty-eight-year term[55]—were silently repealed by his proposal. The 1909 act made compliance with these formalities a condition of copyright protection; failure to comply meant that the work was automatically cast into the public domain. As long as American law made copyright protection for foreign authors turn upon such technicalities, the United States could not hope to join the Berne Convention.[56] Pound's statute was pointedly pro-Berne in this respect.

No sooner had Pound settled upon his perpetual copyright, however, than he dramatically qualified it: "BUT the heirs of an author should be powerless to prevent the publication of his works or to extract any excessive royalties" ("CT," 209; emphasis in original). Pound went on: "If the heirs neglect to keep a man's work in print and at a price not greater than the price of his books during his life, then unauthorised publishers should be at liberty to reprint said works, paying to heirs a royalty not more than 20 per cent. and not less than 10 per cent" ("CT," 209). This provision—effectively creating what the law calls a "compulsory license"—stripped heirs of the power to prevent the reprinting of authors' works or to raise book prices above those that existed during the authors' lifetimes, and substituted a royalty entitlement to be fixed by statute, regulation, or judicial decision. This clause was, in effect, a rule that required heirs "to give a license to use the property to anyone who meets governmentally-set criteria, . . . at governmentally-set rates of compensation."[57]

53. The four largest American cities in 1916, according to population size, were New York, Chicago, Philadelphia, and St. Louis, in descending order. Ralph S. Tarr and Frank M. McMurry, *World Geographies*, 2nd book, rev. ed. (New York: Macmillan, 1919), 413. By 1920, Detroit had replaced St. Louis as the fourth largest city. Frank M. McMurry and A. E. Parkins, *Advanced Geography* (New York: Macmillan, 1921), 481.

54. Copyright Act, 1911, 1 and 2 Geo. 5, ch. 46, § 15 (Eng.).

55. Act of Mar. 4, 1909, ch. 320, §§ 9, 18–20, 35 Stat. 1075, 1077, 1079–1080 (affixation of notice); §§ 15, 21–22, 1078–1080 (domestic manufacture and ad interim copyright); §§ 23–24, 1080–1081 (renewal of copyright).

56. The 1908 Berlin amendments to Berne provided that "[t]he enjoyment and the exercise of such rights are not subject to any formality." Berne Convention, art. 4, § 2 (1908).

57. Wendy J. Gordon, "A Property Right in Self-Expression: Equality and Individualism in the Natural Law of Intellectual Property," *Yale Law Journal* 102 (1993): 1574 n204.

Pound's compulsory license, however, was triggered not so much by aspiring publishers who met certain statutory criteria as by the inaction or greed of heirs who failed to keep authors' works in print at affordable prices.[58] Pound's statute effectively made heirs the stewards of their ancestors' works and gave them an opportunity to profit by their own diligence in keeping those works in print. If heirs did not act as faithful stewards, their exclusive property right vanished and they could no longer seek injunctive relief against unauthorized uses. Their only protection was then found in a liability rule that gave them a legal right to damages in the form of fixed royalties owed by the state-licensed publisher.[59]

Pound's daring blend of property and liability rules did not end there. Declaring that "the protection of an author should not enable him to play dog in the manger," Pound added a second, even more aggressive compulsory license:

> IF, having failed to have his works printed in America, or imported into America, or translated into American, an American publisher or translator apply to said author for permission to publish or translate a given work or works, and receive no answer within reasonable time, say six months, and if said author do not give notice of intending other American publication (quite definitely stating where and when) within reasonable time or desig-nate some other translator, then, the first publisher shall have the right to publish or translate any work, paying to the original author a royalty of not more than 20 per cent. and not less than 10 per cent. in the case of a foreign work translated. The original author shall have right at law to the minimum of these royalties. ("CT," 209)

This complicated limitation on the author's perpetual monopoly is even more startling than the first one. According to this rule, a foreign author retained the

58. Compulsory licenses already existed in copyright law of this period. For example, by the time Pound drafted his statute, both British and U.S. copyright laws had "mechanical license" provisions that allowed anyone to reproduce copyrighted musical works on records, piano rolls, and other devices without permission, as long as the copyright owner had authorized at least one earlier mechanical reproduction of the work and the user paid a fixed royalty per copy. See Act of Mar. 4, 1909, ch. 320, § 1(e); Copyright Act, 1911, 1 and 2 Geo. 5, ch. 46, § 19 (Eng.). In addition, the 1911 British Copyright Act also included a com-pulsory license clause permitting anyone to reprint the published work of an author who had been dead for twenty-five years, upon notice and payment of a 10 percent retail royalty to the copyright's proprietor. See Copyright Act, 1911, 1 and 2 Geo. 5, ch. 46, §§ 3–4 (Eng.).

59. In their classic article, Calabresi and Melamed distinguish between property rules, which permit plaintiffs to obtain injunctive relief to protect their entitlements, and liability rules, which give plaintiffs non-injunctive, monetary remedies only. Guido Calabresi and A. Douglas Melamed, "Property Rules, Liability Rules and Inalienability: One View of the Cathedral," *Harvard Law Review* 85 (1972): 1092, 1106–1110.

exclusive right to control reproduction, distribution, and translation of a work in the United States *unless* the author failed to have it printed in or imported into the country, or did not grant translation rights for an American edition. If the author slumbered on these rights or refused to exercise them—and Pound did not indicate how long authorial inaction must continue before the exception would be triggered—an American publisher or translator could step forward and apply to the author for permission to make use of the work. If the author did not reply within a reasonable time and gave no notice of specific plans for authorized American uses, the publisher or translator could proceed with the proposed use, with the sole duty—enforceable at law—of paying a royalty of between 10 percent and 20 percent.[60] Once again, Pound had fashioned a penalty for the copyright owner's failure to make works available to the public: the author lost the protection of a strong property rule, at least within the United States, and had to be content with a liability rule in the form of a fixed royalty. Thus, Pound's statute allowed an author to maintain exclusive rights in the United States only if he or she performed certain mandatory duties. If the author did not do so, publishing rights could be involuntarily transferred to users who, in effect, assumed control of disseminating the author's work within the United States.

Pound then added an exception to the exception: "But no unauthorised translation should inhibit the later publication of an authorised translation. Nevertheless, an authorised translation appearing later should not in any way interfere with preceding translations save by fair and open competition in the market" ("CT," 209). Thus, once a translation entered the marketplace pursuant to the compulsory-license provision, the author (or the author's heirs) could grant permission for a new translation to compete with the unauthorized one, and the only limitations on competition between the negotiated-license edition and the compulsory-license edition would be those arising from supply and demand, the quality of the translations, the tastes of the public, and other nonlegal factors.

Finally, Pound included a special exception for extremely successful works: "After a man's works have sold a certain number of copies, let us say 100,000, there should be no means of indefinitely preventing a very cheap reissue of his work. Let us say a shilling a volume. Royalty on same payable at rate of 20 per cent. to author or heirs" ("CT," 209). According to this rule, even if an author complied fully with Pound's statute by supplying the American market with copies of a work and

60. Though Pound did not make the point explicit, presumably the same rule would apply to heirs who did not authorize an affordable translation of a foreign author's work for the American market. Moreover, if the author licensed a translation during her lifetime, her heirs would have the responsibility of keeping the translation in print at affordable rates.

authorizing a translation, and even if the author's heirs were diligent in keeping the work in print at a fair price, once the work had sold 100,000 copies, any publisher would be free to bring out a shilling edition, with royalty payments fixed at 20 percent.[61] As a British shilling was worth approximately twenty-five American cents (in unadjusted 1918 dollars) at the time Pound was writing,[62] a compulsory-license edition would have been regarded as inexpensive. (In a related article also written in 1918, Pound complained of having to pay three dollars for a reprint of an old book; "TC," 191.)

Pound's compulsory license for cheap editions of successful works was an especially radical innovation, representing a significant impairment of the author's copyright. Instead of allowing a best-selling author to control the market for cheap editions and to choose, if she wished, to continue to extract profits from exclusive, pricey editions, Pound treated the author's copyright as if its incentivizing purpose had run its course, and supply-side rewards must now yield to demand-side realities. The *ex ante* incentives of the property right, having served to induce creation and generate profits, were retired in favor of the public's need for inexpensive reprints. Pound thus found a way to mitigate the unconstitutionality of his perpetual copyright. Rather than imposing an external time limitation on copyrights, he rendered them self-limiting—in a sense, self-consuming—by making a work's popularity serve as a proxy for the essentially legislative task of determining the appropriate duration of the property right. When sales of a work reached 100,000, the copyright with respect to inexpensive editions could no longer be enforced by a strong property rule and the author would have to content herself with set royalties on cheap editions. Pound's notion of self-consuming copyrights was fully consistent with his decades-long crusade for "cheap books."[63] His call for a compulsory license for inexpensive editions suggested the depth of his commitment to free trade in cultural works.

In sum, Pound's unusual statute began by granting a perpetual monopoly to authors and ended by carving out extremely broad compulsory licenses that would

---

61. Clemens in "The Great Republic's Peanut Stand" also proposed a perpetual-copyright regime with a special provision for cheap books. After twenty years of copyright protection, a work's publisher would be required to issue a cheap edition and keep it in print forever. See Vaidhyanathan, *Copyrights and Copywrongs*, 76.

62. In 1918, the British pound sterling was worth $4.8665 in U.S. dollars. There were twenty shillings in a pound. Michael Vincent O'Shea et al., eds., *The World Book: Organized Knowledge in Story and Picture* (Chicago: World Book, 1918), 4802.

63. Ezra Pound to Dorothy Pound, Oct. 14, 1945, in *Ezra and Dorothy Pound: Letters in Captivity, 1945–1946*, ed. Omar Pound and Robert Spoo (New York: Oxford University Press, 1999), 131.

permit any qualifying person to issue reprints or translations of works that authors or their heirs had failed or refused to keep in circulation. The statute thus eclectically combined property and liability rules to create an international system for keeping books and translations in print upon pain of loss or impairment of the exclusive property right. As long as the foreign author did not delay in authorizing American publications and translations, he or she retained a strong property right to engage in supra-competitive monopoly pricing and to sue for injunctive and monetary relief in the event of infringement.[64] Likewise, heirs could maintain the author's original monopoly pricing and sue for injunctive and monetary relief, but only if they kept the work in print and did not raise the price. If any of these conditions was not met, the property rule favoring authors and heirs turned into a liability rule favoring the public: the perpetual copyright became a mere right to damages in the form of a fixed royalty.

Pound's conditioning of exclusive rights upon compliance with statutory directives strangely recalls the 1891 Chace Act and the 1909 Copyright Act, under which foreign authors could obtain American copyright only by complying with the manufacturing clause and other formalities—requirements that Pound vehemently opposed. The difference, of course, is that the primary intended beneficiaries of the protectionist manufacturing requirements were American printers and bookbinders, whereas under Pound's statute it was the reading public that was meant to benefit from statutory compliance by authors and heirs. Moreover, by quietly repealing the manufacturing clause and granting perpetual and exclusive copyright protection, his statute restored legal symmetry and reciprocity to the transatlantic publishing scene, effectively elevating all foreign-origin works from second-class citizenship to copyright equality with works manufactured on U.S. soil.

What is perhaps most intriguing about Pound's scheme is that it set up elaborate machinery to arrive at essentially the same result that American publishers of the nineteenth century had brought about through "courtesy of the trade": a wide dissemination of inexpensive books, with a fair payment to authors. What, then, is the difference between Pound's statute and trade courtesy? The chief difference is that, in the latter system, once an American publisher had been the first to reprint and pay for a British work, other competitors in the book trade voluntarily respected the publisher's "courtesy copyright" or "title" in the work. Under Pound's

64. Pound's focus was on the availability of foreign authors' works in the United States, but nothing he said suggests that he did not intend the same rules to be applied to the failure of American authors and their heirs to keep works in circulation abroad, as well as in the United States.

statute, once the compulsory-license provision was triggered by the neglect or obstinacy of authors or their heirs, any and all qualifying publishers could issue the work, non-exclusively and simultaneously (unless publishers began to observe something like trade courtesy again). Of course, under Pound's proposal, foreign authors and their heirs initially had much more control over the publication of their works than they did when American copyright law afforded foreign-origin works little or no protection. But that control was precarious; it would be lost or greatly impaired if authors or heirs failed to meet Pound's criteria. Pound's scheme was radically free-trade in its orientation and deeply committed to the robust dissemination of works as a way of promoting international understanding and a borderless culture.

The tension in Pound's statute between authorial control and public access, between monopoly and multeity, is enigmatically captured in his Canto IV, first published in 1919, a year or so after his *New Age* articles. In the midst of the poem's celebration of the sensuous freedoms of nature, Pound introduces the flattering words of a Chinese poet to his king: "This wind, sire, is the king's wind, / This wind is the wind of the palace."[65] The king's rebuke to this toadying assertion of royal ownership is reported by the poem's disembodied voice-over: "No wind is the king's wind. / Let every cow keep her calf."[66] A public good like the wind, these lines suggest, cannot be annexed to the king's dominions—just as the tide could not be made to halt by the command of Canute the Great, the eleventh-century Viking king of England.[67] Yet the reference to cows and calves complicates the anti-monopoly mood here. As Mary de Rachewiltz reveals in her essay in this volume, Pound glossed the line "Let every cow keep her calf" as a reference to "copyright."[68] Indeed, the line recalls the words of the sixth-century Irish king Diarmid who, the story goes, was asked to determine whether the monk Columba was justified in copying, without permission, the manuscript of a psalter belonging to the abbot Finnian. In a ruling that led to the bloody Battle of the Book, King Diarmid drew

65. Ezra Pound, *The Cantos* (New York: New Directions, 1995), 15.
66. Ibid., 16.
67. The story of King Canute and the tide is of ancient origin. One account is found in Charles Dickens, *A Child's History of England* (London: Chapman and Hall, 1870), 25–26.
68. Mary de Rachewiltz's chapter in this volume is a rich *Cantos*-like meditation on her roles as the poet's daughter, a Pound scholar, and the possessor of physical and intellectual property that was the subject of legal disputes. Aligning herself with a Poundian and Ciceronian sense of law as right reason and justice—as opposed to the fallen world of lawyers and litigation—she notes that Pound was "dead against all forms of monopoly" and concludes by suggesting, in the spirit of her father's copyright statute, that new laws should be enacted to assist the technologies of the digital millennium in "reproducing and making a poet's striving and intentions public."

upon Brehon law concerning vagrant livestock to declare: "to every cow her calf, so to every book its copy."[69] Pound thus juxtaposes contrasting images of the proprietary self: one monarch who is humbled by nature's ability to defeat eminent domain, another who draws upon nature and natural law to give judgment in favor of monopoly. Although Pound evinces here some of the solicitude for authorial rights that he manifests in his *New Age* pieces, he once again appears to stress the virtues of uncontrolled dissemination, concluding the passage with an ode to the uncolonized wind: "'This wind is held in gauze curtains...'; / No wind is the king's..."[70] Some years later, he would reprise this morality play of ownership in one of his polemical prose tracts: "The two extremes: superstitious sacrosanctity of 'property' *versus* Jefferson's 'The earth belongs to the living,' which was part dogma, and part observation of a fact so obvious that it took a man of genius to perceive it."[71]

Pound's copyright statute is also consistent with his later theories of money, which were likewise grounded on principles of utility and free circulation. Notably, he championed Silvio Gesell's system of "stamp scrip" in which paper money would require "the affixation of a monthly stamp to maintain its par value." Instead of rewarding individuals for saving or investing, this system "accelerated the circulation of...money"—that is, encouraged spending—because the monthly stamp imposed a mounting cost for hoarding.[72] Pound's copyright statute was similarly designed to discourage the sterile accumulation of property. The threat of compulsory licenses would promote the circulation of works and translations and impose a penalty on misers of intellectual property: the loss of exclusive control over texts.

It is not hard to see that what Pound initially characterized in his *New Age* articles as perpetual protection for authors' intellectual labor was essentially a scheme for maximizing the availability of works and translations. In the end, Pound was more interested in supplying the market with affordable books than with increasing protections for authors. His was a rare kind of copyright proposal: a consumer-side scheme couched in a plea for creators' rights. Through the mechanism of easily triggered compulsory licenses, Pound managed to preserve authorial rewards

69. The story is told in a number of variant forms. See, for example, William Boyd Carpenter, *A Popular History of the Church of England from the Earliest Times to the Present Day* (London: John Murray, 1900), 27–28.

70. Pound, *The Cantos*, 16.

71. Ezra Pound, "ABC of Economics" (1933), in *Selected Prose*, 256.

72. Ezra Pound, "The Individual in His Milieu: A Study of Relations and Gesell" (1935), in *Selected Prose*, 276.

while sustaining his vision of literary production as a solvent of the limitations of time and place. His statute required publishers to pay authors a just price whenever their books were sold, but at the same time limited the power of copyright law to police the borders of geography and history in the form of customs officials, lawyers, court injunctions, and high damage awards.[73]

The Public Domain: Unfair Competition with the Dead

If the dissemination of works and robust competition among publishers and translators were the primary goals of Pound's statute, why did he grant a perpetual copyright in the first place? Why didn't he propose to abolish copyright altogether and rely on the public domain to achieve these ends? The answer is that, in addition to believing that authors were entitled to royalties that could be enforced through some kind of legal right, Pound distrusted the public domain because he believed that it gave earlier, public-domain authors an unfair competitive advantage over contemporary, copyrighted authors in the economic and intellectual marketplace.

Like many of his fellow modernists, Pound viewed contemporary writers as being in a struggle with literary predecessors who, because they were established and familiar, more readily commanded the attention and respect of readers. Critics have noted that modernist authors' relationships to their predecessors were intensely competitive and often fraught with anxiety. Harold Bloom, for example, has claimed that T. S. Eliot's "true and always unnamed precursor was...an uneasy composite of Whitman and Tennyson."[74] Modernists frequently registered their sense of rivalry with earlier authors in the form of ridicule or dismissiveness. Eliot once wrote that Tennyson had "a large dull brain like a farmhouse clock."[75] Pound wickedly mocked Tennyson's status as poet laureate by pointing to "the edifying spectacle of...Tennyson in Buckingham Palace."[76] "Wordsworth is a dull sheep," Pound wrote in 1916, and "Byron's technique is rotten."[77] Matthew Arnold was

73. Of course, Pound's proposal did not address obscenity law and other legal regimes that policed geographic and historical borders.

74. Harold Bloom, *The Breaking of the Vessels* (Chicago: University of Chicago Press, 1982), 21.

75. T. S. Eliot [Apteryx, pseud.], "Verse Pleasant and Unpleasant," *Egoist* 5 (1918): 43.

76. Ezra Pound, "How to Read, or Why. Part III. Conclusions, Exceptions, Curricula," *New York Herald Tribune Books* (Jan. 27, 1929): 5, reprinted in *Contributions to Periodicals*, 5:117.

77. Ezra Pound to Iris Barry, July 27, 1916, in *Selected Letters of Ezra Pound: 1907–1941*, ed. D. D. Paige (New York: New Directions, 1970), 90.

limited by his "mind's frigidity."[78] In her famous essay "Mr. Bennett and Mrs. Brown," Virginia Woolf took to task precursor novelists such as H. G. Wells and Arnold Bennett for failing to treat "life" and "human nature."[79] These novelists "have made tools and established conventions which do their business," Woolf wrote. "But those tools are not our tools, and that business is not our business. For us those conventions are ruin, those tools are death."[80] The sense of a gulf between the present generation and previous ones, between us and them, pervades the writings of modernist authors.

For Pound, however, rivalry with the past was more than aesthetic competition; it had a distinct economic dimension. If books were too expensive, they would fail to make their mark on culture, no matter how important their contents. "Only cheap good books can compete with cheap bad books," he noted in his discussion of the costs imposed by the U.S. book tariff ("TC," 191). Copyright played an important role in this contest between present and past authors. Among the reasons Pound gave in one of his 1918 *New Age* articles for advocating a perpetual copyright was that "the present law by which copyright expires permits dead authors to compete on unjust terms with living authors. Unscrupulous, but well-meaning publishers, well serving the public, print dead authors more cheaply than living ones BECAUSE *they do not have to pay royalties*" ("CT," 208–209; emphasis in original). Thus, in addition to the advantage they held by having shaped the tastes of present readers and ingratiated themselves through the passage of time, "dead authors" could undersell contemporary authors because their works had shed copyright protection and were free for the taking. "This is to the disadvantage of contemporary literature, to the disadvantage of literary production," Pound declared ("CT," 209). Publishers could reprint Tennyson's or Arnold's public-domain texts without the additional overhead of copyright royalties. In this respect, modernist authors were handicapped even when copyright law *did* succeed in protecting them.

Thus, for Pound, the international anomalies created by copyright law's selective policing of geographic boundaries were mirrored in the same law's unequal treatment of the living and the dead. In addition to inhibiting their movement along the modernist axes of space and time, copyright law was simply unfair to contemporary writers as a matter of economics. In his draft statute, Pound offered a radical corrective by making copyrights perpetual "from present date" ("CT,"

---

78. Pound, *The Spirit of Romance*, rev. ed. (1910; New York: New Directions, 1968), 222.
79. "Mr. Bennett and Mrs. Brown" (1924), reprinted in Virginia Woolf, *Collected Essays*, ed. Leonard Woolf (London: Hogarth, 1966), 1:329.
80. Ibid.

208). Because the public domain, regularly augmented by expiring copyrights, would always contain a ready supply of works of high quality, eliminating this free resource was the only way to redress the competitive imbalance.

But there are questions that Pound did not answer. Would only future works come within his statute, or would existing copyrights be extended for eternity as well? Would the statute retroactively restore copyright to works that had previously entered the public domain when their statutory terms expired? Would it go further and grant protection to works that predated copyright regimes altogether, such as "The Seafarer" and Chaucer's *Canterbury Tales?* Would other classic texts be included, such as *The Odyssey, The Aeneid*, and *The Divine Comedy*—texts that Pound regularly drew upon for his own creative work? These questions are not irrelevant. According to Pound's logic, only a complete abolition of the public domain would place all authors—past, present, and future—on a level economic playing field. Anything less would give some portion of the dead an unfair advantage over the living.

A statutory scheme that left part of the public domain intact—and this would be almost inevitable—would sustain to some degree the competitive imbalance of which Pound complained. But he probably did not have in mind an economic rivalry with Homer, Dante, Shakespeare, and other classic authors. Rather, it was competition from authors who had more recently entered, or were entering, the public domain—Tennyson, Arnold, Dante Gabriel Rossetti—that Pound thought would have the greatest impact on contemporary writers' sales and ambitions.

Moreover, within the United States, the copyright law's double standard had created the extremely anomalous situation in which American authors, already at a disadvantage as comparative newcomers to world literature, saw their books marketed at monopoly prices, while pirated British works could be sold at bargain rates. In 1819, the American author Washington Irving had written that "the public complains of the price of my work—this is the disadvantage of coming in competition with those republished English works for which the Booksellers have not to pay anything to the authors."[81] Nearly a hundred years later, Pound echoed Irving's frustration, with a twist: "As America has less past literature than other countries it is particularly to American disadvantage that the living author should not fare as well as the dead one" ("CT," 209). Pound evidently meant that contemporary American authors had to vie not only with pirated contemporary European authors, but also with centuries of unprotected Old World works. The burden of

81. Washington Irving to Henry Brevoort, Aug. 12, 1819, in Washington Irving, *Letters*, ed. Ralph M. Aderman et al. (Boston: Twayne, 1978), 1:554.

the past weighed even more heavily when economic advantages were added to historical and cultural ones.

Blindness and Insight in Pound's Statute

By including compulsory-license provisions in his copyright statute, Pound ensured that the public would not be deprived of reprints and translations. But his statute did not address other copyright-related rights and activities. For example, apart from translations, Pound offered no discussion of derivative works, such as dramatic or cinematic adaptations, or of performance rights, though by 1918 copyright laws addressed all these issues in one way or another.[82] Nor did Pound show any concern about fair use or fair dealing, a doctrine that had recently been codified in Britain.[83] Yet, adaptation rights and fair use are vital to the creative process, as Pound the poet surely knew. If Pound the legislator felt the need to include statutory provisions preventing authors and their heirs from blocking reprints and translations, why did he not incorporate comparable safeguards for other reasonable uses of copyrighted works?

Most likely, Pound included in his statute only those matters that he believed needed urgent attention on an international level—perpetual copyright and rules for reprints and translations—and left other matters to be dealt with by domestic legislation. After all, the duration of copyright, piracy, cheap reprints, timely translations—these were the issues that had dominated discussions of international copyright for the previous century, and Pound was consciously entering that conversation and proposing a unified theory for the needs of authors and readers. Moreover, the focus of Pound's statute was less on the creative process than on the

---

82. For example, the 1911 British Copyright Act protected an author's right to convert a dramatic work into a nondramatic work, and vice versa, and the right of public performance, including the performance of a translation. Copyright Act, 1911, 1 and 2 Geo. 5, ch. 46, § 1(2) (Eng.). Similar provisions were included in the 1909 U.S. Copyright Act. Act of Mar. 4, 1909, ch. 320, § 1(b)–(e). Pound referred to subsidiary rights in a 1930 article in which he criticized Congress's slowness to amend the copyright law: "[T]he welfare of letters is postponed until cinema and radio, and now I suppose talki-o and smellio, rights have been puddled and muddled and strained out to the satisfaction of all the 'parties interested.'" Pound, "Newspapers, History, Etc.," 229.

83. The British statute defined *fair dealing* as the use of a copyrighted work "for the purposes of private study, research, criticism, review, or newspaper summary." Copyright Act, 1911, 1 and 2 Geo. 5, ch. 46, § 2(1)(i) (Eng.). In the United States, the roughly analogous privilege of *fair use* remained an exclusively common-law doctrine until it was codified in the 1976 Copyright Act.

diffusion of affordable works with fair compensation to authors. That was the pragmatic challenge that he chose to address: putting in place statutory machinery that would facilitate the kind of cross-cultural communication that Henry James had made the focus of his fiction writing.

Yet Pound's omission of any discussion of fair use and derivative works (other than translations) is puzzling, because the freedom to create adaptations of, and to borrow extensively from, others' works is a hallmark of modernist writing. It is well known, for example, that portions of Pound's major poetic sequence, *The Cantos*, were modeled on Homer's *Odyssey* and Dante's *Divine Comedy*, among other literary sources. James Joyce composed and promoted his novel *Ulysses* as a modern-day epic based on *The Odyssey* and, to a lesser extent, on *Hamlet* and other works. Both *The Cantos* and *Ulysses* quote freely from texts that were copyrighted at the time, and there is no indication that Pound or Joyce ever sought licenses.[84] T. S. Eliot likewise perfected the craft of generating strikingly original verse by assembling mosaics of previous authors' work, both ancient and modern.[85] Various poems by Marianne Moore contain precise and sometimes lengthy quotations from contemporaneous sources, such as books and magazines.[86] And many other examples could be cited.

It is hard to imagine literary modernism without its extensive and overt use of texts by others, yet that aspect of the writer's craft does not seem to have concerned Pound in 1918 when he proposed his copyright statute. Although some of the most celebrated achievements of modernism, such as *Ulysses* and *The Waste Land*, were not yet published, or not yet fully published, when Pound wrote his *New Age* articles, the use of quotation, allusion, and textual collage was already well established in Pound's own literary practice and in that of his contemporaries. That Pound saw no need to address issues of adaptation rights and fair use in any of his discussions of copyright suggests that he did not regard these kinds of literary borrowing as unlawful, unethical, or otherwise controversial. Moreover, there is no record of

---

84. Saint-Amour discusses potentially copyrighted sources that Joyce freely drew upon in *Ulysses* (see *Copywrights*, 193–198). Interestingly, for his study of medieval literature, *The Spirit of Romance*, Pound obtained permission to use lengthy quotations from modern, copyrighted translations of writings by Dante and Michelangelo. See Pound, *Spirit of Romance*, 7.

85. Eliot's "Notes" to *The Waste Land* indicate that the poem contains quotations from and paraphrases of numerous works potentially still in copyright in 1922 in various parts of the world, including works by F. H. Bradley, Hermann Hesse, Paul Verlaine, Richard Wagner, and Jessie L. Weston. T. S. Eliot, "Notes on 'The Waste Land,'" in his *Collected Poems: 1909–1962* (New York: Harcourt, Brace and World, 1963), 70–76.

86. A noted example of Moore's penchant for incorporated quotation is her poem "An Octopus" (1924). See *The Poems of Marianne Moore*, ed. Grace Schulman (New York: Viking, 2003), 167–172, 381–382.

Pound, Eliot, Joyce, or other modernist writers being challenged by copyright owners, either informally or by means of legal process.

Had Pound and his fellow modernists produced their writings under today's regime of intellectual property laws, it is likely that they would have met with legal obstacles, or that they would have found it necessary to alter their literary practice to conform to a climate more jealously protective of authors' rights and the potential for capitalizing on them than was the case in 1918. As Paul Saint-Amour has noted of Joyce's signature use of quotation and parody, "It is difficult to imagine that *Ulysses*, had it been written and published under [the current copyright] regime, would have made nearly as extensive use of its protected source texts or of the unpublished writings…of others." Many other works of modernism likewise would have been different had they been created under "a standard that recognizes the smallest reuse of material as a potential infringement and reduces fair use to the quotation of brief passages for review."[87]

The more permissive and less propertized climate in which Pound and other modernists produced their richly allusive and collagist experiments was an enabling condition which those writers evidently were able to take for granted. Nor did they record any gratitude for copyright laws that left intact a public domain brimming with raw materials that the individual talent could use without cost to situate itself in relation to tradition. Although Pound in his *New Age* article complained about the impact on contemporary writers of unequal competition with public-domain authors, he did not seem to consider the real cost savings that he and his fellow writers enjoyed by being able to borrow freely from those same authors.[88] It could be argued that any competitive disadvantage that modernist writers experienced with respect to earlier literary periods was at least mitigated by modernists' ability to mine those periods for literary material without having to contend with permissions fees, transaction costs, or threats of litigation. The cost savings that allowed publishers to issue Shakespeare more cheaply than T. S. Eliot arose from the same free public resource that allowed Eliot in *The Waste Land* to quote from and adapt Shakespeare without having to acquire a license[89]—although this does not alter the fact that in 1922 a publisher of Shakespeare's sonnets could presumably undersell a publisher of *The Waste Land*. In drafting his copyright statute, Pound was concerned with inequities in the marketplace, not with the economics of the creative process.

87. Saint-Amour, *Copywrights*, 197.

88. See William M. Landes and Richard A. Posner, *The Economic Structure of Intellectual Property Law* (Cambridge, MA: Belknap, 2003), 52.

89. Eliot quotes from or echoes Shakespeare at numerous points in *The Waste Land*. See *Collected Poems*, 54, 56–57, 59–60, 62 (ll. 48, 77–78, 125, 128, 172, 191–192, 257).

In sum, except in his poetic practice, Pound did not overtly acknowledge modernism's dependence on the public domain and fair use, though he often paid tribute to what he called the "cultural heritage."[90] Problems of distribution and compensation, not the scene of writing, captured his imagination as a volunteer legislator. Unlike recent lawmakers who have argued that stronger intellectual property rights are needed to spur authors to creation, Pound did not treat authorial labor as something that needed to be incentivized by enhanced copyright protection. True creativity, his statute seemed to suggest, would exert itself through the stress of internal compulsions, once the doors of space and time were thrown open by a sensible legal regime. Perpetual copyright could provide an income stream and make for a fairer marketplace, but Pound did not offer his eternal monopoly as an *ex ante* stimulus to literary production. By requiring state-licensed publishers to make royalty payments, he simply acknowledged the right of authors and their heirs to *ex post* remuneration. Pound's legislative energies were stirred by the prospect of unchecked dissemination of books and art, not by economic stimulus packages for creators. His philosophy of copyright was therefore essentially a consumer- or demand-side philosophy, though he did not ignore the plight of pirated writers.

Coda

Ezra Pound did something that few advocates of a perpetual copyright would dream of doing: he candidly faced and articulated some of the dangers to which such a strong property right could give rise. Wordsworth, another great poet-polemicist who believed that copyrights should be everlasting, never conceded the harm that concentrating such potent rights in a single owner might inflict on the public interest. Pound was a man whose *idées fixes* about politics and economics ultimately led him into foolish and tragic errors, yet on the question of copyright he was open-minded and flexible enough to see beyond his own interests as an author and property owner. That flexibility was so great that, in proposing an international copyright law, he combined a powerful monopoly right with extremely broad exceptions to that right.

Although he did not pursue his copyright proposal in later years, Pound avidly followed the efforts of others to reform copyright law along somewhat similar

---

90. Pound defined the "cultural heritage" broadly as "the whole aggregate of human inventions, ameliorations of seed, of agricultural and mechanical process belonging to no one man, and to no group, escaping the possibilities of any definition of patents under any possible system of patent rights." Pound, "The Individual in His Milieu," 275.

lines. In particular, he admired the attempts of Congressman Albert Henry Vestal (1875–1932) in the 1920s and early 1930s to conform U.S. copyright law to international standards. Pound praised Vestal's work in drafting a "decent and civilized copyright act,"[91] and declared that "those impeding Vestal's reform of copyright dishonesty ought to be suspended in chains."[92] But Vestal died before his pending legislation could be pushed through. Had they been enacted, his proposals would, among other things, have extended the copyright term to the author's life plus fifty years, eliminated formalities as conditions of copyright protection, reduced the impact of the manufacturing clause on foreign authors, and permitted the United States to join the Berne Convention.[93] Indeed, Vestal's draft legislation anticipated many features of the 1976 Copyright Act, a law that would not come into force until January 1978, more than five years after Pound died.

Pound passionately believed that communication should not be hampered by the monopoly power that copyrights confer. He was a copyright free-trader at heart. Yet he did not feel that the work of dissemination could be left to an unfettered public domain, because he believed that authors and their heirs were entitled to remuneration for as long as works remained of interest to the public, and he worried that the expiration of copyrights created unequal competition between past and present writers. Moreover, in proposing special safeguards against the abuse of copyrights by authors' heirs, Pound showed himself to be presciently alert to the dangers posed by lengthy copyright terms unaccompanied by limitations that adequately protect the public interest. Today, the estates of James Joyce, T. S. Eliot, Samuel Beckett, and other modernist authors use extended copyrights to discourage or control use of those authors' works by scholars, critics, and others. Pound's perpetual, royalty-based copyright would, at least in principle, have removed or reduced such obstacles to the study and enjoyment of modernism. His statute reminds us that the law cannot safely continue on a course of unqualified maximalist protection for copyright owners. If the labor of translation among generations and cultures is to continue, if the modernist dream of unregulated travel in space and time is to be realized, the law must find a better balance between authorial entitlements and the public weal.

91. Pound, "Program 1929," *Blues* 1 (Mar. 1929): 29, reprinted in *Contributions to Periodicals*, 5:131.

92. Pound, "The Exile," 17.

93. See H.R. 12549, 71st Cong., 2nd sess., §§ 1–2, 12, 28–29, 34, 41, 61 (1930). See also H.R. 6988, 71st Cong., 2nd sess., §§ 1–3 (1929) (authorizing the president to proclaim U.S. adherence to international copyright conventions and providing copyright protection for foreign authors). For Pound's support of Vestal's proposals, see Walkiewicz and Witemeyer, *Ezra Pound and Senator Bronson Cutting*, 28–29, 45–46.

2 Thinking Back through Copyright

Individual Rights and Collective Life in Virginia Woolf's Nonfiction

Celia Marshik

Virginia Woolf's *A Room of One's Own*, famed since its 1929 publication for witty and incisive feminist polemic, explores the literary tradition as Woolf knew it, including both its general import and its originary legal and social horizons. Like *Room* as a whole, Woolf's model of tradition appears to be characterized by possessive individualism: individual writers need access to individual rooms, which offer the kind of private space in which "one" can think, write, and experience intellectual freedom.[1] By focusing on the professional status and remuneration that women writers require in order to participate in this tradition, *Room* appears, in the eyes of some readers, to offer a vision of individual exceptionalism in which limited numbers of women might rise above the material limitations placed upon others to enjoy the privacy and economic independence Woolf thought were crucial conditions for intellectual freedom. And yet, in their focus on the singular nouns that characterize Woolf's title, scholars and readers have missed the radically *collective* implications of both the book's argument and its intertex-

---

1. As a study by Alison Light contends, *Room*'s "ideal state of mind" is "singular, complete and self-contained" (*Mrs. Woolf and the Servants: An Intimate History of Domestic Life in Bloomsbury* [New York: Bloomsbury Press, 2008], 198). Although Light works to persuade readers that this ideal never matched the reality of Woolf's domestic life, my argument suggests that the ideal itself is a misconception.

tual practices: ownership is less importantly pinned to the one than to the many, and a room might shelter more than one without any loss—indeed, with a gain—in its powers of protection and habitability.

This strand of *Room* emerges through examining copyright, one of the elemental legal forces that govern literary traditions through the transformation of imaginative works into literary property. Copyright, for all that it applies to intangible realms of expression, is rather like a room: it makes distinctions between inside and outside, occupant and guest, tenant and owner. Like *Room's* title, copyright is generally possessed by the "one." This singular individual decides who may access the room/text and what activities may take place within the confines of the property; the one can also limit access to the point that the property becomes difficult or unappealing to visit. In this chapter, I will explore the fundamental tension between an individual writer's need to secure economic stability—a need at the center of *A Room of One's Own*—and Woolf's simultaneous argument that "books continue each other," a model of literary production and creativity that serves as a counterweight to Woolf's title and to contemporary copyright regimes alike. In both *Room* and *Three Guineas* (1938), her most famous works of nonfiction, Woolf's arguments suggest that the "rooms" of copyright and possessive individualism often limit, instead of enable, intellectual freedom. While Woolf seldom wrote explicitly about copyright, her work emphasizes the role of the "mass"—of a collective body of thought and expression—in the creation of literary works. Such arguments frame the authorial mind as necessarily distributed, an example of collectivized creative and cognitive processes misunderstood as individual.[2]

As I advance this argument, my own focus on Woolf might seem in opposition to the collective model of authorship advanced by *Room* and *Three Guineas*. My essay is thus a symptom, as well as an analysis, of a particular model of literary history, one that has placed "the man [*sic*] and his work" at the center of interpretation and pedagogy.[3] The figure of this isolated genius is seductive: if reading

2. Anthropology has employed the concepts of the "distributed person" and the "distributed mind" to explore how material objects allow selfhood to be distributed through space. See Marilyn Strathern's *The Gender of the Gift* (Berkeley: University of California Press, 1988), which is generally credited with formulating this model. For my purposes, the concept of distribution helps to articulate the way that ideas and specific expression are distributed through space and time when cited, amplified, and reinvented by subsequent writers.

3. This essay might thus be seen as, in Michel Foucault's formulation, an example of "the-man-and-his-work criticism." See "What Is an Author?" in *The Essential Foucault*, ed. Paul Rabinow and Nikolas Rose (New York: New Press, 2003), 377. Instead, my goal is to demonstrate that Woolf's "author function" has obscured important tenets of major texts—has, in Foucault's words, operated as "a principle of thrift in the proliferation of meaning" that those texts might otherwise set in motion (ibid., 390).

habits are any indication, readers long for it, and our laws and education systems collaborate in the creation of literary auras and "icons."[4] I hope that my single-author optic will be offset by the implications of my argument: we should read Woolf differently, but we should also recognize that modernism, more broadly speaking, has always called attention to the populousness of literature, which is never created in a single room by a sole occupant.

Given Woolf's iconic status, it is surprising how little attention scholars have paid to the question of copyright in (and of) her texts.[5] Julia Briggs is unique in her brief examination of the influence of copyright on Woolf's revision process. In 1919, Woolf wrote a letter to Lytton Strachey requesting corrections to *The Voyage Out* and *Night and Day*. Woolf was preparing the novels for publication in the United States, and she asserted, "the more alterations the better—because of copyright."[6] Briggs observes, "The wording of this letter and her subsequent practice suggest that Woolf thought that any differences she introduced would help to establish a distinctive American copyright, and thus make piracy from the British editions more difficult."[7]

This incident raises the surprising possibility that Woolf might have been locked out of the "room" of copyright early in her career. Indeed, Woolf's first two novels may never have enjoyed legal copyright coverage in the United States. As Robert Spoo has observed in his chapter in this volume and elsewhere, authors of English-language books first released abroad needed to publish—in fact, to manufacture—a book in the United States within thirty days of foreign publication to secure their U.S. copyrights. As a stopgap, authors could deposit a copy of the book with the Copyright Office and have ad interim protection for an additional thirty days from deposit, allowing time for the book to be printed and bound in the United States. Once this small window closed, however, copyright

4. Brenda Silver's incisive *Virginia Woolf, Icon* (Chicago: University of Chicago Press, 1999) has shed important light on the process by which Woolf achieved this status. Other scholarship on modernism and celebrity continues to develop our understanding of how particular authors become famous as personalities through strategies that often mystify their creative process. See, for example, Aaron Jaffe's *Modernism and the Culture of Celebrity* (Cambridge: Cambridge University Press, 2005).

5. This striking vacuum is certainly changing. At the 2008 International Virginia Woolf Society Conference, a panel organized by Bonnie Kime Scott took up the topic of Woolf and intellectual property. The Spring 2010 issue of the *Virginia Woolf Miscellany*, edited by Maggie Humm, also takes up the topic.

6. Virginia Woolf, *The Letters of Virginia Woolf*, ed. Nigel Nicolson and Joann Trautmann (New York: Harcourt Brace Jovanovich, 1978), 2:401. Subsequent references to this six-volume edition, published between 1975 and 1980, will be cited by volume and page number.

7. Julia Briggs, *Reading Virginia Woolf* (Edinburgh: Edinburgh University Press, 2006), 217.

protection for the text terminated.[8] Because *The Voyage Out* was published in London by Duckworth on March 26, 1915,[9] Woolf's thirty-day stopgap had long expired when George H. Doran Co. published the novel in the United States on May 20, 1920. *Night and Day* similarly missed the deadline: almost a full year elapsed between the October 20, 1919, Duckworth edition and Doran's September 29, 1920, U.S. edition.[10] Woolf's deliberate alterations to her fiction demonstrate that she was aware of—and tried to protect her own work through—copyright law, but because her books were not pirated, the author probably never knew that her intellectual property remained vulnerable despite her revisions. Woolf was thus locked out of the copyright to her first novels in the United States, a circumstance that demonstrates how difficult it was for British authors to secure their intellectual property in one of their largest foreign markets.

While this history points to an alternative path that Woolf's career might have taken because of the copyrights *of* her books, I am here more interested in Woolf's thinking about copyright *within* her works. As Paul Saint-Amour writes, copyright "in the late-modern literary imaginary" asserts its "presence *within* literary texts."[11] As she wrote about literary history—and later, in *Three Guineas*, about women's history more generally—Woolf focused on the importance of passing down literary ideas and styles. She argued that political and social movements were equally susceptible of inheritance; at her most radical, she suggested that life itself is not discrete but collective. Such arguments about the sources (and borrowings) of ideas and modes of expression might be subsumed under the familiar concept of intertextuality, but Woolf's model of intertextuality tests (and possibly transgresses) the boundaries of copyright. Indeed, Woolf's nonfiction suggests that this blanket term covers a highly varied field that ranges from allusion to quotation and even plagiarism. The legal status of such practices varies, of course, depending upon whether the property of individual rights-holders is violated. But *Room* and *Three Guineas* suggest that radical intertextuality is the norm rather than an exception; as a norm, it demands that writers, readers, and legal systems privilege the economic needs of the collective and the living above those of the singular and the dead.

---

8. Robert Spoo, "Copyright Protectionism and Its Discontents: The Case of James Joyce's *Ulysses* in America," *Yale Law Journal* 108 (1998): 646, 647.

9. Mark Hussey, *Virginia Woolf A–Z* (Oxford: Oxford University Press, 1995), 335.

10. In 1919, the ad interim and reprinting terms were extended to sixty days and four months, respectively, to compensate for the disruptions of World War I (Act of Dec. 18, 1919, ch. 11, § 21, 41 Stat. 368, 369).

11. Paul K. Saint-Amour, *The Copywrights: Intellectual Property and the Literary Imagination* (Ithaca, NY: Cornell University Press, 2003), 12.

Woolf held the pragmatic view that copyright law is important in enabling writers, and women writers in particular, to support themselves. Her vision of literary history and her limited participation in protest efforts demonstrate that, like writers before and after her, Woolf accepted the premise that copyright protection needed to vest in individual, living authors so that they could continue to produce additional work. Even when Woolf does not mention literary property or copyright specifically, they serve as fundamental conditions that enable ongoing creative work. For example, in her brief account of literary foremothers in *Room*, Woolf points out that Aphra Behn "made, by working very hard, enough to live on. The importance of that fact outweighs anything that she actually wrote."[12] This materialist argument positions intellectual and literary work as insufficient in and of itself; according to Woolf, Behn's writing gains import because it became valuable property, a "room" that sheltered Behn and allowed her to create. The quality of Behn's works is almost beside the point for Woolf: *Room* positions women's literary production as important because it became property, which helped to secure economic and social benefits. While Behn lived and published before the 1710 Statute of Anne enacted authorial copyright for the first time in Great Britain's history, Behn made "enough to live on" by selling her manuscripts to selected publishers, who in turn possessed the rights to her works. Although Behn wrote at a time when, in the words of Mark Rose, "no clearly defined set of authorial rights existed,"[13] Woolf retrospectively inscribed Behn as marking the historical moment when a middle-class woman "proved that money could be made by writing," however insecure that means of making a living remained (*Room*, 64).

Woolf's awareness of the significance of copyright protection for individual women emerges most clearly when she writes about nineteenth-century authors. Her ambivalent treatment of Charlotte Brontë in particular serves to emphasize how the possession and management of copyright influenced literary production. After commenting on the "awkward break" between Jane Eyre's reflections on her limited sphere and Grace Poole's laugh, Woolf's narrator speculates on the possibility of an alternative life history for her subject: "[o]ne could not but play for a moment with the thought of what might have happened if Charlotte Brontë had possessed say three hundred a year—but the foolish woman sold the copyright of

---

12. Virginia Woolf, *A Room of One's Own* (New York: Harcourt Brace Jovanovich, 1981), 64. Further references cited in the text as *Room*.

13. Mark Rose, *Authors and Owners: The Invention of Copyright* (Cambridge, MA: Harvard University Press, 1993), 25.

her novels outright for fifteen hundred pounds" (*Room*, 70).[14] Because Brontë's literary works were her sole means of earning personal income after she gave up working as a teacher and governess—because, through the ongoing payments her copyrights would have secured, her rights in these works were the portal to the writer's creative, intellectual, and social futurity—*Room* pronounces the sale of her copyrights "foolish." For Brontë, it meant that she did not have "more knowledge of the busy world, and towns and regions full of life; more practical experience, and intercourse with her kind and acquaintance with a variety of character" (*Room*, 70). For Woolf, copyright here emerges as a highly cathected matter. It is more than a simple legal protection or title to an intangible property: copyright's economic benefits allow access to a "room of one's own" that women must enter *and* possess in the interest of their future.

Woolf would only have needed to look at her own account books to see how valuable—and life changing—copyright could be. Although family inheritance always provided Woolf with a degree of middle-class comfort, profits from her books led to concrete material improvements in her life, such as an indoor bathroom and a new car.[15] Because of her success, Leonard Woolf writes, "we got more of the things which we liked to possess . . . and we did more of the things we wanted to do, for instance travel, and less in the occupations we did not want to do, for instance journalism."[16] Because Woolf's own valuable literary property enabled her to travel, she made a connection between the control of one's copyright and the ability to explore the wider world.

In one instance, Woolf's investment in copyright took a public and collective form: in 1927, she joined 161 other prominent writers in signing an international protest against Samuel Roth's "pirating" of *Ulysses*.[17] The protest appealed to the

14. This specific comment on Brontë's sale of her copyright is not in the Monk's House manuscript of *Room*, so Woolf added that information to her discussion of the author in revision. See Virginia Woolf, *Women and Fiction: The Manuscript Versions of "A Room of One's Own,"* ed. S. P. Rosenbaum (Oxford: Blackwell, 1992), 106.

15. Leonard Woolf provides detailed information about Woolf's earnings, which began to climb with the 1928 publication of *Orlando*. See *Downhill All the Way: An Autobiography of the Years 1919 to 1939* (New York: Harcourt Brace Jovanovich, 1967), 142–143. Woolf and her siblings also inherited tangible literary property in the form of Thackeray and Meredith manuscripts. The sale of these documents provided an infusion of cash that enabled Woolf to purchase the first Hogarth hand press. But these sales did not always realize the amounts the sellers hoped for and never, of course, secured ongoing revenue.

16. Ibid., 145.

17. Although *Ulysses* was made vulnerable because of ongoing censorship, Joyce's experience demonstrated that U.S. copyright law worked against foreign authors who did not quickly follow their initial publication with an edition manufactured in the United States. For the text of the protest, see James Joyce, *Letters of James Joyce,* ed. Richard Ellmann (New York:

American public to boycott Roth's *Two Worlds Monthly*, which was serializing a bowdlerized edition of Joyce's novel. The document also asked the editors and publishers of other serials to refuse his advertisements, "in the name of that security of works of the intellect and the imagination without which art cannot live."[18] Here, copyright is framed as "security"—an undisputed possession of one's text—enjoyed by a living author. The inverse of such security is clearly reflected in Joyce's experience as well as in Woolf's account of Charlotte Brontë; although one author was unable to find an American publisher who would help to secure U.S. copyright in a purportedly obscene work and the other sold a secure copyright to raise money quickly, both suffered economically because their property passed out of their hands. Together, Woolf's writing and activism reflect the presumed damage that alienated copyright would do to an author's economic and creative futurity.

While Woolf regarded copyright protection as important to the material well-being of individual authors, her nonfiction understands the creative process and textual production as fundamentally resistant to the possessive individualist model of literary production. This model reifies individual works characterized by original thinking and expression. As Saint-Amour writes, copyright law "seems to posit individual genius as the mystified source of innovation." At the same time, "it also recognizes and defends the collective as both the destination *and* source of creation."[19] This recognition takes the form of the public domain, which in time receives all intellectual property for the purpose of inspiring further creative acts. In Woolf's lifetime and our own, however, such recognition has been diminished as (short) copyright terms have been repeatedly extended. The private room of copyright has become, in effect, not just a dwelling place but a kind of mausoleum. Thin copyright regimes—the laws that specify short terms—have been replaced by thick regimes that prevent works from entering the public domain for generations, leaving the rights conferred by copyright in the hands of heirs and estates long after the deaths of individual writers. This has the effect of mystifying the creative process as individual, isolated, and rare, a kind of solo performance instead of a multivocal engagement with an inherited tradition.

Virginia Woolf's nonfiction, however, continually runs counter to such framing. Even as she points out the tragedy of alienated copyright in *A Room of One's*

Viking, 1966), 3:151–153. For details of Roth's dealings with Joyce, including the publisher's rationale for his actions, see Paul K. Saint-Amour's "Soliloquy of Samuel Roth: A Paranormal Defense," *James Joyce Quarterly* 37 (2000): 459–477. As Spoo has argued, Roth's work was not, in law, piracy because *Ulysses* was not published in the United States within the four-month window following its Parisian publication ("Copyright Protectionism," 653).

18. Joyce, *Letters*, 3:152.

19. Saint-Amour, *Copywrights*, 2–3.

Own, she emphasizes the importance of tradition—and collective, as opposed to individual, thinking—and thus makes it difficult to identify the sources of ideas and means of expression as well as who, if any one person, should benefit from their publication. Early in the book, she introduces one of *Room*'s major themes: "the effect of tradition and of the lack of tradition upon the mind of a writer" (*Room*, 24). The meaning of "tradition" might appear obvious, but if we think of it as a body of work by others, we already see that creativity cannot be an isolated or independent act. It needs to take place in a context, even if part of its meaning comes (as in the case of Woolf's work and modernism more generally) from resisting that context.

As Woolf's brief tracing of female literary history attests, women writers were initially hampered by a lack of tradition: "they had no tradition behind them, or one so short and partial that it was of little help. For we think back through our mothers if we are women" (*Room*, 76). Such familial thinking is enabled by tradition, which is made up of works under copyright protection and those in the public domain. The latter, however, are particularly helpful for writers as only those items are available without restrictions: they can be quoted, parodied, assimilated, continued, and borrowed from with no fear of reprisal. They are thus more open to "thinking back through" than works under copyright protection. *A Room of One's Own* illustrates this principle through its numerous examples. Many of the older works Woolf cites were in the public domain at the time of the book's publication, and when she turns to her own moment, Woolf avoids quoting extensively from protected works by *inventing* contemporary novelists and their writings.[20]

The importance of an openly available tradition emerges most distinctly when Woolf writes about her fictional twentieth-century writer Mary Carmichael.[21]

---

20. My thinking about *Room*'s treatment of public-domain and copyrighted texts has been inspired by chapter 5 of Saint-Amour's *Copywrights*, which analyzes the impact of copyright on Joyce's "Oxen of the Sun," particularly the chaotic ending of the episode.

21. Christine Froula has noted that Carmichael is a figure for Woolf herself and that "[a]s Mary Carmichael, Woolf places her own writing and its future on the line." See *Virginia Woolf and the Bloomsbury Avant-Garde: War, Civilization, Modernity* (New York: Columbia University Press, 2005), 191. This argument makes Woolf's assertion of Carmichael's connection to the past an autobiographical admission. There actually was a "Marie Carmichael" (nom de plume of Marie Carmichael Stopes), who published a book called *Love's Creation* (versus Woolf's invention, *Life's Adventure*) in 1928. See Elizabeth Abel, *Virginia Woolf and the Fictions of Psychoanalysis* (Chicago: University of Chicago Press, 1993), 88. Stopes's controversial publications on contraception, family planning, and women's rights place her in parallel with the fictional Mary Carmichael, whose novel depicts women working and inspires *Room*'s narrator to think about censorship. Woolf's device is thus a compound of found materials, the self, and the counterfactual.

When she reads the work of Carmichael, the narrator of *Room* asserts, "[i]t seems to be her first book...but one must read it as if it were the last volume in a fairly long series, continuing all those other books that I have been glancing at." The narrator then makes her point clear: "books continue each other, in spite of our habit of judging them separately" (*Room*, 80). Authors extend and develop what has been written by other writers before; no work appears *ex nihilo*. *Room* thus makes a claim that readers might be willing to assign to a single author's oeuvre and applies it to literature in general. Although Woolf's title suggests that individual authors must possess specific property in order to create, the logic of Woolf's argument dictates that no author works in that room alone. Divisions between books are arbitrary and illusory; instead, as she wrote later that year, "It is one brain, after all, literature."[22]

Woolf's theory of the "masterpiece" similarly articulates a profound connection between new art and previous works. The term *masterpiece* often connotes the work of isolated genius. As the *OED* defines it, the word signifies "the greatest work of a *particular* artist, writer, etc." (emphasis mine), an individuating definition applied to works by men and women who have risen above the ordinary due to singular skills. *Room*, instead, suggests the opposite: "masterpieces are not single and solitary births; they are the outcome of many years of thinking in common, of thinking by the body of the people, so that the experience of the mass is behind the single voice" (*Room*, 65).[23] This construction begins to undermine possessive individualism—a concept at the heart of intellectual property—by blurring the boundaries between texts and authors. Works are not created in isolation; instead, a collective "body" thinks and speaks with one voice, through the pen of an individual. This image of the "single voice" might initially appear to hedge the sentence's bets, and to reinscribe the book's titular "one," by suggesting that the individual is, in the end, the *one* who can enable the mass to speak. But *Room* complicates the boundaries around individual lives, an argumentative development that further undermines the model of the person as a self-determined whole who could or should possess intangible intellectual property.

22. Woolf, *Letters*, 4:4.

23. In *Women and Fiction*, Woolf used a simile to illuminate her theory of the masterpiece, which she there describes as "like the waves of the sea" (100). In revision, this image was edited out. Michael Tratner has noted that the passage cited in the text "describes the role of the mass mind in the development of literary works" and argues that "modernism was an effort to escape the limitations of nineteenth-century individualist conventions and write about distinctively 'collectivist' phenomena." See his *Modernism and Mass Politics: Joyce, Woolf, Eliot, Yeats* (Stanford, CA: Stanford University Press, 1995), 3. Tratner does not discuss *Room* in any detail, but my argument is clearly in sympathy with his larger claims.

As Woolf's narrator closes Carmichael's book, *Room* predicts a positive future for the first-time author: "Give her another hundred years...and she will write a better book one of these days" (*Room*, 94). The author of *Orlando* (1928) was clearly capable of imagining a writer who could transcend the normal human life span, but Woolf's comment does not posit a Methuselah-like existence for her creation. Instead, Carmichael here represents the "body of the people"—a collective process of thinking, creating, and publishing that might eventually produce a "single voice." This "body" and "voice" are expressed most movingly when Woolf writes about the possible return of Judith Shakespeare. At the end of *Room*, when Mary Beton (Woolf's fictional narrator) ceases to speak, Woolf provides a vision of the future. While Judith's body might be buried, "great poets do not die;...they need only the opportunity to walk among us in the flesh." This opportunity will be made available "if we live another century or so—and I am talking of the common life which is the real life and not of the little separate lives which we live as individuals" (*Room*, 113).

Woolf here provides readers with a means of thinking through the fundamental paradox of creativity and intellectual property. Individuals gain copyright protection, which they must possess during their lifetimes in order to support their "little separate lives." Woolf's title, with its single room and sole occupant, has attracted attention to this aspect of her argument; writing at a time when women's right to possess any manner of property was historically novel, Woolf asserts the importance of individual women's ongoing efforts to enter the economy and law on the same terms as men. If these individual gains are necessary, it is, however, the "common life which is the real life," a *collective* and *dividual* model of the creative process that is not reflected by possessive individualism (whether enjoyed by men or women) or by a copyright law that preserves works in isolation over long terms. Woolf's argument is underscored by her use of "we" at the end of *Room*, a shift that encourages readers to reexamine the "one" posited by the book's title. Although "one" might refer to a particular individual, the pronoun simultaneously occupies a liminal position between "my" and "our." This one word functions as a kind of embodiment of the rapprochement between individual rights and the collective life Woolf seeks throughout her nonfiction.[24]

Room's celebration of the collective as opposed to the individual is continued in *Three Guineas*, a book that focuses on the history of women's activism. In her

---

24. Froula argues that "*Room*'s 'one'...subsumes feminism within the Enlightenment struggle for the rights and freedoms of *all* and, by the same token, makes women's emancipation representative of the move from personal oppression to political claims that any oppressed group must make" (*Virginia Woolf*, 28).

response to a male correspondent who requests that she donate to and join a society for the prevention of war, Woolf takes her readers through an account of women's fight for equality, a fight that she frames as part of national and international efforts to resist tyranny at home and abroad. Like *Room, Three Guineas* represents the mass (in this case, the daughters of educated men) as behind the single voice. Woolf's very first example, Mary Kingsley, fills this role when she testifies to the disparity between her education and that of her brother. Kingsley's words appear to offer a singular experience and testimony, but Woolf argues, "Mary Kingsley is not speaking for herself alone; she is speaking, still, for many of the daughters of educated men."[25] Kingsley's speech is thus not singular: it is enabled by and makes sense within the context of the experience of a larger group. Again, it is the common life and not the individual existence that matters.

As *Three Guineas* unfolds, Woolf's treatment of individual lives follows this same pattern. While the details of specific women's lives add compelling nuance to and energize Woolf's argument, these details seldom insist on a *particular* story.[26] As Georgia Johnston has observed, *Three Guineas* "questions the validity of segregating one woman's life from women's lives as a whole" and conflates "lives into one life."[27] In Woolf's book, "[t]he witness of biography . . . is unanimous" (*TG*, 24). While the paths of individual lives vary, biography speaks with one voice on important points, such as the legal and social barriers women encounter when they try to pursue education or enter the professions. As women's lives are generalized in *Three Guineas*, the book identifies the common economic, political, and social conditions that create a common experience for women, further emphasizing the common life made important by *Room*. As a rhetorical strategy—and as an assertion of feminist identity—this is a powerful gesture. At the same time, this construction of collective lives and literary traditions raises several questions. Who should possess intellectual property produced by "thinking in common"? What

25. Virginia Woolf, *Three Guineas* (New York: Harcourt Brace Jovanovich, 1966), 4. Further references cited in the text as *TG*.

26. One exception is the example of Mr. Leigh Smith and his daughter Barbara, which demonstrates what "one father who was immune from infantile fixation could do by allowing one daughter £300 a year" (*TG*, 137). Sadly, Leigh Smith was unique in his treatment of his daughter, so his case remains singular.

27. Georgia Johnston, "Women's Voice: *Three Guineas* as Autobiography," in *Virginia Woolf: Themes and Variations*, ed. Vara Neverow-Turk and Mark Hussey (New York: Pace University Press, 1993), 321–322. Alison Booth similarly observes that Woolf's "many writings imagine a lively tradition of collective biographical history, the common life." See her *How to Make It as a Woman: Collective Biographical History from Victoria to the Present* (Chicago: University of Chicago Press, 2004), 227.

does it mean to possess rights over works that "continue" others? Who can use or enter into the property of others, and under what circumstances? Who should profit from a published work, and for how long?

To answer these questions, readers must move beyond Woolf's theories about collective lives and creations to examine her practices of citation. Woolf's arguments assert that individuals are not wholly (or even largely) responsible for the works they create, and study of her use of examples makes this claim concrete, demonstrating Woolf's own radical intertextual praxis. Although there are numerous citations in both *Room* and *Three Guineas*, I will here examine what I see as limit cases: places where Woolf continues published texts through undocumented borrowing or lengthy quotation. By examining Woolf's most extensive borrowing, I want to locate precisely how and where the mass is behind Woolf's single voice and to argue that Woolf's treatment of sources performs the collective authorship she advances in *Room* and *Three Guineas*. Moreover, Woolf's writerly practice suggests the importance of limiting the individual possession of intellectual property through short copyright terms, exactly the opposite of the laws that were passed during her lifetime and that continue to govern our own.

In most cases, Woolf's debts to her sources are clearly documented. At times, however, the mass behind Woolf's single voice disappears from view. While it would be inaccurate to describe such moments as plagiarism, it is clear that Woolf either continued, or thought along with, contemporaries she didn't cite in some of the most famous passages in *Room*. A case in point is Olive Schreiner's *From Man to Man or Perhaps Only...* (1926). As Susan Stanford Friedman has noted, Schreiner's text presents the idea of a female Shakespeare. In this novel about the frustrated lives of two South African sisters, Schreiner writes:

> [W]e have a Shakespeare; but what of the possible Shakespeares we might have had, who passed their life from youth upward brewing currant wine and making pastries for fat country squires to eat, with no glimpse of the freedom of life and action,...stifled out without one line written, simply because, being of the weaker sex, life gave no room for action and grasp on life?[28]

Because Woolf's exposure to this text is uncertain—in contrast, her readings of Schreiner's *The Story of an African Farm* and Schreiner's letters are documented—Friedman, following Susan David Bernstein, can only speculate that "Woolf's more aphoristic tropes...may have their unacknowledged 'origin'...in Schreiner's less

---

28. Olive Schreiner, *From Man to Man or Perhaps Only...* (London: Virago, 1982), 219.

resonant formulation."[29] Schreiner's possible influence on Woolf reminds readers that the documented sources in *Room* and *Three Guineas* are necessarily accompanied by ideas—and even expressions—that were either in the air of the period or come from unacknowledged sources. Such examples underline Woolf's sense of literature as "one brain,"[30] one room that many writers inhabit as they work and publish. The Schreiner illustration importantly reminds us that the mass working behind and beside Woolf's single voice is inevitably more multiple and significant than we can imagine. It is impossible to conceive of *A Room of One's Own* without Shakespeare's sister, and this formulation may have been suggested to Woolf by a Schreiner text that was published prior to *Room* and that was under copyright protection. If that protection had discouraged Woolf from attempting to enlarge and invigorate Schreiner's rather basic concept, *Room* and our tradition would have been impoverished.[31]

If Woolf's continuation of Schreiner's novel demonstrates the one brain that produces radically intertextual works, scholars might chalk this up to a rare but happy parallel between two feminist authors writing at roughly the same historical moment. In *Room*, however, the mass behind Woolf's single voice includes writers less overtly sympathetic to the author's argument. Woolf's words are enmeshed within a web of quotations from and conversations with copyrighted works by authors whose words energize Woolf's feminist polemic. Sir Arthur Quiller-Couch's *On the Art of Writing*, first published in 1916, allows Woolf to defend herself from the charge that writers should rise above poverty. This strikingly long quotation assesses the chances of success for poor poets:

> What are the great poetical names of the last hundred years or so? Coleridge, Wordsworth, Byron, Shelley, Landor, Keats, Tennyson, Browning, Arnold, Morris, Rossetti, Swinburne—we may stop there. Of these, all but Keats, Browning, Rossetti were University men; and of these three, Keats, who died young, cut off in his prime, was the only one not fairly well to do. It may seem a brutal thing to say, and it is a sad thing to say: but, as a matter of hard fact, the theory that poetical genius bloweth where it listeth, and equally in

29. Susan Stanford Friedman, "Migration, Encounter, and Indigenisation: New Ways of Thinking about Intertextuality in Women's Writing," in *European Intertexts: Women's Writing in English in a European Context*, ed. Angela Leighton, Ana María Sánchez-Arce, and Patsy Stoneman (Oxford: Lang, 2005), 237.

30. Woolf, *Letters*, 4:4.

31. Catherine Gallagher calls such moments "dormant counterfactual possibilit[ies]" that, however imaginary, can expand "our sense of plausible chronologies." See her "Undoing," in *Time and the Literary*, ed. Karen Newman, Jay Clayton, and Marianne Hirsch (New York: Routledge, 2002), 19 and 11.

poor and rich, holds little truth. As a matter of hard fact, nine out of those twelve were University men: which means that somehow or other they procured the means to get the best education England can give. As a matter of hard fact, of the remaining three you know that Browning was well to do, and I challenge you that, if he had not been well to do, he would no more have attained to write *Saul* or *The Ring and the Book* than Ruskin would have attained to writing *Modern Painters* if his father had not dealt prosperously in business. Rossetti had a small private income; and, moreover, he painted. There remains but Keats; whom Atropos slew young, as she slew John Clare in a mad-house, and James Thomson by the laudanum he took to drug disappointment. These are dreadful facts, but let us face them. It is—however dishonouring to us as a nation—certain that, by some fault in our commonwealth, the poor poet has not in these days, nor has had for two hundred years, a dog's chance. Believe me—and I have spent a great part of ten years in watching some three hundred and twenty elementary schools—we may prate of democracy, but actually, a poor child in England has little more hope than had the son of an Athenian slave to be emancipated into that intellectual freedom of which great writings are born. (*Room*, 107–108)[32]

Quiller-Couch's strong language and inexorable logic enable the narrator to conclude, "Intellectual freedom depends upon material things. Poetry depends upon intellectual freedom" (*Room*, 108).

The significance of Quiller-Couch's work for *Room* emerges when Woolf repeats the phrase "a dog's chance" twice after quoting the longer passage, thus borrowing both ideas and specific expression from a work protected by copyright.[33] While Woolf applies Quiller-Couch's argument to a group undreamed of by the original writer—his argument examines male writers, while *Room* is concerned with the economic limits that hamper women's creativity—she does not read against the grain of this writer so much as expand and amplify his ideas. In so doing, she models the collective creative process theorized throughout *Room*, illustrating in her selection of examples how books continue each other through lengthy quotation and thoughtful response. Indeed, the rhetorical room inhabited by the text's narrator(s) seems rather crowded: Quiller-Couch, Olive Schreiner, and many other writers

32. The passage Woolf quotes is from Arthur Quiller-Couch, *On the Art of Writing: Lectures Delivered in the University of Cambridge, 1913–1914* (Cambridge: Cambridge University Press, 1916), 38–39.

33. Woolf's original notes for this conclusion do not mention Quiller-Couch (*Women and Fiction*, 179); she seems to have introduced material from *On the Art of Writing* later in her process of writing and revision.

contribute their personas, words, and ideas to the creative process. Through his status as a professor of literature, Quiller-Couch helps to protect *Room*'s narrator and author from charges that she exaggerates; through her parallel vision of a female Shakespeare, Schreiner offers a kind of intellectual companionship to the apparently lone author. While it is always tempting to focus on Woolf's masterly argument, the seductiveness of her single voice can encourage readers to think of *Room* as a work of isolated genius instead of the product of complicated negotiations with a vocal—and legally regulated—literary and intellectual tradition.

Because Quiller-Couch's work would have been protected by copyright law, Woolf might have requested permission to include the long quotation from *On the Art of Writing* in *Room*. Other writers wrote to Woolf to ask permission to use her words, which she readily granted.[34] If Woolf gave any thought to this decision at all, she may have felt that her use of these sources was protected by the fair dealing clause in the copyright law. While we take the privileges conferred by such clauses for granted in the twenty-first century, copyright law underwent several important revisions during Woolf's lifetime. For example, the 1911 British Copyright Act extended the length of copyright protection to "the length of the author's life plus 50 years." Before that date, copyright law "protected works for 42 years from publication, or author's life plus 7 years, whichever was longer."[35] Woolf was thus born into a copyright regime with a modest de facto postmortem term, but by the time she began her work as a published author in earnest, that term, now pinned definitively to the author's death, had lengthened dramatically.

The introduction of the fair dealing clause was another important change to the law during Woolf's lifetime. Similar clauses had been proposed as early as 1837, but the 1911 act was the first to include such language, which protected "any fair dealing with the work [of another] for the purposes of private study, research, criticism, review or newspaper summary."[36] In practice, fair dealing has been distinguished from infringement if a new text responds to, rather than supersedes, the copyrighted work. Although infringement seems rather clear when one text

34. For example, Catherine Carswell requested permission to include a passage from *Night and Day* in an anthology she published in 1934. Woolf had "no objection" to her request. See "A Letter from Virginia," ed. Stephen Barkway, *Virginia Woolf Bulletin* 17 (2004): 13. This passage was of the same approximate length as the Quiller-Couch quotation cited in the text. Thanks to Stephen Barkway for drawing my attention to this correspondence.

35. Saint-Amour, *Copywrights*, 262n37, 180.

36. Ibid., 182. This type of exemption was not codified into U.S. law until 1976, although the courts had applied the concept throughout the previous century. For a clear discussion of how the boundaries of fair use have been contested and established in the U.S. courts, see Robert Spoo, "Fair Use of Copyrighted Works in the Digital Age," *California Business Law Practitioner* 23 (2008): 37–47.

supplants another through reproduction, it can also apply when a successor dimin-
ishes the appeal of an extant text through parody or other means. In the case of
Room, fair dealing might have become infringement if a reader in 1929 had been
likely to consult Woolf's book *instead of* the work of those she quotes. But in this
text, such an outcome seems unlikely.

I will conclude by examining a case that fits less neatly under the fair dealing
clause and that illustrates most fully the communal, populous authorship of *A
Room of One's Own* and *Three Guineas:* Woolf's creative engagement with Margaret
Todd's *The Life of Sophia Jex-Blake* (published by Macmillan in 1918) throughout
Three Guineas.[37] There can be no doubt that Woolf quotes from and references this
biography extensively.[38] Each citation is carefully documented, so Woolf's intellectual debts are clearly acknowledged. Woolf relies on this work because she sees it
as generalizable, and it thus assists with her argument that it is "the common life
which is the real life" (*Room*, 113). At the same time, she quotes and borrows freely
from the rich specificity of Todd's particular biography in order to advance her
argument. I want to suggest that Woolf's use of this particular text may have been
motivated as much by its status as quasi-orphaned property as by its usefulness for
her argument. In the absence of limited copyright protections, Woolf's deployment of Todd's literary property suggests that works administered by inactive
estates are particularly amenable to quotation and emendation.

Woolf explains her interest in Sophia Jex-Blake's life as a function of its repre-
sentability: "Her case is so typical an instance of the great Victorian fight between
the victims of the patriarchal system and the patriarchs, of the daughters against
the fathers, that it deserves a moment's examination" (*TG*, 64). Here, Woolf's language quickly moves from the singular ("her case") to the plural ("victims" and
"daughters"), and on this occasion and others, it appears that Jex-Blake is comparatively unimportant as an individual. Her father, similarly, was an "admirable
specimen of the Victorian educated man" (*TG*, 64). Later, Woolf writes, "The case
of Mr. Jex-Blake is very easily diagnosed, but it is a very important case because it
is a normal case, a typical case. Mr. Jex-Blake...was an ordinary father; he was
doing what thousands of other Victorian fathers whose cases remain unpublished

37. The relationship between Todd's *Life* and *Three Guineas* has been examined by
Hilary Newman, who details the aspects of the biography—such as Jex-Blake's religious
faith—that Woolf ignores. Newman also points out that Todd's book was published the
same year as Lytton Strachey's *Eminent Victorians* and compares the approach of the two
works to their respective subjects. See Newman, "*Three Guineas* and *The Life of Sophia
Jex-Blake*," *Virginia Woolf Bulletin* 25 (2007): 23–31.

38. See, for example, *TG*, 64–65, 131–134, and 156.

were doing daily" (*TG*, 132). With words like "specimen," "typical," and "ordinary," Woolf turns a father into the fathers. Throughout *Three Guineas*, Woolf's argument about the relationships between the private and public spheres depends upon seeing the individual life as most important in its reflection of the collective life.

At the same time, Jex-Blake's specific experience—and her specific words in communicating that experience—receives close attention. These words are necessarily Margaret Todd's words; although the biography was based on documents quoted, as she admits, "*in extenso*,"[39] Todd destroyed these materials after completing *Life*, thus rendering her book the only source for the material Woolf deploys. Woolf's most extensive quotations come from letters exchanged between Sophia and her father when the young woman was offered a paid job as a tutor. These letters—the exact words of this particular conflict between a specific father and daughter—are quoted in both the second and third "chapters" of *Three Guineas*, which address women's relationship to the professions and an antiwar society, respectively. The repeated citations from the same section of Todd's biography indicate that Woolf found the precise expression of this father-daughter conflict noteworthy even as she wanted to generalize this type of struggle.

While Woolf's intellectual debts to Margaret Todd—and, through her, to Sophia Jex-Blake—are usually documented, Todd's biography seems to have energized Woolf's argument more generally. For example, Todd writes about Jex-Blake's siblings and wonders "whether it ever occurred to the child [Sophia] to compare her brother's education with her own. If she had done so, the reflection might well have made her bitter."[40] This is a clear parallel to "Arthur's Education Fund," Woolf's powerful critique of the unequal educations offered to the sons and daughters of the same family (*TG*, 3–5).[41] Similarly, Todd later quotes Jex-Blake's observation that women are handicapped "by the greater reluctance of parents to spend money on their education, and the more inconsiderate claims made on their time, etc., at home."[42] Woolf's critique of the demands parents place upon their daughters thus thinks along with Todd and Jex-Blake.[43] Here and elsewhere,

39. Margaret Todd, *The Life of Sophia Jex-Blake* (London: Macmillan, 1918), 67.
40. Ibid., 29.
41. Woolf cites William Makepeace Thackeray's *Pendennis* as the source of this specific formulation, but Todd's text (and, no doubt, others) underpins the contrast between the educations offered to sons and to daughters.
42. Todd, *Life*, 480.
43. For example, Woolf writes, "[I]t is difficult to see how any incentive can make women free to give 'their gifts and their presence' to the service of the state, unless the state will undertake the care of elderly parents; or make it a penal offense for elderly people of either sex to require the services of daughters at home" (*TG*, 160n8).

readers can see how Todd's biography animated and enlarged *Three Guineas*, reminding us of *Room*'s observation that "books have a way of influencing each other" (*Room*, 109). Through repeated quotation, and through a reformulation of Todd and Jex-Blake's less evocative constructions, Woolf's book "continues" Todd's *Life* as well as other sources.

Although Woolf extensively deploys Todd's biography in *Three Guineas*, she clearly didn't perceive her actions as infringing upon Todd's property. Instead, her use of *Life* echoes the theories of creation and inspiration that *Room* and *Three Guineas* elsewhere advance. At the same time, it is possible that Woolf selected Todd's biography for particular attention because the text was not jealously guarded by rights-holders. After Woolf published *Three Guineas*, she received a number of letters that praised the book and offered tales of ongoing discrimination against women. Hilary Newman has noted that, in view of such letters, "perhaps the only surprising thing is that Virginia Woolf should have chosen Sophia Jex-Blake to illustrate her argument. Contemporary sources could have made the points as forcefully and perhaps explain Margaret Llewelyn Davies' comment, 'I am not quite sure I might have chosen some different women.'"[44] Davies' comment and Newman's speculation encourage readers to imagine other versions of *Three Guineas*, versions that would have relied upon the lives and biographies of Woolf's contemporaries instead of upon nineteenth-century struggles and the histories of women long dead. Such speculation, however, ignores the limits that copyright protection placed upon the work of "different women," limits that might have prevented the kind of extensive deployment exemplified by Todd's *Life* in *Three Guineas*.

While "contemporary sources" were protected by the same copyright law that propertized Todd's biography, they would nevertheless have presented Woolf with a distinct challenge: copyright law is policed when authors or their estates bring suits for infringement, and while some estates vigorously guard their property until it enters the public domain, the work of living and recently dead authors is most jealously guarded. Woolf may have felt free to think and create with Todd's *Life* in part because Todd had been dead for nearly twenty years: she committed suicide three months after the 1918 publication of her biography. Because Todd did not marry or have children, she did not leave behind an immediate family that might have been invested in and protective of her copyright. Her estate was divided between Eugenia Barbara Todd and Emma Clarke Beilby, a relative and a supporter

---

44. Newman, "*Three Guineas*," 31. For the full text of Davies' letter to Woolf, see "*Three Guineas* Letters," ed. Anna Snaith, *Woolf Studies Annual* 6 (2000): 43.

of Sophia Jex-Blake's hospital in Edinburgh, respectively.[45] Although Eugenia Todd may have been alive when *Three Guineas* was published, Beilby had died in 1936, leaving Todd's text partially, if not fully, orphaned.[46] At our own historical moment, orphaned works (for which no copyright owner can be found) pose their own set of problems. Users are often deterred by the fact that they cannot find anyone to clear rights and are thus paralyzed instead of liberated by the work's legal status. Because Woolf was not, however, concerned with clearing rights, she appears to have been freed rather than hampered by the status of Todd's biography. Moreover, Todd's *Life* had been in circulation for twenty years when Woolf published *Three Guineas*, so whatever market the book had enjoyed was probably exhausted in 1938.[47] This would not be the case with books published in the late 1920s and 1930s, which could have been on store shelves and whose copyrights might have been zealously guarded by authors and their heirs.

Because Woolf's intertextual dialogue took place with a copyrighted text that had been published two decades earlier by an author long deceased, her work was unlikely to receive—and did not attract—unfriendly scrutiny. In other words, the texts Woolf chose to quote from and to continue in *Three Guineas* freed her to a large extent from the need to think about working within copyright restrictions. As her footnotes demonstrate, Woolf documented (most of) her intellectual debts quite clearly, a gesture that demonstrated the extent of her research and gave credit to the "mass" behind her single voice. That this mass was unlikely to be litigious left Woolf free to use legally protected work however she wanted in her passionate political and social polemic. The use of Margaret Todd's *Life* in *Three Guineas* suggests that Woolf respected strong copyright by avoiding extensive quotation from protected, carefully policed texts. By practicing a model of communal literary creation, Woolf demonstrates the kind of creative work made possible by the public domain and, under a worst-case scenario of intellectual property law, inactive rights-holders, who actively or passively let the published works they control be deployed and reinvigorated by others.

45. According to the Probate Registry, the gross value of Todd's estate was £9,172 when the will was proved and registered on November 28, 1918. Although the rights to Todd's work are not mentioned, it seems likely that these devolved upon her two heirs as well. In addition to her biography of Jex-Blake, Todd's books included six novels, the first of which went into several editions.

46. Eugenia Barbara Todd's life and death remain an enigma as the Probate Registry entry is the sole document in which I have found her mentioned.

47. As the London *Times* obituary for Todd observed, *Life* always had a self-selecting readership as it "was in parts almost too laboriously minute for the general reader" (Sept. 5, 1918, 9).

Tensions at the root of copyright law are dramatized by Woolf's own asser-
tions of intellectual property's importance to individual, living authors and
her representations of creativity and literary production as a collective, distributed process. Her nonfiction can only be understood as the work of a
solitary genius by ignoring the prompts of *Room* and *Three Guineas*, which
together encourage readers to look for the ways that thinking back through
and with the mass enable a single voice. Together, these works suggest that the
room of one's own might best be understood as a room of *our* own, a space
that balances women's hard-fought right to privacy and material comfort with
an intellectual activity that is communal rather than individualized. If "one"
goes into the room made possible by and generative of private property, the
work of thinking back through and with "our" mothers that takes place there
is never isolated (*Room*, 76).

If readers return to Woolf's work newly attuned to the chorus that enables her
aria, they might be led to consider the intellectual and economic implications of
the copyright protections that now cover *Room* and *Three Guineas*. Woolf's books
are regularly read and taught, but many of the works she cites and thinks back
through are not in print. This leads to two outcomes for the authors who populate
her notes. First, Woolf's extensive citation keeps works alive for later generations.
Three Guineas introduces Margaret Todd's *Life*, for example, to readers who might
otherwise never consult it. Indeed, Woolf's work helped to create a life for Todd's
book in the virtual world: *Three Guineas* is cited in the Wikipedia entry on Sophia
Jex-Blake, which also cites Todd. According to the entry's revision history, the reference to Woolf's work was added immediately before the reference to Todd's *Life*,
so Woolf's polemic likely pointed the editor—and subsequent readers of the
Wikipedia entry—to Todd's book.[48]

While *Three Guineas* and *Room* thus preserve and help to circulate ideas (and
texts) that might be forgotten, the economic result is rather one-sided: Woolf's
estate alone controls and profits from this material. The Society of Authors, which
manages the estate, has been more flexible and accommodating to scholars than
some of the more notorious modernist estates, but its judgment is not infallible.[49]

---

48. See the history of the page and particularly the changes dated August 1, 2006, in
"Sophia Jex-Blake," *Wikipedia: The Free Encyclopedia*, http://en.wikipedia.org/w/index.
php?title=Sophia_Jex-Blake&action=history (accessed July 21, 2009).

49. According to its website, the proceeds from the society's work as managers of literary
estates support activity on behalf of the rights and interests of contemporary authors. The
proceeds from the contracts themselves go to the rights-holders, in this case to descendants
of Vanessa Bell.

Woolf's arguments about the collective nature of inspiration and authorship—her sense of "[h]ow little one counts ... how little anyone counts"[50]—encourage readers to consider whether intellectual property shouldn't be managed differently. Unlike rights-holder advocates who favor extended or perpetual terms, Woolf never professed a desire for her work to remain propertized for generations. Given her criticism of property and the professions in *Three Guineas*, scholars and readers might well suspect that she held the opposite point of view.[51]

In her analysis of cultural institutions in *Three Guineas*, Woolf figuratively sets fire to a range of traditions and concepts. She queries whether she should ask women "to buy rags and petrol and Bryant & May's matches and burn the [traditional] college to the ground"; later, she proposes that readers write the word *feminist* "in large black letters on a sheet of foolscap; then solemnly apply a match to the paper" (*TG*, 33, 101). While neither *Three Guineas* nor *Room* explicitly incinerates copyright law as Woolf knew it, her nonfiction suggests that readers need to rethink who owns intellectual property and for what span of time. During her lifetime, Woolf needed the profits from her books to enjoy the intellectual freedom that allowed her to write—to create along and think with the works of others. This freedom, however, was limited by the very copyright law that guaranteed her income because, through a model of individual possession of intangible property, the law restricted whom she could cite and to what extent. More important, since Woolf's death, copyright law has been characterized by what Saint-Amour calls "'copyright creep,' a tendency toward frequent and increasingly substantial term extensions."[52] As I write this essay, Woolf's works are still under copyright protection through 2011 in the United Kingdom and many EU nations, a full seventy years after her death. In the United States, texts like *A Room of One's Own* and *Three Guineas* will remain privatized even longer: *Room* will enter the public domain in 2025, and *Three Guineas* will not join it until 2034.[53] While this long period of protection clearly

50. Virginia Woolf, *The Diary of Virginia Woolf*, ed. Anne Olivier Bell and Andrew McNeillie (New York: Harcourt Brace Jovanovich, 1977–1984), 3:201.

51. For example, Woolf observes, "[T]he professions have a certain undeniable effect upon the professors. They make the people who practice them possessive, jealous of any infringement of their rights, and highly combative if anyone dares dispute them" (*TG*, 66). *Three Guineas* then goes on to outline ways in which women might practice the professions differently.

52. Saint-Amour, *Copywrights*, 4.

53. For information about when the copyrights in Woolf's texts expire, see Robert Spoo, "'For God's Sake, Publish; Only Be Sure of Your Rights': Virginia Woolf, Copyright, and Scholarship," in *Woolf Editing/Editing Woolf*, ed. Eleanor McNees and Sara Veglahn (Clemson, SC: Clemson University Digital Press, 2009), 230.

benefits a few, it prevents Woolf from fully joining the mass behind new voices, the new Mary Carmichaels and Judith Shakespeares. Because Woolf's copyrights no longer create intellectual freedom—because no one would argue that copyright can provide retroactive incentives and support to the deceased—it's time to think honestly and clearly about what, if any, purpose such copyrights serve.

PART TWO

Melodic Properties of the Culture System

3 Rhythm Changes

Contrafacts, Copyright, and Jazz Modernism

Mark Osteen

Birds in the tree sing their dayful of song,
Why shouldn't we sing along?

A paean to satisfaction ("who could ask for anything more?") and fulfilled aspiration ("I got starlight, I got sweet dreams"), "I Got Rhythm" not only expresses good cheer, but exults in music's power to generate such feelings. The song's syncopation produces the very rhythm it celebrates, and its melodic simplicity matches the simplicity of its sentiments. Perhaps that is why the Gershwin brothers' infectious little ditty has undergone more reincarnations than any other Tin Pan Alley tune. These include not only George Gershwin's own variations and the tune's revivals in film versions, but also the uncountable jazz compositions that borrow its harmonic structure. So accommodating was the Gershwin song's chord structure, in fact, that a term was coined to describe its numerous children: "rhythm changes" tunes.

Many of these offspring issued from the peculiar circumstances surrounding the birth of bebop, a new jazz style that emerged in the 1940s from after-hours jam sessions where musicians improvised on familiar tunes. Recording the products of those sessions presented a problem, however, for copyright law required that record companies pay royalties to the composers. To avoid these payments, the musicians were encouraged to create new melodies over standard chord changes, rename the results, and call them original compositions. Such compositions—dubbed "contrafacts" in a seminal 1975 essay by musicologist James Patrick—became an indispensable part of the jazz vocabulary.[1] The history of this subgenre reveals a fascinating confluence of musical, economic, legal, and racial currents. Indeed, I propose that "I Got Rhythm," with its changes and contrafacts, both exemplifies the modernist penchant for blending seemingly incompatible forms into new hybrids, and offers an intriguing test case in the shaping of twentieth-century culture. These changes also epitomize the improvisatory, rebellious spirit of jazz as an African-American art form that "signifies" upon established orthodoxies and sidesteps legal and economic restrictions.

Theme and Variations

> Old Man Trouble,
> I don't mind him,
> You won't find him
> 'round my door.

As Lawrence Levine suggests, early jazz—with its vitality, speed, sexual charge, reliance on new technologies, and sheer raucousness—was the soundtrack of 1920s modernity.[2] It was scandalous, obscene, transgressive; it was also joyful, irrepressible, unpretentious. It was thus, as Kathy Ogren puts it, "the specific symbol of rebellion and of what was new about the decade."[3] So powerful was the jazz impulse that even mavens of European high culture, such as conductor Leopold Stokowski, admitted that "jazz has come to stay because it is an expression of . . . the breathless, energetic, superactive times in which we are living."[4] Jazz embodied the era's fascinating rhythms, but those rhythms were under stress, as the old guard fought to preserve tradition from the onslaught of these new forms. Hence, writes Ogren, to "argue about jazz was to argue about the nature of change itself."[5]

One composer who sought to meld old and new styles was George Gershwin, born Jacob Gershwine in Brooklyn in 1898. George took up the piano at age twelve, performed his first original composition at age fifteen, and by sixteen was working

1. James Patrick, "Charlie Parker and the Harmonic Sources of Bebop Composition: Thoughts on the Repertory of New Jazz in the 1940s," *Journal of Jazz Studies* 2 (1975): 3. Patrick chose the term *melodic contrafact* to recall the common practice of textual substitution in medieval music (*contrafactum;* 3). Further references will be cited in the text as "CP."

2. Lawrence W. Levine, "Jazz and American Culture," in *The Jazz Cadence of American Culture*, ed. Robert G. O'Meally (New York: Columbia University Press, 1998), 433.

3. Kathy Ogren, *The Jazz Revolution: Twenties America and the Meaning of Jazz* (New York: Oxford University Press, 1989), 6.

4. Quoted Ibid., 7.

5. Ibid.

as a song plugger—playing the latest tunes for performers and publishers.[6] His scholarly older brother, Ira, enrolled in New York's City College and learned to write satirical verses (*FR*, 16). George had his first hit, the Al Jolson vehicle "Swanee," in 1918, and by 1921 the brothers were creating Broadway shows. "Rhapsody in Blue" and classic songs like "The Man I Love" soon followed. By the end of the 1920s, they had several successful Broadway productions on their resumes.

The Gershwin name, by then, had come to define jazz for many (mostly white) Americans. Some of the brothers' songs seem to acknowledge this status by commenting on their own powers. "Fascinating Rhythm," for example, presents a mock lament about a "darn persistent" melody that "hangs around me all day," forcing the speaker to shake "just like a flivver." Such songs had much of America in their grip. Yet George still found time to paint and to collect works by visual artists such as Picasso and Roualt (*FR*, 165), while Ira became a devotee of George Bernard Shaw, Theodore Dreiser, Henry James, and Abraham Cahan (*FR*, 15). Ira's lyrics sometimes display a penchant for allusion worthy of his literary contemporaries (for example, "Isn't It a Pity?" is doubtless the only Tin Pan Alley tune to cite Schopenhauer and Heine). In short, the Gershwins were both popular artists and self-conscious modernists.

But most of their "serious" work (aside from the quasi-classical "Rhapsody"), such as *Porgy and Bess*, was still to come, and they continued to trade in the breezy musical comedies that had made their reputation. In October 1930, their latest, *Girl Crazy*, debuted on Broadway. The show—a lightweight story about a city boy banished to the country, and the resulting clash of values—included several songs that later became standards, including "Embraceable You," "Bidin' My Time," and "But Not for Me."[7] The showstopper was sung by an ingénue in her Broadway debut: eighteen-year-old Ethel Merman, playing Kate, a young woman married to a faithless gambler named Slick, belted out "I Got Rhythm" and held one note for sixteen measures. The audience went wild: according to Merman's autobiography, people were on their feet by measure four.[8]

It's easy to see why the tune so pleased crowds, for it is brilliant in its use of that most ancient of devices, the pentatonic scale. Beginning on the fifth note of that scale (F, in the key of B♭), it moves to the sixth, first, second, and third pitches, descends on the same pitches, ascends again, then wraps up the cadence two bars later. It is compact, forceful, singable. Rhythmically, it is no more sophisticated: it

6. Deena Rosenberg, *Fascinating Rhythm: The Collaboration of George and Ira Gershwin* (New York: Dutton, 1991), 21, 28. Further references cited in the text as *FR*.

7. For plot summaries of the original *Girl Crazy*, see *FR*, 167; and William Hyland, *George Gershwin: A New Biography* (Westport, CT: Praeger, 2003), 131.

8. Hyland, *George Gershwin*, 131. See also Ethel Merman, as told to Pete Martin, *Who Could Ask for Anything More?* (Garden City, NY: Doubleday, 1955), 82.

I Got Rhythm

George and Ira Gershwin

1930

starts on the second beat of the first bar and alternates downbeats and upbeats thereafter. But it *does* have rhythm: the tune is not only about syncopation; it embodies it. One cannot sing the line "I got rhythm" properly without "getting" that rhythm.

The song also expresses George Gershwin's credo, according to S. N. Behrman, a close friend, who wrote: "Illuminated and vitalized by his own music, his own voice, his own eager sense of the rhythm of life, Gershwin instantly conveys that illumination and that vitality to others" (quoted in *FR*, 120). Like Kate, he is chipper all the day and happy with his lot. Indeed, "I Got Rhythm" describes the spirit of the Jazz Age, when the world itself seemed to be syncopated, the birth of the new coming either too early (the Great War) or too late (the crash of 1929), a world where automobiles, big money, and airplanes knocked life askew, rendering it hectic, jangly, and hazardous. The changes associated with the coming of modernity are defined and embodied in the tune, which bravely asserts optimism in the wake of the stock market crash: I "don't need what money can buy" and still have my most valuable possessions. So why not party on?

That party turned out to be nearly endless, as numerous variations altered the melody, rhythm, context, or meaning of "Rhythm" while retaining its core. Some of them were the Gershwins' own—not a surprising practice for a team that habitually reused melodic and lyrical fragments. For example, the sentiments of "Rhythm" are echoed in Porgy's "I Got Plenty o' Nuthin'" although, as Deena Rosenberg notes, the earlier tune's "dismissal of other considerations... is only implicit" while in "Porgy's song it is explicit" (*FR*, 290). Old Man Trouble showed his face again in 1938's "I Was Doing All Right," and Ira recycled "who could ask for anything more?" in 1937's "Nice Work if You Can Get It" (George employed the same intervals as well; see *FR*, 357).[9]

Under the influence of classical theorist and composer Joseph Schillinger, in 1934 George rewrote "I Got Rhythm" as a semi-classical piece entitled "I Got Rhythm Variations." This set of pastiches transposes the five-note melody into different keys and encompasses styles from a valse triste to "Chinese" and modal versions.[10] The result, writes Steven Gilbert, is a "complete contrapuntal matrix based solely on that all-pervasive, symmetrical motive of seemingly endless possibilities."[11] The "Variations," that is, enacts the song's endorsement of unlimited rejuvenation. Even so, as Gilbert writes, the piece uneasily blends the new techniques Gershwin absorbed from Schillinger with "the tonal procedures to which he still owed allegiance."[12] The "Variations" thus embodies the encounter between tradition and innovation that epitomizes jazz modernism.

Subsequent "I Got Rhythm" versions further sound the cultural transformations and dissonances of the interwar period. For instance, the highlight of the first movie version of *Girl Crazy*, released in 1932, occurs when Kate (Kitty Kelly), who hails from Chicago, sings "I Got Rhythm" at an Arizona dude ranch. So irresistible is the tune that by the end even a stuffed owl and nearby cacti are tripping the light fantastic. The song thus represents how urban attitudes—particularly, a relaxed sexual morality—can infect the hinterlands, and dramatizes the meeting of the Old West and the Jazz Age. The 1943 version, directed by Norman Taurog, erases Kate and her louche associations, turning the story into a "golly-gosh" juvenile fable in which postmistress Ginger (Judy Garland) and tenderfoot Danny (Mickey Rooney) host a rodeo in order to save dear ol' Cody College. At the end, they throw a huge party at which Tommy Dorsey's Orchestra, clad in cowboy outfits, backs Garland

9. There are other examples of this propensity for self-appropriation. For example, "The Man I Love" employs the same primary melodic device (leaping from the tonic to the minor third) as do the main themes of "Rhapsody in Blue" and "Fascinating Rhythm" (see *FR*, 93). The brothers even reused whole tunes, as when "I've Got a Crush on You," originally written for 1928's *Treasure Girl*, showed up again two years later in *Strike Up the Band*.

10. For partial transcriptions of the "Variations," see Steven E. Gilbert, *The Music of Gershwin* (New Haven, CT: Yale University Press, 1995), 175–181.

11. Ibid., 181.

12. Ibid., 175.

singing "I Got Rhythm." The movie ends with Ginger asking, "Who could ask for anything more?" It would have been difficult to cram more into this seven-minute, Busby Berkeley–directed production number, which features his usual chorus girls and swooping crane shots, along with a great deal of flag waving and pseudo-military marching. Here, "I Got Rhythm" is not only remodeled to fit a bland swing era formula typified by wholesome hayseeds and Dorsey's clean-cut, all-white band; it has also been transmuted into a wartime patriotic hymn.

Its next major cinematic appearance, in Vincente Minnelli's 1951 *An American in Paris*, slightly alters this patriotic theme. A half-hour into the film, Gene Kelly, playing an American painter in postwar France, performs "I Got Rhythm" as a lesson in American values for a group of Parisian street urchins. A different kid contributes an "I got" in turn, which Kelly follows with the list of "possessions." The kids' contributions stretch the tempo—they ain't got rhythm—but Kelly certainly has it, especially in his feet, which he demonstrates by showcasing an array of "American" steps, from the shim sham to the cowboy. The United States is thus depicted as a mélange of diverse styles and, because we have to improvise our way through this hybrid terrain, the film suggests, all Americans have got rhythm. The tune now reflects a jazz version of postwar American hegemony: if Kelly learns high culture from the Parisians, they must learn rhythm from him.[13]

Bebop, Rebop

> Little cullud boys with fears,
> frantic, kick their draftee years
> into flatted fifths and flatter beers
> that at a sudden change become
> sparkling Oriental wines
> rich and strange
>
> —Langston Hughes[14]

"I Got Rhythm" seems almost infinitely adaptable, its many incarnations offering proof of its lyrics' inextinguishable optimism. But its most radical revisions came at the hands of a cadre of young African-American musicians who, around the time that the second *Girl Crazy* premiered, were inventing bebop, a revolutionary

13. At this time, many African-American jazz musicians expatriated to Europe, where they hoped to escape the racism they faced in the allegedly free States and, incidentally, taught thousands of Europeans how to get rhythm.

14. Langston Hughes, "Flatted Fifths," in his *Montage of a Dream Deferred*, in *The Collected Poems of Langston Hughes*, ed. Arnold Rampersad (New York: Vintage, 1994), 404.

style of jazz that, paradoxically, relied heavily on old chestnuts. The new style was born during jam sessions at Harlem clubs, such as Minton's Playhouse and Monroe's Uptown House, where musicians retreated after their big band gigs to jam on tunes that everyone knew: standards such as "Whispering," "Honeysuckle Rose," "Embraceable You," "How High the Moon," and, foremost among them, "I Got Rhythm."

The song is well designed for this function. Its thirty-two-bar structure (in AABA form) begins on the root chord; moves to the submediant, supertonic, and dominant; and then repeats the cadence. In intervallic terms, it goes like this: I vi7 ii7 V7 (played twice). A second four-measure cadence follows: I I7 | IV #iv°7 | I V7 | I. Thus, in B♭ major, the chords are B♭ Gm7 | Cm(7) F(7) | B♭ Gm7 | Cm F(7) | B♭ B♭7 | E♭7 Edim7 | B♭ F7 | B♭. That sounds rather complicated. But well-schooled jazz musicians know that the chords in the first four measures are based on the same scale—B♭ major; the A section modulates to the fourth degree and the diminished sharp fourth degree only briefly before returning to the tonic. Thus, by using what is called harmonic generalization, a player can use the same scale as the basis for improvising over the entire A section, except for measure six.[15] Because the measures pass so quickly, one may even ignore this brief modulation and not be heard hitting a wrong note.[16] The bridge, or B section, moves through the cycle of fifths, beginning on the major third: two bars of D7, followed by two bars of G7, two of C7, and two of F7, which sends us ineluctably back to B♭. This section is a bit more challenging, but any jazz player worth his or her salt peanuts should have little trouble negotiating the dominant sevenths, because the consecutive chords have most pitches in common.[17]

The tune soon began to spawn contrafacts, compositions that overlaid a new melody on the chords of the old song. Some of these evolved from a favorite riff,

15. On harmonic generalization, see Jerry Coker, *Elements of the Jazz Language for the Developing Improviser* (Miami: Studio 224/Belwin/Warner Bros., 1991), 45.

16. The simplicity of the A section helps to explain why accomplished players at these formative sessions would drive novices or self-glorifiers off the bandstand by calling "I Got Rhythm" but altering the chords: they might start in B♭ but then leap to a distant chord—say F#—before gradually cycling back to the tonic (see Eddie Meadows, *Bebop to Cool: Context, Ideology and Musical Identity* [Westport, CT: Praeger, 2003], 119). There are many other possible generalization strategies: for instance, Charlie Parker habitually used the blues scale over the last four measures of the A section.

17. There are variant versions in which musicians replace the cycle of fifths with a series of "two-fives" (i.e., ii7-V7 cadences). Certain tunes based on "I Got Rhythm"—for example, Sonny Stitt's "The Eternal Triangle" and Horace Silver's "Tippin'"—replace the bridge harmonies with alternate chords. For a partial list of "I Got Rhythm" contrafacts, see "Rhythm Changes," *Money Chords*, http://www.angelfire.com/fl4/moneychords/rhythmchanges.html (accessed Aug. 31, 2009).

obbligato, or countermelody.[18] This practice was not in itself a bebop innovation: many early jazz tunes share the same chord structures or borrow from other melodies. As Patrick points out, even the chestnut "Tiger Rag" takes part of its melody from a quadrille ("CP," 4–5). In the early bebop period, however, contrafacts became commonplace because they offered "a way to retain familiar harmonic patterns for…improvisation" while also providing new melodies "more compatible with the peculiarities of…the bop style" ("CP," 11). Blurring the lines between improvisation and composition, contrafacts blended tradition and innovation, permitting musicians to mix old and new ingredients and thereby transform the "flat beers" of the 1920s and '30s into rich and strange hybrid brews.

But this process also required another, commonly misunderstood ingredient: commodification, in the form of recordings. That ingredient was, however, absent for more than a year after James Petrillo, president of the American Federation of Musicians (the union to which virtually all working musicians at the time belonged), instituted a recording ban in 1942.[19] The ban created a lacuna in jazz history as it is often presented: on one side lies the increasingly commercialized music of the swing era; on the other, modern jazz, with its complex rhythms, sophisticated harmonies, and aspirations to high art. Contrafacts bridged the gap, providing a means for swing musicians to modernize while also demonstrating their mastery of classics.

In jam sessions, standard tunes function as a commons or public domain that all are free to prowl, mine, cultivate, and share. They thus partake more of a gift economy than of a mercantile one. Hence, as Scott DeVeaux writes in *The Birth of Bebop*, what separates improvisation from composition in a capitalist economy is that the improviser "renounces the intention of transmuting creativity into published commodity" (*BB*, 11): improvisations cannot be copyrighted, unless they are fixed in some permanent form, such as a recording. But, as he also notes, the young black men who created bebop were first and foremost professionals interested not just in honing their craft, but also in making a living (*BB*, 16). And capitalism, DeVeaux argues, "made their achievements possible," in that bebop was "an attempt to reconstitute jazz…[so] as to give its black creators the greatest professional autonomy *within* the marketplace" (*BB*, 27). But first, those jam session vehicles had to be "converted into

18. See Michael Jarrett, "Four Choruses on the Tropes of Jazz Writing," *American Literary History* 6 (1994): 341–342, for an intriguing discussion of the odd etymology of *obbligato*, which over the centuries has metamorphosed from meaning "obligatory" to meaning "optional." Contrafacts, it seems, follow the same trajectory.

19. Believing that records constituted a threat to musicians' livelihood, Petrillo aimed to force record companies to contribute a fee from each recording to a fund for unemployed musicians. See Scott DeVeaux, *The Birth of Bebop: A Social and Musical History* (Berkeley: University of California Press, 1997), 295. Further references cited in the text as *BB*.

clearly defined economic units...for which authorship could be precisely established" (*BB*, 298). These units had to be *original* tunes, for under existing copyright law, a record company was obliged to pay two cents per side for each 78rpm record—one cent each to the composer and publisher. Saving money was essential, for in the wake of the recording ban, a raft of tiny, underfunded independent companies, such as Dial, Keynote, and Savoy, had sprung up to challenge the major labels' domination. Many of the young musicians playing on these companies' records naïvely eschewed contracts, intending to leave themselves available for freelance gigs. Hence, if the labels could also establish themselves as publishing companies, and if the musicians—most of whom received only a flat fee for their performances—could write some original tunes, the label owners would not only avoid paying royalties on copyrighted songs, but would also pocket publishers' fees and, by giving themselves a co-composer's credit, add the composer's royalty to their take.[20]

But what if those "originals" were merely reworked standards? Wouldn't the companies still owe royalties? The answer was no. Copyright law had defined originality such that contrafacts were not deemed infringements. The key decisions related to the legal definition of an "adaptation" (nowadays called a "derivative work") and emerged from notions about creativity and originality carried over from nineteenth-century aesthetics, as codified by judges who impersonated a fictitious character called the "average person."

Watchdogs

> There's a somebody I'm longing to see.
> I hope that he
> Turns out to be
> Someone who'll watch over me.
>
> —Ira Gershwin

Two general concepts come into play in musical copyright law: the "idea" (as opposed to its expression) and the "adaptation." Copyright law specifies that protection does not extend to "any idea, procedure, process, system, method of operation, concept, principle, or discovery, regardless of the form in which it is described, explained, illustrated, or embodied in such a work."[21] Although the law has consis-

---

20. DeVeaux, in *BB*, 306, cites a short story by critic and producer Leonard Feather that vividly depicts how unscrupulous owners fleeced unsuspecting musicians.

21. The idea/expression dichotomy was famously articulated in *Baker v. Selden* 101 U.S. 99 (1880), which posited that an idea may not be copyrighted but an expression of that idea

tently treated compositions as "expression" and therefore protectable, it has treated their harmonic structure as an "idea," "concept," or "system"—as the idea of a song, not the song itself. An "adaptation" (or "derivative work") is "primarily a new work" but one that "incorporates some previously published material.... To be copyright-able, a derivative work must be different enough from the original to be regarded as a 'new work' or must contain a substantial amount of new material." The statute covers translations, musical arrangements, dramatizations, fictionalizations, abridgments, and "any other form in which a work may be recast, transformed, or adapted."[22] Questions leap to mind. "To be regarded" as a new work by whom? What degree of new material is considered "substantial"? And if an arrangement is considered derivative, why isn't a tune that merely drapes a new melody over *exactly* the same harmonic framework also considered to be derivative?

A 1957 essay by Leon Yankwich, a distinguished California judge, outlines the era's judicial thinking.[23] He cites three important cases that shaped mid-century copyright law and confirmed the idea/expression dichotomy. The first, *Universal Pictures v. Harold Lloyd Corp.* (1947), established that originality could be displayed in "taking commonplace materials and acts and making them into a new combination ... protectible by copyright" so long as the artist uses "his own method or way of expressing his ideas."[24] The second, *Funkhouse v. Loew's Inc.* (1953), confirmed that "ideas as such are not subject to copyright" (quoted in "LP," 378); a third, *Alexander v. Irving Trust Co.* (1955), determined that "a copyright does not pre-empt the field as against others who choose a different means of expressing the same idea" (quoted in "LP," 382). These decisions clear the way for contrafacts, which take "commonplace material"—i.e., a harmonic idea—and transform it.

As significant as these decisions is the seemingly indissoluble link between originality and melody. As Judge Yankwich declares, "[O]riginality lies in the

---

may be. However, the dichotomy was not codified until the Copyright Act of 1976, which also altered the terminology so that "adaptations" came to be called "derivative works." See 17 U.S.C. § 102(b).

22. "Copyright Registration for Derivative Works," http://www.copyright.gov/circs/circ14.pdf (accessed Aug. 31, 2009). The owner of a copyright may create or commission derivative works, such as adaptations or sequels, and may block certain derivative works by others; however, the owner may not prevent the creation of parodies. The copyright statutes of the 1940s (based largely on the copyright act of 1909) do not use the term *derivative works.* See 17 U.S.C. §§ 1(b), 6 (1909 act, repealed).

23. In 1937, Judge Yankwich presided over an important musical copyright infringement case, *Hirsch v. Paramount Pictures.*

24. Quoted in Leon R. Yankwich, "Legal Protection of Ideas: A Judge's Approach," *Virginia Law Review* 43 (1957): 378. Further references will be cited parenthetically in the text as "LP."

arrangement of the musical notes so that they form a tune or air" ("LP," 388). This assumption predates the twentieth century: he cites an 1835 English case in which the judge writes, "the original air requires the aid of genius for its construction, but a mere mechanic in music can make the adaptation or accompaniment" (quoted in "LP," 387). Historians of aesthetics will surely hear echoes of Samuel Taylor Coleridge's influential distinction in *Biographia Literaria* between the secondary imagination and fancy: whereas the former (and superior) capacity "dissolves, diffuses, dissipates, in order to recreate," the latter "has no other counters to play with, but fixities and definites."[25] Coleridge's dichotomy seems to underlie the definition of an adaptation or derivative work in American copyright law, in which cases of musical infringement often come down to counting how many notes are the same—that is, how many "fixities and definites" have been reproduced.

One important mid-twentieth-century case explicitly considered the question of harmony versus melody. In *Northern Music Corp. v. King Record Distributing Co.* (1952), Judge Ryan ruled that the defendants (including noted swing band leader Lucky Millinder) had infringed by plagiarizing the song "Tonight He Sails Again" and giving it a new title. The judge initially asserted that originality must be found in either rhythm, harmony, or melody, but later observed that harmony—the "blending of tones"—is achieved "according to rules which have been known for years. Being in the public domain for so long, neither rhythm nor harmony can in itself be subject to copyright." Judge Ryan concluded that "it is in the melody...that originality must be found. It is the arrangement or succession of musical notes, which are the fingerprints of the composition."[26] Note that the judge borrowed his analogy from criminal law: melody equals fingerprints. Each melody, he assumed, is as unique and unchanging as a person's physical "brand." But as we have seen, this is far from true, even among the Gershwins' compositions. In their quest for definitive measures, judges may create hard-and-fast rules about originality where none exist.

Are these watchdogs of musical property rights even qualified to make such determinations? The judicial system seems aware of this problem; to solve it, the system resorts to invention. Enter that obscure being known as "the average person." It is he or she to whom judges defer and whom they sometimes impersonate in their musical copyright decisions. This actor was cast in his first leading role by Judge Learned Hand in a 1923 case, *Hein v. Harris*, where the judge wrote, "the collocation of notes...becomes an infringement, only when the similarity is

25. Samuel Taylor Coleridge, *Biographia Literaria* (1817), ed. George Watson (London: Everyman's Library, 1975), 167.

26. *Northern Music Corp. v. King Record Distributing Co., et al.*, 105 F. Supp. 393 (S.D.N.Y. 1952).

substantially a copy, *so that to the ear of the average person the two melodies sound to be the same*" (emphasis added).[27] Would Jill Ordinary confuse a recorded trumpet arrangement of "Someone to Watch over Me" with one written for xylophone? Probably not; nevertheless, each arranger would owe royalties to the Gershwin estate. More to the point, would Jack Regular recognize the harmonies of "I Got Rhythm" in, say, Charlie Parker's "Anthropology"? Unlikely. Contrafacts are derivative works disguised as original compositions; as long as their melodic camouflage (as played by any number of learned hands) is artful enough to fool Joe Average, they elude Old Man Trouble, aka copyright infringement.[28]

But would Ms. Ordinary recognize "I Got Rhythm" if it were merely reharmonized? That question—whether reharmonization is subject to copyright—was the issue in a significant 1993 copyright case concerning 1940s music. In *Tempo Music v. Famous Music*, the estates of long-time collaborators Duke Ellington and Billy Strayhorn disputed the copyright for an arrangement of "Satin Doll." Ellington's lead sheet had been the basis for numerous arrangements, and his estate claimed that Strayhorn had "merely" reharmonized Ellington's melody and that these harmonies were not sufficiently original to constitute copyrightable expression. "Harmony," the estate asserted, "is in the common musical vocabulary; only the melody and structure are distinctively original." In his decision, Judge Sand appropriately noted that a primary question here is "whether the harmony and revised melody are included within the scope of the copyrights in the Derivative Works." Showing an unusual sensitivity to the process of composition, he pointed out that "creating a harmony may, but need not, be merely a mechanical by-product of melody," and that "once it is understood that originality, for copyright purposes, looks to creative process rather than novel outcomes or results, it becomes clear that harmony can, as a matter of law, be the subject of copyright." He did cite *Northern Music* to support his recognition that, "in most instances, harmony is driven by the melody," and that reharmonization is "less likely to reflect originality" than the "simultaneous" creation of harmony and melody. But he concluded that removing harmonies from the scope of copy-

27. *Hein v. Harris*, 175 F. 875 (C.C.S.D.N.Y. 1910), *aff'd*, 183 F. 107 (2d Cir. 1923).

28. Judge Yankwich recalled that he himself employed Mr. Average to resolve a dispute between parties quarreling over similar arrangements of recorded songs (*Supreme Records, Inc. v. Decca Records, Inc.*, 90 F. Supp. 90 [S.D. Cal. 1950]). Since neither party owned the copyright, he resorted to unfair competition law to make his ruling. The legal question, he wrote, boiled down to whether "the average person" listening to one record "would confound it with the other;...whether in the mind of such a person, confusion would result" ("LP," 393). Such decisions, he concluded, call for "the exercise of...knowledge, understanding and imagination" ("LP," 395); indeed, they require that the jurist improvise like a jazz musician. Whether such improvisations end up becoming standards is a matter for later courts to determine.

right would be "too broad and perhaps deprive appropriate protection to composition which contains sufficient originality and creativity to warrant such protection."
The judge denied the Ellington estate's motion.[29]

But when the judge "looks to creative process," he has exited the law school and
entered the aesthetics department, where Coleridge lurks in the shadows,
whispering disdainfully about "fixities and definites." Let's ask him: which comes
first, harmony or melody? Wisely, he withdraws, aware that here we open a chicken,
find an egg, then break the egg to find inside a chicken. Judging from my own
experience as a composer and from the anecdotes I've heard from others, there is
no set pattern. Some composers figure out a workable set of chord changes, then
write a melody that fits them; others come up with a melody, then harmonize
around it, altering both as the piece evolves. Often, the two emerge in tandem,
with each measure or cadence of one changing the other. One is tempted to shrug
and quote Tin Pan Alley composers Johnny Burke and Jimmy Van Heusen:
"Imagination is crazy / your whole perspective gets hazy."

Beneath the haze, however, a few considerations stand out. First, Judge Sand's
opinion notwithstanding, the bulk of twentieth-century legal rulings affirm that
melody is the primary consideration in determining originality and infringement.
Why? Mostly because the "average person" recognizes melody more readily than
harmony.[30] The practicality of this stance seems obvious when one considers the
alternatives. How much of a composition's harmony would make it copyrightable?
Four measures? Twelve? Thirty-two? No one, no matter how enterprising, could
copyright the I-IV7-V7 twelve-bar blues cadence, since it was invented so long ago.[31]
But what about variations that use descending chromatic chords, or that replace the
V7 with the vi7? If we object to nonmusical judges' (and their expert witnesses')
deciding cases by counting notes, imagine the chaos that would ensue if they sought

29. *Tempo Music, Inc. v. Famous Music Corp.*, 838 F. Supp. 162 (S.D.N.Y. 1993).
The court did not comment on the enormous irony that representatives of Duke
Ellington, probably the greatest composer in the history of jazz and one of the preeminent
musicians of the twentieth century, would argue that "mere" harmonies are not original.
One doesn't have to listen closely to hear Duke rocking in rhythm in his grave.

30. A few other judges have followed Judge Sand in arguing that, in theory, harmony
may be protectable by copyright. For example, in *Hayes v. Rule*, 2005 WL 2136946 (M.D.N.C.
2005), the judge writes: "As for the melodies, harmonies, rhythms, and accompanying lyrics
on Plaintiff's CD, these are certainly protectable elements under copyright law." Nevertheless,
the harmonic structures in contrafact compositions have never been found to be protectable. I thank Robert Spoo for pointing me to the above-cited case and for helping me to
clarify and refine my discussion of legal matters throughout this essay.

31. Copyright law denies protection to such common harmonic structures. See, for
example, *Tisi v. Patrick*, 97 F. Supp. 2d 539, 549 (S.D.N.Y. 2000): "There is nothing unusual
about the key of A Major, a 'I-IV' chord progression."

to determine how many chords constitute an original harmony. Harmonic structures simply present too many difficulties for intellectual property law to manage, even when expert testimony is brought to bear. It seems appropriate, then, that chord progressions are not copyrightable. Yet even if one applauds this fact, as I do, a second consideration remains troubling: these opinions codify a "strained conception of authorship" founded upon a narrow notion of how musicians think and work.[32] Is there really any such thing as a completely original melody or harmony? Don't musicians and composers borrow from each other all the time? And don't the spirit and value of jazz lie precisely in its capacity to circumvent restrictions, bring together the new and the old, and foster conversations between past and present artists?

Copycats

> It seems to me I've heard that song before,
> It's from an old familiar score
>
> —Sammy Cahn and Jule Styne

Such musical conversations demonstrate what Frederick Garber calls jazz's "richly textured intertextual life."[33] Many soloists, for example, are fond of quoting well-known tunes during improvisations, and beginning improvisers often memorize their idols' solos and insert borrowed phrases into their own improvisations. As Garber remarks, "[T]here is no 'innocent' solo that springs only from its moment, no absolute autonomy within the moment of the solo's making."[34] This condition, which Ingrid Monson dubs "intermusicality," generates a dynamic tension between innovation and tradition.[35] Whether through quotation,

---

32. "Jazz Has Got Copyright Law and That Ain't Good," Note, *Harvard Law Review* 118 (2005): 1941. In a related discussion of the idea/expression dichotomy and its ramifications for jazz improvisation, the author(s) of this unsigned note call for a narrower definition of "derivative work" that would permit musicians to copyright improvisations. Though I endorse the spirit of the argument, which seeks to honor and reward jazz performers' creativity, it seems to me that narrowing the definition of "derivative work" would merely further limit artists' creative freedom. The same note also asserts that chord progressions have acquired "thin" copyright but acknowledges that "while no case explicitly holds that this [i.e., writing new melodies over established chord progressions] is permissible," no court has yet found it impermissible either (ibid., 1949). The copyright protection for harmonies in and of themselves, then, is so thin as to be virtually invisible.

33. Frederick Garber, "Fabulating Jazz," in *Representing Jazz*, ed. Krin Gabbard (Durham, NC: Duke University Press, 1995), 92.

34. Ibid., 72.

35. Ingrid T. Monson, *Saying Something: Jazz Improvisation and Interaction* (Chicago: University of Chicago Press, 1996), 97.

memorization, or the musical dialogues that occur during performances, jazz musicians habitually engage in copy rites. When playing jazz, one is expressing the nexus of connections that have helped to produce the player and the music she plays. These connections comprise part of what I've elsewhere termed the "historicity" of improvisation: to improvise is to converse with one's own fluctuating identity, as well as with all others involved in supporting and creating the music.[36] Improvisation invites (indeed, requires) sociable—both congenial and competitive—responses from others. It asks those who receive it to give something back. In that sense, improvisation does function like a gift: occurring within a social circuit, it lies partly inside and partly outside of the marketplace.

Contrafacts serve a somewhat different function. As we have seen, they enabled the recording of early bebop. In that sense, commodification—the transformation of jam session vehicles into original tunes—advanced the art form by enabling bebop musicians to create their legal plagiarisms. Yet, as Patrick suggests, a good many of the riffs from which bop contrafacts derived had so many antecedents in earlier improvisations that tracking the original is both quixotic and pointless. Just as these phrases were simply in the air, so were certain chord progressions; hence, these musicians' use of these harmonies in contrafacts "was often not a conscious act of borrowing" ("CP," 10).[37]

Nevertheless, bebop composers used contrafacts more systematically than previous jazz artists had, and some composers employed them almost exclusively. Alto saxophonist Charlie "Yardbird" Parker's compositions, for example, are nearly all either variations on the twelve-bar blues or contrafacts based on the harmonies of standards: in addition to more than a dozen tunes using rhythm changes, he derived "Ornithology" from "How High the Moon," "Klact-oveeseds-tene" from "Perdido," and "Quasimado" from "Embraceable You." "Scrapple from the Apple" uses "Honeysuckle Rose" for its A section and the "I Got Rhythm" cycle of fifths for its bridge (see "CP," 11).[38] Even so, many of these "derivative" works display a

36. Mark Osteen, "Introduction: Blue Notes toward a New Jazz Discourse," *Genre: Forms of Discourse and Culture* 37 (2004): 16.

37. Legendary musician and composer Benny Carter, for instance, testified that his use of rhythm changes in "Pom Pom" (1940) was unconscious. See also *Bright Tunes Music Corp. v. Harrisongs Music*, 420 F. Supp. 177 (S.D.N.Y. 1976)—the famous "My Sweet Lord"/"He's So Fine" lawsuit—for an instance of "subconscious" infringement.

38. In *Bebop to Cool: Context, Ideology and Musical Identity* (Westport, CT: Praeger, 2003), 207, Eddie Meadows lists fifteen Parker contrafacts based on "I Got Rhythm" alone. Patrick also cites a discography by Tony Williams that estimates almost 28 percent of Parker's recordings to be contrafacts ("CP," 3). See "CP," 13–25, for useful tables listing the contrafacts from three Parker sessions.

Anthropology

Charlie Parker

wondrous inventiveness. "Anthropology," for example, one of Bird's best-known rhythm-changes contrafacts, varies the harmonies only slightly (substituting Dm7 and G7 for B♭6 and F7 in measure seven). Yet the altered melody and rhythm, packed with intricate syncopations and challenging eighth-note patterns, vastly complicate the source tune. "Anthropology" thus suggests that Parker was qualified to boast about having his own rhythm and music, even while paying discreet homage to Gershwin.

Douglass Parker distinguishes between the "metamorphic" contrafact, which borrows melodic fragments from diverse sources to transform the original(s) into something new (the tune he analyzes, "Donna Lee," being one of them), and the "minimal" type—tunes that merely display the chord changes "before the soloists are turned loose on the theme."[39] Although "Anthropology" fits the former category, many of Bird's songs were of the latter species, in which the line between improvisation and composition is exceedingly thin. A well-known story told by bassist Tommy Potter, for example, relates how Bird composed four tunes on the spot for a September 15, 1944, Savoy session. Given a budget of under $200 for three studio hours, the group spent about a hundred minutes unsuccessfully laboring on three vocal tracks for singer Tiny Grimes. With twenty minutes left, Parker composed "Tiny's Tempo," a blues tune, and "Red Cross," a rhythm-changes contrafact, and with them the group produced three complete master takes ("CP," 12). These contrafacts were simply emergency measures.

Producer Teddy Reig chronicles the similar creation of another bop classic. Herman Lubinsky, the owner of Savoy Records, had advanced Parker $300 for four original tunes and wanted to get his money's worth. At the session, Parker's group was playing around with "Cherokee," the Ray Noble pop song that beboppers habitually performed at breakneck speed. Bird ad-libbed an astonishing introduction over the changes, then improvised his way through the tune. The group ran through the tune again behind Parker's solo. Reig named the results "Ko Ko," and a legend was born.[40] Out of such "seedy economic incentives," writes DeVeaux, "did the independence of bebop from popular song arise."[41]

Most of those incentives, however, didn't go to the musicians. Parker, for example, was notoriously lax about contracts,[42] and Lubinsky collected the

39. Douglass Parker, "'Donna Lee' and the Ironies of Bebop," in *The Bebop Revolution in Words and Music*, ed. Dave Oliphant (Austin, TX: Harry Ransom Humanities Research Center, 1994), 182. Perhaps there is a third form: tunes that substitute modern, dissonant harmonies for a tune's original chords. Among the latter are the two contrafacts cited in note 17 and compositions such as Frank Foster's daunting "A Little Chicago Fire," which stretches the rhythm-changes framework to an extreme degree with its challenging melody and altered harmonies.

40. Like most jazz stories, these have probably been embellished over the years. The original published source for the first one seems to be Ross Russell's *Bird Lives*, a book known for its loose treatment of fact (see *Bird Lives: The High Life and Hard Times of Charlie (Yardbird) Parker* [New York: Da Capo Press, 1996], 169–72).

41. Scott DeVeaux, "'Nice Work if You Can Get It': Thelonious Monk and Popular Song," in *The Thelonious Monk Reader*, ed. Rob van der Bliek (New York: Oxford University Press, 2001), 268.

42. Of all the original tunes he recorded for Dial Records, Charlie Parker copyrighted only four: "Moose the Mooche" (a rhythm-changes contrafact), "Ornithology," "Yardbird Suite" (based on "Rosetta"), and one non-contrafact, "Confirmation." He also signed a bizarre contract awarding half of his Dial royalties to Moose the Mooche himself (real name, Emery Byrd), a Los Angeles heroin dealer. For further details, see Edward Komara, "The Dial Recordings of Charlie Parker," in *The Bebop Revolution in Words and Music*, ed. Dave Oliphant (Austin, TX: Harry Ransom Humanities Research Center, 1994), 89.

publisher's royalties for many of Parker's tunes. More important, did these compositions evince Parker's "independence" from popular songs or his dependence upon them? As many of his contemporaries testified, Bird possessed an encyclopedic knowledge of music, from Stravinsky to the silliest pop tune, and frequently quoted from all types of sources during solos. His practice blended romantic individualism with an almost neoclassical awareness of conventions. This legendary innovator was, in short, deeply embedded in intermusicality. As Patrick concludes, Parker was "a revolutionary" who was also, "by virtue of his background and training,... deeply rooted in tradition" ("CP," 21).

So were other bop pioneers. No one has ever accused Thelonious Monk of being derivative: he is widely recognized as the most idiosyncratic of jazz musicians. Seldom attempting the lengthy eighth-note lines typical of bop horn players and pianists, such as his friend Bud Powell, Monk is known instead for his jagged rhythms, percussive touch, and experimentation with innovations such as tritone substitutions and whole tone harmonies.[43] He declared to a journalist in 1948, "They [other beboppers] play mostly stuff that's based on the chords of other things, like the blues and 'I Got Rhythm.' I like the whole song, melody and chord structures, to be different. I make up my own chords and melodies."[44] Well, not always. Monk's "Rhythm-a-ning," as its title indicates, is a rhythm-changes contrafact, as are his "Fifty-Second Street Theme" and "Little Rootie Tootie" (the former raising the key to C and changing the bridge chords a bit; the latter moving the key from B♭ to A♭ and altering the bridge). "Hackensack" uses the harmonies of another Gershwin tune, "Oh! Lady Be Good" (albeit in F, rather than in G). "Bright Mississippi" is based on "Sweet Georgia Brown," "In Walked Bud" on Irving Berlin's "Blue Skies," and "Evidence" is drawn from "Just You, Just Me." DeVeaux writes that, "in translating these tunes to his own harmonic sensibilities, Monk radically defamiliarized them."[45] Yet the old melodies haunt the new ones like ghosts. For example, if you play "Rhythm-a-ning" against "I Got Rhythm," you hear counterpoint, not contradiction. Monk's tune doesn't so

43. A *tritone* refers to the interval of a flatted fifth or augmented fourth: the interval between, say, C and F#. It strikes many ears as dissonant, but Monk and other modernists habitually substitute tritones for dominant sevenths. For example, instead of using G7 as the second chord in the bridge (B section) of "I Got Rhythm," one might employ its tritone, D♭7. The result still produces a "leading tone" that resolves downward to the next chord, C7. A whole-tone scale uses only full steps instead of the major scale's mixture of whole and half steps. There are only two whole-tone scales in Western music; hence, whole-tone harmonies engender harmonic ambiguity.

44. Quoted in George Simon, "Bop's Dixie to Monk," in *The Thelonious Monk Reader*, ed. Rob van der Bliek (New York: Oxford University Press, 2001), 54.

45. DeVeaux, "Nice Work," 224.

Rhythm-a-ning

Thelonious Monk

"Rhythm-a-ning" written by Thelonious Monk. © 1958 Thelonious Monk and Second Floor Music.

much displace the original as shift it to a spare room. Gershwin's melody outlines Monk's like writing in invisible ink. It is clear that this most revolutionary of bebop composers was deeply invested in intermusicality. Even Monk was part copycat.

Jazz Modernism

> Little cullud boys with beers
> re-bop, be-bop, mop and stop
>
> —Langston Hughes, "Flatted Fifths"

Bebop modernized jazz harmony. Its founders often inserted chromatic substitutions into solos and frequently employed the famous flatted fifth to turn a minor chord into a diminished one and render it "bluer," or to recast a dominant seventh as a quasi–whole tone chord. Bebop also enriched the syncopation of earlier jazz: phrases seem to start in the wrong place and end where they shouldn't, melodies and solos begin and end seemingly without warning, and the whole shebang clips along at a lightning speed that makes dancing nearly impossible and forces listeners to attend closely. If there is something inherently excessive about all jazz—after all, improvisation is a surplus added to melody—this is especially true of bebop. Thus, not only do most bop contrafacts present more complex melodies than their sources, some seem to proffer those complexities as a challenge. "Donna Lee," for example, though based on the antique "Back Home in Indiana," is an obstacle course of gymnastic intervallic leaps and unexpected rests that dares musicians to negotiate it.[46] Charlie Parker's "Ornithology" like-

Ornithology

Charlie Parker

Fine

"Ornithology" written by Charlie Parker. © 1946–1978 Atlantic Music Corporation. Used by permission. All rights reserved. International copyright secured.

46. Though "Donna Lee" is often credited to Bird, Douglass Parker makes a convincing case that the composer was actually Miles Davis, who wrote the tune by borrowing riffs from fellow trumpeter Fats Navarro's solo on a "minimal" "Indiana" contrafact called "Ice Freezes Red." See Parker, "Donna Lee," 183–195.

How High the Moon

Morgan Lewis/ Nancy Hamilton

wise pulls "How High the Moon" deep into the solar system by replacing its square quarter-note melody with syncopated phrases that begin on the "and" of four, as if the melody is so eager to launch that it can't wait for the downbeat.[47]

These compositions enact jazz's call to go too far, break frames, rewrite, and restage. Through such excesses, the boppers appropriated and expanded upon the Gershwins' joyful bravado. These musicians in effect transposed the literary modernists' experiments—Joyce's and Pound's allusive density, Williams's freedom of line, Zora Neale Hurston's revised folk forms—into a musical key. Their musical innovations remolded what had been popular music into an art music aimed at cognoscenti. "Make It New" could have been the bebop credo.

And yet, as I've suggested, the bebop founders were highly self-conscious about their relation to musical traditions. A part of this self-consciousness was racial: bebop announced itself as black music. Langston Hughes, in *Montage of a Dream Deferred*, depicts bop as the soundtrack of a "community in transition"—mid-century Harlem—and a declaration of African-American identity.[48] Therefore, as Mark Harvey comments, some bebop founders "saw themselves...as reclaiming a connection with the older [jazz] tradition that swing...had blurred."[49] Lorenzo Thomas also suggests that bebop musicians extended the high-cultural aspirations of Harlem Renaissance intellectuals by pushing jazz toward the "serious music" that writers such as Alain Locke had envisioned.[50] Further, whereas earlier jazz performers such as Louis Armstrong seem to exemplify what Houston A. Baker Jr. calls the "mastery of form"—the self-conscious and sometimes parodic adoption of "the minstrel mask"—bebop musicians, many of whom cultivated surly or self-involved stage personas, appear to embody Baker's opposing concept: the "deformation of mastery," wherein performers advertise their "unabashed *badness*" and blackness.[51] Indeed, for performers such as drummer Max Roach,

47. In a famous 1960 live recording of "Moon," Ella Fitzgerald puts the two songs together. After singing verses of the source tune, she launches into a lengthy improvisation during which she scat-sings "Ornithology," demonstrating both its debt to and complication of the original.

48. Langston Hughes, *Montage of a Dream Deferred* (1951), in *The Collected Poems of Langston Hughes*, ed. Arnold Rampersad (New York: Vintage, 1994), 387.

49. Mark S. Harvey, "Jazz and Modernism: Changing Conceptions of Innovation and Tradition," in *Jazz in Mind: Essays in the History and Meaning of Jazz*, ed. Reginald T. Buckner and Steven Weiland (Detroit, MI: Wayne State University Press, 1991), 136.

50. Lorenzo Thomas, "The Bop Aesthetic and the Black Intellectual Tradition," in *The Bebop Revolution in Words and Music*, ed. Dave Oliphant (Austin, TX: Harry Ransom Humanities Research Center, 1994), 117.

51. Houston A. Baker Jr., *Modernism and the Harlem Renaissance* (Chicago: University of Chicago Press, 1987), 17, 50. Michael Borshuk similarly connects the beboppers' performance style to Baker's concept in his *Swinging the Vernacular: Jazz and African American Modernist Literature* (London: Routledge, 2006), 70.

contrafacts were a way of "writing back" to whites who had allegedly appropriated jazz from African Americans:[52] by evading copyright, contrafacts withheld royalties from white tunesmiths. Roach would thus place contrafacts "firmly within the prism of cultural nationalism."[53]

Eric Lott similarly emphasizes bop's confrontational stance toward (white) convention. In appropriating old pop tunes and rewriting their melodies, he argues, the beboppers engaged in a "ritual dismemberment" of those songs. Like James Joyce's stance toward literary tradition, he declares, their "relationship to earlier styles was one of calculated hostility."[54] But this formulation ignores both the fondness for popular culture evident in Joyce and the fact that efforts at canon formation also characterized formally "radical" modernists such as T. S. Eliot. The same is true of bebop which, as we have seen, maintained an ambivalent relationship to tradition. Like Anglo-European modernism, bebop used classics as a scaffold; it needed earlier jazz and pop as much as Joyce needed his Homer, Pound his Robert Browning, and Claude McKay his Shakespearean sonnets. DeVeaux thus observes that "to characterize bebop as a revolt of musicians against popular song misses the point," because the "sensibilities of the bebop generation were still intimately connected with the music of Tin Pan Alley."[55] Bebop was at once hostile and respectful, subversive and traditional.

In a witty essay on "Donna Lee," Douglass Parker provides a marvelous example of this ambivalence, showing how that notoriously tricky number thrusts us forward so rapidly only by sailing us back home, not only to James Hanley's 1917 "Indiana" but all the way back to Paul Dresser's 1899 "On the Banks of the Wabash," the tune on which "Indiana" was based. Through meticulous tracking of melodic allusions and recapitulations, Parker demonstrates how this swift, jagged "Classick Bebop Melody has, at its heart...a tripled quotation...from Ye Old Tyme Classic Nostalgic Ballad." As he notes, "any contrafact performs an act of fealty to the original piece." Yet that fealty is also a mutiny. In creating contrafacts, the boppers managed at once to bow and to raise the sword of challenge. Like literary modernists, jazz modernists reformed the canon by harnessing hostility to homage, thereby expanding the tradition.

Contrafact compositions, indeed, provide a signal instance of Henry Louis Gates Jr.'s concept of signifyin(g): they exemplify the "black double-voicedness"

---

52. Dizzy Gillespie, with Al Fraser, *To Be, or Not...to Bop: Memoirs* (Garden City, NY: Doubleday, 1979), 209.
53. Eddie Meadows, *Bebop to Cool: Context, Ideology and Musical Identity* (Westport, CT: Praeger, 2003), 119.
54. Eric Lott, "Double V, Double-Time: Bebop's Politics of Style," *Callaloo* 36 (1988): 601–602.
55. DeVeaux, "Nice Work," 268.

that, he writes, "always entails formal revision and an intertextual relation."[56] Neither exactly a parody nor a pastiche, a contrafact tropes on a previous text as (to use Gates's example) Jelly Roll Morton revised and improvised on Scott Joplin's "Maple Leaf Rag." Contrafacts do not simply surpass or demolish the originals, but "complexly *extend*... figures present in the original."[57] As bebop founder Dizzy Gillespie once pointed out, "We didn't attempt to destroy [pop music]—we simply built on top of it."[58] Yet the success of signifyin(g) depends upon who is listening. Whereas the judicial treatment of infringement often relies upon the hypothetical tastes and capacities of the average person, recognizing contrafacts requires specialized knowledge: only listeners aware that "Anthropology" is based on "I Got Rhythm" or "Donna Lee" on "Indiana" really get it.[59] That's one reason that many of us who improvise over rhythm changes make a point of quoting other contrafacts. For example, a performance of Horace Silver's "Tippin'" is not complete without an allusion to "Rhythm-a-ning" or Sonny Rollins's "Oleo." These practices enact that "thick web of intertextual and intermusical associations to which knowledgeable performers and listeners react."[60] Contrafacts, then, like gifts, both erase boundaries between performers and help to solidify the bonds of the jazz community by simultaneously nodding to a shared tradition and tweaking it.

As the durable foundation of so many contrafacts, "I Got Rhythm" exemplifies the energy, adaptability, and transfiguring power of jazz. Like their source tune, rhythm-changes contrafacts embody a peculiarly American optimism—a belief in the value of reinvention. Contrafacts also evince a specifically African-American modernism that, rather than directly confronting the legal and social system that seeks to contain it, ingeniously works around authority, like the legendary signifying monkey. By transforming improvisations into compositions, contrafacts offer a powerful example of the jazz spirit: the capacity to turn limitations—economic, social, legal—into advantages.

Who could ask for anything more?

56. Henry Louis Gates Jr., *The Signifying Monkey: A Theory of Afro-American Literary Criticism* (New York: Oxford University Press, 1988), 51. See also Borshuk, *Swinging the Vernacular*, 66.

57. Gates, *The Signifying Monkey*, 63; emphasis in original.

58. Gillespie and Fraser, *To Be, or Not*, 294.

59. Ingrid Monson similarly cites a performance of a tune called "Parkeriana" by Jaki Byard and Eric Dolphy, noting that much of the "humor and delight that listeners take" from it "turns on the ability to recognize 'Rhythm' changes." See her *Saying Something: Jazz Improvisation and Interaction* (Chicago: University of Chicago Press, 1996), 123.

60. Ibid., 127.

4 Melody, Theft, and High Culture

Joanna Demers

Igor Stravinsky's ongoing legal troubles over his ballet *The Firebird* stand as one of the funnier sagas in the history of music copyright. Although the story has already received extensive treatment at the hands of Peter Szendy and Michael Tilson Thomas, I want to return to it briefly because it addresses intellectual property, modernism, and the encroaching threats to both at the hands of the culture industry.[1] Stravinsky's first copyright for *The Firebird* was issued in 1911 in Russia to the publisher P. Jurgenson, but after the Russian Revolution, Jurgenson's copyright was considered null and void. Stravinsky wrote a new version of the piece in 1918 and sold the rights to Chester Publishing. Jurgenson sued Chester, claiming that its exclusive rights in the first version of *The Firebird* entitled it to the rights in the second version. Jurgenson won the lawsuit, and then Chester threatened to sue Stravinsky for selling rights that were not his to offer. In 1945, Stravinsky emigrated to the United States and published a third version of *The Firebird* in order to reestablish some control over the piece in his new home country. He sold this version to the Leeds Music Corporation, which then published an unauthorized foxtrot arrangement of the ballet's rondo, complete with new lyrics. What's more, the publisher falsely claimed that Stravinsky himself had written the arrangement.

---

1. See Peter Szendy, *Listen: A History of Our Ears*, trans. Charlotte Mandell (Bronx, NY: Fordham University Press, 2008), 85–86; Michael Tilson Thomas, "Igor Stravinsky's Copyright Blues," http://americanpublicmedia.publicradio.org/programs/mtt_files/mtt_04.shtml (accessed July 16, 2008).

Stravinsky sued Leeds in 1947, explaining his anger in the following public statement:

> These vulgar Broadway people…had the idea of extracting melodies from *Firebird*, to be arranged as popular songs…and of commissioning someone to write words, packaging the little *cochonnerie* under the title "Summer Moon."…The intent was to attract the "juke-box trade."[2]

Stravinsky lost his case but won sympathy from an unlikely source: his rival composer Arnold Schoenberg, who wrote an essay excoriating Stravinsky's publishers as "pirates" and opportunists.[3]

Stravinsky's plight is humorous for several reasons. Throughout his career, he marketed his music for different uses both within and beyond the concert hall and pursued conducting jobs and composition commissions with verve. He had no qualms about rearranging his own works with only slight modifications in order to claim new copyrights and cash in on new revenue streams. And yet, when another party undertook arrangements without his permission, Stravinsky suddenly became a purist, a believer in the cohesion and integrity of *The Firebird*. The motivation behind Stravinsky's complaint is certainly understandable: he objected to an unauthorized appropriation that falsely claimed him as its author. But the elitist twinge with which he expressed his disdain—"vulgar Broadway people" who hope to attract the "juke-box trade"—is striking. Stravinsky was angry because he was cheated out of money, but also because he feared that the reputation of his ballet would be sullied if it became associated with pop tunes.

The Stravinsky episode serves as a point of entry for a larger consideration of the divisions between art music and popular music during the first half of the twentieth century. We tend to think of this period, the height of the modernist era according to the standard musicological narrative, as a time when high art spurned popular culture in a last, febrile assertion of its autonomy from society. Many modernist musicians and composers, from Stravinsky and Schoenberg to John Cage and Karlheinz Stockhausen, were critical of popular music or jazz. Given these individual examples of cultural favoritism, standard accounts of music history would have us believe that the distance between art and popular music was insurmountable. Andreas Huyssen calls this distance the "great divide," a chasm that would only later be traversed as tastes drifted away from modernism and

---

2. Stravinsky, *Stravinsky: Selected Correspondence*, ed. Robert Craft (New York: Knopf, 1984), 2:256.
3. Quoted in Szendy, *Listen*, 89.

toward the collage aesthetic of postmodernism.[4] As with most generalizations concerning history, though, this particular one is difficult either to prove or to disprove. Rather than trying to do either, I shall revisit the divide between high and popular music with two specific concerns in mind: copyright law and melody. This chapter will explore how early twentieth-century high-art musicians and critics perceived melody and, in particular, how they felt about appropriations (licit and illicit) of melody. Melody is a particularly relevant musical parameter because U.S. copyright law protects it to the near exclusion of other formal aspects of a composition, such as harmony or rhythm.[5] But melody is also useful because it has been the site of numerous incursions of popular culture into the supposedly sacred realm of art music. As the popular music industry rapidly accelerated its rate of marketing songs during the first few decades of the twentieth century, the melodies from "classical" music (what we now call "Western art music") proved attractive because many of them resided in the public domain and, for many listeners, bore the associations of high culture.

As Mark Osteen demonstrates in his chapter in the present volume, copyright's nearly unilateral protection of melody facilitated the development of bebop in the 1940s and '50s. By replacing the melodies of well-known songs while retaining their underlying chord changes, publishers (and musicians) avoided having to pay licensing fees that would otherwise have made commercial recording prohibitively expensive. My essay looks to complement Osteen's work by exploring high-art musicians' perceptions and debates about melody. By "high-art musicians," I mean the composers, performers, and critics associated with the European-American tradition of Western art music, a tradition that traces its roots back to baroque composers such as Bach; classical composers such as Haydn, Mozart, and Beethoven; and romantic composers such as Schubert and Wagner. In particular, I focus on the aesthetic philosopher Theodor Adorno, whose writings had considerable influence among mid-twentieth-century modernists. Adorno is an appropriate focal point for this discussion because he wrote extensively about how the popular music and "light" music industries borrowed or stole melodies from the classical repertoire.

4. Andreas Huyssen, *After the Great Divide: Modernism, Mass Culture, Postmodernism* (Bloomington: Indiana University Press, 1986), vii–xii.

5. Although the court in *Tempo Music, Inc. v. Famous Music Corp.*, 838 F. Supp. 162, 169 (S.D.N.Y. 1993[0]) did caution against unilaterally discounting harmony from consideration in questions of copyright infringement, melody receives the majority of attention in most cases. As Mark Osteen points out in his chapter in the present volume, one reason for this is that the "average" listener can recognize melody more easily than harmony.

The chapter will conclude by considering the diverging fates of the two types of music copyright: for compositions and for recordings. The anxiety with which modernist era art musicians regarded melody and its appropriation by mass culture paradoxically coincided with the development of a compositional protection that was porous and relatively permissive of appropriation. In contrast, the sound-recording copyright that arose later in the century offered much further-reaching protection, such that the audible and the ownable were practically coextensive.[6] This late twentieth-century regime of protection, I suggest, was modernism's unlikely counterpart. Although copyright in sound recordings developed largely in response to the recording industry around popular music, it also belatedly fulfilled modernist art music's vision of the fully integrated, totally protected work.

Modernist Music and Melody

Modernism in music is a particularly slippery term for a wide range of tendencies and approaches, many in diametric opposition to one another. It is beyond the scope of this chapter to provide an exhaustive account of modernism, but I present here an encapsulation of the features most relevant to a discussion of copyright, with the caveat that no single definition of modernism can capture all of its facets.[7] Musicologists place the beginning of modernism around 1900, as European and North American art music began to be perceived less as an integral part of society's entertainment and more as a cultural pursuit requiring financial, intellectual, and spiritual support to protect it from the threats of industrialization, mass culture, and listeners' apathy. Even more than their pensive romantic predecessors did, modernists engaged in a constant process of critical reflection about the function, form, and responsibilities of music. This reflection led to a rapid rise in the number of conservatories and university programs devoted to composition

---

6. The sound-recording copyright, while in general more comprehensive in its protection than the composition copyright, is not without its quirks. Sound-alike recordings, or recordings of new performances meant to sound identical to a preexisting recording, are permitted, for example.

7. For general accounts of modernism in music, see Leon Botstein, "Modernism," *Grove Music Online*, ed. Laura Macy, http://www.oxfordmusiconline.com/subscriber/article/grove/music/40625 (accessed Sept. 1, 2008; subscription access); James McHard, *The Future of Modern Music: A Philosophical Exploration of Modernist Music in the Twentieth Century and Beyond* (Livonia, MI: Iconic, 2008); Glenn Watkins, *Soundings: Music in the Twentieth Century* (New York: Schirmer, 1988).

and performance and in the consolidation and growth of the discipline of musicology, the study of the history of music.[8]

Early twentieth-century music's relationship with this newly emergent "music history" was ambivalent. Before the nineteenth century, musical compositions were often discarded or forgotten shortly after their first performance, even in those rare instances when they were notated. Beginning in the nineteenth century, European music began to emphasize its own history, in particular the lineages that connected one generation of composers to the next. By the early twentieth century, most musical family trees in some way connected back to Beethoven or Wagner (or both), figures who cast great shadows as masters of instrumental music and opera, respectively. Wagner's influence was particularly imposing, since the discourse surrounding his chromatic, sinuous harmonies and endless melodies popularized the notion of "modern" music as revolutionary, groundbreaking, and experimental. Thus, the modernist Schoenberg could set about dissolving the very tenets of harmonic language that had governed Western music for the previous five centuries and yet also publish an article entitled "Brahms the Progressive" (1933), an homage to a composer many considered reactionary.[9] In fact, this article accomplished a tidy feat of self-promotion for Schoenberg by implying that he was both continuing and improving upon Brahms's work of developing variations.

Many modernists labored to dissolve or destroy existing musical materials. Schoenberg's task was to dissolve tonality, the hierarchy of harmony that dictated the ineluctable supremacy of the home, or tonic, key and the subservience of a secondary key, either the relative major or the dominant. Schoenberg's melodies thus lost any trace of conventional singability or lyricism, becoming alien collections of atonal intervals supported by the scaffolding of traditional dance rhythms. In contrast, the neoclassical period of Schoenberg's contemporary and rival Stravinsky quoted eighteenth-century music with detachment. Other modernists assailed music by introducing exogenous materials: the Italian futurist Luigi Russolo incorporated urban and mechanical noises into his compositions, and Russolo's champion, the French-American composer Edgard Varèse, incorporated similar noises, calling for new methods of "organizing sound" that would free composers from having to work with an outmoded musical language.

Music historians have tended to associate modernism with cultural elitism. According to Lawrence Levine, for example, early nineteenth-century laborers

---

8. Joseph Kerman, *Musicology* (London: Fontana, 1985), 35–38.
9. See Arnold Schoenberg, "Brahms the Progressive," in *Style and Idea*, ed. Leonard Stein, trans. Leo Black (Berkeley: University of California Press, 1975).

might have whistled opera themes on their morning walks to work, but by the end of the nineteenth century the moneyed elite regarded institutions such as the opera house, the symphony hall, and the art museum as the last islands of high culture amid a sea of barbarian mass culture.[10] Judging by Levine's account, culture in earlier centuries was integrated and democratic but by 1900 had become polarized between high and low poles, with high art growing increasingly effete and irrelevant to the masses. Yet this view simplifies what was in fact a more complicated situation. As Huyssen points out, Wagner was the chief influence for what would eventually become film music, even though Wagner never lived to see the cinema. In particular, Wagner's use of leitmotifs—musical materials associated with ideas or concepts—shaped cinema's use of catchy melodies as "calling cards" for characters or places within a film plot.[11] Some modernist musicians were ambivalent about mass culture; some regarded it as a source of inspiration and rejuvenation, others as a threat to high culture. Many modernist composers relished borrowing materials from non-high-art sources. Claude Debussy cited the Javanese gamelan ensemble he heard at the 1889 Paris Exposition as the basis for his interest in pentatonicism, a scale preference that Giacomo Puccini also adopted for his Asia-based operas *Madama Butterfly* (1904) and *Turandot* (1926). Gustav Mahler routinely interwove rustic country dances, children's tunes, and klezmer instrumentation into his symphonies, while Maurice Ravel explicitly used jazz blue-notes in his *Sonata for Violin and Piano* (1927).

But even as modernist music borrowed from beyond the confines of high culture, it also subscribed to the "work concept," the principle that a composition was an integral, self-sufficient creation. Modernist composers stressed the value of authorship and originality, a habit they inherited from their romantic predecessors. This cult of originality was abetted by the relatively new notion that musical pieces existed as "works." Lydia Goehr has shown that Western art music's work concept emerged around 1800, alongside a growing awareness of musical material as property.[12] For Goehr, the work concept describes the shift from music conceived as a craft or form of transient entertainment to music seen as a fine art. Composers no longer wrote mere pieces but rather works that existed theoretically as sets of instructions, or "scores." These theoretical works were realized through performances whose quality was judged on the basis of their fidelity to the

10. Lawrence W. Levine, *Highbrow/Lowbrow: The Emergence of Cultural Hierarchy in America* (Cambridge, MA: Harvard University Press, 1988), 85–113.

11. Huyssen, *After the Great Divide*, 34–43.

12. See Lydia Goehr, *The Imaginary Museum of Musical Works: An Essay in the Philosophy of Music*, rev. ed. (New York: Oxford University Press, 2007).

originating score as well as to conventions governing music making. The work concept was groundbreaking because it distinguished performances (which could be riddled with mistakes) from works (which were supposedly independent, permanent, and capable of expressing the ineffable). The work concept, in short, allowed music to escape its grounding in ephemeral sound and to aspire to what was seen as a superior quality of the plastic arts: permanence.

Although the evolution of the work concept coincided with larger shifts in theories of aesthetics, it had practical implications for music in particular. Chiefly, the work concept lent credibility to the idea that good composers worked from seemingly divine inspiration as independent geniuses, rather than as participants in the shared musical conversation of a given culture. And as the attitude toward musical works began to resemble that toward other protected cultural products, such as novels and poems, copyright's provisions for music multiplied. In the United States, for example, music was not mentioned explicitly in the first Copyright Act of 1790.[13] Yet because music publishing became a competitive industry in the 1820s, Congress amended the Copyright Act in 1831 to include printed musical compositions under separate statutory protection.[14] The 1831 act also increased the term of protection from fourteen to twenty-eight years with an additional renewal period of fourteen years. But even after 1831, music copyright protected only printed media, not live performances. Subsequent legislation attempted to address this tension by extending coverage to other manifestations of music. The 1856 amendment to the Copyright Act stated that the accompanying music for dramatic stage works enjoyed a right of public performance, meaning that a copyrighted piece could not be reperformed in public without the permission of its copyright holder.[15] A later amendment in 1897 granted copyright holders of all types of musical works (not just accompaniment to dramatic works) the exclusive right to perform their pieces publicly.[16]

By the early twentieth century, the development of player pianos had enabled even wider dissemination of musical content. Yet no law protected authors from having their works reperformed through mechanical means because the 1897 performance right act applied only to live performances by humans, not mecha-

---

13. William F. Patry, "The First Copyright Act," in *Copyright Law and Practice* (Washington, DC: Bureau of National Affairs, 1994), available online at http://digital-law-online.info/patry (accessed Nov. 14, 2008). Patry points out that the first copyright for a musical composition was granted on January 6, 1794, for "The Kentucky Volunteer: A New Song," attributed to Raynor Taylor.

14. Copyright Act of Feb. 3, 1831, 21st Cong., 2nd sess., *U.S. Statutes at Large* 4:436.

15. Copyright Act of Aug. 18, 1856, 34th Cong., 1st sess., *U.S. Statutes at Large* 11:138.

16. Act of Jan. 6, 1897, 44th Cong., 2nd sess., *U.S. Statutes at Large*, 29:481.

nized replay. Congress addressed this issue in the 1909 Copyright Act by granting copyright owners an exclusive right to authorize the mechanical reproduction of a work. This exclusive right held only for the *first* recording, however. Once an authorized mechanical reproduction of a protected work had been released to the public, any recording artist could record her own version of the piece as long as she paid a statutory royalty, or "compulsory license fee." (In later decades, the compulsory licensing provision facilitated the creation of "cover versions," recordings made by musicians other than the original performers.) The 1909 act thus ensured that copyright holders were paid for recordings of their work, as well as for reprints and live performances, while eliminating exclusive contracts between music publishers and piano roll companies. During the same period, UK and continental copyright laws were similarly strengthened and extended, with European countries also attending to the rights of performers.[17] In short, changes to copyright protection acknowledged that musical works existed both in score form and through performances, whereas, previously, performances had been treated as ephemera.

As mentioned above and discussed in detail in Osteen's chapter, copyright protection has effectively been limited to melody and lyrics. There are practical justifications for this: as Osteen points out, the hypothetical "average listener" presumably recognizes melody more easily than harmony or rhythm. But even professional music critics have commented on melodic borrowing much more than on the appropriation of other attributes. Three exemplary articles written in English-language music periodicals within about a hundred years of each other (and straddling the demarcation between the romantic and modernist eras) show the variation in opinions on the topic. The two points on which all three accounts agree are (1) plagiarism is a type of theft; and (2) in music, the plagiarism that matters is plagiarism of melody. F. W. Horncastle, an Irish chorister who sang in Westminster Abbey and was active in attacking Handel for musical theft, wrote an article in 1822 distinguishing between serious and venial examples of plagiarism.[18] Allowing that young composers learn their craft through imitation, the article nonetheless urges them not to engage in note-by-note appropriation of the kind

---

17. The British act of 1911, for example, granted a fifty-year copyright in mechanical reproductions (via record, piano roll, etc.) of musical performances, dating from the manufacture of the recording's original template. By paying a statutory royalty, anyone could make a mechanical reproduction of a piece provided one had first been made by or with the consent of the copyright owner. See Copyright Act, 1911, 1 and 2 Geo. 5, ch. 46, § 19 (Eng.).

18. F. W. Horncastle, "Plagiarism," *Quarterly Musical Magazine and Review* 4 (1822): 141–157.

practiced by Corelli, Handel, and Rossini. Horncastle ruefully acknowledges that some of the most respected composers plagiarized as a matter of course: "Even the greatest composers, beginning from an early period, have not only been guilty of this offence in many instances, but have increased the measure of their guilt in proportion as they were more enlightened, more experienced, and more exalted above 'petty men,' by the splendour of their genius."[19]

Nearly a hundred years after Horncastle, Constantin von Sternberg, a pianist, theorist, and composer most famous for having taught George Antheil, writes that reworking a theme is legitimate, especially when a composer does it throughout the course of a work.[20] He adds that because serious plagiarism is easy to hide from laypersons (and courtroom juries), superficial similarities should not automatically be interpreted as intentional theft. For von Sternberg, originality is to be measured by how the composer treats a subject rather than by the subject itself. Capable composers know how to obscure theft, so obvious similarities are usually coincidental rather than intentional. Style belongs to the period, while substance is the contribution of the individual composer. Mendelssohn and Wagner both reworked materials by Beethoven, but neither is seen as a thief because the public believes in their integrity. "So we see (although stealing is stealing, no matter how cleverly done) that theft changes its aspect considerably if the thief can make of the stolen object something better than the former owner was able to make; in other words: the thief must have the power to *keep* what he stole!"[21]

Finally, in a 1927 article, the British music critic Hugh Arthur Scott at first glance appears more forthright in condemning plagiarism and refusing to accept the excuses provided for Handel's blatant appropriations.[22] Genius, he says, cannot exist without indebtedness, but indebtedness can exist without genius. Yet Scott later appears to recant somewhat when he states that repetition is to be expected in music:

> [T]he greatest composers, when they reach the highest limits of musical expression, will often be found to approach very near to one another in ideas and methods, however wide apart their original starting-points may have been. For, indeed, this is only another way of saying that expressiveness in music, as a whole, is referable to certain general principles and laws.[23]

19. Ibid., 142.
20. Constantin von Sternberg, "On Plagiarism," *Musical Quarterly* 5 (1919): 390–397.
21. Ibid., 395–396.
22. Hugh Arthur Scott, "Indebtedness in Music," *Musical Quarterly* 13 (1927): 497–509.
23. Ibid., 508.

Scott concludes by providing an extensive list of passages that bear intentional or accidental resemblance to other works.

While all three writers are quick to repeat the truism that a good plagiarist can hide the traces of his theft, they then proceed to pinpoint what can be described as the most obvious similarities between pieces, all the while subscribing to the genius of the composers in question. In other words, these testimonials indicate that questions of plagiarism almost always revolve around the most salient feature of a piece: its melodic content. This emphasis on melody appears at odds with the putative goal of the three authors, the assertion that art music composers are superior. Admittedly, the task of detecting more subtle forms of plagiarism may have been beyond their abilities; nevertheless, their focus on melody suggests that the materials they took to be worth stealing in art music were precisely those that even listeners with the most basic skills could discern.

Adorno and Melody

I will now turn to Theodor Adorno (1903–1969), who often wrote about the habit among popular music publishers of (re)arranging classical tunes. Adorno was acutely troubled by the waning influence of Europe's art music tradition, which he attributed to the culture industry, popular music, and jazz.[24] Adorno studied philosophy under Hans Cornelius and Paul Tillich in the late 1920s before joining the philosophy faculty at the University of Frankfurt. He also studied musicology and composition, for a time taking composition lessons from Alban Berg, who with Schoenberg and Webern was a primary figure in the Second Viennese School. Adorno's friendships with Max Horkheimer and Walter Benjamin led to his joining the Institute for Social Research to continue his work in Marxist social and aesthetic criticism. But his teaching career was cut short in 1933 when his right to teach in Frankfurt was revoked because he was a Jew. After a sojourn in Berlin, Adorno left Germany, first for London, then for the United States, where he joined Horkheimer at the relocated Institute for Social Research in New York. In 1941, he moved to Los Angeles, where he collaborated with Horkheimer on their exposé of mass culture's complicity with fascism, *The Dialectic of Enlightenment* (1944; rev. 1947). He also began work in 1941 on *Philosophy of Modern Music* (1949). In it, Adorno sets up a polemic between Schoenberg, whom he praises for creating an

24. For a comprehensive presentation of Adorno's views on music, see Max Paddison, *Adorno's Aesthetics of Music* (Cambridge: Cambridge University Press, 1993).

innovative, subjective musical language, and Stravinsky, whom he excoriates for restoring baroque and classical music and writing with a stilted objectivity. *Philosophy of Modern Music* exerted considerable influence among serialist and experimental composers—Stockhausen, Luigi Nono, Pierre Boulez, and others— who made up the so-called Darmstadt School of the 1950s and 1960s.

Adorno's singularity is apparent when one compares his writings to those of other music critics of the early twentieth century. Musicology at that time concerned itself with ascertainable historical facts, largely ignoring questions about musical meaning and interpretation. Music critics and journalists often provided fanciful blow-by-blow descriptions of works accompanied by banal biographical analyses of composers. Adorno was unique among his peers in engaging directly with compositions to provide sociological, psychological, and Marxist critiques of music. Whereas most writers had fallen prey to the myth of absolute music, Adorno insisted that society inscribed itself onto music and, conversely, that successful art music had to critically reflect the outside world. Yet Adorno was disappointingly rigid in his rejection of popular forms. His essays "On Jazz" (1936) and "On Popular Music" (1941) broadly dismiss mass culture on the basis of extremely narrow examples. ("On Jazz" actually addresses 1920s German dance music more than it does American jazz.)[25] For Adorno, popular music's catchy tunes and rhythms encouraged fascism by discouraging critical listening and lulling audiences into accepting the status quo. He renounced the sort of armchair forensic analysis undertaken by the likes of Horncastle, von Sternberg, and Scott as "fetishized" listening, or listening for the fleeting melodic clues suggesting theft to the untrained ear. Whereas Enlightenment era music (best epitomized for Adorno by Beethoven) balanced private expression with public forms, the modern culture industry produced music that encouraged fetishized listening, providing easily remembered tunes that drew attention away from the alienation endemic to factories and shopping arcades.

By today's standards, Adorno was hardly progressive in his stance toward the ownership of creative output. He subscribed faithfully to the principle that originality was a necessary ingredient for genius. The basis for his musical aesthetics was the assertion that the composer engaged in a dialectic in which his (it was always a male composer) individuality struggled to express itself within the rules of his era. But unlike the three critics discussed above, Adorno resisted making easy accusations of musical plagiarism. In "Musical Thieves, Unmusical Judges" (1934), he laments:

25. J. Bradford Robinson, "The Jazz Essays of Theodor Adorno: Some Thoughts on Jazz Reception in Weimar Germany," *Popular Music* 13 (1994): 1–25.

If a non-musician wants to say something bad about any music he encounters, there is nothing easier at his disposal than to declare that it was stolen.... Those individual elements of music that can be stolen are measurable, countable series of tones: motives and themes. Since in the meantime the harmonic dimension has been loosened such that a chord can be as good an idea as a theme; and since there are no more harmonic conventions that allow one only to use a slim number of sounds, today people can if they wish also look for stolen harmonies; but so far they are still not of the kind one should worry about. So they keep to that which they call melody, longer or shorter successions of tones, usually such that they also resemble each other rhythmically.[26]

Music critics' fascination with the obvious traces of appropriation—"stolen" melodies, above all—implies that music is made up of so many interchangeable building blocks, an assumption that, for Adorno, belies the inextricable relationship between small-scale and large-scale events that superior works display. Distracted listeners, by his account, think that composers borrow large-scale, impersonal forms that they later fill in with expressive content such as melody. Adorno mockingly says that this leads uneducated listeners to entertain false notions of how Beethoven composed, with form coming first and content developing later. In his view, such a misconception clouds the intimate relationship between form and content; form *is* content, with a kernel idea manifesting, in a brief instant, vast possibilities for its trajectory through the ensuing piece.

Adorno also despises the mercantile environment that treats melodies and themes as commodities. He writes in "On the Fetish-Character in Music" (1938):

Melody comes to mean eight-bar symmetrical treble melody. This is catalogued as the composer's "inspiration" which one thinks he can put in his pocket and take home, just as it is ascribed to the composer as his basic property.... The works which are the basis of the fetishization and become cultural goods experience constitutional changes as a result. They become vulgarized. Irrelevant consumption destroys them.... They are transformed into a conglomeration of irruptions which are impressed on the listeners by climax and repetition, while the organization of the whole makes no impression whatsoever.... The more reified the music, the more romantic it

26. Theodor Adorno, "Musikalische Diebe, Unmusikalische Richter," in his *Musikalische Schriften IV* (Frankfurt: Suhrkamp, 2003), 292–296. I am grateful to Inouk Demers for providing what I believe is the only English translation of this article.

sounds to alienated ears. Just in this way it becomes "property." A Beethoven symphony as a whole, spontaneously experienced, can never be appropriated. The man who in the subway triumphantly whistles loudly the theme of the finale of Brahms's First is already primarily involved with its debris.[27]

This point—that listeners can actively participate in the destruction of high culture—is something that never would have occurred to romantic era critics, who conceived of listeners as passive receptors of creative genius. In Adorno's mind, such listeners were complicit with the devaluing of high culture.

Adorno's reaction to light music was predictable enough: he loathed it both for its status as consumer good ("From the middle of the nineteenth century on, good music has renounced commercialism altogether")[28] and for the fact that it encouraged fetishized listening for the ephemeral delights of a sentimental melody or a dance step. But Adorno reserved his greatest disdain for light arrangements of classical works, which he regarded as the ultimate perversions of high culture. He writes of salon music (a synonym for light music), "The practice of arrangement comes from salon music. It is the practice of refined entertainment which borrows its pretensions from the *niveau* of cultural goods, but transforms these into entertainment material of the type of hit songs" ("FCM," 300). Curiously, Goehr's work concept coexisted with the arrangement, an entity that at times seemed to contradict the premises of an autonomous, integral work. Arrangements in their various forms, from transcriptions and adaptations to reorchestrations, are intrinsic to music; it is impossible to conceive of a prehistory during which arrangements did not exist. But arrangements became an object of contemplation and debate with the rise of written musical notation, which empowered musicians to fix in a permanent medium what had previously been ephemeral. With the advent of written arrangements, it became possible not only to compare an original with its different versions but also to trace the migration of a musical work between different social spheres. The nineteenth-century arrangement epitomizes this moment: virtuosi performers such as Franz Liszt used popular opera melodies as the bases for extended concert fantasies, and composers adapted mediocre materials into sophisticated explorations of form and style, as Beethoven did with his *Diabelli*

---

27. Theodor Adorno, "On the Fetish-Character in Music and the Regression of Listening," in *Essays on Music*, ed. Richard D. Leppert, trans. Susan H. Gillespie (Berkeley: University of California Press, 2002), 298. Hereafter, this article will be cited as "FCM" in the text.

28. Theodor Adorno, *Philosophy of Modern Music*, trans. Anne G. Mitchell and Wesley V. Blomster (New York: Continuum, 2003), 8.

Variations. Such arrangements appeared just as a high-art canon of classical works was solidifying. Arrangements thus gave the lie to high culture's myth of impermeability.

In using humble elements as raw material for high-art arrangements, Liszt and Beethoven were following a well-established compositional practice. But during the nineteenth century, a new kind of arrangement stood the older practice on its head, turning art music into a quarry for popular pieces. This emerging form took advantage of the cultural cachet then being attributed to classical music, which, as Levine and Melanie Lowe both point out, was increasingly associated with wealth, prestige, and intellect.[29] Since classical works often resided in the public domain, creating new arrangements of them was also a good business practice for publishers facing stricter copyright policing. A typical example of a popular arrangement of a classical work can be found in the 1831 voice and piano piece "I Pity and Forgive: The Last Words of Simon Bolivar," an adaptation of the second movement from Beethoven's Third Symphony. The title page lists "Music from Beethoven, Arranged with an Accompaniment for the Piano Forte by N. C. Bochsa." Even strictly faithful arrangements usually need to leave out materials from the original. Like most piano arrangements of symphonic movements, Bochsa's retains the essentials of Beethoven's harmonies and consolidates the melody (which in the original travels between winds and strings) in the vocal part. The arrangement takes further liberties in how it treats the second theme of the movement. In Beethoven's version, this theme group comprises its own discrete section that lasts as long as the first thematic group. In the Bochsa version, the second theme is condensed to serve as a bridge section between the two iterations of the first theme in each verse. In other words, what in Beethoven's original is an important section in its own right becomes, in the arrangement, a tool to serve the standard form of a song.

"I Pity and Forgive" no doubt existed because of the prestige afforded to Beethoven. Adorno was not naïve when it came to the economic incentives for arranging such respected works of classical music:

> All sorts of reasons are offered by [arrangers] for instrumental arrangements. In the case of great orchestral works, it will reduce the cost, or the composers are accused of lacking technique in instrumentation. These reasons are lamentable pretexts. The argument of cheapness, which aesthetically condemns itself, is disposed of by reference to the superfluity of

29. See Levine, *Highbrow/Lowbrow*; Melanie Lowe, "Claiming Amadeus: Classical Feedback in American Media," *American Music* 20 (2002): 102–119.

orchestral means at the disposal of precisely those who most eagerly carry on the practice of arrangement, and by the fact that very often, as in instrumental arrangements of piano pieces, the arrangements turn out substantially dearer than performance in the original form.... Above all, arranging seeks to make the great distant sound, which always has aspects of the public and unprivate, assimilable. ("FCM," 298–299)

Adorno's use of the phrase "distant sound" probably gestured to Walter Benjamin's "The Work of Art in the Age of Mechanical Reproduction" (1935), to which "On the Fetish-Character in Music" was a kind of response. Benjamin had described the experience of distance felt by observers of a unique and consecrated object, even one close at hand. This experience of distance he called "aura," going on to argue that methods of copying and mass dissemination, such as photography and cinema, destroy aura because they render accessible what was previously distant or unreachable. By destroying aura, mechanical reproduction also removed the art object from its tradition and its historical context, which for Benjamin was a revolutionary (and positive) development because those previously disenfranchised from art production and consumption could now participate in both activities. Although Adorno admired his friend's essay, he had little enthusiasm for the destruction of aura. His 1938 essay reads aura in musical terms as the prestige attributed to high-art musical works (in Goehr's sense of the "work concept"). Musical works for Adorno were not meant to be immediately "assimilable," but should reveal their secrets only when approached with attentive, critical listening. The constituent parts of a musical work—its melody and harmony, its formal articulations, and its instrumentation—were not separable qualities to be abstracted for single-serving consumption.

To underscore: Adorno's complaint was not that unscrupulous music publishers were trying to pass off popular arrangements as high art. Instead, he felt that the music industry emphasized the differences between high and popular culture in order to make light arrangements more attractive commodities:

If the two spheres of music are stirred up in the unity of their contradiction, the demarcation line between them varies. The advanced product has renounced consumption. The rest of serious music is delivered over to consumption for the price of its wages. It succumbs to commodity listening. The differences in the reception of official "classical" music and light music no longer have any real significance. They are only still manipulated for reasons of marketability.... The more industriously the trade erects wire fences between the musical provinces, the greater the suspicion that without these, the inhabitants could all too easily come to an understanding.... The world of that musical life, the composition business which extends peacefully from Irving Berlin and Walter Donaldson—*"the world's best composer"*—by way of Gershwin, Sibelius and Tchaikovsky to Schubert's B minor Symphony, labeled *The Unfinished*, is one of fetishes. ("FCM," 293; emphasis in original)

With a canny mixture of fealty and aggression, the popular arrangement declares allegiance to its classical source while disavowing any elite pretenses of its own. In the process, the derivative work exercises a privilege more typically reserved for art music: that of drawing the line between elite and mass culture. In the Beethoven/ Bochsa example above, for instance, the great composer's name is prominently displayed as a certification of the work's quality even as the arranger's editorial decisions and the addition of lyrics conspicuously decline to make a bid for high-art status. The man who whistles the theme of a symphony might now flatter himself that he is sophisticated in his musical predilections, but for Adorno and, given his *Firebird* lawsuit, for Stravinsky as well, the dismemberment of classical works for popular uses has destroyed the foundations of art music's separation from mass culture. The arranger and the whistler are not just "involved in" the symphony's ruins; they are the agents of its ruination.

Adorno regarded high-art melodies as easy targets for appropriation and theft. But the status and responsibilities of melody were themselves in flux during this time. In general terms, the melody of a musical work through the mid-nineteenth century was its most distinctive feature, the one that listeners would most easily retain after leaving the salon or concert hall. But starting in the 1860s, European concert music began to drift away from the strict harmonic language that governed how pitches and tones would be organized. And as tonality began to stretch, melody too changed. As the chordal language and harmonic scaffolding in Wagner's operas became more ambiguous, his melodies became longer and more chromatic. By the first decade of the twentieth century, atonality, or the absence of tonal hierarchies, had rendered melodies abstract and strange. Huyssen helpfully recalls Adorno's observation that Schoenberg's twelve-tone, or serialist, procedure, invented in the early 1920s, rebuked commodification by itself commodifying musical material.[30] If the culture industry seized upon the most attention-grabbing portions of a work as fodder for a hit song, Schoenberg would preempt that gesture

---

30. Huyssen, *After the Great Divide*, 34: "[Schoenberg's] turn to atonality is interpreted as the crucial strategy to evade commodification and reification while articulating it in its very technique of composition."

by objectifying the tone row, divesting it of the sort of sentimentality or tuneful-
ness that might open it to popularization and making it the structural basis for a
new work. Such a work would be inoculated from the start against arrangement
and commodification. Unassailable and self-identical, it embodied the work concept—a formal ideal that would not find its legal counterpart until later in the
century.

Melody, Copyright, and Arrangements

Copyright law is partial toward melody thanks to long-standing musical practices
in the West. Because songs, themes, and tunes are the most easily remembered
musical materials, Western art music for the past 500 years has typically made
melody the bearer of a work's core emotions. We speak of the character of melodies in terms of affect: cheerful, lugubrious, obsessive. Simply put, melodies are
anthropomorphized. The law focuses squarely on melodies as protectable property because, of all musical parameters, they seem most closely to approximate
human subjectivity. As Osteen reminds us, the judge in *Northern Music Corp. v.
King Record Distribution* (1952) likened a melody to the fingerprints of a musical
work, the primary index of a piece's singularity.

It is therefore surprising that U.S. copyright law came to accommodate as much
appropriation and borrowing of melody as it did. The 1909 Copyright Act,
remember, permitted arrangements or covers of songs already released in
mechanical format (i.e., through recording), and these usually retain the original
work's melody and lyrics (if any) while taking liberties with its harmony, rhythm,
and structure; the stipulation here is that the cover not change "the basic melody
or fundamental character of the work."[31] Although the 1909 act protected publishers' rights by requiring cover artists to pay a licensing fee, it also stipulated that
no permission was required to license a song. In other words, neither the publisher
nor the song's composer or lyricist could veto an arrangement or cover of a song
once that song had been made available to the public through mechanical
reproduction. As the proliferation of rock 'n' roll covers from the 1950s on would
demonstrate, the compulsory licensing system effectively served the interests of
songwriters, publishers, cover artists, and the public.

Given how the 1909 act stimulated popular music by permitting a fair degree of
appropriation, it is doubly surprising that later copyright provisions would seek to

31. 17 U.S.C. § 115(a)(2).

protect popular music by permitting *less* appropriation. Here, I have in mind the 1976 Copyright Act, the first to provide copyright protection in sound recordings. According to the act, federal copyright protection is enjoyed only by sound recordings created on or after February 15, 1972—just a few years before the emergence of hip-hop music. By the mid-1980s, hip-hop had popularized the use of (usually unauthorized) borrowings, or "samples," of funk and soul recordings. A string of lawsuits against hip-hop artists during the 1990s culminated in 2004, when the Sixth Circuit Court of Appeals tersely ordered, "Get a license, or do not sample."[32] Since this precedent, the decisions in U.S. courts have been to look upon the unauthorized borrowing of *any* sound, no matter how insignificant or negligible, as theft.[33] The forces behind the popular music industry—large multinational content providers scrambling to solidify control over all permutations of their property— had made all recorded material equally protectable. In effect, the recording industry succeeded in doing what the modernist composers, with their dedication to the work concept, could only dream of: they had propertized the integrity of the artwork in a manner that privileges melody neither more nor less than any other audible phenomenon.

Let me end here by observing that the rise of the sound-recording copyright has done nothing less than shift the idea/expression dichotomy. This central principle of U.S. law tells us that copyright protects the *expression* of ideas but not ideas themselves. For most of the twentieth century, the idea of a musical work existed in a composer's or a listener's head, and its expression was the materialized composition, usually a pen-and-paper score in traditional notation. Now that copyright protects all sounds fixed in a recording, however, the category of expression includes not just notation but the full range of audio phenomena that arises from a recorded performance of the score. Meanwhile, the concepts underlying those recorded sounds—especially the melody—receive less comprehensive protection than they did under the 1909 act and have thus assumed, in a sense, the status of ideas. This is a subtle but crucial point because it coincides with a general migration

32. *Bridgeport v. Dimension*, 383 F.3d 390 (6th Cir. 2004).

33. This tension played out in James Newton's lawsuit against the Beastie Boys for borrowing a three-note motive from one of his flute solos in their track "Pass the Mic" (1992). The Beastie Boys had already obtained permission to sample Newton's recording from his record label, and had tried unsuccessfully to ask Newton for permission to borrow from the underlying composition. At both the district court and appellate levels, the court found that the portion of Newton's work in question was neither long enough nor original enough to constitute a copyrightable work. Had the Beastie Boys not obtained a license to borrow the recording, however, they would certainly have been found guilty, no matter how brief the sample. See *Newton v. Diamond*, 204 F. Supp. 2d 1244. (C.D. Cal. 2002), *aff'd*, 349 F.3d 591 (9th Cir. 2003).

in post-1945 Western art music *away* from traditional parameters of melody, harmony, and form, and toward timbre or tone color. Modernist music in the early decades of the twentieth century eventually led to late modernist styles (e.g., the new complexity) that stretched melody and harmony to maximal proportions, as well as to ambient and experimental styles that regarded "sound" itself, not formal or syntactical parameters, as the core of the work. Music copyright, with its growing emphasis on recorded sound over preconceived forms or syntax, has uncannily followed the same trajectory. We can speculate that the parallel between copyright and post-1945 music reflects an underlying shift in views toward listening. Whereas romantic and early modernist works conduced to a hierarchical type of listening that attended to some aspects of musical structure at the expense of others, post-1945 music often obfuscates any easy hierarchy, suggesting that *all* sounds are equally important and, thus, protectable.

PART THREE

The Fall and Rise of Remix Culture

5 Gag Orders
Comedy, Chaplin, and Copyright
Peter Decherney

Many scholars and cultural critics have observed that we are witnessing the reemergence of an active, collaborative, and participatory form of creativity—a mode of creativity that was suppressed by the rise of mass media during the twentieth century.[1] Mashup videos, remixed audio works, and Photoshopped collages are everywhere. These new forms of remix culture, critics often remark, have reawakened the everyday artistry of nineteenth-century folk culture and the collage aesthetics of avant-garde and modernist artists. But if we are in the midst of such a resurgence, what made it necessary in the first place? When and how did imitating, copying, and reusing the material of great artists move from the center of cultural production to the—often legally ambiguous—margins from which those practices have only recently returned? I look for part of the answer to this

I would like to thank Paul Saint-Amour, Rebecca Tushnet, and the attendees of the first meeting of the International Society for the History and Theory of Intellectual Property for comments on earlier drafts of this chapter. And I would like to thank Eric Hoyt and Tamar Lisbona for invaluable research assistance.

1. See, for example, Henry Jenkins, *Convergence Culture: Where Old and New Media Collide* (New York: New York University Press, 2006); Yochai Benkler, *The Wealth of Networks: How Social Production Transforms Markets and Freedom*(New Haven, CT: Yale University Press, 2007); and Lawrence Lessig, *Remix: Making Art and Commerce Thrive in the Hybrid Economy* (New York: Penguin, 2008).

question in the interaction between copyright law and film comedy in the first decades of the twentieth century. Focusing on two cases, one from 1904 and another that stretched over much of the 1920s, we can see how courts shifted from addressing imitation and borrowing as natural forms of cultural development to seeing them as theft.

It is no accident that this is a story about comedy. A great many film copyright cases in the first half of the twentieth century involved film comedy and comedians. Charlie Chaplin, Buster Keaton, Harold Lloyd, Laurel and Hardy, the Marx Brothers, Jack Benny, and Sid Caesar, among others, were all involved in important copyright lawsuits. Together, these cases set the ground rules for the genre of film comedy and, indeed, for the entire entertainment industry. As Chaplin, the Marx Brothers, and many other comedians moved from vaudeville to Hollywood, both the nature of performance and the scope of their celebrity changed; they could now, at least in theory, play in every movie theater around the globe simultaneously. Film comedy stars responded by using copyright law to redraw the boundaries of their field, blunting the culture of imitation in which they had been reared.

Why were comedians on the front lines of copyright battles? While we might dispute whether any artistic creation can be truly original, we would have to agree that comedy would certainly not exist without a referent on which to build, riff, or comment. Comedy is always about something else. It is a parody *of* another work or a joke *about* someone or something. Comedy, at its root, is about imitation, and, as a result, film comedy has consistently pushed the boundaries of copyright law.

Before Hollywood

Before the invention of film, vaudeville comedians and comic performers had all but given up on using copyright to protect their material. In a series of late nineteenth-century cases, vaudeville performers attempted and failed to protect the copyrights in their performances. Courts found that many vaudeville acts didn't meet the constitutional criteria for copyright as it was understood at the time. Particularly in the wake of the Comstock anti-obscenity legislation of the 1870s, nineteenth-century U.S. judges were quick to dismiss obscene works as not "promot[ing] the Progress of Science" and therefore beneath the constitutional threshold for protection. And before the 1909 Copyright Act expanded the range of protected works, the same judges held that works lacking narrative or dramatic content failed to meet the constitutional criteria that a work be a form of "writing."[2] (Today, "writing" is understood to be anything "fixed in [a] tangible medium.") In this climate, vaudeville acts were regularly found to be either obscene or too loosely structured to have a story.[3]

When copyright law proved to be a dead end, vaudevillians began to rely on the self-policing of their industry. Performers and their managers took out ads in trade papers to call out and shame other performers who unabashedly stole their material. Vaudeville theater owners regularly pledged that they would not hire copied acts, although this may have been a sop to performers and managers rather than a real commitment. And a series of short-lived institutions arose to accept documentation about acts and to arbitrate disputes. In some cases, these ad hoc copyright offices or grassroots courts established royalty-sharing agreements between the original performers and the copycats.[4]

But these were extreme solutions. For the most part, vaudeville performers simply permitted and expected a certain amount of imitation from their peers. Live vaudeville performers could only cover so much territory, so there was more room for duplication. It was common, for example, for European performers to copy acts they had seen on the American vaudeville circuit and for American performers to repeat acts they had seen in Europe.[5]

Even in instances where performers sought to protect their acts, they often found the task impossible. Celebrated dancer Loie Fuller, for example, vigilantly

---

2. See Act of Mar. 4, 1909, ch. 320, § 5. According to this act, copyright inhered in the following non-exhaustive list of work classifications:

> (a) Books, including composite and cyclopaedic works, directories, gazetteers, and other compilations; (b) Periodicals, including newspapers; (c) Lectures, sermons, addresses (prepared for oral delivery); (d) Dramatic or dramatico-musical compositions; (e) Musical compositions; (f) Maps; (g) Works of art; models or designs for works of art; (h) Reproductions of a work of art; (i) Drawings or plastic works of a scientific or technical character; (j) Photographs; (k) Prints and pictorial illustrations.

3. See *Broder et al. v. Zeno Mauvais Music Co.*, 88 F. 74 (C.C.N.D. Cal. 1898); *Martinetti v. Maguire*, 16 F. Cas. 920 (C.C.Cal. 1867) (No. 9173); Edward S. Rodgers, "Copyright and Morals," *Michigan Law Review* 18 (1920): 390–404; Jean Thomas Allen, "Copyright and Early Theatre, Vaudeville, and Film Competition," in *Film before Griffith*, ed. John Fell (Berkeley: University of California Press, 1983), 176–187. Even when vaudeville copyright cases were decided on different grounds, the question of moral censorship was always present; see, for example, *Barnes v. Miner et al.*, 122 F. 480 (C.C.S.D.N.Y. 1903).

4. Kerry Segrave, *Piracy in the Motion Picture Industry* (Jefferson, NC: McFarland, 2003), 6, 15, 17, 18, 19.

5. Ibid., 17.

protected her performance style. She held patents on her use of color in stage lighting and on her design for a dancer's skirt frame. She sued lithographers, ultimately unsuccessfully, for distributing her image. And in 1892, Fuller attempted, also unsuccessfully, to protect her signature Serpentine Dance from imitation in a copyright law suit. *Fuller v. Bemis* is one of those cases in which a judge found a vaudeville act to lack sufficient narrative or drama to be protected by copyright.[6] As a result of the decision, Fuller could not prevent dozens of dancers from using her Serpentine Dance routine across the United States and Europe. In the world of vaudeville, this kind of imitation not only was common but also made it possible for the originator, Fuller, and many other dancers to have successful careers. In her autobiography, Fuller recounts several instances in which she thought the presence of emulators or counterfeiters would ruin her career. But she consistently performed her original dance to sold-out crowds even when rivals were performing the Serpentine Dance at nearby theaters. There were many stages on which to perform, and audiences were willing to pay in proportion to the dancers' levels of talent and acclaim. The Serpentine Dance eventually grew into a widely performed genre of dance rather than the property of a single performer, and it remained popular in the United States and in Europe for more than three decades.[7]

From Vaudeville to Early Film

Many of the earliest films made by Thomas Edison and others were simply records of vaudeville acts. Several different dancers, for example, performed the Serpentine Dance before Edison's cameras, though Fuller herself never did. Unlike vaudeville performers, however, early filmmakers were not content to allow self-policing alone to govern their industry. Edison had a long history of using litigation, including intellectual property litigation, to control his other businesses (the phonograph, electricity, etc.), and he brought a litigious business culture to the early film industry. As a result of early filmmakers' efforts, legal decisions in the first years of the twentieth century began to set parameters of imitation and copying in the film industry. Although the early case law continued to preserve the culture of imitation that

6. *Fuller v. Bemis*, 50 F. 926 (C.C.S.D.N.Y. 1892); Mary Louise Fuller, "Garment for Dancers," U.S. Patent 518347 (Apr. 17, 1894).

7. Loie Fuller, *Fifteen Years of a Dancer's Life* (Boston: Small, Maynard, 1913), 41–42, 55–56; Richard Nelson Current and Marcia Ewing Current, *Loie Fuller: Goddess of Light* (Boston: Northeastern University Press, 1997), 40–44, 62.

pervaded vaudeville, film companies would eventually prove more successful than vaudeville performers had been in convincing judges to recognize their copyrights.

Market leaders Edison and Biograph initiated most of the early film copyright cases. Frequent rivals in patent disputes, the two firms threatened each other with copyright lawsuits as well. All of these were settled out of court until Edison's company remade Biograph's *Personal* (1904) without permission—a standard practice at the time. Edison and other companies often made their own versions of competitors' films, which were frequently shot-for-shot copies of the original. But several factors led to the 1904 standoff. First, the case of *Edison v. Lubin* (1903) had outlawed film duping, the practice of making a negative from a competitor's film and then striking new prints from the new negative. Now that courts had frowned on duping, remakes became an even more important part of the film business. Also, in 1903–1904, fictional narrative films began to replace reality-based genres, such as travel films and films of newsworthy events. With the turn to fictional narrative, remakes suddenly had much more value, and for the first time in a copyright dispute, Biograph's lawyer, Drury Cooper, and Edison's, Frank Dyer, failed to come to an agreement after months of negotiations.

Biograph v. Edison asked whether the common practice of remaking a competitor's film violated copyright law and, if so, how courts or filmmakers could determine if and when remakes took too much from the original. Copyright law protects original expression, while the ideas expressed remain free to be borrowed and used.[8] At times, the distinction between ideas and expression can seem meaningless or arbitrary. We might imagine paraphrasing another author's words to express the same idea differently, but how can anyone decouple the underlying idea of an image or a musical phrase from its expression? Fortunately, like many elements of the law, the idea/expression dichotomy does not exist as a Platonic ideal. It is a living concept that changes over time—a sort of valve that responds to social context and artistic trends in order to moderate the exchange of creative ideas at a particular time. Like any valve, it can be turned to increase or decrease the flow of creativity. *Biograph v. Edison* was the first case to take up the idea/expression

8. As Supreme Court justice Louis Brandeis once famously put it, "[T]he noblest of human productions—knowledge, truths ascertained, conceptions, and ideas—become, after voluntary communication to others, free as the air to common use." Another justice, Sandra Day O'Connor, explained years later that the disentangling of ideas from their expression keeps copyright law from hampering free speech. *International News Service v. Associated Press*, 248 U.S. 215 (1918) (Justice Brandeis, dissenting); *Harper & Row v. Nation Enterprises*, 471 U.S. 539 (1985). Also see Yochai Benkler, "Free as the Air to Common Use: First Amendment Constraints on Enclosure of the Public Domain," *NYU Law Review* 74 (1999): 354.

dichotomy in film, and, as we will see, it preserved the imitative culture that the early film industry had inherited from vaudeville.

Biograph's *Personal* tells the story of a European nobleman who takes out a personal ad asking potential brides to meet him in front of Grant's Tomb. When more than one willing prospect arrives at the assigned hour, the nobleman runs. The suitors pursue him until the fastest woman gets her man. The film merged comedy with a chase format, two popular genres at the time. Exhibitors clamored for copies when they read the description of *Personal*, and Biograph immediately sold the film to its licensed distributors. Following its usual practice, however, Biograph refused to sell the film to Edison's distributors or to other competitors. Biograph wanted its own circuit of licensees to enjoy some exclusivity.

When the Edison Company failed to obtain a copy, the head of production followed what was also standard procedure and instructed the company's top director, Edwin S. Porter, to remake the film. Edison was not the only company to remake *Personal*; Siegmund Lubin and the French company Pathé also made their own versions. But Porter's quickie remake, which the Edison Company entitled *How a*

How a French Nobleman Got a Wife Through the New York Herald Personal Columns (1904). Edwin S. Porter's remake of American Mutoscope and Biograph's film *Personal* (1904).

French Nobleman Got a Wife through the "New York Herald" Personal Columns, reached the market before Biograph's original version, and audiences much preferred it to *Personal.* Biograph's management was infuriated, and they petitioned the New Jersey District Court for an injunction against Edison, asking that Edison surrender all prints and negatives to Biograph.[9]

In a series of affidavits, Edison's staff admitted having seen and copied the Biograph film. In Edison's own testimony, he suggested that they were operating in an extralegal realm. "As far as I am aware," he told the court, "it has never been considered that a copyright upon a moving picture photograph covers the plot or theme which the exhibition of the moving picture portrays." Porter, the director, had a more nuanced interpretation of what happened. He saw the Biograph film and immediately recognized it as a genre film, a "chase picture." Moreover, *Personal* was not much more than the elaboration of a joke, something so basic that it could not be protected. Porter stated for the record:

> It occurred to me after seeing the exhibition of the complainant's film *Personal* that I could design a set of photographs based upon the same joke, and which, to my mind, would possess greater artistic merit. My conception of the principal character representing the French Nobleman was entirely different from that of the complainant's film, as regards costume, appearances, expression, figure, bearing, posing, posturing and action.[10]

Porter had had his own films remade by Biograph and other companies for years. He had, in turn, remade many films. Remakes had been a standard of the industry; improving on another director's film was how an international industry of filmmakers exchanged ideas and contributed to the growth of their art form. Porter had not duped any scenes—a practice now both illegal and unfashionable—and he felt entitled to take Biograph's ideas as long as he expressed them differently.

In the court statements, Edison's lawyers accused Biograph's director of having taken the story from a newspaper cartoon, although no one involved in the case was able to produce it. Still, it was a plausible claim. *Personal* does have the quality of a live-action cartoon, setting up a situation that leads to an unexpected result

9. David Robinson, *From Peep Show to Palace: The Birth of American Film* (New York: Columbia University Press, 1996), 122.

10. Quoted in Edison, *Thomas A. Edison Papers: A Microfilm Edition* (Frederick, MD: University Publications of America, 1987–), reel 223, frames 810, 813.

and then turns into a slapstick chase. As in any other work of art, the ideas under-lying jokes, gags, and other kinds of comic routines are part of the public domain, but the specific expression of a joke may be copyrighted. Comic routines, how-ever, pose some extra difficulties when one tries to separate the original contribu-tions of individual performers from the underlying ideas they are building upon.[11] Jokes and gags are generally short; they fall into a few broad structural categories; and they often circulate widely. Because they respond to cultural trends or political events, jokes come in waves, with different comedians creating similar jokes about similar circumstances. (Part of *Personal*'s humor, for example, came from the fact that it responded to a cultural phenomenon, the trend of European nobility marrying American money.) Comic shtick further secures its social rele-vance by using stock characters ("A rabbi, a priest, and a blonde walk into a bar..."). The attributes most basic to jokes and gags—their simple structure, stock characters, broad dissemination, and brevity—are precisely what make them difficult to protect legally.

Both Edison's and Porter's testimonies indicate that an interpretation of the idea/expression dichotomy guided many early filmmakers' creative decisions. But that fact did not make the judge's job any easier. It is always difficult—especially when a medium or genre is new—to separate the generic tropes of an art form from the nuances and individual contributions of a particular work. In 1868, for example, playwright and producer Augustin Daly successfully defended his copy-right in the staging of a last-minute rescue from an oncoming train. How could the judge in the Daly case have known that such scenes would become a stock fix-ture of professional and amateur plays around the world and eventually the stuff of children's cartoons?[12]

Chase films and comedies were already common by 1904. Although filmmakers remade each other's films regularly, there was no legal or normative consensus about acceptable and unacceptable borrowing—about which comic elements were stock "ideas" and which were protectable "expressions." In the absence of such a consensus, Judge Lanning made his decision by closely analyzing the two films; he even requested a shot-by-shot description of *Personal* from Biograph. In Judge Lanning's reading, "the two photographs [as he referred to the films] possess many

---

11. For a great assessment of comedy and copyright, see Dotan Oliar and Christopher Sprigman, "There's No Free Laugh (Anymore): The Emergence of Intellectual Property Norms and the Transformation of Stand-Up Comedy," *Virginia Law Review* 94 (2008): 1787–1867.

12. *Daly v. Palmer*, 6 F. Cas. 1132 (C.C.S.D.N.Y. 1868) (No. 3552).

similar and many dissimilar features." The plot lines were uncannily similar, but the framing and some of the backgrounds were different. Despite the similarities, Judge Lanning concluded, Porter's remake "is not an imitation.... [he] took the plaintiff's idea, and worked it out in a different way."[13] Moreover, the two films had significantly different titles, so exhibitors and audiences were unlikely to mistake one for the other from the advertisements. An appeals court agreed with Lanning, and as a result remakes remained a common practice of production companies during the early years of narrative film.[14]

The high judicial tolerance for remakes fostered an international culture of creative exchange among filmmakers. This open creative environment, as Jay Leyda and others have shown, allowed the nascent art of narrative film to develop extremely rapidly. In one example, suggested by Leyda and elaborated by Tom Gunning and Charles Musser, D. W. Griffith's great masterpiece of cross-cutting, *The Lonely Villa* (1909), turns out to have been the result of an international dialogue among writers, dramatists, and filmmakers. First, Pathé Frères made a film, *A Narrow Escape* (1908), inspired by a French Guignol play, *Au Téléphone*, about a man who receives a phone call and listens to his family being attacked by robbers. Six months later, Edwin S. Porter made a film, *Heard over the Phone* (1908), based either on the English version of *Au Téléphone* or on the Pathé film. The narrative, now too widely circulated to pinpoint the exact chain of influence, was remade and altered by Griffith and, five years later, by Russian filmmaker Yakov Protazanov.

Biograph v. Edison had sanctioned an environment of creative exchange in which plots and themes could be repeated, and this environment helped to solidify early film genres. More than twenty years after *Biograph v. Edison*, Buster Keaton remade *Personal*—or perhaps he remade Porter's remake of *Personal*—as a feature-length comedy, *The Seven Chances* (1925). Some of the simple ideas in Biograph's film became the building blocks of film comedy; they were ideas that no one could own.[15]

13. *American Mutoscope & Biograph v. Edison Mfg. Co.*, 137 F. 262 (C.C.D.N.J. 1905).

14. Charles Musser, *Before the Nickelodeon: Edwin S. Porter and the Edison Manufacturing Company* (Berkeley: University of California Press, 1991), 282. See also Jennifer Forrest, "The 'Personal' Touch: The Original, the Remake, and the Dupe in Early Cinema," in *Dead Ringers: The Remake in Theory and Practice*, ed. Jennifer Forrest and Leonard R. Koos (Albany: State University of New York Press, 2001).

15. See Jay Leyda, "A Note on Progress," *Film Quarterly* 21 (1968): 28–33; Leyda, "Waiting Jobs," *Film Quarterly* 16 (1962–1963): 29–33; Tom Gunning, "Heard over the Phone: *The Lonely Villa* and the de Lorde Tradition of the Terrors of Technology," *Screen* 32 (1991); and Musser, *Before the Nickelodeon*, 424.

"Legally Unique": *Chaplin v. "Aplin"*

Vaudeville and early film comedians accepted the liberal legal standards of owner-ship. In the mid-1910s, however, the loose conglomeration of small film companies began to merge into vertically and horizontally integrated film studios (i.e., Hollywood), with more rationalized models of production, distribution, exhibi-tion, and marketing. The star system was one such form of rationalized marketing, and when some of the vaudeville comedians emerged as slapstick film stars in the 1910s, they began to push for much greater protection of their images and their material. Several of the new stars turned to copyright law, and they fought to rede-fine the idea/expression dichotomy. The case that transformed comic authorship for the age of mass media and finally broke with the imitative cultures of vaude-ville and the early film industry involved Charlie Chaplin.

Chaplin had been an unexceptional member of the British musical hall and vaudeville troupe Karno's Speechless Comedians before Mack Sennett invited him to perform in a film in 1911. But Chaplin's star rose quickly in Hollywood, and only six years later, he enjoyed an almost unparalleled degree of creative autonomy, having established his own studio where he wrote, produced, directed, and starred in all of his films. After co-founding United Artists in 1919, the multitalented Chaplin had a hand in distributing his films as well and even began scoring them after the adoption of sound. In a collaborative medium, Chaplin enjoyed a degree of individual authorship that only a few other filmmakers have ever achieved.

Chaplin helped to redefine the idea of the filmmaker, giving rise to a mythic conception of the director as lone artist. According to one story, he was known to go off on a short fishing trip in the middle of shooting a film just to look for inspi-ration in the stillness of a lake or stream. Art and film theorist Rudolf Arnheim helped to propagate the Chaplin-as-solitary-genius myth, describing him as "a man who, in the middle of the Hollywood film industry, where every day in the studio costs thousands and art is produced with a stopwatch, sometimes disap-pears suddenly and for days paces in solitude with his plans."[16] Indeed, it became a rite of passage for every modernist cultural theorist in the 1920s and 1930s to write a profile of Chaplin as the exception within the commercial sphere of mass culture, as the artist who could work within the capitalist machine of mass production, at the pinnacle of the system, yet remain apart from it. The Frankfurt School theo-rists, in particular, seemed determined not to break ranks in their unified defense

---

16. Rudolf Arnheim, "Chaplin's Early Films" (1929), rpt. in "Walter Benjamin and Rudolf Arnheim on Charlie Chaplin," trans. John MacKay, *Yale Journal of Criticism* 9 (1996): 312.

of Chaplin as the last vestige of a romantic authenticity. Walter Benjamin, building on an essay by surrealist writer Philippe Soupault, called Chaplin the "poet of his films."[17] Siegfried Kracauer, in his obligatory Chaplin portrait, performed great contortions to argue that money and success had not changed Chaplin. "Rather than letting himself be changed by money, like the majority does," Kracauer wrote, "he changes it; money loses its commodity character the moment it encounters Chaplin, becoming instead the homage which is his due."[18] Even the Frankfurt School's severest critic of Hollywood, Theodor Adorno, who elsewhere described laughter as "a disease" of "the false society," made Chaplin an exception by celebrating the actor's imitative genius.[19] As many admirers claimed, Chaplin was simply able to become the characters he mimicked. Only the American cultural critic Gilbert Seldes contested Chaplin's singularity by putting him "wholly in the tradition of the great clowns" and tracing the origins of his style to his film apprenticeship in Mack Sennett's Keystone studio. The "Keystone touch," Seldes wrote, "remains in all [Chaplin's] work."[20]

Was Chaplin a romantic poet of the screen whose inspiration came only from his own genius? Or was he more like Homer, fixing on film a comic performance style that had been developed over decades or even centuries by court jesters, traveling comics, and vaudeville performers? The question of Chaplin's originality grew increasingly important as his films gave rise to thousands of professional and amateur Chaplin imitators. Were the imitators taking and remixing the same ideas that Chaplin had himself lifted from other comics, or were they looting his individual expression?

17. Theodore Huff, *Charlie Chaplin* (New York: Arno, 1972), 125; Walter Benjamin, "A Look at Chaplin" (1929), rpt. in Benjamin, "Walter Benjamin and Rudolf Arnheim on Charlie Chaplin," 310.

18. Siegfried Kracauer, "Two Chaplin Sketches," trans. John MacKay, *Yale Journal of Criticism* 10 (1997): 115–120.

19. Theodor W. Adorno, "Chaplin Times Two," trans. John MacKay, *Yale Journal of Criticism* 9 (1996): 57–61. Adorno's remarks about laughter appear in *The Dialectic of Enlightenment* and are quoted in MacKay's "Translator's Introduction," 57. MacKay points out that Adorno defended his admiration for Chaplin—and at the same time may have explained the soft approach reserved for this Hollywood star—with a personal anecdote: "Perhaps I may justify my speaking about him by recounting a certain privilege which I was granted, entirely without my having earned it. He once imitated me, and surely I am one of the few intellectuals to whom this happened" (Adorno, "Chaplin Times Two," 60).

20. Gilbert Seldes, *The Seven Lively Arts* (New York: Harper, 1924), 41–42. For more essays on Chaplin as artist, see Richard Schickel, ed., *The Essential Chaplin: Perspectives on the Life and Art of the Great Comedian* (Chicago: Dee, 2006).

A Chaplin lookalike contest promoting *The Idle Class* (November 5, 1921). Photo by
J. W. Sandison; Whatcom Museum, Bellingham, WA.

In July 1915 alone, more than thirty New York City movie theaters sponsored
Chaplin look-alike competitions (or were they really Little Tramp look-alike competitions?).[21] Future professional comedian Bob Hope won one such competition,
and Walt Disney, who would draw heavily on Chaplin to create Mickey Mouse,
entered dozens of Chaplin impersonation contests, eventually being ranked the
second best in Kansas City.[22] Professional imitators were also plentiful. The
well-known Chaplin imitator Billy West made over fifty films as a Chaplin-like
character. Actress Minerva Courtney made three films cross-dressing as Chaplin,
and former Chaplin understudy Stan Laurel developed a Chaplin stage act years
before his success as part of the film duo Laurel and Hardy. The Russian clown
Karandash ultimately had to give up his Chaplin routine because he was overwhelmed by competition from other Chaplin imitators.[23] There were both authorized and unauthorized Chaplin cartoons; the most prominent, *Charlie*, was
animated by future *Felix the Cat* creator Otto Messmer and had an unofficial nod
of approval from Chaplin, who sent ideas to Messmer. Even superstar silent comedian Harold Lloyd began as a Chaplin imitator, making fifty-seven films as a
Chaplin-like character named Lonesome Luke. Some companies took Chaplin's
image more directly than did the imitators, selling dupes of Chaplin films or taking

21. Charles Maland, *Chaplin and American Culture: The Evolution of a Star Image*
(Princeton, NJ: Princeton University Press, 1989), 10–11.

22. Kathy Merlock Jackson, "Mickey and the Tramp: Walt Disney's Debt to Charlie
Chaplin," *Journal of American Culture* 26 (2003): 439–444.

23. John McCabe, *Charlie Chaplin* (Garden City, NY: Doubleday, 1978), 88–89; Joyce
Milton, *Tramp: The Life of Charles Chaplin* (New York: Da Capo, 1998), 123–124.

Poster for *His Waiting
Career* (1916), staring
Chaplin imitator Billy
West.

excerpts from his films and mixing them with stock footage, creating "mashups"
(to use an anachronistic term). Other Chaplin mashups mixed footage from
Chaplin films with footage of imitators.[24]

Modernist and avant-garde writers, artists, and performers were also obsessed
with Chaplin. The Dadaists, the surrealists, Fernand Léger, T. S. Eliot, James Joyce,
Gertrude Stein, and countless others copied Chaplin and his Tramp character in a
variety of ways. Critics have made strong cases that Joyce's Leopold Bloom and several Wyndham Lewis characters were, at least in part, explicitly modeled on Chaplin.[25]

24. Terry Ramsaye, *A Million and One Nights: A History of the Motion Picture through
1925* (New York: Simon and Schuster, 1926), 732; Ulrich Ruedel, "Send in the Clones," *BFI
Charles Chaplin Symposium* (July 2005), http://chaplin.bfi.org.uk/programme/conference/
pdf/ulrich-ruedel.pdf (accessed July 31, 2009).

25. See, for example, Susan McCabe, "'Delight in Dislocation': The Cinematic Modernism
of Stein, Chaplin, and Man Ray," *Modernism/Modernity* 8 (2001): 429–452; Anthony Paraskeva,
"Wyndham Lewis v. Charlie Chaplin," *Forum for Modern Language Studies* 43 (2007): 223–
234; Austin Briggs, "Chaplin's Charlie and Joyce's Bloom," *Journal of Modern Literature* 20
(1996): 177–186; David Chinitz, *T. S. Eliot and the Cultural Divide* (Chicago: University of
Chicago Press, 2003), 87–88, 101; Haim Finkelstein, "Dalí and *Un Chien andalou:* The Nature
of a Collaboration," in *Dada and Surrealist Film*, ed. Rudolf E. Kuenzli (New York: Willis
Locker and Owens, 1987), 129–130; Paul Hammond, ed., *The Shadow and Its Shadow: Surrealist
Writings on the Cinema*, 3rd ed. (San Francisco: City Lights, 2000).

Felix in Hollywood (1923).

Eastern European poets used Chaplin and the Tramp character as figures in their poetry during the 1920s and 1930s. The tradition included poems by German-French writer Yvan Goll and by Russians Osip Mandelstam and Anna Akhmatova, the latter imagining herself sitting on a bench in conversation with Chaplin and Kafka. Cubist painter Fernand Léger, who had a deep obsession with Chaplin, illustrated an edition of Goll's *Chaplinade*. Léger went on to animate a dancing Charlot—the French diminutive for Chaplin—in his 1924 avant-garde film *Ballet mécanique*, which premiered in New York on a program with Chaplin's *The Pilgrim* (1923).[26]

Neither Chaplin nor his attorney, the legendary copyright and entertainment lawyer Nathan Burkan, was happy about the massive proliferation of imitators and derivative works. Their first attempt to contain the spread of Chaplin's image was to go after a company that mixed footage from Chaplin's film *The Champion* (1915) with footage of an undersea film to create a new film. (It is difficult to imagine how

26. Matthew S. Witkovsky, "Surrealism in the Plural: Guillaume Apollinaire, Ivan Goll and Devĕtsil in the 1920s," *Papers of Surrealism* 2 (2004): 1–14; Clare Cavanagh, "Rereading the Poet's Ending: Mandelstam, Chaplin, and Stalin," *PMLA* 109 (1994): 71–86; Susan Delson, *Dudley Murphy: Hollywood Wild Card* (Minneapolis: University of Minnesota Press, 2006), 60.

boxing footage might have been mixed with undersea shots, but that is what the accounts describe; the film isn't extant.) Chaplin had made *The Champion* for the Essanay Film Manufacturing Company, and he did not own the copyright. When Essanay failed to take action, Burkan sued the company responsible for the new film, claiming that the filmmakers had unfairly adopted Chaplin's Little Tramp character.

It was a novel argument at the time, but one would expect no less of Burkan, a pioneering lawyer and lobbyist who had organized composers in 1908 and led the campaign for compulsory licensing to be included in the 1909 revision of the Copyright Act. The judge in the first Chaplin case eventually rejected the argument that one performer could own a character independent of a particular work, but he did force the Crystal Palace Theatre in New York to stop misleading the public by advertising the film as if it were a real Chaplin film.[27] It is not clear, however, that the decision accurately assessed the situation nor that it had the intended effect. According to Terry Ramsaye, writing in 1926, the Crystal Palace's attendance dropped by half when it attempted to pass off a Chaplin imitation as an original, which suggests that filmgoers were not as susceptible to misleading advertising as the judge thought. And if audiences knew the difference between Chaplin and his imitators, devoted fans were nonetheless willing to watch imitators' work in between the star's sporadic releases. Despite Chaplin and Burkan's partial victory, Chaplin biographer Joyce Milton notes, the decision led to even more imitators, who could now legally borrow the Tramp character as long as they did not mislead the public through advertising.[28]

But Chaplin and Burkan were not deterred. In a lawsuit against Mexican actor Charles Amador, who made several films under the name "Charlie Aplin," they reprised the argument that Chaplin owned his Little Tramp character. Burkan spent three years trying to settle with Amador before the case went to trial. But Amador and his lawyers were stubborn, maintaining that they had a right to use the comic elements that Chaplin used too. Hollywood insiders and movie fans paid close attention to the case, which dragged on for six years, garnering dozens of op-ed pieces and occasionally making front-page news.[29]

---

27. Milton, *Tramp*, 124; Maland, *Chaplin and American Culture*, 317.

28. Milton, *Tramp*, 124. Ramsaye, *A Million and One Nights*, 732, 737.

29. See, for example, "Charlie Chaplin Protests," *Los Angles Times* (Mar. 8, 1922); "Delay of Chaplin Suit," *Los Angeles Times* (Apr. 7, 1922); "Chaplin Papers Here," *Los Angeles Times* (Apr. 23, 1922); "Chaplin Injunction," *Los Angeles Times* (Jan. 5, 1924).

When the trial court heard testimony in the case in 1925, Amador's lawyers bravely let the charismatic celebrity take the stand and discuss his creative method. In a later copyright case involving the 1918 film *Shoulder Arms*, the opposition's attorney would try to stop Chaplin from swaying the court with his charm and wit.[30] But in the Amador case, Chaplin's testimony may not have helped him. Chaplin adopted an aloof and aristocratic tone. "My inspiration," he explained to the court, "was from the whole pageantry of life. I got my walk from an old London cab driver, the one-foot glide that I use was an inspiration of the moment. A part of the character was inspired by Fred Kitchen, an old fellow-trouper of mine in vaudeville. He had flat feet." When Amador's lawyer, Ben Goldman, cross-examined Chaplin about his costume, Chaplin was dismissive. "Where did you get that hat?" Goldman asked. "Oh, I don't know. I just conceived the idea of using it," replied Chaplin. "Did you ever see anyone wear pants such as you wear?" Goldman continued. "Sure," replied Chaplin, "the whole world wears pants."[31] Chaplin's answers had both a dismissive and a mystical quality: ideas just came to him, he suggested, or else he extracted them from his observations of life.

Goldman and Amador, however, had another theory. Goldman called a vaudeville reviewer, Joseph Pazen, to the stand, and asked him if Chaplin imitated any of the comics who had preceded him. Pazen named dozens of performers who had used similar elements in their routines. George Beban, for instance, had a similar moustache; Chris Lane had a similar hat; Harry Morris had baggy pants; Billy Watson used the same combination of baggy pants, big shoes, and a glide-walk. A member of Les Petries Brothers used the same makeup and a similar costume in his tramp character. This actor had even performed as a tramp in a film for Chaplin's old employer, Mutual. As later critics have noted, Chaplin's costume also invoked circus clowns and real tramps who rode railway cars and took odd jobs.[32]

When Amador took the stand, he was as unsympathetic as his opponent, shiftily claiming that his contract engaged him to imitate the Chaplin look-alike Billy West, not Chaplin. Amador, however, did have one powerful argument: if Chaplin won, the precedent would create a new monopoly on performance. Amador's team made the case that Chaplin was only the most famous in a long tradition of comic tramps, and he could not be given a proprietary right in staples of the trade.[33]

30. "Chaplin to Testify in Loeb Film Suit," *New York Times* (May 6, 1927), 20.

31. "Charlie Chaplin Sues Chaplin Imitator," *Los Angeles Examiner* (Feb. 20, 1925).

32. "Chaplin Garb Is Called Old," *Los Angeles Times* (Feb. 21, 1925), A1.

33. Ibid.; "Fears Monopoly in Acting," *Los Angeles Times* (Mar. 24, 1925), A10; "Aplin Will Call Chaplin," *Los Angeles Times* (Feb. 26, 1925), A1.

When Burkan attempted to respond to the specifics of Amador's criticisms, he fell into rhetorical quicksand, fumbling in the attempt to name Chaplin's original inventions. Reporters following the case had the same problem as they combed the testimony for some element that Chaplin had contributed to the art of comedy. "Chaplin Pants Real Issue," read one headline.[34] But Burkan stuck to his larger strategy by insisting that Chaplin was a unique genius, endowed with an ineffable quality that people could see for themselves. Chaplin's genius, Burkan maintained, could not be described or broken down into distinct elements. In one show of courtroom theatrics, he claimed that a clip from a Chaplin film would have to be placed in the court's decision, because words could not describe him.[35] The romantic vision of the solitary artist is always compelling, but it was a particularly powerful part of the Chaplin myth. In addition to the German theorists mentioned earlier, people as varied as Winston Churchill and Graham Greene, Edmund Wilson and Dwight Macdonald had perpetuated the myth of Chaplin as an individual genius—perhaps the sole individual genius—working in the collaborative and commercial Hollywood system.

But the prevailing argument would end up being a humbler, more pragmatic one. In addition to calling for the protection of Chaplin's unique genius, Burkan argued that the Charlie Aplin name and appearance confused potential filmgoers because they resembled Chaplin's own name and iconic image too closely. This argument carried more weight with Judge John Hudner, who enjoined the distribution of Amador's film *The Race Track* and prohibited Amador from further misleading the public by advertising his films as if Chaplin had made them. By focusing not on the proprietary right in character but instead on the confusion that imitators unleashed in the market, Judge Hudner's decision itself sowed confusion: the press and the film industry were not sure who had won this round of the case. The *Los Angeles Times* declared "Chaplin Legally Unique." The *New York Times* agreed at first, running the headline "Chaplin Wins Suit to Protect Make-Up." But after revisiting Judge Hudner's final ruling with its limited emphasis on Amador's deceptive intent and advertising, the paper reevaluated its conclusion and ran a new headline, "Chaplin Loses Fight on Exclusive Make-Up." Chaplin had successfully

---

34. "Chaplin Pants Real Issue," *Los Angeles Times* (Feb. 25, 1925), A1.

35. *Chaplin v. Western Feature Prods.*, No. 103571 (Cal. Super. Ct. July 11, 1925), *aff'd sub nom; Chaplin v. Amador*, 269 P. 544 (Cal. Dist. Ct. App. 1928); "Chaplin Trial Ends Today," *Los Angeles Times* (Feb. 28, 1925), A11.

prevented Amador from using his image, but he had failed to protect his character from imitation.[36]

Amador's lawyer, Goldman, claimed victory: "we can continue to produce pictures featuring Amador in the characterization as long as we specifically state in the titles that Amador is playing the character.... [Chaplin] has no patent or copyright on the character."[37] The decision raised more questions about originality and ownership than it answered. While Chaplin waited for an appeals court to rule on the Amador case, he was himself sued for copyright infringement—twice. The legal skirmish over the exchange of comic ideas was heating up.

Star Power

When the appeals court heard the case, it refined Judge Hudner's decision, giving more weight to the idea that Chaplin owned the Tramp character. As Judge H. L. Preston stated plainly in his decision, "the record reveals that Charles Chaplin...originated and perfected a particular type of character on the motion picture screen." Elements of Chaplin's character may have been in the public domain, free to be used by other comics. But Chaplin owned this particular expression of the Tramp character; he was the first to use it on-screen; and he could prevent others from confusing the public by adopting his look and actions.[38]

The appeals court in *Chaplin v. Amador* did not entirely adopt Burkan and Chaplin's model of romantic authorship, but Chaplin had succeeded in forging a new and greatly expanded legal definition of comic authorship and, indeed, of authorship and performance in general. The stated goal of both the trial and the appellate decision was to protect the public from confusion, and both decisions used copyright to control unfair competition. In his decision in the Chaplin appeal, for example, Judge Preston made it clear that Chaplin had the right to protect his character from "the fraudulent purpose and conduct of [Amador]"

36. "Challenges Title of Film Comedian," *Los Angeles Times* (May 20, 1925), A1; "Chaplin Loses Fight on Exclusive Make-Up," *New York Times* (July 12, 1925), E2; "Chaplin Legally Unique," *Los Angeles Times* (July 12, 1925), B16.

37. "Chaplin Legally Unique," B16.

38. "Chaplin to Testify in Loeb Film Suit," 20; "Sues Chaplin for $100,000," *New York Times* (Nov. 15, 1928), 25; *Charles Chaplin v. Charles Amador*, 93 Cal. App. 358, 69 P. 544 (1928); *Kustoff v. Chaplin*, 120 F.2d 551 (9th Cir. 1941); and *Roy Export Company Establishment of Vaduz, Liechtenstein, et al. v. Columbia Broadcasting System*, 672 F.2d 1095 (2d Cir. 1982).

and "against those who would injure him by fraudulent means; that is by counterfeiting his role."[39] There is no indication, however, that the existence of coun-
terfeit Chaplins injured the original, at least not by deceiving his audience
into misspending their ticket money. In a statement that Chaplin submitted,
ostensibly in support of his case, Lee Ochs, the former president of the Motion
Picture Exhibitors League of the State of New York, told the court that Amador's
film "is very poor and failed to embody the elements of comedy and pathos that
so aptly distinguish the Chaplin pictures. Nevertheless, to the casual observer, it
might readily be mistaken for a Chaplin picture." Yet, as we saw in the wake of
the trial court decision, audiences were not easily deceived. On the contrary,
vaudeville had taught theater owners and audiences of popular amusement to
expect repetition and imitation. The box office dips when imitators' films were
shown at the Crystal Palace demonstrate that audiences were well aware of the
differences between Chaplin and pseudo-Chaplin films. The limits that *Chaplin
v. Amador* placed on imitation did not serve to clarify the options available to
audience members; it only limited their choices.[40]

By protecting Chaplin the great artist from co-optation by average screen
comics, both the 1925 and 1928 decisions made unprecedented levels of protection
the reward for reputation and standing. Although the courts did not announce
this innovation explicitly in their decisions, it became clear in the cases that
adopted *Chaplin v. Amador* as precedent. Lawyers began to invoke the case, often
successfully, to protect performers from defamation, trademark infringement,
unfair competition, and lower-echelon imitators who tarnished their clients' reputations. The Chaplin precedent emerged as a tool for policing performers' reputations rather than for protecting their originality.[41]

Chaplin v. Amador also inaugurated the development of character protection in
copyright law, but Chaplin's Tramp character didn't resemble the kinds of characters that copyright has since come to protect. As Judge Learned Hand would write
in 1930, character copyright protects the specific traits of "sufficiently developed"
characters. Chaplin, however, used a stock vaudeville figure, the tramp, and made
it his own. Although the individual elements of Chaplin's Tramp remained part of
the public domain, Chaplin's global celebrity so identified him with the Tramp
that it became impossible for other performers to play a tramp without evoking

39. *Chaplin v. Amador* (1928), p. 8.
40. Affidavit of Lee A. Ochs, *Chaplin v. Western Features* (1925).
41. See, for example, *Bert Lahr v. Adell Chemical Co.*, 300 F.2d 256 (1st Cir. 1962); *Lone
Ranger v. Cox*, 124 F.2d 650 (4th Cir. 1942).

Chaplin. As a result, the new precedent of character protection gave a significant advantage to pioneering media stars who drew, as Chaplin did, on centuries of stage tradition to create their characters.[42]

Chaplin v. Amador signaled a cultural shift from vaudeville to Hollywood, from live to recorded performance, and from local celebrity to global stardom. Many other vaudeville performers, especially comics, were confounded by the new limits on imitation. Former vaudeville stars the Marx Brothers, for example, were mired in lawsuits over comic authorship after they made the transition to film.[43] Because film fixed performances permanently on celluloid and circulated exact copies rapidly and globally, the nature of imitation had undoubtedly changed. The vaudeville model of peer policing and tolerance for some degree of imitation no longer provided enough control and protection to satisfy performers, and the courts responded with new tools that constricted the flow of ideas between artists. The casualties of this change were future Bob Hopes, Stan Laurels, and Harold Lloyds, who were no longer free to learn their trade through emulation. The vaudeville circuit could house droves of clowns and tramps, but on film there was room for only one.

42. *Nichols v. Universal Pictures Corporation*, 45 F.2d 119 (2d Cir. 1930); Robert C. Osterberg and Eric C. Osterberg, *Substantial Similarity in Copyright Law* (New York: Practicing Law Institute, 2004), ch. 5. Both the trial and appellate decisions carefully noted that Chaplin was "the first person to use the said clothes, as described herein and as described in the complaint, in his performing as an actor *in motion pictures*" (*Chaplin v. Amador*, emphasis added). This is a dubious claim—there were many other screen tramps before Chaplin—but it also reveals the great advantage of performers adapting characters to a new medium.

43. The Marx Brothers' copyright lawsuits include *Henry Barsha v. Metro-Goldwyn-Mayer*, 32 Cal. App. 2d 556, 90 P.2d 371 (1939); *Marx Bros. v. United States*, 96 F.2d 204 (9th Cir. 1938); *Clancy v. Metro-Goldwyn Pictures Corp. et al.*, 37 U.S.P.Q. (BNA) 406 (S.D.N.Y. 1938).

6 Marked by Modernism

Reconfiguring the "Traditional Contours of Copyright Protection" for the Twenty-first Century

W. Ron Gard and Elizabeth Townsend Gard

For centuries, a small number of writers were confronted by many thousands of readers. This changed toward the end of the last century.... [T]he distinction between author and public is about to lose its basic character.... At any moment the reader is ready to turn into a writer.

—Walter Benjamin, "The Work of Art in the Age of Mechanical Reproduction" (1935)

Copyright law is presently in the midst of a crisis. Seventy-five years after Walter Benjamin's forecast, user-generated content has become ubiquitous.[1] Examples

This chapter benefited from suggestions by Keith Werhan, Jancy Hoeffel, Mark Rose, Pamela Samuelson, Diane Zimmerman, Kenneth Crews, Peter Hirtle, Glynn Lunney, Catherine Hancock, James Boyle, Mark Davis, Onnig Dombalagian, Claire Dickerson, Pamela Metzger, William Patry, Robert Spoo, and Peter Jaszi. We began thinking about many of these ideas with Caren Deming and the Frankfurt School Reading Group at the University of Arizona over the summer of 2002, and we are grateful for the opportunity to present the paper at the Works in Progress I.P. Colloquium 2008, the Intellectual Property Scholars Conference 2009, and the Tulane Faculty Brown Bag Summer Workshop 2009. Thanks in particular to Evan Dicharry (3L, Tulane Law School) for his suggestions, research, and assistance. And to SKG and RJT, who weathered our writing together. We also would like to especially thank Paul Saint-Amour for his suggestions on various drafts and his patience and kindness throughout the publication process.

1. For us, the word *ubiquitous* emanates from Paul Valéry's prescient "La Conquête de l'ubiquité" ("The Conquest of Ubiquity"; 1928): "Just as water, gas and electricity are brought into our houses from far off to satisfy our needs in response to minimal effort, so we shall be supplied with visual or auditory images, which will appear and disappear at a

abound: fans filming their own fifteen-second versions of the original *Star Wars*,[2] software that pairs your latest Tweet with someone else's Flickr photos,[3] CNN iReports, and Amazon user reviews are just a few examples of consumption's fusion with creation. Digital media allow users to copy original works, manipulate and recombine them into derivative works, and disseminate them freely, easily, and instantaneously via the internet. Creators, publishers, and end-users have become harder to distinguish from one another.

The crisis arises from the fact that U.S. copyright laws were not designed to accommodate creator-publisher-consumers. Anglo-American copyright gives authors incentives to create and publish new works. These incentives consist of exclusive rights over the use of the work "for limited Times," after which the work enters the public domain and becomes, in Judge Brandeis's famous phrase, "free as the air to common use."[4] For most of copyright's history, the law functioned principally as a boundary between one publisher and another, there being little reason to police users' deployments of particular works. Individuals merely

---

simple movement of the hand, hardly more than a sign." This English version is in Paul Valéry, *Aesthetics*, trans. Ralph Manheim (New York: Pantheon, 1964), 226. The expression *user-generated content* entered common usage in 2005, and the following year *Time* magazine named "You" as its Person of the Year:

> But look at 2006 and you'll see another story, one that isn't about conflict or great men. It's a story about community and collaboration on a scale never seen before. It's about the cosmic compendium of knowledge Wikipedia and the million-channel people's network YouTube and the online metropolis MySpace. It's about many wresting power from the few and helping one another for nothing and how that will not only change the world, but also change the way the world changes.

Lev Grossman, "*Time*'s Person of the Year: You," *Time* (Dec. 13, 2006).

2. See http://www.starwarsuncut.com, a project in which fans collaborate to remake the *Star Wars* films by individually recreating fifteen-second segments of the films.

3. Portwiture won mashup of the day on February 25, 2009, and is described as software that "grabs photography from Flickr that matches content of your most recent Twitter updates." See http://mashupawards.com/portwiture.

4. U.S. Constitution, art. I, § 8; *Int'l News Serv. v. Associated Press*, 248 U.S. 215, 250 (1918) (Brandeis, J., dissenting). The context of the quote:

> The general rule is, that the noblest of human productions—knowledge, truth ascertained, conceptions, and ideas—become, after voluntary communication to others, free as the air to common use. Upon these incorporeal productions the attribute of property is continued after such communication only in certain classes of cases where public policy has seemed to demand it.

See, for example, Yochai Benkler, "Free as the Air to Common Use: First Amendment Constraints on Enclosure of the Public Domain," *NYU Law Review* 74 (1999): 354–446; and Diane Zimmerman, "Is There a Right to Have Something to Say?" *Fordham Law Review* 73 (2004): 297–375.

purchased works; they rarely had the ability to create and publish market-replacement copies or derivative works. Digital technology has now made these practices common, but copyright law remains grounded in a world where creator, publisher, and consumer are separate entities. As a result, the law is ill equipped to separate pernicious forms of reproduction and dissemination from permissible ones—to distinguish, say, between downloading *Shrek* from a torrent found through Pirate Bay and uploading to YouTube a video of one's toddler dancing to a half-audible Prince song.[5] The difference between the two activities—market replacement by illegal download and the incidental reproduction of protected material in a context of personal expression—may seem intuitively obvious. Yet how do we understand this difference within a legal context that sees both as potentially infringing?[6]

Many copyright scholars believe the law is overdue to be harmonized with the practices and expectations of the user-generated digital-content age.[7] But as we argue about the shape such reforms might take, we should bear in mind that copyright has had to respond to previous sea changes in the speed and circuits of cultural production. The current situation is a crisis long in the making, one we will locate along a continuum the courts are now referring to as the "traditional contours" of copyright law. This chapter's grounding claim is that copyright's twenty-first-century crisis should be seen as the digital-age extension of a modernist crisis, one whose most legible evidence in the United States was the 1909 Copyright Act. If, as we shall argue, we continue to be marked by the modernism that both prompted and was embodied in the 1909 act, then current reform in our own moment, if it is to be productive, must look not only forward to the digital future but also back to 1909. To the extent that modernism is the quintessential narrative of crisis, we might say that modernism is not yet done with us. At the same time, we should revisit the 1909 Copyright Act not as a monumental event

---

5. For a good introduction to the clash between copyright and remix culture, see *Good Copy Bad Copy*, a documentary about the state of copyright and culture (Denmark, 2007; dir. Andreas Johnsen et al.), available at http://www.goodcopybadcopy.net (accessed July 14, 2009). On the dancing baby video, see "Dancing Baby v. Universal: Baby Wins!" *Register* (Aug. 25, 2008), available at http://www.theregister.co.uk/2008/08/25/dancing_baby_universal_dmca (accessed Oct. 12, 2009). "Copyright holders must assess whether material has been used fairly before they demand that it be taken off the Internet, a U.S. court has ruled. The case involved a YouTube video clip of a baby dancing to a Prince song."

6. Some copyright scholars have called for a doctrine of noncommercial personal exception or fair use to cover instances like the dancing baby. See, for example, Jessica Litman, "Lawful Personal Use," *Texas Law Review* 85 (2007): 1871–1920.

7. See, for example, Pamela Samuelson, "Preliminary Thoughts on Copyright Reform," *Utah Law Review* 3 (2007): 551–571.

that happened *to* us but as a moment and a document that should always be rein-terpreted according to our own needs and categories—and as a resource to be drawn on as we wrestle with crisis and reform today. Which is another way of saying that we are not yet done with modernism.

A note about terminology: *modernism* tends to be defined as a set of ideologi-cally inflected formal properties that respond in some manner to the condition of "modernity." Rather than continue relegating modernism to the belated, reactive category of superstructure, we wish to take modernism to the base—to the economic core—to ask what was already modernist about the means and condi-tions of production. Modernism being, as we have suggested, the narrative par excellence of crisis, a reading of modernism "at the base" will be attentive to the volatile, critical state of the economic core and its self-presentations. One site where this crisis will be especially legible, we submit, is in laws, such as copyright, that have governed and calibrated the development of new technologies of repre-sentation, duplication, and dissemination, bearing a close witness to both the pro-liferation of realia and the incipient dematerialization of expression in late modernity. Whether the works protected by copyright are formally "modernist" or not is, for us, beside the point. It is the modernism of the law—its being-in-cri-sis—that concerns us.

The 1909 Copyright Act arose out of the sense that industrially mass-produced objects were insufficiently protected. It's true that copyright protects the expres-sive dimensions of a "work" rather than its material embodiment as an object; nonetheless, the broadening of the expressive aspects considered eligible for pro-tection conferred both a new legitimacy and a new security on industrial objects with copyrightable elements. In bringing a far wider range of objects under pro-tection, the act embodied a certain materialization of culture that would attract the attention of Walter Benjamin and others throughout the twentieth century. But the modernist moment also witnessed the rise of disembodied media forms—including film, radio, and (later) television—that the materialist 1909 act would struggle to accommodate. Cries of protest arose even before the 1909 act became law, and demands for copyright reform continued through most of the century, eventually culminating in the enactment of the 1976 Copyright Act. Yet certain modernist assumptions inscribed in the 1909 act were carried forward into the 1976 act, and they largely persist today. The cultural and technological transfor-mations of the twenty-first century require us to rethink copyright law again, this time moving it more fully from its modernist foundation in analog objects to one more supportive of the digital exchanges that make up so much of our culture in the present. In this essay's final pages, the "circulation of value" will emerge as the theoretical underpinning of both the analog and digital worlds. But before it can emerge, we need to introduce the "traditional contours of copyright protection," a nascent doctrine that can illuminate the law's core functionality without stripping it of its historical context. As we will suggest in the next section, the formulation of the traditional contours to this point has failed to account for the materialist bias of the doctrine's originary historical moment. When reinscribed in its present-day deployments, this failure threatens to undermine the benefits the doctrine might yield.

Traditional Contours of Copyright Protection Today

Since 2003, courts have been turning to the notion of the "traditional contours of copyright protection" as a tool for evaluating whether new amendments to the 1976 Copyright Act are constitutionally allowable. The phrase first appeared in the Supreme Court's opinion in *Eldred v. Ashcroft* (2003), a case whose petitioners questioned the legality of the 1998 Sonny Bono Copyright Term Extension Act, which had effectively frozen the public domain for twenty years. Most of the petitioners in *Eldred* were publishers who made inexpensive reprints of public-domain works; they wanted the court to find that a copyright term extension of twenty years on existing works required First Amendment scrutiny.[8] The Court found to the contrary, however, with Justice Ginsburg writing, "[W]hen Congress has not altered *the traditional contours of copyright protection*, further First Amendment scrutiny is unnecessary."[9] Congress had on numerous previous occasions extended the term of copyright protection for both new works and works already in existence. The Court held that the present situation was no different.

The *Eldred* Court used the phrase "traditional contours of copyright protection" off-handedly toward the end of the opinion, without offering further elaboration. In *Golan v. Gonzales* (2007), the Tenth Circuit observed as much: "The *Eldred* Court did not define the 'traditional contours of copyright protection,' and we do not find, nor do the parties suggest, that the phrase appears in any other federal authority that might shed light on its meaning. Nevertheless, the term

8. Dover Publications, perhaps the best known of the petitioners, republishes fiction and children's novels that have entered the public domain. The company's website reads, "Welcome to Dover Publications! Since 1941, we've offered great books at amazing prices, including over 600 titles that sell for less than $2.00!" See http://www.doverpublications. com (accessed Oct. 19, 2009).

9. *Eldred v. Ashcroft*, 537 U.S. 186, 221 (2003), emphasis added.

seems to refer to something broader than copyright's built-in free speech accommodations."[10] Undeterred by the *Eldred* Court's vagueness, the *Golan* court applied the "traditional contours of copyright protection" phrase in analyzing the constitutionality not of term extension (as in *Eldred*) but of the reactivation of lapsed copyrights.

In 1994, the Uruguay Round Agreements Act (URAA) had restored U.S. copyrights in foreign-origin works that had previously entered the public domain either from failure to comply with earlier mandatory U.S. copyright formalities or because no treaty obtained between the United States and the country of origin. The plaintiffs in *Golan* were, again, groups or individuals who relied on the availability of public-domain works and who had either to cease utilizing those works or to obtain licenses from their (restored) rights-holders. Many of the plaintiffs were groups with small or no budgets for licensing fees, so any cost attaching to the works would effectively bar their use. Also quoting the *Eldred* opinion, the plaintiffs argued that the legislature's removal of works from the public domain, as implemented in § 104A of the copyright code, violated the traditional contours of copyright protection and therefore required First Amendment scrutiny.

The *Golan* court defined the traditional contours as a three-step process consisting of a work's creation, a period during which it enjoyed copyright protection, and its finally entering the public domain. The court explained, "Until [§ 104A restored copyrights in foreign-origin works], every statutory [copyright] scheme preserved the same sequence. Thus, by copyrighting works in the public domain, [§ 104A] has altered the ordinary copyright sequence." After further review, the court concluded that "[§ 104A] deviates from the time-honored tradition of allowing works in the public domain to stay there."[11]

Because of the nature of the case, the *Golan* court concentrated its analysis on copyright's third step or phase, the public domain. We see this as a good beginning but would like to extend the analysis in two ways. First, we will concentrate on the transition between phases one and two, asking how a work moves from creation to

---

10. *Golan v. Gonzales*, 501 F.3d 1179, 1184 (10th Cir. 2007) (Congress's removal of works from the public domain in URAA implicated the free-expression rights of users by altering the traditional contours of copyright protection and was therefore subject to First Amendment scrutiny). See also *Golan v. Holder*, 611 F. Supp. 2d 1165 (D. Colo. 2009) (On remand, the district court ruled that URAA was a content-neutral regulation of speech that was broader than necessary to achieve the government's interest in complying with the Berne Convention, and it therefore violated the First Amendment rights of public-domain-reliant parties by altering "the bedrock principle that works in the public domain remain in the public domain").

11. *Golan v. Gonzales*, 1189.

legal protection.[12] And second, we will broaden the historical discussion of the traditional contours beyond a single step or a transition between steps. We see nothing less than the whole process of copyright law and its historical progression as encoded in the traditional contours of the law.

How, within a traditional contours analysis, does the transition from creation to legal copyright protection occur, particularly given the disparities between the 1909 and 1976 copyright acts as to this very transition? Under the 1909 act, federal legal protection commenced upon *publication* coupled with proper notice of copyright; a new work published without the proper copyright notice fell immediately into the public domain. In contrast, federal copyright protection under the 1976 Copyright Act arises automatically upon *creation* of the work, requiring no specific formal step, such as publication, notice, or registration, so long as the work is "fixed in any tangible medium of expression." A work published under this system remains under copyright for its full term without the need for renewals or further formalities.[13] The moments at which the two acts bestowed protection were disparate to be sure, but they may be seen as congruent with a single theory if we understand the work protected by copyright as relational rather than material. Like property law generally, copyright addresses the social relationships among people in regard to things. The moment designated by copyright law as the start of protection, then, tells us at what point the law understands a work's mediating role in social relations to begin. That the 1909 act granted protection from the moment of publication tells us that the work's propertizable role in social relations was held to begin with its public dissemination within the marketplace, whether that entailed the reproduction of mass-produced novels or the sale of a single painting.[14]

12. Oren Bracha has discussed the transition from creation to legal protection in "The Ideology of Authorship Revisited: Authors, Markets and Liberal Values in Early American Copyright," *Yale Law Journal* 118 (2008): 103–163. See also chapter 3 of Bracha's "Owning Ideas: A History of Anglo-American Intellectual Property" (S.J.D. diss., Harvard University, 2005), which discusses the historical development of the legal protections offered by copyright. Bracha pinpoints the 1879 Drone copyright treatise as a moment of transition when the right to control derivative uses, excepting the provisions of fair use, was added to the already-extant right of reproduction.

13. The range of subject matter to which copyright applies is laid out in 17 U.S.C. § 102(a) and importantly clarified in *Feist Publications v. Rural Telephone Company*, 499 U.S. 340 (1991). The duration of copyright under the 1976 act and subsequent amendments is at 17 U.S.C. § 302.

14. For more on whether the sale of a single painting counts as general publication, see *Gottsberger v. Aldine Book Publishing Co.*, 33 F. 381 (C.C.D. Mass. 1887); *Werckmeister v. American Lithographic Co.*, 134 F. 321, 325 (2nd Cir. 1904); *Bobbs-Merrill Co. v. Straus*, 147 F. 15, 19 (2nd Cir. 1906), *aff'd*, 210 U.S. 339, 28 S. Ct. 722 (1908); and *Burke v. National Broadcasting Co.*, 598 F.2d 688 (1st Cir. 1979). The category of "limited publication"—one "which communicates the contents of a manuscript to a definitely selected group and for a limited

In contrast, by starting the copyright clock with a work's fixation in a tangible medium of expression, the 1976 act made *that* moment the inception of the work's valuable, protectable role in social relations. Although the courts seem hard put to explain why the dramatic change introduced by the latter act does not alter the traditional contours, we suggest there is an underlying mechanism that explains both processes: the *circulation of value.*

The creation-to-copyright-to-public-domain sequence of the traditional contours analysis would seem to focus on a work's physicality, whether by privileging the moment of its dissemination as a physical, saleable good or by emphasizing the moment of its fixation in a tangible medium of expression. But as debates and developments in the last hundred years demonstrate, a work's material incarnation is not always its most legally valuable aspect. Although the 1909 act deemed works valuable and worthy of protection when they became saleable goods, more and more first encounters between user and work have taken the shape of hearing or viewing rather than of purchase. We suggest that rather than depending on a work's materialization, the transition from creation to protection should hinge on a more pliable and historically responsive concept, the circulation of a work's value. Our suggestion is based on the observation that the value of an expressive work is not an indwelling property that precedes its circulation; rather, value arises in and through the work's circulation. The means of circulation, in turn, are dictated not just by technology but also by copyright's response to it. Because both technology and value are mutable, the law must be able to renegotiate the relationship between them, like a flexible bridge between shifting riverbanks. Far from solidifying some rigid notion of what a work is or how it should be protected and used, copyright should calibrate the social relations through which we recognize a work as a work and constitute it as valuable. As long as it fails to function in this manner, copyright can deform our expressive practices in the name of superseded technologies and regimes of value.

The circulation of value, as we have discussed it here, may seem abstract, but it gains substance and specificity when read back into a particular historical moment.

---

purpose, without the right of diffusion, reproduction, distribution or sale"—provides an illustrative case for our claim that copyright protection is commensurate with a work's mediating role in social relations. Limited publication was not considered "publication" in the terms of the 1909 act: it neither required copyright notice nor resulted in a divesting of common-law protection for the work. The above definition is Judge Napoli's, from *The Letter Edged in Black Press, Inc. v. Public Building Commission of Chicago*, 320 F. Supp. 1303 (1970), citing *White v. Kimmell*, 193 F.2d 744, 746–747 (9th Cir. 1952). For a more comprehensive discussion of publication, see Thomas Cotter, "Toward a Functional Definition of Publication in Copyright Law," *Minnesota Law Review* 92 (2008): 1724–1795.

We will now take a closer look at the modernism of the 1909 act—at both its materialist metaphysics and its prescient creation of a copyright in "works...not reproduced for sale." Although marginal, the latter provision marked the beginning of a shift both from publication as the main criterion for legal protection and from the presumption of a saleable, tangible work. The 1976 act extended but did not complete this shift, remaining indentured to the materialist assumptions of the 1909 act in a manner that is less and less compatible with the twenty-first century's digital remix culture. We will then return to the concept of the circulation of value, which can help us to identify the moment at which a work both acquires and requires legal protection. The chapter will conclude by suggesting how a traditional contours analysis infused by the circulation of value principle might guide the next wave of reforms.

The Making of the Modernist "Traditional Contours" of Copyright Law

Ironically, the traditional contours invoked by the *Eldred* and *Golan* courts are a relatively recent creation. The contours in question belong variously to the 1909 and 1976 copyright acts rather than to something innate within all copyright regimes, and the tradition to which they belong dates back only to the period of industrial mass production that we have called modernist-at-the-base. The four-plus decades from the conclusion of the Civil War in 1865 to the passage of the 1909 act were a period of profound change in the United States. The U.S. economic system was radically restructured and the lived cultural experience of the citizenry concomitantly transformed.[15] Agrarian and merchant-based capitalist economies (and, indeed, even financial markets) were first matched and then outstripped by mass manufacturing.[16] This emerging sector sought to produce and distribute everything that individuals might desire. And marketers quickly came to recognize that, with a little help from the growing advertising industry, desire itself could be reproduced.[17] While books, magazines, and other printed matter traditionally protected by copyright were certainly among the swelling tides of desirable

15. Alan Trachtenberg, *The Incorporation of America* (New York: Hill and Wang, 1982), 121–122.
16. William G. Roy, *Socializing Capital* (Princeton, NJ: Princeton University Press, 1997), 4–5.
17. Paul A. Baran and Paul M. Sweezy, *Monopoly Capital* (New York: Monthly Review Press, 1966), 114–131; Richard Ohmann, *Selling Culture* (New York: Verso, 1998), 74–75.

commodities, they were being joined by a burgeoning variety of saleable, mass-reproducible expressive forms—objects and media that were not yet protected by the law but whose potential value became an argument for their inclusion under an expanded intellectual property regime.

With high industrialism's massive reordering of the social relations of exchange came a shift in the dominant notions of economic value.[18] There are many ways to narrate this shift, but it is most vividly described as transferring the determinant scene of a commodity's value from labor to consumption.[19] Brad Sherman and Lionel Bently have traced this transformation in value theory through design, patent, and copyright law in Great Britain, noting its beginnings in the mid-nineteenth century. "What we witness, in effect," they observe, "is the beginning of an epistemic shift within intellectual property law whereby reason, experience, and wisdom were displaced by the consequential positivities that had come to characterize modern law." They go on to explain that, "rather than valuing the labour embodied within a particular object, the law came to focus on the macro-economic value of the object; on the contribution it made to learning and progress or, as we would now say, GNP or productivity."[20]

The 1909 Copyright Act responded to these economic, commercial, and cultural transformations by vastly increasing the range of expressive forms that were eligible for copyright. Some scholars and historians of law remain troubled by the act's provisions, which represented a move away from creative and intellectual labor and a regrounding of the law in the teeming materiality of the mass marketplace. As recently as 1991, L. Ray Patterson and Stanley W. Lindberg blamed the 1909 act for a "trivialization of copyright," adding that the act's deleterious effects have been "too seldom discussed."[21] They attributed this trivialization to the extension of copyright protection

18. A great deal of scholarship since the 1980s has sought to demonstrate the historical and cultural contingency of economic value and to reveal homologous notions of value among sociological, economic, linguistic, psychological, and aesthetic realms. See, for instance, Marc Shell, *Money, Language and Thought* (Baltimore, MD: Johns Hopkins University Press, 1982); Jean-Joseph Goux, *Symbolic Economies*, trans. Jennifer Curtiss Gage (Ithaca, NY: Cornell University Press, 1990); and David Graeber, *Toward an Anthropological Theory of Value* (New York: Palgrave, 2001).

19. For a discussion of this shift in terms of copyright law, late nineteenth-century economic theory, and models of literary value, see chapter 1 ("Neoclassicisms: The Tectonics of Literary Value") in Paul K. Saint-Amour, *The Copywrights: Intellectual Property and the Literary Imagination* (Ithaca, NY: Cornell University Press, 2003).

20. Brad Sherman and Lionel Bently, *The Making of Intellectual Property Law: The British Experience, 1760–1911* (Cambridge: Cambridge University Press, 1999), 39, 174.

21. L. Ray Patterson and Stanley W. Lindberg, *The Nature of Copyright* (Athens: University of Georgia Press, 1991), 88.

to such "writings" as "statuettes, bookends, clocks, lamps, door knockers, candlesticks, inkstands, chandeliers, piggy banks, sundials, salt and pepper shakers, fish bowls, casseroles, and ash trays." Compare these "copyrightable works" with newspapers—for which one court in the nineteenth century had actually refused to recognize copyright protection, on the grounds that they did not contribute to learning! That overly narrow ruling led to the 1909 act's designation of newspapers as being copyrightable, but in the process the fundamental intent of copyright was seriously compromised with the simultaneous inclusion of so much extraneous baggage.[22]

The 1909 act's critics were right to be disturbed by its materialism. Its portrait of cultural production located a work's value not in its laborious origins or even in its aesthetic or propositional content but in the fact of its reproduction for sale—in the physical publication by which it entered into the socially mediating realm of the market. As we noted above, the act viewed a work as valuable, and thus as deserving legal protection not afforded to unpublished works, when it was transformed into a good. This emphasis on a work's materiality and saleability would ill adapt the 1909 act to the coming eras of broadcast and digital connectivity, eras whose cultural works could be consumed without sale or material reproduction. Yet in its provision for "works…not reproduced for sale," the 1909 act did make a single exception to its rule that protection began with publication. With the privilege of hindsight, we can now recognize this exception as the loophole through which the future could be glimpsed.

The Curious Case of "Works…Not Reproduced for Sale"

Fascinatingly, this loophole in the 1909 act was lobbied for not by representatives of the emerging media but by representatives of a long-established one: the stage. In the hearings leading up to the act, it was a theater man who insisted on the need for certain works to enjoy copyright protection despite their being unpublished. Ligon Johnson, representing the National Association of Theatrical Producing Managers ("which embraces practically all the producing managers of America"), explained that the scripts used by theatrical companies were often both unpublished and vulnerable to copying by competitors.[23] Representative Currier, one of

22. Ibid.
23. *Legislative History of the 1909 Copyright Act*, vol. 5, ed. E. Fulton Brylawski and Abe A. Goldman (South Hackensack, NJ: Rothman, 1976), 24, 31. Hereafter cited in the text as *LH5*.

Johnson's congressional questioners, had difficulty understanding: "The people whom you represent do not publish these plays?"

> Mr. JOHNSON. No; they do not.
>
> Representative CURRIER. They do not multiply copies of them?
>
> Mr. JOHNSON. No, sir.
>
> Representative CURRIER. They do not sell them?
>
> Mr. JOHNSON. No, sir.
>
> Representative CURRIER. They do not receive royalties from the copies, but the royalty comes from the production of the unpublished play....
>
> Mr. JOHNSON. That is sometimes done abroad, but I have never known of an instance of it in America. I think the dramatists desire to reserve the right to publish, but from the producer's end of it we know nothing about the publishing of any manuscript nor am I now familiar with a single instance of it.
>
> The CHAIRMAN. You recognize the fact, however, that if it were published it would occupy an entirely different position as far as the law is concerned than if not published. (*LH5*, 33)

Although Currier continued to misunderstand him, Johnson eventually succeeded in describing the scenario most feared by his fellow theatrical managers. It was the theater's form of industrial espionage—or, if you like, its version of the film duping so common in the early years of cinema: a member of a rival company would sit in the audience, taking notes on everything from dialogue to stage directions, costumes, and scenery, with the intent of putting on a duplicate performance or publishing an unauthorized copy of the script.[24]

In asking for a federal tool to combat this sort of "initial play piracy" (*LH5*, 31), Johnson argued that more hung in the balance than a few theater companies' profit margins. According to a statement he filed on behalf of his association, more than $200 million was "now invested in theatrical enterprises dependent upon adequate copyright protection" (*LH5*, 24). The statement explained:

> There are more than 100,000 persons directly dependent upon these enterprises for their means of livelihood; that the investments thereunder reach from the Atlantic to the Pacific and from the Great Lakes to the Gulf; that there is annually paid in salaries by these enterprises about $5,000,000; that there is annually paid by them to railroads approximately $2,000,000;

24. On film duping, see Peter Decherney's chapter in this volume.

that there is annually paid to newspapers and in printing and advertising in excess of $3,000,000; there is annually paid to costumers, bootmakers, scene builders and others for the equipment of productions approximately $10,000,000; that more than $1,000,000 per annum is paid for trucking [each] year...and that other large amounts are directly or indirectly paid to hotels, shops and stores and other interests throughout the country. Petitioner hereto attaches communications from individuals at interest showing in detail as to the investments in theatres and theatrical enterprises directly concerned in the full protection by copyright of the dramatic author.[25]

The Theatrical Producing Managers' statement had an immanent value theory of its own. The value of a cultural work, it implied, lay not in its material embodiment but in the totality of economic relations in which it participated. If plays were not federally protected in their unpublished condition, a vast network of jobs, industries, and investments could collapse. At least in the case of such dramas, publication could not be the trigger for copyright protection.

Thanks in part to the theater managers' efforts, § 11 of the 1909 act made the following provision:

That copyright may also be had of the works of an author of which copies are not reproduced for sale, by the deposit, with claim of copyright, of one complete copy of such work if it be a lecture or similar production or a dramatic or musical composition; of a photographic print if the work be a photograph; or of a photograph or other identifying reproduction thereof, if it be a work of art or a plastic work or drawing.[26]

Copyright law in the United States had never previously needed such a category as "works...not reproduced for sale," but the theater managers testified to the economic benefits to be had from protecting works that were performed but not sold as goods, which is to say not "published" in the material sense. In both case law and in later amendments to the 1909 act, federal protection for circulating works not reproduced for sale covered film, radio, television, and other media operated without tangible, saleable commodities. Circulation without publication: what had been an exceptional case in 1909 was fast becoming the general one.

Over the course of the twentieth century, the category of works not reproduced for sale grew from an exception to a series of industries and became a crucial

25. *LH5*, 31.
26. Act of Mar. 4, 1909, ch. 320, § 11.

measure of the 1909 Copyright Act's obsolescence. William Strauss, writing in 1957, explained:

> In earlier days when the public dissemination of copyrightable works usu-
> ally meant the reproduction and distribution of copies, it may have been
> logical and practical to define publication in those terms, to protect unpub-
> lished manuscripts against unauthorized publication under the established
> common law, and to limit the copyright statute to published works. Today,
> when copyrightable works are disseminated widely by public performance
> to audiences of millions over radio and television and by sound recordings
> and audiovisual films, the dichotomy of common law and statutory copy-
> right based on the historic concept of publication may be thought to be
> outmoded.[27]

The 1976 Copyright Act sought to eliminate the problem by having federal protection begin from the moment a work is "fixed in any tangible medium of
expression"—from the moment of creation. The move not only responded to
international pressures to adopt the Berne Convention's standards of protection
but also recognized that the 1909 act's confidence in the materiality of goods had
been misplaced.[28]

On Circulation

Let us return to the evolving traditional contours framework, which courts have
used to test the validity of new amendments to the 1976 Copyright Act. According
to the *Golan* court, remember, these contours emplotted a work's progress from
creation to copyright protection to the public domain. As with any highly sche-
matic framework, both the danger and the usefulness of the traditional contours lie
in the concept's implicit claim to be a kind of legal master plot that underlies

27. William S. Strauss, *Protection of Unpublished Works* (1957), rpt. in Senate Committee
on the Judiciary, 86th Cong., study no. 29, *Copyright Law Revision* (Washington, DC: Comm.
Print, 1961), 197.

28. One can hear an echo of the 1909 act's "works not reproduced for sale" in an amendment of the 1976 act, the Artists' Rights and Theft Prevention Act, which allows suit for
certain works (motion pictures, sound recordings, musical compositions, literary works,
computer programs, etc.) that are still being prepared for commercial distribution. See 17
U.S.C. § 411(a). A preregistration procedure allows content industries to get ahead of
infringers who, for example, hack and distribute movies over the internet even before they
have been released to theaters. See 17 U.S.C. § 506(a)(3) (defining works "being prepared for
commercial distribution") and 37 C.F.R. § 202.16 (setting forth rules for preregistration).

multiple historical periods. The danger in this case is that, in projecting a traditional contours analysis back upon an earlier moment, we shear off the historical
specificities of both moments. The usefulness lies in the prospect of finding unlikely
continuities and homologies between periods we tend to assume are discontinuous.
In the foregoing analysis, we have tried to anchor both the traditional contours
analysis and the 1909 Copyright Act on which we have trained it firmly in their contexts. With that anchoring in place, we are in a position to say more about the
implicit circulation of value criterion that was shared by the 1909 and 1976 acts and,
in our view, should guide our thinking about the next iteration of legal reform.

Two things have emerged for us as axiomatic: a work's passage from creation to
legal protection is the moment at which the law recognizes and constitutes it as
valuable; and the legal manner in which a society defines value should change with
that society's technological and cultural horizons. When left unexamined, legal categories enacted under one set of historical conditions can persist under subsequent,
quite different ones in which they are either invisibly presupposed or consecrated
as "traditional." If we are not careful, even the emerging doctrine of traditional contours might be lumbered by legal remnants of the 1909 act, in particular its emphasis
on the physicality and saleability of expressive works. To be compatible with twenty-
first-century technological and cultural practices, a traditional contours analysis
must be animated by the recognition that expressive works' value is created neither
by isolated genius nor by ossified entitlements but rather by expression's movement
through the world—a movement whose speed, media, and propagative patterns are
always in flux. This recognition is what we have called the *circulation of value*, and
it leads to a view of law as flexible, corrigible, and responsive to historical change. In
this spirit, we would look at the questions of the day not just as a matter of, say,
moral rights or commercial versus noncommercial uses but with the goal of understanding the system's historical conditions and how they interact with copyright's
core functionality. Peter Jaszi wondered if it were possible for copyright law to
become harmonized with a culture in which the creation of derivative works has
become a crucial form of personal expression.[29] In trying to achieve such a harmonization, we would analyze how remix culture embodies the values of our society
and how copyright law might respond to the many circulatory needs of creators,
consumers, and consumers-as-creators.

We are now living in a future that the 1909 Copyright Act, with its high industrial
metaphysics and its modernist ambivalence toward new media, could glimpse

---

29. Peter Jaszi, "Is There a Postmodern Copyright?" *Tulane Journal of Technology and
Intellectual Property* 12 (2009): 105.

only in its exceptions and omissions. The expressive practices and cultural forms of 2109 are probably just as latent and unprovided-for in the margins of today's law. But the examples of 1909 and 1976 bid us to do what we can to unforeclose those future forms and practices by keeping the law as flexible as possible. For us, this means keeping copyright rooted in its traditional contours: its irreversible progression from creation to protection to the public domain; its incentives not just to create but to disseminate expressive works; and, above all, its commitment to the shared benefits of fresh creation as the end to which exclusive rights are nothing more than a delimitable means. At the same time, we must not misrecognize what we call "traditional" as immutable or self-evident. Rather, our sense of tradition and all that follows from it—the permissible uses of a protected work, the phases and dimensions of its life span as intellectual property—will be remade periodically by the convergence of two forces: the weight of the past and the exigencies of the present. And in this one way, copyright may remain deeply modernist after all.

PART FOUR

Regimes of Attribution and Publicity

7 The Modern Author at Work on Madison Avenue

Catherine L. Fisk

No poet, no artist of any art, has his complete meaning alone.

—T. S. Eliot, "Tradition and the Individual Talent" (1919)

If we become large at the expense of the individual's pride in himself, in the perfection of his own individual powers, we will reach a stage when the individual either is not happy in this organization, or when the organization is unable to attract the kind of individuals necessary to its perfection. It seems to me that if we become larger, we shall have to stress individual progress, individual cultivation of individual talents, very much more than we have been stressing them during the past four or five years.

—Bill Day, J. Walter Thompson executive (1950s)

In 1957, Howard Kohl, a senior executive of the J. Walter Thompson Company—then the largest advertising agency in the United States—sent a memo to members

I am grateful to Duke law students Josh Mayer and Sowmya Krishnamoorthy for superb research assistance; to the archivists of the Hartman Center for Sales, Marketing, and Advertising in the Perkins Library at Duke University in Durham, North Carolina; and to the J. Walter Thompson Company for assistance and permission to use materials in the JWT Collection. All citations to JWT records are to those in the Perkins Library at Duke University. I am extraordinarily indebted to Paul Saint-Amour for superb editing and to Nan Goodman, Jane Anderson, Dick Langston, Andy Russell, Ariela Gross, Clyde Spillenger, Hilary Schor, Amy Adler, Nomi Stolzenberg, Jennifer Mnookin, Seana Shiffrin, Susan Sterrett, and Erik Zitser for thoughtful advice on previous drafts of this chapter.

of the New York office of the firm.[1] The memo was part of a decades-long series of company efforts to bring professionalism and efficiency to the management of the creativity involved in advertising. The J. Walter Thompson Company, or JWT as the firm had come to be known, prided itself on having modernized the business of advertising during the 1920s and 1930s. At JWT, an account representative was in charge of relations with the client and coordinated the work of the writers, artists, and market researchers to design an advertisement. Kohl's memo warned that "the tendency of Representatives to use creative people and specialists in daily and regular contact work with our clients…does not serve the best interests of the client…and can be dangerous to the well-being of the company." Kohl identified several problems with allowing creative workers to have direct relationships with clients. It would undermine the company's ability to present clients with "our completely objective viewpoint…. The Representative should be a buffer between client and agency, should serve as a filter of the client's subjective points of view…. In addition, the fine work of a creative man or specialist can, on occasion, be rendered ineffective or unusable because of personality problems." Moreover, contact with clients could reduce both "the time creative people and specialists have available for actually producing and working on the problem" and "the number of problems creative people and specialists can work on," which would in turn "obviate their ability to bring a broad experience and the invaluable stimulation that comes from working on a variety of problems." Finally, the account representative would "reduce his value to that of a messenger boy if he places on others the major responsibility in presenting the agency's work."[2]

The company's executives were fond of saying that in advertising—an economic sector in which the firm's "assets ride down the elevator every night"—the key to success is the wise management of creativity. By assimilating the manufacturing of ideas, text, images, and sounds into the dominant system for manufacturing cars or managing finance, Kohl's memo embraced three aspects of the classic management theory of the twentieth-century office or factory. First, to be a professional, even in the world of writing and design, was to remove the idiosyncrasies of personality and individual point of view from the work process and product. Second, efficient workplace management demanded a sharp division of labor between creativity and management, an adaptation of Taylorist "scientific management" to creative production. And third, the success of the firm depended

1. Howard Kohl (long-time senior executive of JWT) to Winfield Taylor (senior executive at the New York office), memorandum, Mar. 8, 1957, Colin Dawkins Papers, box 2, Howard Kohl file.
2. Ibid.

upon managers maintaining control over the creative workers. Kohl's memo exerted just this type of managerial control even in the course of describing it.[3]

While Howard Kohl was urging that creative people be kept away from client meetings, other JWT executives were advocating just the opposite. They feared that bureaucratic management of the creative process was alienating creative labor. One cited a writer's complaint that he had been reduced to working in a "storyboard factory."[4] Other employees had complained about feeling "lost" in a large firm where they churned out ideas, artwork, or texts and stuck them in the "out" box on their desks each day.[5] Worried that bureaucratic employment practices could not easily be reconciled with individual creativity in writing, art, and design, one executive proposed that especially talented staff were "deserving of greater publicity," while another proposed that the public recognition of creative staff could reduce alienation and improve the company's reputation for creativity. Bill Day, a JWT executive who eventually left to form his own agency, urged the firm "to stress individual progress, individual cultivation of individual talents, very much more than we have been stressing them."[6] According to this view, creative work could not be assimilated to the managerial model of manufacturing or office work.

This chapter will use the work relationships of creative employees at the JWT agency to explore the roles of the law and legal norms in mediating creation, ownership, attribution, and public recognition as dominant features of twentieth-century authorship. It might seem that modernism, which is conventionally associated with elite, formally difficult, autonomous works of art, would have nothing to do with the corporate production of mass culture, the anonymous and collaborative creative process of advertising, nor the legal rules that made mass culture a profitable industry. I hope to dispel that impression by showing that copyright is not the only place, perhaps not even the most important place, to study the role of law in shaping the nature of creative work in modernism. In both legal and literary studies, scholars have tended to focus on the relationship between

3. John Guillory argues that the memorandum was not "a bit player" in the development of modern corporate management but rather "a central instance of the control revolution." See Guillory, "The Memo and Modernity," *Critical Inquiry* 31 (2004): 108, 122.

4. Thomas Naegele to Dan Seymour, End of Year Report, Dec. 1956, p. 5, Dan Seymour Papers, box 2. Dan Seymour was the head of the JWT Los Angeles office.

5. Elton to Strouse and other executives, memorandum, 1957, and "Program for Growth and Development," JWT Company Policies file, Wallace W. Elton Papers, box 1.

6. This quote is drawn from an unpublished manuscript written in the late 1970s by another JWT vice president, Colin Dawkins, "Ain't It Hell on a Windy Day," 281–282. The manuscript is in the Colin Dawkins Papers, box 22.

copyright law and an individual, literary model of authorship. This scholarly focus on authors and owners has been incommensurate with the relatively small percentage of twentieth-century creative people whose efforts were rewarded through copyright ownership. Once we realize that much modern creativity is exercised in an employment setting where salaried creators sign away their rights in their work as a condition of hire—sign away, in effect, their very status as authors—we can see that the *attribution* of work, rather than *ownership* of the intellectual property represented in it, defines the modern connection between many creators and work of all kinds.

Modern authorship, I argue, is only partly defined by sole creation or by individual rights and incentives. Just as significantly, authorship is constituted by social and legal processes of *recognition*, processes that pertain to both individuals and firms. Like the working class in E. P. Thompson's description, modern authors were present at their own creation,[7] which occurred through their recognition as public persons to whom works were attributed. Attribution often supplanted ownership because the work-for-hire doctrine, which was introduced into U.S. copyright law in 1909 and matured alongside modernism in the arts, defined employers as the authors of works made for hire. The project I undertake here is to show that modernism did not *coincidentally* grow at the same time as the corporatization of creativity. Rather, they unfolded in complex relation to each other. Advertising mimicked and capitalized on modernism as an aesthetic style, and it attracted employees with its promise of steady and lucrative compensation for the exercise of creative genius. Modernism, for its part, adopted a combative attitude toward mass culture even as many canonical works borrowed freely from it. What's more, modernist authors were more dependent for their livelihoods and reputations upon the techniques of modern advertising than is often acknowledged. If we look a little to the side of canonical modernists and their works, we can see how the borders of modernism overlap with an area of cultural production that previously seemed remote from it. And if we look to areas of law adjoining copyright, we will see how the author/artist was constructed, in part, through such neighboring regimes.

The argument proceeds in four parts. First, I will explain that, because law enabled employers to claim ownership of a huge swath of cultural production, many people who created texts and images for a living saw the attribution of the

---

7. E. P. Thompson, *The Making of the English Working Class* (New York: Vintage, 1963), 9 ("The working class did not rise like the sun at an appointed time. It was present at its own making").

work, not ownership of it, as the essence of authorship. And attribution was important not only for creative work in mass culture but also for the Arts and Crafts movement, which celebrated the creative labor embodied in beautiful and useful objects. Attribution also mattered for modernism, notwithstanding many modernists' insistence on the sharp divide between art and mass culture. Second, I will argue that social relations, particularly economic hierarchy and gender segregation within bureaucratic employment cultures, determined how work was attributed. While this is true to some extent of all work, we can learn more about the complex nature of authorship if we look away from the "great" artists and focus instead on the cultural practices of attribution within firms like JWT. The third section will explore attribution in the context of late twentieth-century debates about the legal meaning of authorship. Finally, in the last section, I will suggest that the tendency to propertize authorship—which became a tendency to propertize attribution—led to the late twentieth-century blurring of distinctions among the authorship of art, the authorship of persona, and celebrity. In sum, this chapter argues that, in the world of commercial cultural production, authorship has been an unstable blend of individual and collective creation and attribution. What authorship has meant was determined largely outside the purview of copyright law, and often outside any other formal law, bouncing endlessly back and forth between the individual and the corporation.

Attribution, Authorship, and Modernism

To be an author came to mean many things in the twentieth century, with particularly wide variation in the nature and degree of creativity involved and in the status accorded to different types of authorship. An author is an *originator.* An author is the one whose *name* is on the work. An author is one who is *recognized* as an originator. Under copyright law, an author is a presumptive *owner.* But under the work-for-hire doctrine, an author is the *employer* of a creator.[8] Finally, in some contexts, authorship merged into the concept of a trademark or corporate brand and, eventually, into the concept of celebrity, in which an author is a *persona* or the creator of a persona. Authorship during the modernist decades partook of all of these meanings.

A major political project of modernism was to critique the alienation and exploitation of labor, which had its roots in factory production that redefined

8. 17 U.S.C. § 201; Catherine L. Fisk, "The Origin of the Work for Hire Doctrine," *Yale Journal of Law and Humanities* 15 (2003): 1.

creative labor. In the nineteenth century, the "art" of a worker was the particular skill and learning that defined respectable occupations and the people who performed them. Possessing an art conferred worth on the people who labored at those tasks, made them independent, useful, and therefore valuable members of society.[9] One had not only to possess an art but also to be recognized as possessing it. For Marx, the worker's recognition of and for the products of her labor was essential to her well-being, and the loss of that recognition—the alienation of the worker's labor—was of course central to the Marxist critique of capitalism. In the twentieth century, what had formerly been the art of the skilled worker became the human capital of the workforce and, simultaneously, the human assets of the firm. But one thing remained constant: the desire to see the products of one's labor as one's own—if not in the ownership of the products, then at least in their attribution to oneself. The same concern with labor alienation existed, I argue, in the bureaucratic production of works customarily attributed to authors.

During the late nineteenth century, the Arts and Crafts movement prefigured modernism's concern with the relationships among individual and collective creativity, artistic authenticity, and commerce. Where industrialism had weakened the connections among workers, their art, their labor, and consumers, Arts and Crafts insisted that those connections must be apparent and immediate. By attributing works to individuals, Arts and Crafts sought an antidote not only to the dehumanizing labor relations of the factory but also to the anonymity of mass production.[10] Despite the movement's anti-industrialism, however, its practice of individual attribution was short-lived; as time wore on, Arts and Crafts works tended to be sold under their founder's or company's name rather than being attributed to a particular artisan. The Craftsman ideal persisted with respect to high quality and pride in the work, but Madison Avenue increasingly dictated the names under which Tiffany glass, Rookwood pottery, and Stickley furniture were sold; commercial viability seemed to demand some degree of labor alienation.

An exhibit of Tiffany lamps at the New York Historical Society in 2007 revealed that some of the most celebrated creations of the glass design studio that bore the name of Louis Tiffany were the work of Clara Driscoll, the head of the Women's Glass Cutting Department. Driscoll worked at Tiffany Studios from 1888 until 1909

9. Sean Wilentz, *Chants Democratic* (New York: Oxford University Press, 1984); David Montgomery, *The Fall of the House of Labor* (New York: Cambridge University Press, 1983); Paul E. Johnson, *Sam Patch, the Famous Jumper* (New York: Hill and Wang, 2003).

10. Eileen Boris, *Art and Labor: Ruskin, Morris, and the Craftsman Ideal in America* (Philadelphia: Temple University Press, 1986).

and designed or supervised the creation of most Tiffany lamps, yet she was absent from the studio's publicity.[11] After a dragonfly lamp designed by Driscoll won a prize at the 1900 World's Fair, a 1904 article about the lamp credited it to her rather than to Tiffany, but this was a rare moment of recognition. Driscoll and the thirty-five other women who worked in the Women's Glass Cutting Department enjoyed considerable autonomy within the firm; they worked on their own designs and successfully resisted attempts by the Lead Glaziers and Glass Cutters Union to eliminate them or reduce their sphere of influence.[12] Yet, as significant as the women's role may have been, their names and their work were largely forgotten over time. Tiffany knew, as did modern art dealers and publishers, that attribution creates value both in the work and in the name of the person or firm to which the work is attributed. Today, some might deem Clara Driscoll's lamps more valuable because they represent the creative and physical labor of women whose story was long forgotten and who struggled to exercise their creativity in a world dominated by men.[13] To others, the value of the lamp depends on its attribution to Tiffany; they prize the value of the brand rather than the labor relations within the studio. But either way, value depends upon attribution of the work to a creator, not—as copyright law would have it—on the ownership of the intellectual property rights in the work.

This complex negotiation among artistic authenticity, labor alienation, and financial success persisted in the development of modernism, which, like Arts and Crafts, celebrated the individual talent of the artist. Of course, modernism exhibited a more individualistic notion of the creative process and a different relationship to commerce than did Arts and Crafts or Madison Avenue. It tended to imagine the creative process as an act of sustained rebellion against the industrial and commercial circuits of mass production. Thus, for many practitioners and critics of modernism, authorship was the unique individual's exercise of total compositional control over a unique work. According to the critic Clement Greenberg, the "great works" are derivative of nothing and are about nothing; they

11. Jeffrey Kastiner, "Out of Tiffany's Shadow, a Woman of Light," *New York Times* (Feb. 25, 2007); Martin Eidelberg and Nina Gray, *A New Light on Tiffany: Clara Driscoll and the Tiffany Girls* (New York: New York Historical Society, 2007).

12. Eidelberg and Gray, *A New Light on Tiffany*, 34, 49, 119–121.

13. Feminist art historians have enjoyed discovering that many of the late nineteenth- and early twentieth-century artworks sold under the company names of men were in fact executed or designed by women. For example, many famous Currier and Ives lithographs were done by Frances Flora Bond Palmer. Ellen Mazur Thomson, "Alms for Oblivion: The History of Women in Early American Graphic Design," *Design Issues* 10 (1994): 27, 29–30.

"maintain the high level of... art by both narrowing and raising it to the expression of an absolute."[14] A celebrant of what Andreas Huyssen has called the "great divide" between high and mass culture in modernism's self-conception, Greenberg insisted on the artwork's autonomy and dismissed as kitsch the cultural forms— "popular, commercial art and literature with their chromotypes, magazine covers, illustrations, ads, slick and pulp fiction, comics, Tin Pan Alley music, tap dancing, Hollywood movies, etc., etc."—created and marketed by firms like JWT.[15] In response to Greenberg, Huyssen observes that a modernism defining itself in opposition to mass culture depends intimately on that mass culture for its identity.[16] And now we are in a position to see that Madison Avenue and modernism were secret sharers in another, more specific way: their tendency to define authorship by recognition and attribution.

The Madison Avenue model of authorship emphasizes the mixture of hard work, fortuity, and marketing that enables works to come into existence and those who create them to capture the public eye. This model derives some of its energy and much of its cachet from the modernist idea of the author as visionary rebel. But Madison Avenue insists that an author's economic viability and social relevance come primarily from the *perceived* relation between an author and her work. And it embraces the fact that this perception is created by the investment of time and resources in marketing. To be an author is to be a felicitous mix of inspiration, labor, money, cleverness, talent, and luck, which together enable a person and her work to seize fifteen minutes of fame. Madison Avenue knows that the genius of the author cannot be divorced from the cleverness of the publicist. This mingling of authorship and attribution may be parasitic upon modernism, but it is distinct. Whereas modernists, like the romantics before them, insisted publicly on the aesthetic purity of their motives while deemphasizing their commercial canniness,[17] Madison Avenue openly embraced the interdependence of creativity and commerce in producing and disseminating *all* work.

As I have already intimated, neither the modernist nor the Madison Avenue view of authorship is a pure type. As scholars of modernism have demonstrated since the 1990s, the reputations enjoyed by many modernists both during their

14. Clement Greenberg, "Avant-Garde and Kitsch," *Partisan Review* 6 (1939): 34–49.

15. See Andreas Huyssen, *After the Great Divide: Modernism, Mass Culture, Postmodernism* (Bloomington: Indiana University Press, 1986); Greenberg, "Avant-Garde and Kitsch," 5.

16. Huyssen, *After the Great Divide*, ix.

17. Clement Greenberg, "Modernist Painting," in *Modern Art and Modernism: A Critical Anthology*, ed. Francis Frascina and Charles Harrison (London: Harper and Row, 1982), 5, 6; see also Amy Adler, "Post-Modern Art and the Death of Obscenity Law," *Yale Law Journal* 99 (1990): 1359, 1363–1364.

lifetimes and in the present are partly the result of successful marketing.[18] Conversely, in the heart of Madison Avenue, right alongside the norm of corporate attribution that governed any JWT ad campaign, there was a deep faith in the transformative power of originality approaching that of modernism à la Greenberg. Both the creative people and the company managers valued some of the same qualities in agency employees that they valued in "noncommercial" writers and artists: creative and compelling uses of words, images, and sounds. The talented and highly educated people who worked at JWT esteemed both *modernity*, the condition of a mass-produced now, and *modernism*, an array of critical and symptomatic responses to modernity. At times, they saw themselves as "apostles of modernity,"[19] at others as purveyors of modernism to the world at large. In 1923, Helen Landsdowne Resor, an influential company leader, hired Edward Steichen to bring his modernist photographic eye to several ad campaigns.[20] A lifelong admirer and collector of modern art and a trustee of the New York Museum of Modern Art, Resor clearly saw the potential to blend "serious" and commercial art. Steichen himself embraced the artistic merit of the

18. In addition to Huyssen, see Robert Jensen, *Marketing Modernism in Fin-de-Siècle Europe* (Princeton, NJ: Princeton University Press, 1994); Kevin J. H. Dettmar and Stephen Watt, eds., *Marketing Modernisms: Self-Promotion, Canonization, Rereading* (Ann Arbor: University of Michigan Press, 1996); Lawrence Rainey, *Institutions of Modernism: Literary Elites and Public Culture* (New Haven, CT: Yale University Press, 1998); and Catherine Turner, *Marketing Modernism between the Two World Wars* (Amherst: University of Massachusetts Press, 2003). Lawrence Rainey, for example, has shown that the publication of the 1922 *Ulysses* involved clever marketing deeply attuned to the possibilities of capitalizing on wealth and a whiff of scandal—as against the received account in which a heroic author (Joyce) and literary promoter (Sylvia Beach) succeed despite "a benighted legal system, philistine publishers, and a hostile or indifferent public." Rainey, *Institutions of Modernism*, 42. Later, when Samuel Roth was publishing a bowdlerized *Ulysses* in the United States, Joyce's lawyers had recourse to a state law of unfair competition because the book was not under U.S. copyright. As Robert Spoo puts it, Roth was enjoined "from using the name of the plaintiff [Joyce] for advertising purposes or for purposes of trade." Thus, attribution did for Joyce what copyright could not. See Robert Spoo, "Copyright Protectionism and Its Discontents: The Case of James Joyce's *Ulysses* in America," *Yale Law Journal* 108 (1998): 633–667, 640, quoting *Joyce v. Roth* (N.Y. Sup. Ct. Dec. 27, 1928), in *Letters of James Joyce*, vol. 3, ed. Stuart Gilbert and Richard Ellmann (New York: Viking, 1966), 185.

19. Roland Marchand's classic study of advertising in the 1920s and 1930s said, "The American advertising man of the 1920s was the most modern of men...an exuberant apostle of modernity." Marchand, *Advertising the American Dream: Making Way for Modernity 1920–1940* (Berkeley: University of California Press, 1986), 1.

20. Staff Meeting Minutes, Oct. 16, 1932, box 5. In describing the history of the Jergens Lotion campaign, Ruth Waldo noted the contributions of "Miss E. Lewis," whose "copy gives the story an unusually human and moving quality." Waldo added: "Mr. Steichen, by the way, has taken the photographs almost from the beginning of the [Jergens] Lotion advertising." Waldo commended those who "worked with Mr. Steichen and succeeded in getting some very charming illustrations on what hands can do in building romance."

commercial work he did for JWT, taking care to include many of his advertising photos in exhibitions of his work during the 1920s and 1930s. As for fine art's supposed purity, Steichen pointed out that patronage made the artist "a glorified press agent for the aristocracy" and confessed that, having produced fine art, "wrapping it up in a gold frame, and selling it to a few snob millionaires who could afford it—after I got to thinking about it, I did not feel quite clean." But in his work for JWT, he said, "I have an exhibition every month that reaches hundreds of thousands of people through editorial and advertising pages."[21] In the work practices of JWT, as indeed in much contemporary art, the modern and the modernist converged.[22]

Authors on Madison Avenue

Advertising, then, was both an agent and a site of the dramatic twentieth-century changes in the nature of cultural production and the meaning of authorship. Advertising agency employees were reminded daily that copyright did not fully capture the social and economic significance of authorship. What mattered to them, and to consumers and corporate clients, was whose name was attached to the product as its creator and in what contexts. They valued the claim of an authentic connection between creators and works, but the criteria of authenticity, and the varieties of connections between creators and works that could satisfy these criteria, were flexible.

Like other advertising agencies, JWT competed for clients on the reputation of its human capital, in today's corporate parlance. Company lore claimed that JWT had played a crucial role in transforming advertising from nineteenth-century hucksterism into a modern profession through the particular talent of its staff in applying science to marketing and modernism to art and design.[23] The modernization and professionalization of advertising, as they saw it, entailed hiring Yale

21. Patricia Johnson, *Real Fantasies: Edward Steichen's Advertising Photography* (Berkeley: University of California Press, 1997), 35, 37, quoting Carl Sandburg, *Steichen the Photographer* (New York: Harcourt Brace, 1929), 51–52; and Presentation of Edward Steichen, Minutes of the Representatives Meetings, Jan. 31, 1928.

22. Jackson Lears, *Fables of Abundance: A Cultural History of Advertising in America* (New York: Basic, 1994), 224–227.

23. On the role of JWT in introducing professionalism and "science" into advertising, see Robert Haws interview, Nov. 18, 1964, pp. 1–2, Bernstein Company History files, box 1; biographical file on Paul T. Cherington, Bernstein Company History files, box 4; *JWT News*, Feb. 1984, Bertram Metter Papers, box 2. *JWT News* was the company's internal newsletter.

graduates as writers and university professors to conduct market research.[24] Internal office memorandums portrayed excellence as the result of collaboration, and executives insisted that JWT, not the individual writers, artists, or account representatives, was the author of the advertisements it produced.[25] Stanley Resor, the long-time head of the agency, "would never let anyone have credit for even an ad. It was a 'Company' job. The whole thing was 'Company.' No one person." Walter Lord, who was a copyeditor for the firm before he published *A Night to Remember* (1955), said, "The Thompson Company deliberately beclouded the matter as to who was responsible for a particular ad. Mr. Resor believed so firmly in the team idea...that an individual was never known as the person who wrote such-and-such an ad....Keep yourself out, if you want to get your idea across, is the cardinal rule in dealing with the Old Gentleman."[26] Excessive attention to individual contributions—indeed, almost any form of obvious self-promotion—was considered unprofessional, gauche, and counterproductive. Because the name of the firm was valued above the names of those who worked for it, there weren't names on office doors, and senior JWT employees described the corporate form of the organization as "a picket fence" rather than a pyramid. There was supposed to be no hierarchy, just collective achievement through individual creative effort and spirited collaboration. "That's why we depreciated titles—we didn't have labels or titles," said one employee; "we didn't sign our names individually to projects, we signed our work 'J. Walter Thompson,'" said another.[27]

By contemporary standards, JWT was somewhat relaxed about intellectual property rights in employees' work. The company employed thousands of creatives to produce a range of materials that were protected (or protectable) as intellectual property, including photographs, texts, symbols, music, films, and radio programs. Employees also generated less tangibly fixed creations, including ideas and ad campaigns, that were valuable but not protectable by copyright. The firm did not use written contracts for any of its employees for most of the twentieth century, nor does the paper trail left by the employees deal much with copyright and trade secret law. Nonetheless, it was generally understood as a matter of the corporate culture that both the intellectual property and the ideas that workers

24. Robert Haws interview, Nov. 18, 1964, pp. 1–2, Bernstein Company History files, box 1; biographical file on Paul T. Cherington, Bernstein Company History files, box 4.

25. Henry Flower interview, pp. 6–7, Helen and Stanley Resor file, Colin Dawkins Papers, box 3. "The phrase he said, 'I don't ever want to hear you say that's your account. It belongs to the Company. It belongs to your partners.' He kept emphasizing that over and over again."

26. Walter Lord interview transcript, Colin Dawkins files, box 17.

27. Interview with Sam Meek, Bernstein Company History files, box 1.

generated belonged to the firm.[28] J. Walter Thompson made its money by selling its employees' ideas and works to its clients, so it generally acted as if both the intellectual property rights and the credit for creating the property were the agency's to sell.[29] Yet the agency did not always claim ownership of the work vis-à-vis its employees. In the days when the agency wrote and produced radio programs for its clients to sponsor, the show's writer might own the script even though he or she was technically a JWT employee (they were only sometimes independent contractors).[30] Composers of music for radio programs often retained the rights to the music, and JWT licensed the songs under the ASCAP system just as a broadcaster would have. In some of the shows it produced for clients as sponsors in the early days of television, JWT hired writers without a written contract and simply assumed that it owned the scripts as works made for hire. In some cases, the writer owned the script although it had been written for JWT or its clients.[31]

Just as the agency did not uniformly insist on the property side of authorship, it was inconsistent about attribution. In the early days of JWT's move into radio advertising, the company's handling of credit still reflected its general culture of anonymity and corporate attribution. As one executive recalled:

> As you look back at the credits for writing, directing, and producing these and other JWT shows another striking thing stands out. The credits look like a roster of JWT Radio Department talent.... In those days, JWT wrote all of the material their stars used on the air. The stars might be getting five thousand to seventy-five hundred dollars a week, and the writers and

28. William Howard to John Devine, June 16, 1949 ("I emphatically share your views on the lack of desirability of contracts with employees"), Edward Wilson Papers, box 48. Readers might object to my claim that ideas were the firm's property by adducing that only expressions, and not ideas, are copyrightable. But ideas can be owned as trade secrets, even if they cannot be copyrighted, and JWT insisted that it owned its employees' ideas.

29. Employee work that was not copyrightable, such as ideas and concepts for campaigns, was protectable under trade secret law. I found no evidence in the JWT files of disputes between employees and the firm over the ownership of ideas as trade secrets. Sometimes, the agency's lawyers negotiated with clients about whether JWT or the client owned unused material. For example, the JWT agreement regarding a print advertising campaign for Parker Pens in 1969 provided that all of the agency's work product—"sketches, layouts, art work, copy, plans, ideas, trade names and product concepts"—"shall, as between agency and client become client's exclusive property when paid by client." The general counsel of JWT rejected the idea, initially proposed by Parker, that the agency would convey the property to the client when the client *approved* the work: "Unless the client actually uses and pays for material which we have shown him, we should not be precluded at a later time from using it for another client." Edward Wilson Papers, box 51.

30. Edward Wilson Papers, boxes 48, 65.

31. Edward Wilson Papers, box 65.

directors might be getting that much a year, and no credits on the air or in the trades. Ours was an anonymous society, and our only accolade, after a particularly fine show and one which "broke new ground," was an orchid, which we would find on our desks the morning after—from [JWT Vice President] John Reber.[32]

Later, when JWT began producing television shows for its clients to sponsor, screen credit was handled on the same terms and under the same collective bargaining agreement provisions used for any other TV program, which meant that sometimes JWT employees received screen credit and sometimes they did not.[33] But those were the early days of TV, when the authorship of programs had not yet been regularized by the elaborate system the Writers Guild of America later constructed to wrest authorship away from the whims of studio moguls, who had previously doled out credits like party favors.

Privately, and within the world of ad agencies, JWT did attribute work both to itself as a firm (in the case of ads that were nominated for awards) and to individual employees. Attribution was made for many purposes. It was a strategy of bureaucratic rationality. The business of managing creative talent required processes for spotting and nurturing talent, which in turn required tracking the work of individuals.[34] Dossiers of employees' accomplishments were used, for example, to set their salaries "as nearly as possible in proportion to individual contributions."[35] These same dossiers were used to match the talents of individual employees to the

32. "Ain't It Hell on a Windy Day," 335–336, Colin Dawkins Papers, box 22 (some internal punctuation omitted).

33. In the lengthy labor negotiations in 1950–1952 between television producers and networks, on one hand, and the Writers Guild, on the other, the ad agencies (including JWT) attended as interested observers (ad agencies typically produced the shows they prepared for clients). It was understood that the agencies would adhere to the collective bargaining agreement for all shows they produced.

34. Robert Haws, the long-time personnel director of JWT, described the process of finding an account representative in the early 1960s: "Is he very exciting from the standpoint of what he *may* be able to do here? Either in the form of talent or your estimate of the way he will grow in a general way." "[W]e keep sort of like an executive recruiting file, internally here, of people that we know. So we immediately call over there for background, on all sorts of fellas. In addition to that, we start an intelligence team working" to spot talent. Robert Haws interview, Nov. 1964, pp. 5–7, Bernstein Company History files, box 1. Later, each JWT office was directed to compile a list of its "top ten contributors." The goal of inventorying names and qualifications, as the company's general counsel explained to a manager of the London office, was so that "we can receive the qualifications of outstanding persons we already have when we are in need of particular talents in another office." Edward Wilson to George D. Johnston of JWT London, cable, Jan. 12, 1971, Edward Wilson Papers, box 43.

35. "Notes on JWT Compensation Policies, Written 1949 by EGW-LL," Bernstein Company History files, box 7.

demands of particular clients and campaigns.[36] Other mid-twentieth-century tenets of bureaucratic management insisted that the organization should present a human face to its employees. The company newsletter, which was published weekly or biweekly for decades, routinely profiled individual employees and often attributed slogans, ideas, or other aspects of ad campaigns to them.[37] In addition, the background and development of particularly successful ad campaigns—like the "Uncola" 7-Up campaign of the late 1960s and early 1970s, or the "She's Lovely, She's Engaged, She Uses Pond's" campaign of the 1940s—were covered in the newsletter and typically credited to group leaders and at least some of their team. Company lore sometimes lionized the past accomplishments of particular company leaders as a way of dignifying the firm and inspiring younger employees. For example, Helen Landsdowne Resor was praised for her uncanny ability to understand what would appeal to the female consumer, for her pioneering work in introducing emotion and, especially, sexuality to advertising campaigns ("A skin you love to touch"), and even for the development of managerial strategies (she was credited with hiring and promoting women into creative and responsible positions within the Women's Editorial Department).[38] And, sometimes, authorship was attributed as a matter of what seemed to be common decency but may also have been a motivational tactic; when particular commercials garnered unusual praise, the account representative considered it gracious to pass along the compliments to the head of the group that had worked on it.[39]

When authorship was acknowledged, there were discussions about how it should be done fairly. The desire that credit be given where it was due, without

36. Interview with Robert Haws, Bernstein Company History files, box 1.

37. JWT Newsletter files. See *JWT News*, Nov. 21, 1962 (Pan Am ad campaign won awards; firm credited as a whole); *JWT Michigan Avenues*, May 1, 1970 ("Uncola" campaign credited to a group headed by named individuals).

38. James W. Young interview transcript, Nov. 1963, p. 6; client file on Chesebrough-Pond's, Bernstein Company History files, box 5 (the Pond's slogan); biographical file on Ruth Waldo, Bernstein Company History files, box 5 (gender segregation of departments); Colin Dawkins Papers, box 1, Offers and Staff file on Carroll Carroll (attributing the Woodbury Soap slogan, "A skin you love to touch," to Landsdowne in 1911).

39. Robert Castle to Peggy King, memorandum, June 25, 1956, John F. Devine Papers, box 37 (Personnel):

> The favorable reaction to our 1½ min. Skol commercial has exceeded the usual response. The client has repeatedly spoken of its high quality and has asked me to express their thanks for an excellent job to all concerned. In addition to this, I have heard from several people in the industry already—who have gone out of their way to contact me and comment favorably on this commercial. One of these was a long distance call from Mr. Walter H. Annenberg, owner and Managing Editor of *TV Guide*, who wanted me to know it was the finest commercial he had ever seen on television.

regard to interpersonal power dynamics, explains some significant and otherwise mystifying features of the organization. In particular, it was often cited as a reason that JWT maintained separate men's and women's editorial groups. As at Tiffany Studios, women decided to maintain a gender-segregated creative department precisely so that they could be, and be recognized as, autonomous authors of their work within the firm, knowing that the company would be recognized as the sole author of their work outside the firm. They used gender as a tool to prevent the total alienation of their creative labor.

The origin of the separate departments was typically attributed to Helen Landsdowne Resor, who had been employed as a copywriter around 1911 and married Stanley Resor, the head of the company, in 1917. Mrs. Resor insisted, and other senior women agreed, that if women worked with men in gender-integrated departments the men would get all the credit for the good ideas, copy, and artwork created by women. In an early 1960s interview, recently retired senior executive Ruth Waldo, who had joined JWT in a clerical position in 1915 and became its first female vice president in 1944, explained why she supported the policy even though women newer to the firm thought of it as discriminatory:

> When a woman works for a man or in a men's group, she becomes less important, her opinion is worth less, her own progress and advancement less rapid. Then she does not have the excitement and incentive to work as hard as she can, nor, in a men's group, does she get the full credit for what she does.... But with the knowledge and confidence of Mrs. Resor's support, a woman at Thompson could advance in her own group without having to compete with *men* for recognition of her ability. She has greater independence and freedom; a woman's ideas could be judged on their value alone. It was one less handicap.[40]

As another woman put it, "I think you cannot have a strong woman's department unless it is separate.... [O]f course the men have had women writers, over the years. But no woman writer in the men's department has ever been made group head, for instance."[41]

The agency thus maintained a flexible array of practices with regard to individual attributions and branding itself through its employees' creativity. Its business was to focus on promotion of the client's brand. It persuaded its clients of its fitness to do so by focusing on the abilities of its creative staff, and this attention

40. Ruth Waldo bio, Bernstein Company History files, box 5.
41. Interview with Margaret King Eddy, Bernstein Company History files, box 1.

in turn required JWT to promote its own brand of professionalism and polish. It prided itself on a workplace culture in which some individual contributions were lauded but no person was a brand on his or her own. It was a clever and adaptable blend of individual and collective authorship. And none of it rested on a creator's copyright in a work. Authorship was determined largely outside the purview of the law, and it was both claimed and obscured for reasons of bureaucratic rationality according to a variety of management theories pervading the large mid-century corporation.

The Many Facets of Authorship in the Legal Imagination

Having looked at the workplace practices at JWT to understand the attribution of authorship in commercial art, I now will consider a range of legal means by which authorship in a more general sense was constructed during the twentieth century. The many facets of authorship—origination, ownership, attribution, and recognition—are reflected in the multiple legal theories that people invoked to assert their claims of authorship. In law, as in culture, the value of genius became inextricably tangled with the value of regard. Twentieth-century copyright law embraced modernism's portrait of the artist as innovative dissident at every opportunity. Lawyers seeking to expand property rights in valuable mass-cultural commodities, such as movies, photographs, or popular music, frequently invoked the iconic modernist notion of the creator's unique and transformative vision as the reason that law must protect property rights in the work. Yet these encomiums to the creative genius of individual authors usually served the goal of securing corporate legal rights to mass-cultural artifacts. Modernism became Madison Avenue's friend, at least so far as copyright law is concerned.

Because this claim may seem counterintuitive, it is worth going over again more slowly. The oppositional aesthetic of many modernists linked the power of artistic creation to a project of social transformation aimed at reducing labor alienation, economic exploitation, and social conformity. To some, then, modernism was part of the class struggle.[42] By the time this oppositional aspect of modernism filtered into the world of mass culture, it had been simplified to something like "alienation of labor is bad and creativity is good." This version of the modernist critique,

42. This is, of course, an oversimplification of a complex phenomenon. See Raymond Williams, *The Politics of Modernism: Against the New Conformists* (New York: Verso, 1989); Matei Calinescu, *Five Faces of Modernity: Modernism, Avant-Garde, Decadence, Kitsch, Postmodernism* (Durham, NC: Duke University Press, 1987).

watered-down as it was, had a surprisingly strong influence on the law relating to creative work. It was one source for the development of legal rules that, in theory if not in fact, insisted upon a right of attribution and a right of self-ownership, which became the right of publicity. As studies of modernist icons have pointed out, authors, publishers, lawyers, marketers, and others exploited the market value of marquee names like Virginia Woolf or James Joyce, wholly apart from the value of the books that bear their names.[43] The result was a conscription of the right of privacy and trademark law, legal categories that came into being separately in the early twentieth century, to the formation of a new property right in the manufactured or imagined self. Emerging around mid-century, this new right of publicity benefited the entertainment elite but turned out to be unavailable to those anonymous company employees who helped to turn the reputations and images of modernist icons into valuable commercial properties.[44] The legal regime under which such creators worked deprived them of the material conditions—the intellectual and financial independence of an entrepreneur-in-ideas—conducive to the kind of creativity imagined by modernism. What remained, then, was just the reputation for being innovative and the ability to market oneself as a generator of novelty—the Madison Avenue version of authorship.

In the popular imagination, authorship has little to do with copyright ownership. High school students learn that Shakespeare was the author of *Hamlet* and Woolf of *Mrs. Dalloway* without being asked to consider those works' copyright status. (At the same time, the moral force of copyright law still rests on the equation of authorship and ownership, as those students learn when they are lectured about the evils of unauthorized downloading of music and movies.) Yet scholarly debates about authorship in copyright law continue to underplay the extent to which authorship and ownership have been disarticulated. Setting aside the canonical works of modernism—poetry, novels, concert hall music, gallery art—a huge amount of the creative work of the twentieth century, including much that is an essential part of how we today envision twentieth-century culture, was done by employees who did not own the copyrights in their work. A great deal of the work that translated the modernist aesthetic to a mass audience—including writing, designs, illustrations, and music created by anonymous, creative ad agency employees who were admirers of modernism—was owned by and, in law, was "authored" by the agencies.

43. See, for example, Brenda R. Silver, *Virginia Woolf, Icon* (Chicago: University of Chicago Press 1999); Maurizia Boscagli and Enda Duffy, "Joyce's Face," in Dettmar and Watt, *Marketing Modernisms*, 133–162.

44. Jane M. Gaines, *Contested Culture: The Image, the Voice, and the Law* (Chapel Hill: University of North Carolina Press, 1991).

Although legal rules developed to protect authors, companies, and publishers from the misattribution of work, none protected creative employees from misattributions by their employers or co-workers. After the divorce of creation from ownership made attribution a new, *cultural* form of authorship within companies and in the market at large, the question arose whether attribution, in turn, would become as alienable from creative labor as copyright had become. It did. As attribution became a valuable commodity in a highly mobile labor market, and as advertising created awareness of the value of a brand, the law allowed companies to treat attribution as a form of property that, like everything else, was alienable from the labor of creation.

In economic terms, an innovation or someone's talent or a bit of knowledge can produce two separate revenue streams: one from the intellectual property itself (e.g., the copyright to *Mrs. Dalloway*) and one from the attribution of the intellectual property to a person (Virginia Woolf's valuable reputation as the author of *Mrs. Dalloway*).[45] Together, attribution and reputation help to constitute a valuable persona. The right of publicity has evolved to protect a person's right to the revenue stream associated with that persona. Like copyright, it embraces multiple visions of what it means to be a creator, including the modernist conception of the author as a unique, transformative force. To be a persona is to be an author of oneself, which has come to entitle one to be recognized as the author of one's creative work. Here again, advertising has been both an agent and a site of the legal change in the meaning of authorship. The 1988 case *Midler v. Ford Motor Company* involved a car ad whose soundtrack was a song made famous by Bette Midler and performed, without the singer's permission, by a Midler sound-alike. In finding for Midler, the court deployed the modernist image of the creative genius and emphasized the uniqueness of the self: "The human voice is one of the most palpable ways identity is manifested.... The singer manifests herself in the song. To impersonate her voice is to pirate her identity."[46] The court also embraced the anticommercial posture we have come to associate with modernism, pointing out that Midler was harmed by the unauthorized use of a sound-alike because she refused as a matter of personal philosophy to perform in advertisements.

Yet the right of publicity also drew heavily upon the Madison Avenue vision of authorship. A leading case involved an advertisement parodying Vanna White, the on-screen assistant on the TV game show *Wheel of Fortune*. The ad depicted a robot wearing a blonde wig and sparkly jewelry turning over letters on a board.

45. Catherine L. Fisk, "Credit Where It's Due: The Law and Norms of Attribution," *Georgetown Law Journal* 95 (2006): 49.
46. *Midler v. Ford Motor Co.*, 849 F.2d 460, 463 (9th Cir. 1988).

Finding that the robot ad infringed White's right to control depictions of her persona, the court reasoned:

> Television and other media create marketable celebrity identity value. Considerable energy and ingenuity are expended by those who have achieved celebrity value to exploit it for profit. The law protects the celebrity's sole right to exploit this value whether the celebrity has achieved her fame out of rare ability, dumb luck, or a combination thereof.[47]

In White's case, there may have been no essential genius, no transformative authorial vision, but there was a "trademark" wig, gown, smile, and gesture, and the law protects those. Yet the modernist attribution of a creative accomplishment to an individual, not the Madison Avenue habit of noting the promoter, played a role in the case too. The court treated the case as if White alone were the author and owner of her persona; the opinion entirely disregarded the fact that she had developed her persona while employed by a TV program. Neither the case nor the voluminous commentary on it has asked whether White or her employer owns the right to defend (and profit from) her persona when what was parodied was not White herself, but White in her customary poses and costume at work.

Like JWT's creatives, Hollywood celebrities came to be seen as the corporate assets that rode down the elevator every night. Because the human capital of employee reputation was so easily slotted into the category of a firm's marketable assets, it could become one more thing that the employee signed away to the employer as a condition of hire. A famous case involving the image of Bela Lugosi as Count Dracula probed the question of whether employees sell their personas along with their copyrights as a condition of employment. When Universal Pictures made money selling Lugosi's image as Dracula on T-shirts and trinkets, Lugosi's heirs filed a lawsuit claiming that his image was their inherited property. The California Supreme Court eventually ruled against the heirs on the basis that the right to exploit one's name and likeness ends with death and cannot be passed to heirs. But one justice who joined the majority opinion also pointed out the following in a separate opinion: because Lugosi had created the Dracula persona while employed by Universal and had signed an employment contract giving Universal the right to use and exploit his name, voice, and likeness, that persona had not belonged to him even during his life.[48] It is at best unclear, then, under what cir-

---

47. *White v. Samsung Electronics America, Inc.*, 971 F.2d 1395, 1399 (9th Cir. 1992).

48. *Lugosi v. Universal Pictures*, 25 Cal. 3d 813, 824–828, 603 P.2d 431, 434 (1979) (Mosk, J., concurring).

cumstances employee-creators are the authors of their personas. If voice and persona manifest a person's uniqueness such that their impersonation violates her identity, then the sale of one's persona as a condition of employment begins to look like a sale of identity, a profound alienation of the self from the self.

Modernism, Branding, and the Persistence of Interest in the Author's Labor

The long shadow cast by modernism over mass culture invited constant artistic and commercial engagement with the relationship between artist and creative work. As we have seen, advertising was both a provocateur and a field of battle in that engagement. The commercial value of attribution and anxiety about what that entailed for art became subjects of "high culture" at the same time that anxiety about creativity in a work setting became a subject of "popular culture." Everyone knew that marketing mattered; the relationship between publisher and author, dealer and artist, was an important feature of the modernist world in the 1920s. But the fraught relationship between the artist and the marketers, and the arm wrestling between modernism and Madison Avenue over the nature of authorship, gained new attention with the rise of pop art and postmodernism. Andy Warhol mimicked advertisements for soup cans, referred to himself as a brand and to his studio as "the Factory." He disclaimed authorship of some of his paintings by deflecting questions about the intent of his work to his assistants who, Warhol said, actually created them.[49] Warhol's combination of artistic talent, transformative vision, and hype does not make sense except against the backdrop of modernism's insistence on the separation between art and commerce; it invited ever more thorough conflations of authorship, attribution, branding, and celebrity in the twentieth century's final decades.

Warhol's critique notwithstanding, the emphasis on individual, artisanal creation that modernism shared with the Arts and Crafts movement persisted in the late twentieth century. In the 1960s and 1970s, it animated various trends in visual art and, especially, in popular music. Music audiences wanted some element of authenticity in rock groups despite (or perhaps because of) the growing

---

49. Amy Adler recounts this incident in her article "Against Moral Rights," *California Law Review* 97 (2009): 263, 296. "Boasting his lack of connection with his own objects, addressing a group of admiring interviewers, Warhol said: 'Why don't you ask my assistant Gerry Malanga some questions? He did a lot of my paintings.'" Quoted in Caroline A. Jones, *Machine in the Studio: Constructing the Postwar American Artist* (Chicago: University of Chicago Press, 1996), 422n35.

influence that producers and record companies exerted on the composition and sound of bands.[50] The search for authenticity through attribution continues even into the making of musical instruments. Thanks to internet discussion groups, Fender guitar aficionados began to discover a shared preference for electric pickups hand-wound in the 1950s by Fender employee Abigail Ybarra. A market grew for vintage guitars with Ybarra pickups. One can imagine this as Marx's revenge: an anonymous worker is valorized because her routine, factory-style work proved to be distinctive. But the Madison Avenue view of attribution is ever flexible: the Fender company began marketing "re-issue Abbys": new pickups wound and signed by Ybarra. The company thus capitalized upon the reputation of Ybarra— who had been entirely unknown to the world until guitar fans discovered her work—to enhance its own reputation, even as skeptics doubted whether vintage Stratocaster mojo could be attributed to the winding of a coil around magnets.[51]

Studies of the economics of artistic labor markets identify the crucial importance of reputation in determining the market value of creative labor. The law has both facilitated and reacted to a modern conceptualization of talent not as merely inhering in a person, nor even as being the product of an expressive person's effort, but as reflecting the investment of the promoter and the impresario, the TV hosts, the DJs, and even the social and serendipitous relation between the artist and the crowd. As the social theorist Pierre-Michel Menger has observed, one should understand the value of artistic labor as a matter of reputation as much as talent:

> [T]he appraisal of art and artists varies with the organizational traits of each art world, since it reflects the cooperative and competitive activities of the various members....Rather than being a causal factor, talent becomes a dependent variable, socially determined by the behavior of employers on one side of the market and consumers on the other side. This is why talent may be conceived as embodying not only artistic abilities and technical skills, but also behavioral and relational ones.[52]

50. Matthew Stahl, "Authentic Boy Bands on TV? Performers and Impresarios in *The Monkees* and *Making the Band*," *Popular Music* 21 (2002): 307, 319.

51. I am grateful to Clyde Spillenger for pointing this out to me based on his reading of guitarists' internet discussions. For Fender's marketing of the Abbys, see www.fender.com/products/search.php?partno=0992114000 (accessed Aug. 22, 2009). Spillenger's observation that the craft involved in the manufacture of electric pickups may not be distinctive enough to merit the term "authorship" illustrates the term's elasticity. The cachet of being an author is great enough to provide the incentive to expand the definition as far as sense will allow.

52. Pierre-Michel Menger, "Artistic Labor Markets and Careers," *Annual Review of Sociology* 25 (1999): 557–558 (internal citation omitted). See also Howard Becker, *Art Worlds* (Berkeley: University of California Press, 1982), ch. 4.

Attribution was thus a function of the labor market and the consumer market, but it was distinctly valuable to the creative worker. As with other things of value, people began to think of both attribution and persona as species of property, and they did so principally by analogy with copyright. Where copyright propertized expression, the right of publicity propertized the commercial use of a name, likeness, and persona. And where copyright proscribed unauthorized copying, the right of publicity forbade misattribution and unauthorized mimicry. By 1988, Madison Avenue's marketing of pop songs and pop stars had made it possible to say that, when an ad agency asked a singer to sing too much like Bette Midler, it was doing nothing less than "pirat[ing] her identity."

Throughout the twentieth century, the relationship between creators and law was staked as much to matters of attribution and reputation as it was to copyright. The latter, a right to (try to) control the sale and duplication of a work, was usually managed and often owned by someone other than the artist: the employer, the publisher, the dealer, the heir. But because reputation was more intimately tied to the author's or artist's very self, it seemed that it should be at least partly inalienable. Modernism, after all, insisted that the author's genius was as inalienable as it was inimitable. Yet once reputation became really valuable (in the form of celebrity), it too became something that could be sold. And the work of reputation making—for example, the advertising that made Tiffany Studios a valuable brand—was often done by artists whose greatest talent lay in the creation and obscuring of others' reputations.

I have used "Madison Avenue" as a metonym for one of two contrasting twentieth-century visions of authorship, each accompanied by a rationale for its legal protection. But Madison Avenue was also, in both a figurative and a literal sense, a place where creators worked for intellectual property owners and, in so doing, worked out the nature and meaning of modern authorship. It was a place where the meaning of authorship mutated to emphasize the value of attribution over the value of creation. But by harboring these mutations, and by modeling how and why attribution should be alienable, Madison Avenue created the conditions that would give rise to a backlash—the search for the "real" artist or author behind the company name—even as the terms *artist* and *author* became ever harder to define.

8 Modernism and the Emergence of the Right of Publicity

From Hedda Gabler to Lucy, Lady Duff-Gordon

Oliver Gerland

So, if a likeness, once lawfully taken, were, without permission to be multiplied for gain, the artist reckoning on the beauty or distinction of the original for an extensive sale, it might be considered whether there was not a violation of a sort of natural copyright, possessed by every person of his or her own features, for which the courts would be bound to furnish redress.

—John A. Jameson (1869)

This chapter considers modernism in relation to copyright's neighboring "right of publicity." J. Thomas McCarthy, author of the leading treatise on the topic, defines it as "the inherent right of every human being to control the commercial use of his or her identity."[1] This is a strong statement, declaring that the publicity right originates deep in people, that it is "a sort of natural copyright," in Judge Jameson's words. Whereas copyright laws give owners a statutory monopoly in certain kinds of original works fixed in a tangible medium of expression, publicity laws give one a property-like right in one's name, signature, likeness, photograph, and other indices

This chapter's epigraph is a quotation from J. A. J. (John A. Jameson), "The Legal Relations of Photographs," *American Law Register* 17 (1869): 8.

1. J. Thomas McCarthy, *The Rights of Publicity and Privacy*, 2nd ed. (Eagan, MN: Thomson Reuters, 2009), 1:3.

of identity. Because the right of publicity underpins the economics of celebrity endorsements, it is an essential component of twenty-first-century mass culture.

The birth of the right of publicity was beset with complications. Scholars see its roots in "The Right to Privacy," an 1890 *Harvard Law Review* essay by lawyer Samuel Warren and future Supreme Court justice Louis Brandeis, which argued that people have the right "to be let alone" by a meddling, intrusive media. In 1900, a New York state court decided the first U.S. case involving the unauthorized commercial use of a living person's picture: *Roberson v. Rochester Folding Box Company.* The plaintiff, a young woman whose image had been used without her permission to advertise a brand of flour, brought suit against the manufacturer, claiming mental distress and violations "of her right to privacy and the right of property in her own likeness."[2] Judge Davy found for the plaintiff, but his decision was overturned on appeal, inspiring the New York state legislature to take action. In 1903, it passed a law establishing that "a person, firm, or corporation that uses for advertising purposes, or for the purposes of trade, the name, portrait, or picture of any living person without having first obtained the written consent of such person...is guilty of a misdemeanor."[3] Although it protects the right of publicity under McCarthy's definition, this statute appeared (and still appears) under the heading "Right of Privacy" in the New York State Civil Rights Code. McCarthy unravels the tangled history of the privacy and publicity rights:

> The right to control the commercial use of one's identity first historically developed within the domain of "privacy" law, focusing upon the indignity and mental trauma incurred when one's identity was widely disseminated in an unpermitted commercial use....
>
> However, "famous plaintiffs" began to appear in court to complain that their identity was used in advertising without their permission. Their complaint sounded out of tune with the concept of "privacy." Their complaint was not that they wanted no one to commercialize their identity, but rather that they wanted the right to control when, where, and how their identity was so used....The situation was ripe for some courageous judge to break out of the "privacy" mold of thinking. This is what Judge Jerome Frank [of the Second Circuit Court of Appeals] did in the 1953 *Haelan* case [concerning the exclusive right to use famous ballplayers' photographs for commercial purposes]. He saw that what the law needed was an alternative way of

---

2. *Roberson v. Rochester Folding Box Company*, 65 N.Y.S. 1110 (1900).
3. New York State Civil Rights Code, art. 5, "Right of Privacy," § 50.

viewing the right to control commercial use of human identity. For this purpose, Judge Frank chose the new label the "right of publicity."[4]

In *Haelan*, the Second Circuit formally recognized a kind of property right that had emerged during the first half of the twentieth century. Distinct from the right of privacy, this right of publicity enabled one to exploit one's image and name for commercial purposes. "We think the New York decisions recognize such a right," Judge Frank stated, citing, among others, a 1917 case called *Wood v. Lucy, Lady Duff-Gordon*, which I will consider in detail below.[5]

Scholars may debate exactly when "modernism" began and ended, but the dates framing McCarthy's account of the emergence of the publicity right—1890 to 1953—are reasonable bookends. This rough historical alignment raises my main question: what is the relationship between modernism and the rise of the right of publicity? To answer that question, I will consider the complementary figures of Hedda Tesman, the protagonist of Henrik Ibsen's 1890 play *Hedda Gabler*, and Lucy, Lady Duff-Gordon, the celebrity dress designer known as "Lucile." As McCarthy states, the right of publicity developed in two phases: first, in the guise of the right to privacy; and, second, on its own as a way to protect the commercial value of a famous person's identity. Ibsen's dramatic character and the real-life fashion maker embody these phases, the former desperately seeking privacy for herself and the latter successfully branding and marketing herself. I will tell a story of elites working in different cultural registers—law and theater—who responded in similar ways to the increasingly pervasive use of mass communication technologies in the late nineteenth and early twentieth centuries. Viewing this development as the promotion of a mass society, they placed new and extraordinary value upon personal uniqueness, personality, identity. In the legal register, this resulted in the development of the rights of first privacy and then publicity; in the theatrical register, it resulted in sometimes shocking works characterized by a signature style, what Aaron Jaffe has called the modernist "imprimatur."[6]

The Media and Modernism

Europeans and Americans witnessed tremendous advances in communications technology during the last quarter of the nineteenth century.[7] These were the

4. McCarthy, *Rights of Publicity and Privacy*, 9–10.

5. *Haelan Laboratories v. Topps Chewing Gum*, 202 F.2d 868 (2nd Cir. 1953).

6. Aaron Jaffe, *Modernism and the Culture of Celebrity* (New York: Cambridge University Press, 2005), 20.

7. For a detailed account, see Asa Briggs and Peter Burke, *A Social History of the Media* (Cambridge: Polity, 2005), 121–187.

years when Alexander Graham Bell outdid telegraphy with the telephone, a device that he both invented (1876) and worked to put into people's homes. Before Thomas Edison created the gramophone in 1877, one could not capture and reproduce sounds; by 1897, when Guglielmo Marconi incorporated the Wireless Telegraph and Signal Company, it had become possible to transmit sound through the ether. Meanwhile, driven by high-speed rotary presses and news-gathering organizations like the Associated Press, newspaper circulation quadrupled between 1870 and 1900.[8] In 1881, according to one estimate, more than 5 million penny newspapers, weeklies, and monthlies could be found in London alone.[9] After decades as a cumbersome and error-laden process, photography took its first steps toward the mainstream with George Eastman's introduction of roll film and the hand-held Kodak camera in 1888. Moving pictures drawn from real life, like the Lumière brothers' *L'Arrivée d'un train en gare de la Ciotat* (*The Arrival of a Train at Ciotat Station;* 1895), would follow before the century's end.

These developments were welcomed by some people, but they disturbed others who feared that the exceptional individual would disappear beneath a tide of media-fed conformism. In the opening essay of his *Unmodern Observations* (1874), Friedrich Nietzsche tied this concern directly to the drivel of the press. "The bulk of the German's daily reading material can be found, almost without exception, on the pages of the daily papers and standard magazines. This language, its continual dripping—same words, same phrases—makes an aural impression."[10] He concluded, "When the flat, hackneyed, vulgar, and feckless are accepted as the norm,... then the powerful, the uncommon and the beautiful fall into disrepute."[11] Henry James made the connection between mass media and social leveling, writing in 1887:

> One sketches one's age but imperfectly if one doesn't touch on that particular matter: the invasion, the impudence and shamelessness, of the newspaper and the interviewer, the devouring *publicity* of life, the extinction of all sense between public and private. It is the highest expression of the note of

8. Amy Henderson, "Media and the Rise of Celebrity Culture," *Organization of American Historians Magazine of History* 6 (1992): 49–50.

9. Briggs and Burke, *A Social History of the Media*, 198.

10. Friedrich Nietzsche, "David Strauss: Writer and Confessor," trans. Herbert Golder, in *Unmodern Observations*, ed. William Arrowsmith (New Haven, CT: Yale University Press, 1990), 58.

11. Ibid., 59.

"familiarity," the sinking of *manners*, in so many ways, which the democratization of the world brings with it.[12]

As these examples attest, members of the social and intellectual elite felt threatened by nineteenth-century media developments, which they saw as a means of
promoting mediocre sameness over individual—and class—differences.

Raymond Williams states that any explanation of modernism

> must start from the fact that the late nineteenth century was the occasion
> for the greatest changes ever seen in the media of cultural production.
> Photography, cinema, radio, television, reproduction and recording all
> make their decisive advances during the period identified as Modernist,
> and it is in response to these that there arise what in the first instance
> were formed as defensive cultural groupings, rapidly if partially
> becoming competitively self-promoting. The 1890s were the earliest
> moment of the movements, the moment at which the manifesto (in the
> new magazine) became the badge of self-conscious and self-advertising
> schools....
>
> The movements are the products, at the first historical level, of changes
> in public media...the technological investment which mobilized them,
> and the cultural forms which both directed the investment and expressed
> its preoccupations.[13]

Williams suggests here an intriguing vision of modernist artists as rivals of public
media. Modernism began near the end of the nineteenth century when artists
formed "defensive cultural groupings" against the technological and financial
changes that were turning newspapers, photography, sound recording, and cinema
into awesomely powerful cultural forces. They responded as rivals always do, with
a combination of aggression and imitation, using mass media while striking back
at the conformist values they claimed the media advanced. We can see this complex gesture in the collage, a characteristic modernist form. Picasso and Braque
did not simply read newspapers; they tore them up, glued the scraps, and made art
out of them.[14]

---

12. Henry James, *The Notebooks of Henry James*, ed. F. O. Matthiessen and Kenneth B.
Murdock (New York: Oxford University Press, 1961), 82, quoted in Richard Salmon, *Henry
James and the Culture of Publicity* (New York: Cambridge University Press, 1997), 14,
emphasis in original.

13. Raymond Williams, "When Was Modernism?" *New Left Review* 175 (1989): 50.

14. See David Cottington, "What the Papers Say: Politics and Ideology in Picasso's
Collages of 1912," *Art Journal* 47 (1988): 350–359.

In other words, modernists were ambivalent toward mass media. While they saw it as a threat to individual difference, they also recognized its power and used it to promote themselves and their works. As Williams indicates, the manifesto—a signature modernist document—was a kind of advertising. Martin Puchner elaborates: "The avant-garde manifesto had been intimately connected to advertising ever since Marinetti launched futurism through a series of advertising techniques, including posting his manifestos as ads in newspapers and on billboards and distributing them as leaflets on the street."[15] Malcolm Bradbury and James McFarlane argue that the modernist literary magazine was similar in kind, "often an analogue or extension of the manifesto formula. Virtually a new phenomenon, [the little magazine] represented a privatization of the publishing process....It was largely through such magazines that the evolving works of Modernism achieved their transmission."[16]

Scholars disagree about how best to characterize modernists' relationship to the media and the mass culture it was thought to advance. Williams's image of defense portrays a relationship of opposition, a cultural war in which artists gathered together to protect against invasion. Along similar lines, Fredric Jameson suggests that modernist writers invented a highly individualized literary style in response to the pablum of public media. "[T]he great modern writers have all been defined by the invention or production of rather unique styles," he writes. "[T]hink of the Faulknerian long sentence or of D. H. Lawrence's characteristic nature imagery; think of Wallace Stevens's peculiar way of using abstractions."[17] Jameson continues:

> The great modernisms were, as we have said, predicated on the invention of a personal, private style, as unmistakable as your fingerprint, as incomparable as your own body. But this means that the modernist aesthetic is in some way organically connected to the conception of a unique self and private identity, a unique personality and individuality, which can be expected to generate its own unique vision of the world and to forge its own unique, unmistakable style.[18]

15. Martin Puchner, *Poetry of the Revolution* (Princeton, NJ: Princeton University Press, 2006), 159.

16. Malcolm Bradbury and James McFarlane, "Movements, Magazines, and Manifestos: The Succession from Naturalism," in *Modernism: 1890–1930*, ed. Malcolm Bradbury and James McFarlane (Atlantic Highlands, NJ: Humanities, 1978), 203.

17. Fredric Jameson, "Postmodernism and Consumer Society," in *The Anti-Aesthetic: Essays on Postmodern Culture*, ed. Hal Foster (Port Townsend, WA: Bay, 1983), 113.

18. Ibid., 114.

We may resist Jameson's general sense of this "unique self and private identity" as a capitalist mystification without contesting his more specific point: imaginary or not, the modernist writer's singular interior was expressed by means of an idiosyncratic style, one that was often as difficult for the general public to interpret as it was for the literary expert to mistake. The work itself, in other words, became an index of the author's identity. Jaffe's term *imprimatur* designates this feature of modernist writing: "At once as a distinctive mark and a sanctioning impression, the imprimatur, as I define it, turns the author into a formal artifact, fusing it to the text as a reified signature of value."[19] To use more commercial terms, the modernist imprimatur was a sort of literary self-branding.

Jameson's emphasis on the writer's "unique self and private identity" coordinates his view with subjectivist accounts of modernism that set the individual artist against the masses. Michael Tratner has complicated this picture by tracing the origin of the modernist's authorial voice to the masses themselves. He argues that Virginia Woolf did not develop her idiosyncratic, stream-of-consciousness style to express her unique personality; rather, her unique style results from her channeling the dynamic, image-based consciousness of the crowd. "Masterpieces are not single and solitary births," she writes in *A Room of One's Own*. "They are the outcome of many years of thinking in common, of thinking by the body of the people, so that the experience of the mass is behind the single voice."[20]

Jameson's subjectivist theory of modernist literary creation conflicts with Tratner's collectivist one: the former links the author's voice to "the conception of a unique self and private identity," the latter to the masses.[21] Rather than resolve that tension, I shall use it to help characterize the principal figures in this study. Hedda Tesman and Lucy, Lady Duff-Gordon, occupy distinct places along this tense continuum: where Hedda opposes private to public and individual to mass, Lucy aligns private with public, individual with mass.

Hedda Gabler and the Right of Privacy

In act 2 of Ibsen's play, Eilert Løvborg comes to visit his former rival George Tesman and Tesman's new wife, Hedda. Daughter of the aristocratic General

19. Jaffe, *Modernism and the Culture of Celebrity*, 20.
20. Virginia Woolf, *A Room of One's Own* (New York: Harcourt, Brace and World, 1957), 113, quoted in Michael Tratner, *Modernism and Mass Politics: Joyce, Woolf, Eliot, Yeats* (Stanford, CA: Stanford University Press, 1995), 3.
21. Tratner, *Modernism and Mass Politics*, 2.

Gabler, Hedda feels constrained by her husband's academic ambitions and medi-ocre earning potential. One part of her life that Tesman cannot touch is her past relationship with Løvborg. Now a recovering alcoholic and, like Tesman, a historian, he was in his youth a die-hard reprobate with a curious confessional relationship to the general's daughter: after carousing in notorious downtown establishments, he would secretly confess his profligacies to her. As his confessor during those years, Hedda built up an image of Løvborg as a heroic individual, able to transcend social norms as if he were a Greek god "with vine leaves in his hair—fiery and bold."[22]

In one scene, Hedda and Løvborg sit on a sofa, downstage, flipping through an album with photographs from her wedding trip. She is ostensibly showing him the pictures, but what they are really doing is using the album as a shield behind which to reconstruct their youthful intimacy, a "secret closeness—[a] companionship that no one, not a soul, suspected" (*HG*, 738). No one but Hedda knew about Løvborg's scandalous debauchery, the details of which she pried from him through sly interrogation. "Ah, what power was it in you, Hedda," he remarks, "that made me tell you such things" (*HG*, 738–739). Whatever power it was, it appears to be in force again. The audience sees the couple in a physical situation strikingly like the one that they're discussing: sitting close together under the nose of a male authority figure supposedly looking at pictures but, really, secretly conversing. The male authority figure in the present scene is Tesman, who chats blithely with Judge Brack in the small curtained room upstage; in the past, it had been Hedda's father who would read his newspapers by the window while his daughter and her friend sat side by side on a sofa. "Always with the same illustrated magazine in front of us," Løvborg remembers. "Yes, for the lack of an album," she jokes (*HG*, 738). It is a signature Ibsen moment, an example of his artistic imprimatur. Past and present merge as the characters verbalize a historical narrative while physically reenacting it. Even General Gabler is there in the form of his portrait, which hangs on the back wall of the inner room just over the head of Mrs. Tesman's uncomprehending spouse. In this past-present scene, Ibsen employs elements of public media—pho-tographs, newspapers, an illustrated magazine—to carve out a private space around his protagonist and her secret companion. The play's dramatic question can be framed in these terms: will Hedda retain her private space and her treasured image of the exceptional individual, the vine-crowned hero, or will she lose them

---

22. Henrik Ibsen, *Hedda Gabler*, in *Ibsen: The Complete Major Prose Plays*, trans. Rolf Fjelde (New York: Farrar, Straus and Giroux, 1978), 745. Further references are cited in the text as *HG*.

to the society of bourgeois sameness that newspapers and illustrated magazines have helped to generate? She plays a dangerous game.

As mentioned earlier, many of Hedda's real-world counterparts among the privileged classes also felt threatened by new media developments. Warren and Brandeis certainly did, as the latter's biographer records: "[Warren and his wife] set up housekeeping in Boston's exclusive Back Bay section and began to entertain elaborately. The *Saturday Evening Gazette*, which specialized in 'blue blood items,' naturally reported their activities in lurid detail. This annoyed Warren, who took the matter up with Brandeis. The article ["The Right to Privacy"] was the result."[23] It was a common headache for wealthy and well-connected persons of the late nineteenth century. Newspaper owners had discovered that scandal was a way to increase readership. Some, like Joseph Pulitzer of the *New York World* and William Randolph Hearst of the *New York Journal*, became notorious for this "yellow journalism," but the basic principle was widely practiced. Boston's *Saturday Evening Gazette* specialized in stories involving the social elite. To produce them, reporters began to put pressure on the customary limits of decency and decorum; they were early versions of today's paparazzi. The inhabitants of exclusive neighborhoods like Boston's Back Bay felt victimized. To their rescue rode Warren and Brandeis in the pages of the *Harvard Law Review*. A self-admitted coward fearing public scandal (*HG*, 739), Hedda Tesman, too, would have greeted their arrival with relief.

"The Right to Privacy" marshals theory and precedent to advance the proposition that "the existing law affords a principle which may be invoked to protect the privacy of the individual from invasion either by the too enterprising press, the photographer, or the possessor of any other modern device for rewording or reproducing scenes or sounds."[24] According to the co-authors, "the intensity and complexity of life, attendant upon advancing civilization, have rendered necessary some retreat from the world, and man, under the refining influence of culture, has become more sensitive to publicity, so that solitude and privacy have become more essential to the individual" ("RP," 196). On this view, privacy aligns with personal identity, and publicity is the enemy of both. Public media, in its search for saleable content, violates the privacy necessary for the person's free development: "To occupy the indolent, column upon column is filled with idle gossip, which can only be procured by intrusion upon the domestic circle" ("RP," 196).

---

23. Alpheus Thomas Mason, *Brandeis: A Free Man's Life* (New York: Viking, 1946), 70.

24. Samuel D. Warren and Louis D. Brandeis, "The Right to Privacy," *Harvard Law Review* 4 (1890): 206. Further references are cited in the text as "RP."

To protect oneself, then, it is necessary to withdraw into a private, domestic, interior space. Only there can one cultivate one's identity or individuality—what Warren and Brandeis name the "inviolate personality" ("RP," 205). Victoria Rosner observes an "essential resemblance or interdependence" between architectural and personal interiors:

> As Walter Benjamin has suggested, the increasing symmetry between these two senses of the interior is part of the advent of modern life, the origin of what he terms "the phantasmagorias of the interior." "For the private individual," he writes, "the private environment represents the universe. In it he gathers remote places and the past. His drawing room is a box in the world theater." As the private environment detaches from the place of work, the individual's inner life aligns with the domestic interior.[25]

Ibsen's stage setting exhibits this alignment. It is divided in two: a large dark-colored drawing room downstage and a small inner room upstage, behind a wide curtained doorway. Tesman and Brack sit in the small upstage room during the act 2 wedding album scene but, by the end of the play, it has become Hedda's private space where, as Benjamin says, she "gathers remote places and the past"—that is, the piano, pistols, and portrait of General Gabler that were, apparently, the extent of her inheritance. Because it is located deep in the stage space, this inner room seems like the interior of an interior, more private than the downstage drawing room. It is to this deep interior that Hedda retreats in the play's final moments, when she places her father's pistol to her temple and pulls the trigger.

Taking this extreme action, Hedda performs the private image of extraordinary personality that was forged during her secret conversations with young Løvborg. She has hoped that he will commit a deed worthy of the vine-crowned hero she imagines him to be, but he fails her by drinking to excess and losing the manuscript of his revolutionary new book. Løvborg is depressed when he returns to his confessor the following morning. Instead of comforting him by returning the book manuscript that has fallen into her hands, she directs him to commit suicide "beautifully." "With vine leaves in my hair, as you used to dream in the old days," he muses, smiling. "No. I don't believe in vine leaves anymore," she replies. "But beautifully all the same" (*HG*, 762). She gives him one of her father's pistols, and Løvborg leaves, never to reappear. Once again, however, he fails to enact her design. Judge Brack, one of Hedda's long-time admirers, reveals that Løvborg died from a

25. Victoria Rosner, *Modernism and the Architecture of Private Life* (New York: Columbia University Press, 2005), 129.

pistol shot to the abdomen (rather than to the temple, as she had hoped). More troubling is the fact that the weapon is now in the hands of the police. Judge Brack knows to whom it belongs but promises to remain silent in exchange for sex. What will happen if she does not agree? "Well, Hedda—there'd be a scandal…the kind you're so deathly afraid of. Naturally, you'd appear in court" (*HG*, 775). Judge Brack is not just a member of the legal bureaucracy but also a media informer, with connections to the police and the newspapers. At the end of the play, he brings the threat of two presses to bear upon Hedda: the private press of his flesh and the public press of the media. Unwilling to yield to either, she retreats to her private sanctum, the inner room upstage, and shoots herself in the temple "beautifully."

Hedda's suicide is a characteristically modernist gesture in Jameson's sense of modernism: the shocking display of a singular interior rendered in a private idiom that members of the general public cannot comprehend. "But good God!" a prostrate Judge Brack cries. "People don't *do* such things" (*HG*, 778). Yet her suicide is also, strangely, a sort of public act. This oddity is embedded in the architecture of the inner room upstage. Framed "by a wide doorway with curtains drawn back" (*HG*, 695), it looks like a stage upon the stage: the curtain-hung doorway reads as a second proscenium arch. Hedda's inner room might have been placed behind folding doors. Rosner explains the customary architecture of the Victorian drawing room:

> Women appear to have been the ones who sought the refuge of the folding doors.…the nether half of the drawing room served as an impromptu boudoir, a room for the lady of the house that was typically designed, as J. J. Stevenson noted in *House Architecture* (1880), for "the very commendable purpose of allowing ill-humor to be got rid of in private."[26]

By placing Hedda's impromptu boudoir behind curtains, Ibsen indicates its theatrical nature. Her inner room is not only a site for the private expression of emotion; it is also a site for making those private expressions of emotion public.

Lucy, Lady Duff-Gordon, would build a fashion empire on just this principle. But unlike Hedda, who died to preserve her privacy, Lucy sought media attention for herself and her creations, including those designed for the masses. She would become party to a proto-right-of-publicity lawsuit when she breached a contract with an advertising agent for the commercial use of her name. To understand how her name became worth an advertiser's attention, it is necessary to consider her extraordinary life and career.

26. Ibid., 75.

Staging Fashion at Maison Lucile

The British fashion designer widely known as Lucile was in many ways a mirror—which is to say, a congruent but reversed—image of Ibsen's Hedda Tesman. She was born Lucy Christiana Sutherland in London in 1862, older by a year than her sister, Elinor, who would find fortune and Hollywood fame writing risqué fiction for women under the name Elinor Glyn. The girls came from aristocratic Scots stock but little money. Indeed, they had to make their own dresses. Lucy proved so adept that, by the age of eighteen, she was designing and constructing frocks for herself, her mother, and her sister.[27] In 1884, she married James Wallace and, the following year, bore her one and only child, a daughter named Esmé. After Wallace ran off with a pantomime dancer sometime in the late 1880s, Lucy divorced him, a scandalous action at the time. By 1889, she was a twenty-seven-year-old single mother, living in her own mother's house and wondering how to make ends meet. Although made of different ontological stuff, Ibsen's Hedda Gabler would have been twenty-eight that year, single but with similar money worries. But where Hedda addressed her problems by marrying George Tesman, the real-life Lucy Wallace took matters into her own hands. One morning, while making a dress for Esmé, she had a flash of inspiration: "Whatever I could or could not do I could make clothes. I would be a dressmaker."[28] She borrowed some money from her mother and set to work, cutting out patterns on the dining room floor (*DI*, 39). Lucy quickly found her first client, a socialite friend of the family who needed a tea gown for a house party. Worn in the late afternoon, after shooting tweeds but before formal evening wear, tea gowns were loose and uncorseted, suggesting "if not a state of undress, then at least a private and introspective state on the part of the wearer."[29] It was a fortunate commission not just because it brought money and more clients but also because it shaped Lucy's signature design style: layered, soft-hued chiffons that gave slightly scandalous expression to intimate emotional states.

This signature style was evident in her so-called personality dresses. Years later, she would contrast these creations to the off-the-rack garments that were then threatening to eclipse them:

27. Meredith Etherington-Smith and Jeremy Pilcher, *The "It" Girls* (New York: Harcourt Brace Jovanovich, 1986), 24.

28. Lady Duff-Gordon, *Discretions and Indiscretions* (New York: Stokes, 1932), 36. Further references will be cited in the text as *DI*.

29. Alistair O'Neill, "Lucile," in *Encyclopedia of Clothing and Fashion*, ed. Valerie Steele (Farmington Hills, MI: Scribner's, 2005), 2:364–365.

> I studied the type of each [client] and designed a gown for her which I thought would harmonize with her individuality, and they were all immensely intrigued at rediscovering themselves in my eyes. I think that many designers of the younger school [post–World War I] are far too inclined to turn out their models *en masse*, regardless of the special needs of the women who will wear them, and so they lack personality and interest. I always saw the woman, not the frock as detached from her, and so women loved my clothes, because women are above all other things personal in every thought and action. (*DI*, 38)

This is a statement reminiscent of Jameson's view of modernism. Lucy positions herself as a depth psychologist and publicist whose special talent is to discover each client's individual personality and to design a dress that makes it visible. Cloth, in her view, is a medium, like words or paint, that can be used to signify, externalize, and make public an individual's private, interior states. In the words of a publicity puff piece: "She has gone to the silent worlds of desires and temperaments and sensations and translates their secrets into wondrous colors and entrancing forms" (*DI*, 93). She followed the personality dresses with a more daring inner-to-outer expressive gesture: "I started making underclothes as delicate as cobwebs and as beautifully tinted as flowers, and half the women in London flocked to see them, though they had not the courage to buy them at first" (*DI*, 41–42).

Lucy combined a (Jamesonian) modernist's desire to express singular interiors with a businessperson's desire to profit by showing them to others. Her diaphanous frocks and flimsy camisoles became the talk of high-society London in the 1890s and business boomed, forcing moves to larger premises. She took her physical relocations as opportunities to reposition her brand. Leaving her mother's house for her first stand-alone shop, she named herself Lucile and her place of business Maison Lucile. The word *Maison* is important, for it announced Lucy's desire to model her commercial environment after the interiors of fashionable homes. In 1897, she moved the business again, to a thoroughly refurbished eighteenth-century residence on Mayfair's Hanover Square. The new Maison Lucile, with its bedrooms turned into studios and its drawing room into a showroom, had no precedent in the fashion business: "Nobody had thought of developing the social side of choosing clothes, of serving tea and imitating the setting of a drawing-room" (*DI*, 67). Having visited with Hedda, we are in a position to appreciate the brilliance—and perversity—of Lucy's plan: she took the private interiors cherished by the social elite and opened them to market and to public view, commodifying the precious intimate spaces enjoyed by women like Hedda Tesman.

In seeking, as she put it, "to lure women into buying more dresses than they could afford" (*DI*, 67), Lucy settled on two interlocking stratagems. The first was to make women feel comfortable, which she accomplished by imitating the manners and architecture of their homes. The second was to provide women with living embodiments of their wishes and dreams—figures of rare and striking beauty onto whom they could willingly project themselves. Her attempts to stage this drama of surrogacy would produce her most significant contribution to twentieth- and twenty-first-century fashion performance: the runway show. She described the process of its invention: "Slowly the idea of a mannequin parade, which would be as entertaining to watch as a play, took shape in my mind. I would have glorious, goddess-like girls, who would walk to and fro dressed in my models, displaying them to the best advantage to an admiring audience of women" (*DI*, 69). Incredible as it seems, this had never been done before. To buy a dress meant either inviting a private dressmaker to one's home—a prohibitively expensive option for many women—or visiting a cramped shop where plain-faced girls showed dresses while wearing clumpy lace-up boots and, for modesty's sake, a close-fitting, long-sleeved, black satin undergarment that went from neck to waist. Lucy wanted exposure. She found tall, slender beauties, all from working-class backgrounds. She taught them poise and deportment, assigning them exotic names like Gamela, Dolores, and Hebe. And she stripped them of the black satin *maillot* and taught them to move with grace. The result was profitably persuasive: "When the lights are lowered to a rosy glow, and soft music is played and the mannequins parade, there is not a woman in the audience, though she may be fat and middle-aged, who is not seeing herself looking as those slim, beautiful girls look in the clothes they are offering her. And that is the inevitable prelude to buying the clothes" (*DI*, 78).

Lucy's first show completed the work begun by her renovations—the work of converting the drawing room of an old house into a theater. Recall the arrangement described by Rosner: the drawing room was a large comfortable seating area at whose nether end folding doors formed a small, private area to which the woman of the house could retire when emotionally overtaxed. Ibsen theatricalized this impromptu boudoir in *Hedda Gabler* when he hung it with curtains, but Lucy turned it, literally, into a stage. "I had a soft, rich carpet laid down in the big showroom, and beautiful, gray brocade curtains to tone with it were hung across the windows. At one end of the room I had a stage, a miniature affair, all hung with misty olive chiffon curtains, as the background, which created the atmosphere I wanted" (*DI*, 69–70). Lucy created a new line of dresses for the event that she called "gowns of emotion." They were flowing embodiments of moments in a woman's romantic life, with names such as "Do You Love Me?" "Give Me Your Heart," and "When Passion's Thrall Is O'er" (*DI*, 73). Attended by celebrities such as Queen Victoria's daughter Princess Alice and actress Lillie Langtry, the show was a huge hit. It was the start of Lucy's spectacular success, the moment about which she could later conclusively state, "My star had risen" (*DI*, 74).

Her career would endure for another twenty-plus years, until after World War I, when tight economies and a more slender or "boyish" female silhouette would consign the name of Lucile, along with most of its associations, to a vanished world. But from 1897 until 1922 or so, Lucy was the queen of the fashion world, inventing new feminine styles and marketing them in exciting new ways. What's more, her innovative use of media, reputation, and endorsement extended her influence well beyond the precincts of expensive dressmaking. By lending her name to a wide range of luxury products, and by disseminating her views through syndicated newspaper and magazine columns, Lucy may have been the first multimedia promoter of a branded lifestyle. She was Martha Stewart's modernist ancestor.

Lucy, Lady Duff-Gordon, and the Right of Publicity

By 1915, branches of Maison Lucile could be found in London, Paris, New York, and Chicago. But Lucy's fashion and financial empire was already in peril. England and France were engaged in the Great War, meaning greatly reduced sales in London and Paris, and the high-flying life of a celebrity dress designer was expensive—particularly now that Lucy was, in essence, just a highly paid employee of the company that she had founded. She had married Scots aristocrat Cosmo Duff-Gordon in 1900, and it was he who now controlled the Lucile label, giving Lucy an allowance of $200 a month in return for which she was bound to go on creating Lucile dresses.[30] Living apart from Sir Cosmo by the war's second year, Lucy rebelled by reinventing herself once again. She began to sign contracts with American marketers and advertisers under a new name, no longer "Lucile" but "Lady Duff-Gordon."

On April 1, 1915, Lucy entered into such an agreement with advertising agent Otis Wood, assigning him the exclusive rights to market goods under the name Lady Duff-Gordon. It was Wood's job to seek out endorsement opportunities and submit them to her for approval. If Lucy approved, then she would collect half of

---

30. Etherington-Smith and Pilcher, *The "It" Girls*, 196.

the licensing revenues. Both parties got something out of the deal: Lucy freed her-self from her husband's tight financial grip, and Wood gained control of the name of the famous designer. The arrangement appeared to satisfy both parties for the first year or so. Wood began to place her name on goods affordable to the many middle-class readers of her columns in *Harper's Bazaar*, Hearst's *Sunday American*, and other mass publications. He arranged for Lucy to endorse the opening of the Bedell fashion shop of New York "where the one great, actuating idea is to supply authenticated styles at the LOWEST figures possible."[31] Wood pushed Lucy's name further down-market the following year, when he negotiated a deal with the Oliver Typewriter Company to send to the "business girls of New York" paper patterns of her latest creation," 'The Ideal Office Gown' for Business Women and Stenographers, with full directions showing how you can make this model at a cost of only $18.00."[32]

The wartime economy was not the only motivation for Lucy's shift to middle- and working-class markets. She had announced her agenda in early 1915, in a letter to her daughter: "I'm getting dead sick of working for the 'few' rich people that go into the four Luciles with their personal fads. They don't like this and that. I am going to work for the millions....I'm going to be a help to the great 'Middle Class' of America; the workers and the great struggling poor."[33] Lucy's populist turn was striking but not without foundation in her own life. She had begun her high-flying fashion career while living in her mother's house, a single mother on her knees cutting out patterns on the dining room floor. Moreover, her famously beautiful mannequins all hailed from the lower classes. Lucy reported that, following their day at Maison Lucile, "they took off their splendid clothes, and caught trams and buses to their homes. There they cooked the family supper, did their own washing and performed a hundred and one prosaic tasks" (*DI*, 76). In September 1916, without Wood's knowledge, she entered into an agreement with Sears, Roebuck and Company to sell her dresses through its catalog. An advertisement in the *Ladies' Home Journal* of October 1916 presented her rationale in the form of an interview:

> Yes, of course, I have designed gowns for most women of note in the world...and I shall continue to do this through the "Lucile" establishments in London, Paris, New York, and Chicago.

31. [Display Ad 54—No Title], *New York Times* (Oct. 3, 1915), 85, emphasis in original.

32. [Display Ad 4—No Title], *New York Times* (Oct. 21, 1916), 4. Although it is not clear whether Wood or Lucy made this deal, the fact that he did not mention the Oliver Typewriter Company in his complaint implies that he was responsible.

33. Quoted in Etherington-Smith and Pilcher, *The "It" Girls*, 171.

> But what of it? It is nothing.... [I]t has been *my one dream* to make clothes for the women who have *not* hundreds of dollars to spend on one frock.... I am going to design clothes for the women who have twenty-five or fifty or ten dollars to spend.[34]

This passage illuminates Lucy's self-branding strategy. She began her career as Lucile, designing dresses for high-society women. Having ceded that name to her husband, she sought to extend an alternative, Lady Duff-Gordon, to the middle-class and working-class women who read her syndicated columns. Lucy was no political revolutionary but, like the modernists cited by Tratner, she sought to align herself—or at least her aristocratic name—with the masses.

The problem was that, given her agreement with Wood, she no longer controlled the commercial use of that name either. When he learned of her deal with Sears, Roebuck, he sued. She answered by declaring her contract with him void for lack of mutuality, claiming that he had promised her nothing in return for the exclusive right to place endorsements under the Lady Duff-Gordon label. The case moved swiftly through the courts, ending in the New York Court of Appeals, which upheld the validity of their agreement. *Wood v. Lucy, Lady Duff-Gordon* concerned contractual obligations, yet it was prominently cited by the Second Circuit Court of Appeals in the 1953 *Haelan* decision that gave the right of publicity its name. Judge Frank could have foregrounded any number of other decisions granting individuals, even celebrities, control over the commercial use of their names, signatures, photographs, and like indices of identity. What was it about Lucy's case that attracted him?

I suggest there were two factors. First was the stature of the decision. Contract law in the United States was in flux during the late nineteenth and early twentieth centuries. The technological and financial innovations that were informing modernism were also creating a dynamic business environment that led parties to construct agreements with more "open" terms than was customary.[35] Courts struggled to find principles that would allow them to determine the enforceability of open contracts like Lucy's agreement with Wood. In deciding the case, the New York Court of Appeals was pronouncing upon an unsettled area of the law. Its decision, written by future Supreme Court justice Benjamin Cardozo, became influential soon after its delivery in December 1917. "The law has outgrown its

---

34. Quoted in Victor Goldberg, *Framing Contract Law: An Economic Perspective* (Cambridge, MA: Harvard University Press, 2006), 56.

35. Walter F. Pratt Jr. makes this argument in "American Contract Law at the Turn of the Century," *South Carolina Law Review* 39 (1987–1988): 415–464.

primitive stage of formalism when the precise word was the sovereign talisman, and every slip was fatal," Cardozo wrote. "A promise may be lacking, and yet the whole writing may be 'instinct with an obligation,' imperfectly expressed. If that is so, there is a contract."[36] First-year law students pored over these words as early as 1921, when *Wood v. Lucy, Lady Duff-Gordon* was included in two contract law casebooks.[37] Victor Goldberg's claim that "[e]veryone knows about *Wood v. Lucy, Lady Duff-Gordon*... [because] it is in virtually every Contracts casebook and is still widely cited by courts" was already true in 1953 when the Second Circuit decided *Haelan*.[38] Identifying this case as a precedent for the right of publicity, Judge Frank was associating a novel idea with a thoroughly examined legal classic. If there was a problem with this newly articulated right, he was suggesting, it would have been noted long ago.

The second factor leading the *Haelan* court to *Wood v. Lucy, Lady Duff-Gordon* was that the disputed contract acknowledged the commercial value of Lucy's name and her right to exploit it. As a legal doctrine distinct from the right to privacy, the right of publicity developed as courts determined that plaintiffs held property rights in the indices of their identity. Warren and Brandeis constructed the right to privacy as a protection of human dignity, arguing that a person should have the right to authorize the commercial use of his or her persona because unauthorized commercial uses could be harmful. In other words, they staked out the right to privacy in the field of tort (personal injury) law rather than property law. This difference is important because right-of-publicity claims are property claims, declarations of ownership of one's name, signature, likeness, photographic image, and so on. As early as the aforementioned *Roberson* case, judges were holding that a person has property rights in the indices of his or her identity. By 1907 and *Edison v. Edison Polyform Mfg. Co.*, the idea had matured and been extended to a celebrity plaintiff.[39] From Judge Frank's point of view, these cases posed problems because they promoted the right of privacy. To cite them as precedents for the right of publicity would only have blurred the line that the Second Circuit wished to draw between a right that protects feelings and a right that protects property. The significance of *Wood v. Lucy, Lady Duff-Gordon* was that it presented as a contractual condition the ownership of celebrity identity. Obviously, Lucy held property rights in her famous name: that was how she could grant to Wood her exclusive rights to

---

36. *Wood v. Lucy, Lady Duff-Gordon*, 118 N.E. 214 (N.Y. 1917).

37. Arthur L. Corbin, *Cases on the Law of Contracts* (St. Paul, MN: West, 1921); and George P. Costigan Jr., *Cases on the Law of Contracts* (Chicago: Callaghan, 1921).

38. Goldberg, *Framing Contract Law*, 43.

39. *Edison v. Edison Polyform Mfg. Co.*, 67 A. 394 (N.J. Ch. 1907).

its commercial use. Just as obviously, her name had economic value. One recital in the contract read: "Whereas, [Lucy, Lady Duff-Gordon's] personal approval and endorsement over her own name of certain articles and fabrics used not only in the manufacture of dresses, millinery and other adjuncts of fashion, but also divers other articles to people of taste has a distinct monetary value to the manufacturers of such articles used."[40]

The issue in *Wood v. Lucy, Lady Duff-Gordon* was the plaintiff's implied promise, not the value of the defendant's name or her ownership of it. If Lucy's name had not been a valuable subject as property, Wood would never have bargained for it. Upholding their contract, Judge Cardozo implicitly acknowledged her right of publicity. For this reason, Judge Frank cited the case thirty-six years later when he stated on behalf of his Second Circuit colleagues: "We think the New York decisions recognize such a right."

We cannot know exactly what Lucy was thinking when she inked the deal with Sears, Roebuck and Company. Perhaps, like many actresses of the age, she was uncomfortable that she had granted a businessman rights to her name and, given the fluid state of the law concerning personality rights, thought that reasserting her control of it was worth the risk.[41] This supposition jibes well with other elements in Lucy's story. From the start of her career, she understood that she could use an index of her identity as a marketing tool. Having abandoned her maiden and (first) married name, she became Lucile, designer for the stars. Having lost control of that brand, she invented another, Lady Duff-Gordon, which she aimed at the masses. But a name is more than a marketing tool. It is also an indicator of one's personality, one's "unique self and private identity," in Jameson's words. Perhaps Lucy broke her agreement with Wood because she could not tolerate giving yet another man exclusive control of her identity. Perhaps, like Hedda Tesman née Gabler, she found it hard to surrender her name.

40. Quoted in Goldberg, *Framing Contract Law*, 51.
41. See Marlis Schweitzer, "The Mad Search for Beauty: Actresses' Testimonials, the Cosmetics Industry, and the Democratization of Beauty," *Journal of the Gilded Age and Progressive Era* 4 (2005): 255–292.

PART FIVE

Biography, Privacy, and Copyright

9 "The Quick in Pursuit of the Dead"

Ian Hamilton and the Clash between Literary Biographers and Copyright Owners

Mark A. Fowler

The novelist and essayist Elizabeth Hardwick once lampooned biographers as "the quick in pursuit of the dead."[1] The contest between biographers and their subjects—living or dead—is not, however, as unequal as Hardwick's quip might suggest. In order to substantiate their interpretations of their subjects' lives and works, biographers are generally expected to quote from published and unpublished source materials authored by their subjects. This is especially so in a biography of a novelist, poet, playwright, or other literary figure whose way with words may be the subject's most notable achievement. Primary materials such as diaries and letters often provide the most contemporaneous record of what a person was thinking. And writers or their estates, the rights-holders in such materials, enjoy considerable bargaining power in dealing with biographers. Indeed, it is commonplace for copyright owners to demand the opportunity to review and approve a biography as the quid pro quo for authorizing quotations from the

This chapter is intended to provide general information about U.S. copyright law and not specific legal or professional advice. If legal assistance is required, the reader should consult an experienced attorney who can review and assess all of the facts and circumstances relevant to the reader's situation and provide appropriate counsel.

1. Elizabeth Hardwick, *Sight Readings: American Fictions* (New York: Random House, 1998), 299.

subject's works when those quotations exceed the limited and uncertain bounds of fair use.

Copyright may constrain the biographical enterprise in several ways. The duration of copyright has grown progressively longer over the course of history. As of 2010, only works first published prior to 1923 can be said with immediate certainty to be in the public domain in the United States; determining the copyright status of later works—particularly works that may not have been published—may require careful and time-consuming research.[2] In countries where duration of copyright has long been computed from the date of the author's death, even some pre-1923 works remain copyright protected. As a result, many, if not most, of the published and unpublished writings of many prominent twentieth-century literary figures continue to be protected by copyright many decades after their deaths. The doctrine of fair use (or fair dealing, as it is known in the United Kingdom) does allow for some quotation without permission of the copyright owner for purposes such as criticism, comment, news reporting, teaching, scholarship, or research.[3] There are, however, few bright lines in fair use, no clear assurances that quoting, for example, thirty words from a two-page unpublished letter is always fair use, while quoting a hundred words from the same letter is not. When biographers and copyright owners cannot come to an understanding on permissions, there is always the risk that litigation may ensue, generating unwelcome legal expenses, potentially disrupting publication plans, and even adversely affecting a scholar's reputation. In short, copyright gives the subjects of literary biographies or their estates legal leverage to influence and, to a limited degree, censor biographers, as this chapter's touchstone figure, Ian Hamilton, discovered to his regret.[4]

2. For a useful guide to the duration of copyright in the United States, see Laura N. Gasaway, "When Works Pass into the Public Domain," www.unc.edu/~unclng/public-d. htm (accessed June 13, 2009). For a more detailed discussion of the copyright status of James Joyce's works in the United States, the European Union, the United Kingdom, Ireland, Canada, and Australia, see Paul K. Saint-Amour, Michael Groden, Carol Shloss, and Robert Spoo, "James Joyce: Copyright, Fair Use, and Permission: Frequently Asked Questions," *James Joyce Quarterly* 44 (2007): 753–784, or the online version: http://english.osu.edu/research/organizations/ijjf/copyrightfaqs.cfm (accessed July 23, 2009).

3. 17 U.S.C. § 107.

4. Living individuals may sometimes also invoke libel laws to attack unflattering biographies, as in the 2002 case brought by Clint Eastwood against the author and publisher of the book *Clint: The Life and Legend* by Patrick McGilligan (New York: St. Martin's, 2002). In the United States, at least, libel actions cannot be brought to vindicate the reputations of the dead. Moreover, in civil libel actions, requests for injunctive relief barring publication are almost never granted; the remedies are usually limited to money damages. It should be noted that a few states continue to have antiquated criminal libel statutes on the books, some of which purport to prohibit defamation of both the living and the dead.

Even when the subjects of biographies are dead, copyright law gives them certain advantages over their living pursuers. Hardwick's term *pursuit*, moreover, captures the sense in which the biographer trails behind her subject, who might be said to have both a legal and a temporal head start. This chapter focuses on how developments in U.S. copyright law since the mid-1980s have influenced the craft of scholarly life writing. Partly because biographers labor in the wake of their subjects, the last few decades have been rich ones for biographies of modernist writers, composers, and artists. They have sometimes been embattled ones, too, for those who study modernists and their circles, with a number of high-profile copyright cases pitting biographers against estates. Although I do not focus explicitly on modernism here, I do provide a narrative survey of late twentieth- and early twenty-first-century U.S. copyright law as it pertains to literary biography. I hope that such a survey may be of use to scholars who study modernism. After all, those modernist writers who published actively during the interwar period are among the earliest figures whose post-1922 work is still protected, and this requires their biographers to become schooled in the particulars of the fair use doctrine and proficient in "writing around" material that cannot be directly quoted at length. In what follows, I will pay particular attention to fair use and writing around in both their technical and practical aspects as well as to the typical course and financial stakes of infringement litigation. My aim is neither to discourage scholars and biographers from pursuing projects involving protected works nor to spur them to reckless confrontations with copyright owners. Instead, I want through a combination of hopeful and cautionary accounts to suggest that copyright generally permits biographers to quote less than they wish but more than they fear it will; that the question of permissions should inform biographical projects from the outset; and that many literary biographies entail, of necessity, some compromise between the quick and the dead.

The Salinger Case

In 1983, Ian Hamilton began work on a biography of the reclusive novelist and short story writer J. D. Salinger. Hamilton was no Kitty Kelley; he was a poet and an editor of good reputation and had just published a well-reviewed biography of his friend the poet Robert Lowell. And as an admirer of Salinger, he was by no means bent on diminishing the novelist's personal or literary reputation. Early on, Hamilton wrote Salinger a letter to advise him of the project and to seek his cooperation. Salinger refused, advising Hamilton that he preferred not to have his biography written and that he had "borne all the exploitation and loss of privacy I can possibly bear in a single lifetime."[5]

Despite Salinger's rebuff, Hamilton "continued to regard the publication of a study of the relationship between [Salinger's] life and work as an appropriate effort."[6] He went forward with research on the biography, tentatively entitled *J. D. Salinger: A Writing Life*, locating several repositories of unpublished Salinger letters that the recipients had donated to libraries at Harvard, Princeton, the University of Texas, and other institutions. Several acquaintances of the writer also shared with Hamilton their private collections of letters that Salinger had written to them. These documents had been largely overlooked by other scholars who had set out to chronicle Salinger's life and literary career. Hamilton believed that the letters offered significant insights into Salinger's life and thoughts, and he quoted from many of them in his manuscript, which was scheduled to be published by Random House in 1986. "I regard these letters as a tremendous autobiographical source," he said. "In my view, it would be totally inconsistent with the craft of biography to omit such materials."[7]

It may be useful here to summarize the respective rights of the author and the recipient of a letter under the copyright laws of the United States. The recipient becomes the owner of the tangible physical property and may therefore show the letter to others, sell it, give it away, or destroy it.[8] The recipient does not, however, obtain the right to reproduce or publish the letter. This "reproduction right" is reserved exclusively to the owner of the copyright—that is, to the author or his heirs or transferees, except to the limited extent authorized by the doctrine of fair use.[9]

---

5. J. D. Salinger letter to Ian Hamilton (undated), Exhibit B to Affidavit of J. D. Salinger, sworn to Oct. 1, 1986, filed with the district court in *Salinger v. Random House, Inc., and Ian Hamilton*, 650 F. Supp. 413 (S.D.N.Y. 1986) (Leval, J.) (hereafter cited as *Salinger*). I was one of the attorneys representing Hamilton and Random House. My firm and I also represented the biographers and publishers in the *New Era* and *Wright* litigations described below.

6. Affidavit of Ian Hamilton, sworn to on Oct. 3, 1986, filed with the district court in *Salinger*.

7. Ibid.

8. Compare 17 U.S.C. § 106 with 17 U.S.C. § 109. See also *Grigsby v. Breckinridge*, 2 Bush 480, 1867 WL 4043 (Ky. App. 1867) (recipient may destroy original letters). It has, however, sometimes been contended, usually in the context of actual or threatened litigation, e.g., in *Wright v. Warner Books, Inc.*, 748 F. Supp. 105 (S.D.N.Y. 1990) (Walker, J.) (hereafter *Wright*), that a recipient who has retained original letters may have an equitable duty to provide copies to the copyright owner, if requested to do so, for the purpose of preserving the intellectual property or allowing the copyright owner to register the copyrights.

9. Or, to put it another way, absent an express writing to the contrary, transfer of ownership of the tangible physical property of the letter does not carry with it the transfer of the copyright.

Fair use, as I indicated earlier, holds that some reproduction of copyrighted works is permissible for purposes such as criticism, comment, news reporting, and scholarship. However, several court cases decided prior to the enactment of the 1976 act suggested that fair use of unpublished letters and diaries was more restricted than the use that could be made of published materials.[10] And again, even with respect to published works, fair use has always been one of the murkiest areas of copyright law, with no clear-cut means for determining the amount of unauthorized quotation that may reliably be considered "fair."

Although not a lawyer, Hamilton knew that he could not, consistent with fair use, quote the entirety of Salinger's letters. At the same time, he believed that some verbatim quotation was necessary in order to capture the nuances of Salinger's thinking and the expressiveness of his prose even in casual correspondence. In addition to including limited verbatim quotation in his manuscript, Hamilton tried, as he put it,

> to report the factual material contained in the letters as accurately as I could, recognizing my obligation under the copyright laws to express these facts in my own words. I will not pretend that this was an easy task. Mr. Salinger, after all, was an eyewitness to the events he describes, and his great talent has enabled him to depict those events vividly and precisely.[11]

A book dealer obtained a reviewer's copy of Hamilton's work while it was still in page proofs and sent it to Salinger's literary agent, who in turn shared it with Salinger. Shortly thereafter, Salinger's attorneys filed suit in federal district court in New York, primarily alleging copyright infringement of the letters.[12] They sought a preliminary injunction barring publication of the biography in its then-current

10. See *Harper & Row, Publishers, Inc. v. Nation Enterprises*, 471 U.S. 539, 551 (1985) (discussing the status of the law pertaining to unpublished works prior to the enactment of the 1976 Copyright Act and its virtual per se refusal to apply fair use thereto). See also William Patry, *The Fair Use Privilege in Copyright Law* (Washington, DC: Bureau of National Affairs, 1985), 436–441 (noting that the common law in the United Kingdom denied the application of fair use, or "fair dealing" as the corresponding doctrine is usually called there, to unpublished works).

11. Affidavit of Ian Hamilton, sworn to on Oct. 3, 1986, filed in *Salinger.*

12. The litigation gave rise to a deposition of Salinger, which would be one of the few interviews (albeit involuntary) he gave during the last four decades of his life. Much of the transcript was designated confidential, but the following exchange between Salinger and my partner, Robert Callagy, was not:

> Q. Have you written any full-length works of fiction during the past 20 years which have not been published?
> A. Could you frame that a different way? What do you mean by a full-length work? You mean ready for publication?

form. The case was randomly assigned to Judge Pierre Leval, who found that Hamilton had made fair use of the letters. "Hamilton's use of copyrighted expression is so minimal," he concluded, "it is difficult to perceive any harm to Salinger. The wound he has suffered is not from infringement of his copyright but from the publication of a biography that trespasses on his wish for privacy. The copyright law does not give him protection against that form of injury."[13] On appeal, a three-judge panel of the Second Circuit Court of Appeals reversed Judge Leval's decision and directed entry of a preliminary injunction. Central to the court of appeals' decision was the view that unpublished works "normally enjoy complete protection against copying any protected expression." The court of appeals also criticized the lower court for the perceived failure to include all instances of impermissibly close paraphrase in its analysis of the "amount and substantiality" of the portions of the letters that were used. "The biographer has no inherent right to copy the 'accuracy' or the 'vividness' of the letter writer's expression," the court said.[14] The U.S. Supreme Court declined to review the court of appeals' decision.

The L. Ron Hubbard Case

Over the next several years, the courts and Congress struggled to clarify the scope of fair use of unpublished source materials in biographies. The next judicial showdown involved a very different variety of biography: *Bare-Faced Messiah*, written by journalist Russell Miller, which chronicled the life of the science fiction writer and founder

---

Q. As opposed to a short story or a fictional piece or a magazine submission.
A. It's very difficult to answer. I don't write that way. I just start writing fiction and see what happens to it.
Q. Maybe an easier way to approach this is, would you tell me what your literary efforts have been in the field of fiction within the last 20 years?
A. Could I tell you or would I tell you?

Ultimately, Salinger acknowledged that, during his years of isolation in New Hampshire, he had been writing "a work of fiction." He disclosed no details. Deposition of J. D. Salinger, taken on Oct. 7, 1986, 5–6. See also Ian Hamilton, *In Search of J. D. Salinger* (New York: Random House, 1988), 202.

13. *Salinger*, 650 F. Supp., 426. Judge Leval went on to become one of the federal judiciary's recognized authorities on copyright law. For his retrospective thoughts on *Salinger* and related cases, see Pierre N. Leval, "Toward a Fair Use Standard," *Harvard Law Review* 103 (1990): 1105–1161.

14. *Salinger*, 811 F.2d 90, 96 (2d Cir. 1987) (Newman, J.) (court of appeals decision reversing and remanding to the district court with instructions to enter a preliminary injunction). Like Judge Leval, Judge Jon Newman is regarded as especially well versed in copyright law.

of the Church of Scientology, L. Ron Hubbard. To some (certainly to Miller), Hubbard was a far less likable figure than Salinger. Under his leadership, Scientology established hundreds of counseling centers worldwide, which took in approximately $2 million per week from adherents who underwent a one-on-one counseling process known as "auditing." As Hubbard's followers proliferated, his legal entanglements multiplied. In the United States and abroad, he was accused of fraud and other crimes, and in 1979 several church members were convicted of charges stemming from the alleged infiltration of U.S. government agencies by means of burglaries, illegal wiretapping, and theft of government documents. Although he was a prolific novelist, Hubbard's greatest work of fiction may have been the mythical account he gave of events in his own life. One of the principal objectives of Miller's highly uncomplimentary biography was to contrast the discrepancies between Hubbard's invented public persona and the facts contained in his unpublished letters and diaries, to which Miller had gained access from various sources. According to court submissions, for example, in one letter quoted by Miller, Hubbard discusses converting Scientology into a "religion" for business reasons. In another letter (also according to the defendant's submissions), Hubbard falsely told his daughter that he was not her father.

Hubbard died in 1986 under circumstances that were as mysterious as his life. From 1987 through 1989, the church and its publishing arm, New Era Publications International, made every effort to frustrate publication of Miller's highly critical biography. They hired investigators to look into Miller's life, and they commenced whack-a-mole legal proceedings to block publication in England, Canada, and Australia; all three jurisdictions declined to enjoin Miller's book. Undaunted, New Era sued again in a last-ditch effort to prevent publication in the United States.

The international parade of litigation seemingly had little to do with the literary expressiveness of Hubbard's prose.[15] In declining to enjoin publication, the British courts concluded that the lawsuit there was instituted to "stifle criticism." In the United States, the church and New Era went so far as to offer to buy out Henry Holt's rights to publish the biography. The buy-out effort was scarcely motivated by admiration for Miller's work. As Judge Oakes noted in one of the saltier footnotes to appear in a federal court decision, the executor of the Hubbard estate, in his deposition, described *Bare-Faced Messiah* as "a scumbag book....full of bullshit."[16]

By the luck of the draw, the U.S. case, which was filed in federal court in New York, was assigned to none other than Pierre Leval, the judge who had handled the

15. Not that Hubbard's literary works are without economic value; the church claims that his fiction and nonfiction books have sold more than 100 million copies worldwide.

16. *New Era Publications International, ApS v. Henry Holt and Company, Inc.,* 873 F.2d 576, 594 (2d Cir. 1989) (Oakes, concurring) (hereafter cited as *New Era*).

Salinger case. In a remarkably detailed and scholarly thirty-five-page opinion, accompanied by an elaborately color-coded appendix, Judge Leval documented his findings with regard to the fair use justification for each and every quotation from Hubbard's published and unpublished materials. He concluded, "As to the book overall, I would conclude that fair use had been adequately demonstrated.... Hubbard's expression is taken primarily to show character flaws in a manner that cannot be accomplished without use of his words."[17] But Judge Leval went on to say that, "given *Salinger's* strong presumption against a finding of fair use for unpublished materials, I cannot conclude that the Court of Appeals would accord fair use protection to all of Miller's quotations, or that the biography as a whole would be considered non-infringing."[18] Despite the finding of infringement, Judge Leval nevertheless went on to take the extraordinary step of declining, on First Amendment grounds, to enter an injunction. "The grant of an injunction would...suppress an interesting, well researched, provocative study of a figure who, claiming both scientific and religious credentials, has wielded enormous influence over millions of people." After reviewing the legal authorities suggesting that an injunction in a case of infringement need not be automatic, Judge Leval wrote, "I have no difficulty concluding that this is one of those special circumstances in which the interests of free speech overwhelmingly exceed the plaintiff's interest in an injunction."[19] In essence, Judge Leval was politely telling the higher court that it was dead wrong in *Salinger* and that it had unnecessarily created a circumstance where copyright was impinging on fundamental free speech values.

New Era immediately appealed the denial of the injunction. Also by the luck of the draw, Judge Miner, who had been one of the three judges on the Second Circuit panel that had decided *Salinger*, ended up writing the majority opinion in the *New Era* appeal. Unrepentant in the face of Judge Leval's scarcely disguised disdain for the appellate decision in *Salinger*, Judge Miner reiterated his view that there is a "strong presumption against fair use of unpublished work," and unpublished primary source materials "normally enjoy complete protection" from any fair use quotation. "Since the copying of 'more than minimal amounts' of unpublished expressive material calls for an injunction barring the unauthorized use," he concluded, "the consequences of the district court's findings seem obvious."[20] In other words, an injunction would ordinarily follow as the night the day, with no special

17. *New Era*, 695 F. Supp. 1493, 1520 (S.D.N.Y. 1988) (Leval, J.; district court decision).
18. Ibid., 1524.
19. Ibid., 1528.
20. *New Era*, 873 F.2d 576, 584 (2d Cir. 1989) (Miner, J., court of appeals majority decision with separate concurrence by Oakes, C.J.).

breathing room because of First Amendment concerns. Nevertheless, Judge Miner found another way to avoid enjoining *Bare-Faced Messiah*. He seized on laches, an equitable defense against a plaintiff's "sleeping on its rights" that Miller's attorneys had invoked in the district court. Judge Miner concluded that because New Era had waited too long to seek injunctive relief against publication in the United States, and because the publisher of the biography had been damaged by that delay (incurring the expenses of printing, distribution, and marketing), New Era had lost any right to equitable relief. So publication could go forward, although New Era could pursue a claim for money damages.

In a concurring opinion, Judge Oakes agreed that an injunction should not issue against *Bare-Faced Messiah*, but went out of his way to express his concern that the language of the *Salinger* opinion restricting fair use of unpublished materials "might be taken too literally in another factual context [and] come back to haunt us." He emphasized, "Responsible biographers and historians constantly use primary sources, letters, diaries, and memoranda. Indeed, it would be *irresponsible* to ignore such sources of information."[21] Judge Oakes concluded that Judge Leval's novel First Amendment reasoning for denying the injunction should have been affirmed by the majority.

There was one more round in *New Era*. Miller and his publisher, Henry Holt, asked all of the judges of the appeals court to rehear the appeal *en banc*—a form of review rarely granted in the Second Circuit. In an extraordinary 7–5 vote, the Second Circuit declined to grant rehearing. Four of the five judges who dissented from the denial of rehearing felt compelled to state their belief that "copying some small amounts of unpublished expression to report facts accurately and fairly" must be deemed fair use and that an injunction should not automatically follow when a biographer or historian steps over the line.[22] But a separate concurrence by four judges who supported the denial of rehearing rejected the idea that there may be some added leeway for the quotation of unpublished works when it is necessary to convey facts. And they qualified only slightly the prospect that "under ordinary circumstances" an injunction must issue when "'more than minimal amounts' of unpublished expressive material is quoted."[23] This unabashed concurrence (the

21. Ibid., 596 (Oakes, concurring), emphasis in original.
22. *New Era*, 884 F.2d 659, 663 (2d Cir. 1989) (Newman, J., dissenting from the denial of request for rehearing *en banc*). The fact that Judge Newman wrote the *dissent* was striking since he had authored the court of appeals decision in *Salinger*. In the *New Era* case, Judge Newman candidly acknowledged that the *Salinger* opinion had gone too far in saying that "under ordinary circumstances, the copying of 'more than minimal amounts' of unpublished expressive material calls for an injunction barring the unauthorized use."
23. Ibid., 660 (Miner, J., concurring).

only insight into the thinking of the seven-judge majority of the Second Circuit that declined rehearing) left open the possibility that some small, but not clearly defined, amount of quotation from unpublished source materials was, simply put, against the law—an intolerable prospect for scholars. The Supreme Court declined to review the Second Circuit's remarkable disagreement in *New Era*.

Two commentators succinctly summarized the central problem with the Second Circuit's analysis in *New Era*:

> The Second Circuit majority in *New Era* departed from basic fair use principles that require an accommodation of competing interests and equities. Instead, it elevated one fact—the unpublished status of Hubbard's writings—to an almost insurmountable obstacle to a successful fair use defense. By handcuffing future considerations of the fair use defense in the context of unpublished writings, the Second Circuit ignored the explicit mandate that the equities must be flexibly balanced case by case.[24]

As to the practical effect of the decision in *New Era*, Pulitzer Prize–winning historian Arthur Schlesinger told *Newsweek*, "If the law were this way when I wrote the three volumes of *The Age of Roosevelt*, I might be two volumes short."[25]

The Richard Wright Case

The tide was, however, about to turn. The third case in the unpublished works trilogy involved a biography entitled *Richard Wright: Daemonic Genius* written by Margaret Walker (Alexander), an African-American poet. Ellen Wright, the novelist's

---

24. David J. Goldberg and Robert J. Bernstein, "Fair Use: The Biographer's Bane," *New York Law Journal* (May 19, 1989): 2.

25. David Kaplan, "The End of History," *Newsweek* (Dec. 25, 1989): 80. In the wake of *New Era*, Victor Kramer, an author and professor at Georgia State University, felt compelled to take the extraordinary step of commencing a declaratory judgment action seeking to establish, among other things, that his quotations from the manuscripts of James Agee, which Kramer sought to include in a book about Agee, qualified as fair use. See *Kramer v. Newman*, 749 F. Supp. 542 (S.D.N.Y. 1990). Another example of how bad the climate had become: an amicus brief submitted by PEN American Center and the Authors Guild, Inc., in support of the biographer's application to the Supreme Court for certiorari in *New Era* (which was denied) indicated that, prior to the publication of the biography of John Connally entitled *The Lone Star*, the publisher insisted that James Reston Jr. remove all quotations from Connally's letters to Lyndon Johnson, which were deposited in the public files of a presidential library.

widow, objected to a series of quotations in the biography drawn primarily from unpublished letters that Wright had written to Margaret Walker after the two had become friends when they were both working with the Works Progress Administration in Chicago during the Great Depression. There was no dispute that the physical letters belonged to Walker but, remember, the "reproduction right" did not. The reasons for Ellen Wright's objections to the quotations were never entirely clear. However, they appeared to have been partly political and partly personal. Ellen Wright, who was white, and Richard Wright, who was black, had both been members of the American Communist Party. Ellen contended that her husband had consistently adhered to a Marxist view that racism was cultivated by the ruling economic class in order to divide white workers from black workers and that it could best be overcome by a united, multiracial workers' movement. Margaret Walker, however, saw Richard Wright as a herald of black power, with its emphasis on African Americans seeking to gain political and economic control within their own communities. Ellen Wright objected to Margaret Walker's use of Richard Wright's correspondence in a biography that (Mrs. Wright believed) fundamentally misinterpreted her late husband's political world view. Additionally, by some accounts, there was a romantic aspect to Margaret Walker's friendship with Richard Wright in Chicago; Walker believed, rightly or wrongly, that Ellen Wright resented her for that reason, even though Ellen first met Richard Wright in 1941, years after his stint with Walker in the WPA.

At the trial court stage, Judge John Walker (no relation to Margaret Walker) found that the quotations from Richard Wright's letters qualified as fair use. While he acknowledged that *Salinger* continued to be an authoritative statement of the law in the Second Circuit, he emphasized that the unpublished status of materials, while an important factor, is not the only consideration in analyzing the second fair use factor, "the nature of the copyrighted work":

> [I]t is first important to remember once more what the Second Circuit said in *Salinger:* unpublished works *"normally* enjoy complete protection against copying any protected expression." *Salinger,* 811 F.2d at 97 [emphasis added]. The court's admonition compels two conclusions. First, by saying "normally," *the court refused to adopt a* per se *rule and left intact its instruction to proceed on a case-by-case basis;* and second, the court sought to protect expression, not merely any facts that might be set forth in unpublished materials. Having carefully reviewed the letters in question, and the ways in which Walker has paraphrased them, I conclude, without much difficulty, that Walker has used the letters not to recreate Wright's creative expression,

but simply to establish facts necessary to her biography, which often relies on her personal association with the late novelist.[26]

In *Salinger* and *New Era*, the Second Circuit had sounded very much like it *was* imposing a per se rule—in this case, a blanket rule that fair use does not apply at all to unpublished source materials, no matter what the individual circumstances may be. Judge Walker's reemphasis of a "case-by-case" analysis was implicitly an acknowledgment that the language in those cases ran the risk of being overprotective of copyright owners.

On appeal, a host of publishing and scholarly organizations submitted amicus briefs in support of the publisher and biographer.[27] While the Second Circuit did not run away from the overprotective language in the *Salinger* decision, it affirmed Judge Walker's central finding that the quotations did not infringe Ellen Wright's copyrights in her husband's letters:

> In *Salinger*, we held that unpublished works "*normally* enjoy complete protection against copying any protected expression."…Neither *Salinger, Harper & Row*, nor any other case, however, erected a *per se* rule regarding unpublished works. The fair use test remains a totality inquiry, tailored to the particular facts of each case.[28]

Biographers could at last breathe a bit easier.

In 1992, Congress completed the job of undoing the mischief that the Second Circuit had wrought by its nearly absolutist language in *Salinger* and *New Era*. In direct response to the two decisions, Congress amended § 107 of the Copyright Act to add the following language: "The fact that a work is unpublished shall not itself bar a finding of fair use if such finding is made upon consideration of all the [fair use] factors."[29] The amendment had an immediate salubrious effect; in 1993, the

---

26. *Wright*, 748 F. Supp., 111 (district court decision; first emphasis in original as indicated; second emphasis added). Judge Walker, a first cousin to George Herbert Walker Bush, was and is a member of the Second Circuit Court of Appeals; he handled the *Wright* case in the district court by designation.

27. These included the Association of American Publishers, PEN American Center, the Authors Guild, Inc., the American Council of Learned Societies, the American Historical Association, the American Political Science Association, the Modern Language Association of America, and the Organization of American Historians.

28. *Wright*, 953 F.2d, 740 (2d Cir. 1991) (majority opinion by Judge Meskill; court of appeals decision), internal citations omitted.

29. Congress added this sentence to § 107 of the Copyright Act at the urging of book publishers, writers groups, and scholarly organizations, which argued that the *Salinger* and *New Era* decisions were chilling the preparation and publication of, in particular, scholarly biographies and works of twentieth-century history. See *Fair Use and Unpublished Works:*

Ninth Circuit held in *Norse v. Henry Holt & Company* that biographer Ted Morgan had not infringed the copyright of beat poet Harold Norse in quoting phrases from his unpublished letters in *Literary Outlaw*, a biography of William Burroughs. And since 1992, the frequency of major cases against biographers and historians has markedly declined.

The Salinger-Hubbard-Wright trilogy of cases is striking for the fact that money was not the immediate motivation for any of the plaintiffs. Neither Salinger, nor the Church of Scientology, nor Ellen Wright ever signaled that, for a fair fee, they would consider granting the biographers permission to quote freely from the letters and diaries at issue. In each case, the plaintiff's goal was to discourage publication of a biography or, at the very least, to radically alter its contents.[30] In this regard, the cases are the high-water mark in the long tradition of granting or withholding copyright permissions to shape literary reputations.

Aside from the five-year span from 1986 to 1991, actual litigation over quotation in biographies has not been especially common, but over the years there have been many instances of threatened litigation. Indeed, the implicit threat of litigation underlies many communications between copyright owners and biographers, resulting in too many instances of self-censorship where scholars forbear from quoting extensively from their subject's published or unpublished works for fear of being sued. Indeed, some projects die in the cradle because a scholar believes that a literary estate will never grant permission to quote and will not tolerate quotation that flirts with the outer limits of fair use. There is no means of determining the number of projects that have been scuttled or drastically re-engineered in the face of opposition from copyright owners. The accounts of censorship or self-censorship are mostly anecdotal. But one veteran litigant, having lost his case and altered his book accordingly, chose to chronicle some of the noteworthy battles between literary estates and biographers over the last five centuries.

Joint Hearing on S. 2370 and H.R. 4263 before the Subcommittee on Patents, Copyrights and Trademarks of the Senate Committee on the Judiciary and the Subcommittee on Courts, Intellectual Property, and the Administration of Justice of the House Committee on the Judiciary, 101st Cong., 2nd sess., 196–197 (1990) (written statement of American Historical Association, the Organization of American Historians, the National Writers Union, the Authors Guild, Inc., PEN American Center, and the Association of American Publishers). As one legal commentator has explained, it was "a very modest amendment" that "endorses *Wright v. Warner Books*" and "merely cautions the courts not to erect a *per se* rule barring fair use based solely on the unpublished nature of the work." William Patry, *Copyright Law and Practice* (Washington, DC: Bureau of National Affairs, 1994), 1:767.

30. Judge Oakes noted that the executor of Hubbard's estate testified in his deposition that "any biography that is not objectively favorable to Mr. Hubbard" would not be approved for publication. *New Era*, 873 F.2d, 594.

A Tradition of Conflict

Even though he had suffered through eighteen months of court proceedings, Ian Hamilton did not abandon his study of Salinger. By law, injunctions that implicate First Amendment concerns must be narrowly tailored, and Hamilton had been enjoined only from publishing his book in its "then current form." During the year after the final ruling, he rewrote his manuscript, excluding virtually all direct quotations and close paraphrases from the letters that he had discovered. He then added a blow-by-blow account of his legal battle with Salinger. In 1988, the revised work appeared under the new title *In Search of J. D. Salinger*. It was not the book that Hamilton had wanted to publish, but it has much to offer, including insights into the autobiographical origins of short stories such as "For Esme—with Love and Squalor" and the models for the Glass family who populates many of Salinger's works. Hamilton's book is also an engaging work of literary criticism: "When the Hamilton mind goes to work on the [Salinger short] stories, it's something to see," Nick Hornby said in 2003.[31]

The legal battle scarred Hamilton, and even after he published *In Search of J. D. Salinger* he was not yet ready to put the experience entirely behind him. Hamilton wrote a series of essays on the long history of animosity between copyright owners and literary biographers, which were collected in *Keepers of the Flame* and published in 1993. The collection describes campaigns of literary reputation shaping carried out by the heirs of Donne, Pope, Burns, Byron, Carlyle, Tennyson, Stevenson, James, and others. Rupert Brooke's mother, for example, was described as a "dragon in the path" of her son's literary co-executor who, through her control over the copyright in his letters, succeeded in micromanaging the early accounts of Brooke's life to suppress evidence of his sexual entanglements; the early authorized depictions of Brooke contained no mentions of his "gloomy, flippant, and sardonic sides, there was no offensive language, no girlfriends"—and certainly no boyfriends.[32] Hamilton also described the determined efforts of the famous to manage their own legacies. George Orwell instructed his heirs to countenance no authorized biographies (*KF*, 292). W. H. Auden shared the sentiment, directing his executor, Edward Mendelson, to assist in "making biography impossible" and asking friends to destroy

---

31. Nick Hornby, *The Polysyllabic Spree* (San Francisco: McSweeney's Believer Books, 2004), 18. This volume collects a year's worth of Hornby's "Stuff I've Been Reading" columns from the *Believer;* his discussion of Hamilton originally appeared there in September 2003.

32. Ian Hamilton, *Keepers of the Flame: Literary Estates and the Rise of Biography* (London: Pimlico, 1993), 233. Hereafter cited in the text as *KF*.

all of his letters: "Biographies are always superfluous and usually in bad taste," he said. (As it turned out, Mendelson decided that Auden's instructions were "flexible enough to be bent backwards"; *KF*, 292). Franz Kafka famously directed, "Everything I leave behind me is to be burned unread...even to the last page," but his executor, Max Brod, equally famously disregarded the instruction and rescued Kafka's novels from the flames (*KF*, 291–292). In order to confound unauthorized biographers, Thomas Hardy went so far as to author his own "biography" and "[have] it put out, post-mortem" under the name of his second wife, Florence. Hardy "toiled on his grand deception for ten years," and it was not until 1940, twelve years after his death, that "the subterfuge was publicly exposed" (*KF*, 241).

Hamilton mostly confined his studies to what he called "dead, out of copyright, estates," adding, "I learned enough from my study of these to shy away from too much probing of the present-day, and not just for legal reasons" (*KF*, viii). This reluctance probably explains his decision not to write at length about the dispute between Valerie Eliot, T. S. Eliot's widow, and Peter Ackroyd. But he knew it well, the Ackroyd-Eliot contretemps having been cited by the defendants in their submissions in the *Salinger* case as evidence of the perils of a per se rule against the quotation of unpublished source materials. In the preface of his 1984 biography of Eliot, Ackroyd had noted: "I am forbidden by the Eliot estate to quote from Eliot's published work, except for purposes of fair comment in a critical context, or to quote from Eliot's unpublished work or correspondence." As Ackroyd explained in a later essay, "I wrote to Mrs. Eliot explaining my intentions; but since she is bound by her husband's wishes that there should be no biography, she could offer me no help. Faber and Faber, Eliot's publishers, were charmingly oblivious to my pressing need to write such a book and they declined to help."[33]

Valerie Eliot was not moved by Ackroyd's public complaints: "Ackroyd knew when he set out that Tom had said: No biography. So to start bleating at the end about not being able to quote from the poetry, when everyone else has to obey the same rules, is pretty feeble."[34] No authorized biography of Eliot has yet appeared, owing to his widow's continued tight control over the copyrights in his work and particularly in his unpublished letters.[35]

33. Peter Ackroyd, *The Collection: Journalism, Reviews, Essays, Short Stories, Lectures* (London: Random House, 2001), 374–376.

34. Quoted in Ian Hamilton, "Keepers of the Flame," *New Statesman* (May 29, 2000) (article with the same title as Hamilton's book, which noted that Valerie Eliot has also said that, despite her husband's wishes, she will probably commission an authorized biography some day, "after I've done the letters").

35. Karen Christensen, "Dear Mrs. Eliot," *Guardian* (Jan. 29, 2005) (arguing that "Eliot's reputation is done no good by the delay").

The Costs of Copyright Litigation

Estates have two potential sources of legal leverage over biographers. Sometimes, a copyright owner will control access to the tangible physical works, making them available only to those who will contractually agree to conditions governing their use.[36] More often, however, the power of a copyright owner to sue for infringement is the implicit threat that underlies all negotiations over permission to quote and any fees to be charged. Most negotiations between biographers and literary estates are conducted, amicably or grudgingly, without the involvement of lawyers and the courts. But sometimes, a scholar's aims will not be compatible with the demands of the rights-holder. Scholars who are unwilling to accede to the copyright owner's terms (whether they be editorial or financial) must either limit their quotations and close paraphrasings of the copyrighted work so that they fall within the (again, imprecise) bounds of fair use or push those bounds at the risk of legal action.[37]

In order to provide some perspective on the balance of power in a dispute over permission to quote, it may be useful to trace the trajectory and financial implications of a typical copyright infringement dispute. When a copyright owner notifies an author and publisher that she may assert a copyright infringement claim, it sets in motion a complex series of events. The economics of threatened litigation may have a profound effect on the outcome, and the risk-averse tendencies of universities, insurance companies, and some (but not all) publishers often predispose the outcome in favor of the rights-holder.

Before commencing a lawsuit, a copyright owner will often authorize his attorney to send a cease-and-desist letter warning that such an action is imminent unless the scholar cures any perceived infringement. A warning letter is not a prerequisite to

36. For example, estates sometimes donate manuscripts to archival libraries, subject to a contractual requirement that any requests for permission to photocopy or quote will be referred to the estates. Similarly, even though Salinger had not donated any of his letters to the libraries in which Hamilton located them, his attorneys argued (unsuccessfully) that Salinger was a "third-party beneficiary" of certain library access agreements that Ian Hamilton had signed and that Salinger could therefore pursue a breach-of-contract claim against Hamilton. *Salinger*, 650 F. Supp., 427. For a discussion of the role that library agreements play in literary scholarship, see Robert Spoo, "Copyright Law and Archival Research," *Journal of Modern Literature* 24 (2000–2001): 205–212.

37. Of course, even if a scholar has conformed to fair use, the copyright owner may nevertheless sue for purposes of intimidation. However, a plaintiff does incur some risk in bringing a less than meritorious lawsuit. Unlike most other litigation under the American system, the losing party in a copyright case may sometimes be required to pay the prevailing party's reasonable attorneys' fees and court costs.

filing a civil complaint. It does, however, provide a quick and inexpensive way for the copyright owner to impress upon the scholar and her publisher that a lawsuit is likely and therefore the copyright owner's demands should not be ignored. A cease-and-desist letter may give rise to a number of legal and financial consequences. First, if the accused work has not yet been published, the publisher must decide whether it dares to proceed with publication. Once the publisher has been put on notice of the potential infringement claim, the stakes in any ensuing litigation may be higher because, as described below, "willful infringement" may be grounds for increasing certain money damage remedies available to a prevailing plaintiff under the Copyright Act. Second, regardless of whether the work has or has not been published, if the publisher has media perils insurance that covers copyright infringement claims, it may be contractually obligated under the terms of its policy to notify the insurer promptly of the potential claim or else run the risk that the insurer will have a basis to refuse to pay for the cost of the legal defense and any damages or settlement.[38] The obligation to notify the insurer may also have other financial implications, for example, the publisher will likely be concerned that infringement claims may push up the price it pays for insurance. Third, if the publisher has no prior knowledge that a copyright dispute is brewing, a cease-and-desist letter may, rightly or wrongly, cause the scholar some professional embarrassment because of the possible implication that the scholar has submitted a work for publication without due regard for the intellectual property rights of another.

Too often, a simple cease-and-desist letter causes a publisher and scholar to abandon all plans to publish a work in order to avoid the costs and uncertainties of litigation or the effort and delay of revising the work to bring it safely within the bounds of fair use.[39] Scuttling publication is a regrettable outcome because, as I

38. Commercial publishers, university presses, and major periodicals often have insurance that covers infringement claims. Smaller journals and smaller print or internet publishers with limited budgets may not.

39. Many publishers will balance the cost of litigation against the revenues that the publication is likely to generate. In the case of journal articles, the revenues are, of course, small or nonexistent, ensuring that the economic balance (taken in isolation) will almost always weigh against going forward with publication. With respect to books, disputes over fair use quotation most often involve scholarly works, which also have limited commercial potential. (Hamilton's biography of Salinger was an exception.) Therefore, if a work has not yet been published, a publisher that resists a rights-holder's demand is often called upon to make a stand on principle. If the issue arises after books have already been printed, the economic balance shifts because the publisher has a substantial stake in establishing that it can lawfully sell its costly inventory. If a publication has already been released to the public, the balance shifts again because the publisher may face not just the possibility of an injunction, but also the risk of money damages for infringement, and therefore it has little choice but to vigorously defend the litigation.

will discuss below, with the benefit of detailed legal advice, it is usually possible to rewrite an accused work in a way that greatly reduces, if not eliminates, the risks of a successful lawsuit. Whether this can be done without significantly compromising the quality of the work is another question, one whose answer will depend on the nature and importance of the excised or paraphrased material.

If a copyright owner does commence a lawsuit, the ante is upped substantially. In the cities where most major publishers are located, the costs of full-blown litigation are very high, with experienced attorneys charging anywhere from $200 to $800 per hour. Depending upon the case and the law firm, the preparation and filing of the plaintiff's complaint (or the defendant's answer), by itself, may cost only a few thousand dollars.[40] Thereafter, the costs can quickly spiral upward. If a plaintiff's lawyer believes that he has a strong case, he is likely, as in the *Salinger* and *New Era* cases, to seek a preliminary injunction prohibiting the printing and distribution of the work until the court decides the ultimate merits of the case. A preliminary injunction proceeding is often an expensive proposition, sometimes involving expedited discovery (i.e., an exchange of documentary evidence and depositions of witnesses), sometimes involving a short trial, and almost always involving extensive legal briefing and oral arguments before the court. The issuance of an injunction can be a nightmare scenario for a publisher, leaving it with a warehouse filled with thousands of books that it has paid to print and bind but cannot sell. Indeed, the economic consequences of an injunction are often far greater than the money damages a defendant would face in the event of a final judgment in the plaintiff's favor. As a result, preliminary injunction proceedings tend to be hard fought, and when major law firms are involved it is not unusual for the defendants' legal fees alone to amount to many tens of thousands of dollars. A preliminary injunction usually entails a finding by the judge as to the plaintiff's likelihood—or unlikelihood—of success on the case's ultimate merits, at which point the parties to a copyright litigation often settle the case.

If the parties proceed with the case, however, full-blown discovery, summary judgment motions, or a trial on the merits will further tax the litigants' economic

---

40. Plaintiffs may sometimes be able to retain an attorney on a contingency fee basis, typically one-third of the amount recovered, although payment based upon an attorney's hourly rate is more common. Defendants have no comparable method of controlling their out-of-pocket costs, unless they have insurance that covers the infringement claim. As indicated above, some publishing companies have insurance that covers infringement claims; individuals rarely do. Some insurance companies will write media perils policies for individual authors for a particular work, but they generally require that a lawyer (acceptable to the insurer, paid by the author) review the manuscript before providing coverage, which can run several thousand dollars for a book-length work.

resources. In a forum such as New York or Los Angeles where lawyers' rates tend to be high, it is not unusual for each side's legal fees in a case involving a commercially significant work to amount to $100,000, $200,000, or (especially when technological issues are involved) even more. And there is the potential for money damages. A prevailing plaintiff is entitled to recover any actual damages she suffers as a result of the infringement plus the defendants' profits attributable to the infringement—to the extent that those profits are not taken into account in computing actual damages. The operational word is "profits," not "revenues." As a result, during the damages phase of a copyright infringement case, the defendant will seek to prove that its expenses offset most, if not all, of the revenues. Moreover, a plaintiff is only entitled to profits "attributable to the infringement." While the computation of such profits can involve a complex, qualitative assessment of what has been unlawfully copied, sometimes it amounts to little more than a simple mathematical proportion. For example, if 20 pages of A's 400-page book were unlawfully copied from B, the judge or jury might award B $\frac{20}{400\text{ths}}$ or 5 percent, of A's profits.

Because actual damages and profits attributable to an infringement may not amount to much or may be difficult to compute, the Copyright Act provides, at the election of a prevailing plaintiff, an alternative remedy known as "statutory damages." Imagine, for example, a situation where the defendant published, without authorization, an entire poem written by the plaintiff. Because even the *New Yorker* does not pay very much for poetry, the most that a prevailing plaintiff might hope to recover in actual damages or profits attributable to the infringement might be a few hundred dollars—scarcely enough to deter infringers or to provide an incentive to copyright owners to vindicate their rights. Recognizing this fact, Congress enacted the "statutory damages" scheme, which allows the judge or jury to award to a prevailing plaintiff an amount that it "considers just" between $750 and $30,000 for an inadvertent infringement and up to $150,000 in the case of a "willful infringement."

Finally, under certain circumstances, the Copyright Act allows a prevailing plaintiff or prevailing defendant to recover from the other party his costs and reasonable attorneys' fees.[41] Because, as we have seen, copyright litigation can be

---

41. The attorneys' fee shifting provision in the Copyright Act is in stark contrast to the usual practice under U.S. law where each party typically pays his own fees, regardless of whether he wins or loses. But there is a catch: to oversimplify somewhat, a prevailing copyright owner may only recover statutory damages and attorneys' fees if she has registered her copyright with the Copyright Office before the onset of the infringement. 17 U.S.C. § 412. This is, by far, the single most important advantage of registering copyrights.

extraordinarily expensive, the possibility that one side may end up paying the other side's attorneys' fees is a powerful dynamic in many copyright cases. An attorney who is confident that her client will prevail has a significant economic incentive to press her case aggressively, and an attorney who believes that her client is in the wrong has much to fear from the fee-shifting rule.

The expense of litigation, the possibility of an award of attorneys' fees, and the risk of an injunction barring the distribution of an allegedly infringing work largely account for the power of copyright holders who become embroiled in disputes with scholars.[42] The potential compensatory damages or profits attributable to the alleged infringement are often minimal by comparison.

Writing Around the Problem

One should not overestimate the power of copyright owners, but biographers and critics have recourse to two legal safety valves that limit rights-holders' control over protected works. The first is the doctrine of fair use, which permits some quotation of source material, including unpublished sources, so long as the quotation satisfies the imprecise standard set forth in 17 U.S.C. § 107. The second is a fundamental principle of copyright called the "idea/expression dichotomy." According to § 102(b) of the U.S. Copyright Act, "In no case does copyright protection for an original work of authorship extend to any idea, procedure, process, system, method of operation, concept, principle or discovery, regardless of the form in which it is described, explained, illustrated, or embodied in such a work." As the Second Circuit once put it in an important ruling on copyright, the idea/expression dichotomy "strike[s] a definitional balance between the First Amendment and the Copyright Act by permitting free communication of facts

---

42. *Shloss v. Estate of James Joyce* was a rare and interesting example of a scholar filing suit to obtain a declaratory judgment of non-infringement against a copyright owner who allegedly was improperly using the implied threat of litigation to discourage publication of a work that the copyright owner may have found objectionable for reasons having little to do with copyright. The ultimate settlement favored the biographer Carol Shloss. Regrettably, few authors are so fortunate to have such spirited, creative, pro bono legal representation. The cost of paying a lawyer an hourly rate to wage such a case would be prohibitive, and few lawyers would handle an alleged infringer's counterattack on a contingency basis, even if it were likely meritorious, because, despite the fee-shifting provision in the Copyright Act, the likelihood of recovering attorneys' fees in such a case would be the longest of long shots. Shloss was fortunate in this regard. Her motion seeking reimbursement for her reasonable attorneys' fees was granted by the court. See *Shloss v. Sweeney*, 515 F. Supp. 2d 1083, 1086 (N.D. Cal. 2007). Ultimately, a settlement was reached on the amount, and in September 2009 the estate paid $240,000 of the fees for and costs incurred by Shloss's attorneys.

while still protecting an author's expression."[43] In other words, a biographer or critic may restate in her own words the gist of what she finds in her subject's letters, diaries, and other source materials without violating the copyright in those works. In many cases, it is possible to write around protected material in this manner while still conveying the facts and ideas essential to analysis.

That said, extracting the ideas and facts from a protected work without intruding upon the author's expression is sometimes easier said than done. As one commentator, invoking Yeats, said, it can be like trying to "know the dancer from the dance."[44] According to the Second Circuit Court of Appeals, Ian Hamilton too often failed in that effort, replacing direct quotations from Salinger's letters with impermissibly close paraphrases that closely echoed Salinger's own original expression. The court illustrated its point with this example, among others:

> Salinger, expressing his unfavorable opinion of the 1940 presidential candi-
> date Wendell Willkie wrote [to Whit] Burnett: "He looks to me like a guy
> who makes his wife keep a scrapbook for him." Hamilton reports that
> Salinger "had fingered [Willkie] as the sort of fellow who makes his wife
> keep an album of his press clippings."[45]

In this particular instance, the court was probably correct in concluding that, by tracking Salinger's comparison, Hamilton had copied Salinger's expression. As Judge Newman put it, "The copier is not at liberty to avoid 'pedestrian' reportage by appropriating his subject's literary devices."[46] The court also included as another

---

43. *Harper & Row v. Nation Enterprises*, 723 F.2d 195, 203 (2d Cir. 1983), *rev'd on other grounds*, 471 U.S. 539 (1985).

44. Gregory J. Wrenn, "Comment: Federal Intellectual Property Protection for Computer Software Audio-Visual Look and Feel: The Lanham, Copyright and Patent Acts," *High Tech Law Journal* 4 (1989): 279, 297–307, quoting W. B. Yeats, "Among School Children," in *W. B. Yeats: The Poems*, ed. Richard Finneran (New York: Scribner's, 1983), 217.

45. *Salinger*, 811 F.2d, 93. In another unpublished letter, Salinger who, in 1941, had dated Oona O'Neill, the daughter of playwright Eugene O'Neill and the future wife of Charlie Chaplin, wickedly imagined a scene from the couple's married life: "I can see them at home evenings. Chaplin squatting grey and nude, atop his chiffonier, swinging his thyroid around his head by his bamboo cane, like a dead rat. Oona in an aquamarine gown, applauding madly from the bathroom." Here is Hamilton's report on the letter: "At one point in a letter to Burnett [Salinger] provides a pen portrait of the Happy Hour Chez Chaplin: the comedian, ancient and unclothed, is brandishing his walking stick—attached to the stick, and horribly resembling a lifeless rodent, is one of Chaplin's vital organs. Oona claps her hands in appreciation." Here, again, the Second Circuit believed Hamilton's summary tracked Salinger's expression too closely and therefore the paraphrase was tantamount to verbatim copying for the purpose of determining whether Hamilton had exceeded the bounds of fair use.

46. Ibid., 97.

example of impermissibly close paraphrasing Hamilton's treatment of Salinger's observation that "I suspect that money is a far greater distraction for an artist than hunger." Hamilton rewrote this to attribute to Salinger the view that "[m]oney, on the other hand, is a serious obstacle to creativity." Given that the structure, sound, and phrasing of the Salinger and Hamilton sentences are entirely different, in this instance the court of appeals was, in my view, protecting ideas, not expression, under the guise of copyright. The lesson is that deliberate "non-copying" must be carefully done and may be the subject of close scrutiny in the event of litigation.

Robert Spoo, for one, has deplored the advent of what he calls the "era of forbidden quotation," in which scholarly works are legally sanitized to avoid conflicts with copyright owners:

> By trimming quotations to the bone or forgoing them altogether, by deleting all unpublished material or paraphrasing it nearly out of existence, by using public-domain editions in place of better, copyrighted ones, academic authors are practicing the art of designing around copyrights....Design-around scholarship often amounts to a kind of perverse self-denial—perverse because not warranted by the porous nature of copyrights.

As Spoo argues, design-arounds come at a price—often in the form of "timid, bloodless paraphrase."[47] He also reminds us that the law does not by any means require the elimination of all quotations when permission cannot be obtained. However, there are times when it is only prudent to cut back, as artfully as possible, on the amount of quotation in order to bring a scholarly work safely within the bounds of fair use.

On the Practical Side: Dealing with Copyright Permissions

It happens all too often: a historian, biographer, or critic has spent years writing a book-length manuscript on the assumption that permission to use published or unpublished source materials will be forthcoming, only to be told as the book is about to go into production that permission is denied. Sometimes, the crisis is not the author's fault, but more often than not it could have been avoided or at least defused. How might the author have maximized her chances of avoiding a

---

47. Robert Spoo, "Copyrights and 'Design-Around' Scholarship," *James Joyce Quarterly* 44 (2007): 566–567, 578.

showdown over copyright? Above all, it makes sense to assess one's vulnerability to the objections of a copyright owner early in a major project.[48]

When a scholar is writing a book-length manuscript or some other work that is likely to consume months or years of effort, she should consider at the outset whether it might be desirable to quote at length from copyrighted source materials. Letters, poems, and song lyrics present special problems because the quotation of even a few lines from short works has, in some instances, been deemed to be pushing the limits of fair use. Similarly, even though it is now clear that the doctrine of fair use applies to quotations from unpublished works, some of the cases continue to suggest that unpublished status may be an important factor limiting the amount of fair use quotation, while not barring it entirely. Accordingly, the quotation of diaries, letters, poems, songs, and unpublished works may potentially give rise to legal questions. Some types of work, such as a scholarly study of a single novel, may also require more in the way of direct quotations than the few hundred words that permissions editors at publishing houses use as their rule of thumb in deciding whether permissions are needed.[49] It may be useful to know from the outset whether or not the owner of the copyright in the novel will freely grant permissions, whether there will be a sizable permissions fee, and whether there will be other conditions, such as a request to review the manuscript before publication.

In some instances, it may be prudent to seek legal advice from an experienced copyright attorney at the outset. In the case of a book-length project that has already been accepted for publication, the publisher's in-house counsel may provide free legal advice. Journals, by contrast, are unlikely to be able to provide any legal assistance. Scholars affiliated with an academic institution might seek help from the general counsel's office or a colleague-professor who specializes in

---

48. Some editors prefer to encourage authors to write their books as they want to write them without regard to legal considerations—reserving all legal review for the editing stage. Often, this works well enough. However, for a full-length work that is heavily dependent on quotations from copyrighted works, a belated rewrite to bring the amount of quotation within the bounds of fair use may be time consuming and burdensome or, in some instances, impossible. A rewrite may also entail significantly greater legal costs than an early consultation with a lawyer who can provide practical guidelines.

49. Some publishers, university presses, and journals have reputations for championing their authors in fair use matters, countenancing more liberal quotation and showing a willingness to stand up to literary estates that take an overly restrictive attitude toward quotation. Usually, this stance is attributable to the courage of a few commendable editors. If a scholar expects trouble with an estate and has a choice in the matter, she may wish to take into account a publisher's supportiveness of fair use quotation in choosing where to submit her manuscript.

copyright at a law school affiliated with the scholar's institution.[50] A lawyer can help a scholar to determine whether the quoted works are still protected by copyright; provide guidance regarding how much may be safely quoted consistent with the doctrine of fair use; offer practical suggestions on writing around copyrighted material, if necessary; or prepare a suitable form for seeking permissions from copyright owners, if the scholar decides to do so.[51]

If it appears that permissions from copyright owners will be needed, it is usually preferable to obtain them in writing at the beginning of the project and in a form that is irrevocable.[52] The problem, of course, is that the copyright owner may make permission conditional on his review and approval of the relevant portions of the final manuscript. This quid pro quo should ordinarily be resisted when possible, but resistance is often unavailing. The risk is that the copyright owner will decline permission at the last moment, pulling the rug out from under the entire project. Some estates are, of course, notorious for declining virtually all permissions requests. Contacting a rights-holder known to be hostile to scholarly projects may only serve to provoke a cease-and-desist letter threatening legal action even for quotations that should safely qualify as fair use, which will only complicate the prospects for publication. In such instances, it may be prudent to resign oneself, from the inception of a project, to quoting within the bounds of fair use. Yet many authors have successfully negotiated with prickly literary estates, reluctantly sharing the draft text with the literary executors, making some changes requested by the executors without compromising the basic integrity of the works, and ultimately obtaining the desired permissions. One should keep in mind that most copyright owners are not as unreasonable as Rupert Brooke's mother; flat refusals to grant permissions are the exception rather than the rule.[53] Usually, copyright owners and literary executors regard requests for permission to quote as

50. In some cities, there are also organizations, such as Volunteer Lawyers for the Arts, that can provide assistance, although some may have income limitations.

51. Note that some publishers have model forms that make clear that the copyright permission extends to all editions of the work (without any limitations on print quantities) and to all pertinent media, including electronic books, print on demand, websites, and the like.

52. As a matter of copyright law, a non-exclusive permission to quote need not be in writing. But publishers will frequently—and rightly—insist on a signed permission form to eliminate the risk of any dispute over the existence of an agreement with the copyright owner and its terms.

53. Of course, quotations beyond the bounds of fair use are essential for some projects. Some scholars have successfully negotiated needed permissions even with the James Joyce estate, while, as described elsewhere in this volume, others have found such discussions beyond hopeless.

welcome occurrences (and not occasions for confrontation) either because the quotations may draw favorable attention to the quoted authors and their works or because the copyright owners stand to earn permissions fees.[54]

"The Subject Would Have to Be Very, Very Dead"

Ian Hamilton, however, was confronted with a copyright owner who testified that he would *never* grant permission to quote from his correspondence. Salinger was an uncommonly sympathetic plaintiff; the Second Circuit opinion seemed to agree that Salinger's concern for personal privacy had a bearing on the case, even though he had mailed his letters to the recipients with no assurances that the letters would not be shared with others. (Hamilton had, after all, tracked down most of the letters in library collections that were open to the public.) One wonders whether, if the first in the trio of unpublished works cases had been brought not by Salinger but by the estate of L. Ron Hubbard, arguably a far less endearing plaintiff, the Second Circuit would still have made the sweeping statement (now overturned by Congress's 1992 amendment to 17 U.S.C. § 107) that unpublished works "normally enjoy complete protection against copying any protected expression."

After his landmark battle with Salinger and his subsequent study of the history of clashes between estates and scholars, Hamilton remained skeptical—perhaps unduly so, given the outcome of *Wright v. Warner Books, Inc.* and the 1992 amendment—about undertaking the biographical effort too soon.

> Any potential or probable biographees should follow Henry James and try to serve as their own keepers of the flame. If they don't, or if they fail to cover all the angles (as James did), then it seems to me that fifty years is not too long for us to wait for the "whole truth" about a private life. In the

---

54. Authors sometimes mistakenly assume that literary executors will be hostile to their projects. For example, a number of years ago, one of our firm's clients was contemplating publishing a work that reinterpreted George Orwell's *1984* and quoted many thousands of words in the process, vastly exceeding the comfort zone of fair use. The author and publisher both assumed that the Orwell estate would be hostile to the project, but reducing the quotations to bring the book within the usual fair use guidelines would have necessitated completely rewriting—and rethinking—the manuscript. Ultimately, the author and publisher decided to seek permission. The Orwell estate surprised everyone. The estate not only granted permission, but agreed to accept a small percentage of the author's royalty rather than the more typical "per word" permission rate, which would have been prohibitively expensive for the scholarly work at issue.

meantime, no one should burn anything however certain he or she might feel about what the lost loved one "really would have wished." All this may sound fishy, coming as it does from the biographer of Robert Lowell (d. 1977), and the near, would-be or failed biographer of J. D. Salinger ([b.] 1919), but there it is. We live and learn. (*KF*, viii)[55]

In a similar vein, a news magazine once asked Hamilton whether he would have written about Salinger if he had known what was in store for him. "'No,' he says emphatically. How does he feel about writing other biographies? 'Extremely reluctant. The subject would have to be very, very dead.'"[56] Ian Hamilton died in 2001 at the age of sixty-three. J. D. Salinger died on January 27, 2010, at the age of ninety-one. His literary agent issued a statement: "In keeping with his lifelong, uncompromising desire to protect and defend his privacy, there will be no service."[57]

55. Hamilton's view that "fifty years is not too long for us to wait for the 'whole truth' about a private life" refers to the fifty-year postmortem copyright term in effect when *Keepers of the Flame* was published in 1993. The Sonny Bono Copyright Term Extension Act passed in 1998 would prolong that postmortem term an additional twenty years.

56. R. Z. Sheppard, Helen Gibson, and Raji Samghabadi, "Trespassers Will Be Prosecuted: In Search of J. D. Salinger," *Time* (May 23, 1988).

57. Audie Cornish, "Rest in Privacy, J. D. Salinger," National Public Radio (Jan. 30, 2010), www.npr.org/templates/story/story.php?storyId=123140347 (accessed April 8, 2010). See also Charles McGrath, "Still Paging Mr. Salinger," *New York Times* (Dec. 30, 2008): C1 (noting that "[Salinger's] been so secretive he makes Thomas Pynchon seem like a gadabout").

Salinger initiated other litigation over the years. He successfully sued to block the staging of *The Catcher in the Rye* by a college theater group and the publication of an unauthorized volume of previously uncollected short stories. And, in 2009, the lawyer who had acted on Salinger's behalf in the dispute with Ian Hamilton and Random House brought suit on Salinger's behalf to block publication of a sequel of sorts, entitled *60 Years Later: Coming through the Rye*, written by Fredrik Colting, which the publisher described as "an unauthorized fictional examination of the relationship between Mr. J. D. Salinger and his most famous character." A. G. Sulzberger, "Holden Caulfield, a Ripe 76, Heads to Court Again," *New York Times* (June 17, 2009): C1. A federal district court preliminarily enjoined publication in the United States; in April 2010, the Court of Appeals affirmed that Salinger (through his Estate) is likely to succeed on the merits on the infringement claim, but remanded the case to the district court for findings on whether the continued distribution of Colting's book, while the litigation was pending, would cause irreparable harm to the interests protected by the copyright in *The Catcher in the Rye*. David Itzkoff, "Author Appeals Ban of Salinger Sequel," *New York Times* (July 25, 2009): C2.

10 Privacy and the Misuse of Copyright

The Case of Shloss v. the Estate of James Joyce

Carol Loeb Shloss

In a 1967 *New York Times* article, Archibald MacLeish wrote, "History is like a badly constructed concert hall [with] dead spots where the music can't be heard."[1] The history of modernism is especially prone to this kind of constructed silence, its dead zones managed and manipulated by the practices of active literary estates. In *Shloss v. the Estate of James Joyce* (2007), four issues were assembled for adjudication.[2] The primary one was fair use: when quotations from protected works are used in contexts that transform them, to what extent are those quotations subject to the control of the rights-holder in those works? On its own, this is a common question in copyright suits. What set the case apart were two intertwined subsidiary claims: the allegations of "unclean hands" and "copyright

---

1. Archibald MacLeish, untitled article, *New York Times* (Jan. 21, 1967).

2. *Carol Loeb Shloss v. Seán Sweeney and the Estate of James Joyce*, 515 F. Supp. 2d 1083, 1086 (N.D. Cal. 2007). The case is generally (and herein) referred to as *Shloss v. the Estate of James Joyce*. The four causes of action in support of the request for declaratory judgment and injunctive relief in the suit were: (1) that Shloss's planned online Supplement, containing quotations excised from the print edition of *Lucia Joyce: To Dance in the Wake*, did not infringe any of the estate's copyrights; (2) that where Shloss used the estate's copyrighted material in the Supplement, that use was a presumptively fair use; (3) that the estate had misused its copyrights; and (4) that the estate's unclean hands prohibited enforcement of its copyrights against Shloss.

misuse" on the part of the Joyce estate.[3] According to the complaint in the case, the estate acted inappropriately in prohibiting the plaintiff, Carol Shloss,[4] from using materials that were not under the estate's control; in denying her permission to use manuscript material held in both private and public institutions; and in interfering with the permission-granting decisions of other literary estates. These behaviors, the estate had maintained, were guided by the criterion of "Joyce family privacy" and the desire to protect it.

In the course of examining the particular criterion of "Joyce family privacy," this chapter will pause to consider how the desideratum of privacy arose, charting the genesis of attitudes toward privacy in the West alongside the evolving structures of law that arose to protect it. Delving back to "The Right to Privacy," Warren and Brandeis's 1890 essay in the *Harvard Law Review*, it will chart how the invasion of privacy evolved into a tort grounded in the belief that society in some way depends upon privacy and secrecy, that secrecy can serve a definite social good. The essay will then consider how the right to privacy, which was designed to build a wall around the lives and reputations of respectable people, came to be confused with copyright law, whose function is to provide financial incentives for innovation and expression. Looking at the confluence of two kinds of torts—copyright infringement and the invasion of privacy—in *Shloss v. the Estate of James Joyce* lets us examine how certain dead zones in the history of modernism have arisen, why their re-enlivening should occupy us, and what legal tools might assist us in that work.

The Background of the Case

In this particular case, the narrative of silence and its resistance is a long one that began many years ago with the sale of some Joyce letters to Cornell University. During his research in the 1950s, Richard Ellmann, Joyce's biographer, had discovered that the widow of Stanislaus Joyce was living in poverty. She had an

---

3. The doctrine of "unclean hands" prevents one party from obtaining equitable relief from another when the first party has acted unethically or in bad faith. Rooted in unclean hands is the emerging doctrine of "copyright misuse," an equitable defense against infringement when the rights-holder has abusively enforced copyright. For a discussion of the doctrine of copyright misuse, see William F. Patry and Richard A. Posner, "Fair Use and Statutory Reform in the Wake of *Eldred*," *California Law Review* 92 (2004): 1658–1659.

4. I have chosen to write about myself in the third person throughout this piece. Doing so has allowed me, first, to understand and describe experiences with a greater sense of myself as an actor at a certain moment in social history; and, second, to distance myself from the emotions that still accompany my memory of the proceedings discussed here.

unexpected resource: letters that Joyce had sent to his partner, Nora Barnacle, in 1909. Cornell's purchase of the trove in 1957 seemed a simple transaction, but the letters, charged as they were with erotic memories and fantasies, aroused immediate controversy. Their sale also brought discord to the trustees of the Joyce estate, for Stephen James Joyce, the author's grandson, objected to the release of the letters. At this point, he was a beneficiary of the estate but not a trustee; hitherto he had remained a silent recipient of moneys, but he apparently felt that the reputation of his grandparents would be damaged by the revelations contained in their correspondence. Despite these protestations, the trustees permitted Ellmann to publish some of the 1909 correspondence in *Letters of James Joyce*, volume 2 (1966), followed by a more complete offering in *The Selected Letters of James Joyce* (1975). In the early 1980s, Stephen Joyce renewed his complaints in the wake of the latest publication of the letters. Trustee Peter du Sautoy wrote at length to explain that he and his colleagues had given these issues consideration, that they had the Joyce family's interests at heart, and that it was, indeed, their sole reason for serving. In the end, they differed with Stephen Joyce, refusing both his logic and his influence.[5] Two years later, at an International James Joyce Symposium in Frankfurt, Stephen

5. Peter du Sautoy to Stephen James Joyce, Dec. 7, 1982, Richard Ellmann Papers, McFarlin Library, University of Tulsa. The letter was wide ranging, responding to a number of complaints: Stephen Joyce wanted a "trunk/suitcase"; he was upset about the publication of Richard Ellmann's edition of *Selected Letters of James Joyce* (1975), and he had apparently accused the trustees of some kind of financial mismanagement, for du Sautoy took pains to reassure him that "your interests are being carefully watched." For Shloss's purposes, the letter was important simply because of its adversarial stance: it revealed that Stephen Joyce was a potential, partial beneficiary of Giorgio Joyce's estate but not in control of the estate itself. Du Sautoy was clear: "I don't think there is any doubt about the ownership of the box and its contents. They belong to your father's Estate. In other words they are owned (legally) by the Trustees of the George Joyce Estate who are Lionel Monro [the son of Joyce's solicitor] and John Ferrar, the present senior partner of the firm Monro Pennefather & Co." That is, Stephen could complain and cajole, but he had no legal claim even to a trunk belonging to his father. Giorgio's will had specified that his wife, Asta, should receive the income from the Joyce estate (she was still alive), and that after her death the estate should be divided so that "you can receive one half while a quarter each goes to Hans Jahnke and his sister." Du Sautoy was conciliatory in his letter, but he also made it clear that he didn't want even to raise the question of Stephen's receiving the box without stipulating that "the contents should not be lost or destroyed." Du Sautoy also explained Lucia's will to Stephen (she was still living as he wrote, although she would die five days later). She had designated that her share of the Joyce estate should be divided between her nephew Stephen and her paternal aunt Nelly. Upon Nelly's death, her son, Lucia's cousin Jimmy Joyce, would become the next legal heir. Stephen Joyce was the one-half beneficiary of each will but shared this status with Hans, Hans's sister, and Nelly and Jimmy Joyce. What rights did these other beneficiaries have in matters of the James Joyce estate? By its very existence, du Sautoy's letter seemed a tacit acknowledgment that none of the legatees had legal authority; they had rights to financial profit, which was a separate matter. While Stephen Joyce was owed courtesy, du

Joyce was still adamantly insisting upon Ellmann's violation: "Intimate very personal private letters, which were never meant for the public eye, have been sold, pirated, and published. I condemn and deplore this intolerable shameless invasion of privacy as would my grandparents, were they standing beside me here today."[6] Ellmann was just as adamant, writing across a typescript on his desk that the privacy of a dead person would never be a guiding principle of his work.[7]

Stephen Joyce continued to deprecate the incursion into the Joyce family's privacy as a concerned individual until he was able to reorganize the internal structure of the estate so that he would have a greater voice in its decisions. In 1988, he used that increased influence to abridge the contents of Brenda Maddox's biography of Joyce's wife, Nora,[8] forcing Maddox to delete the book's epilogue about Lucia Joyce and engineering a very limited and specific use of Joyce's, Nora's, and Helen Fleischman's letters. The settlement bound all of the parties to silence, but another consequence of its execution was Stephen Joyce's decision to destroy his aunt Lucia's letters to him.[9] "I didn't want to have greedy little eyes and greedy little fingers going over them," he told Caryn James of the New York Times. "My aunt may have been many things, but to my knowledge she was not a writer."[10]

Sautoy made it clear that the estate was controlled legally by the trustees. Since Ellmann's time, Shloss knew that the trustees of the estate had changed, obviously with Stephen's influence, until now its sole administrator was Seán Sweeney, Stephen's friend from their undergraduate days at Harvard University. If he held no more legal authority than he had in 1982, he clearly held moral sway, but to her this distinction between legal and moral rights continued to be essential.

6. Brenda Maddox, *Nora: The Real Life of Molly Bloom* (Boston: Houghton Mifflin, 1988), 398.

7. Richard Ellmann, n.d., Richard Ellmann Papers, McFarlin Library, University of Tulsa. He was equally explicit in the introduction to the *Selected Letters:* "The editor has sought to publish all the letters in their entirety," and in the preface to volume 2 he wrote, "for a new generation does not confirm the privacy of a dead author's conjugal life." "Preface," James Joyce, *Letters of James Joyce*, ed. Richard Ellmann (New York: Viking, 1966), 2:xxix.

8. James Joyce and Nora Barnacle married in 1931, predominantly to secure their children's and potential grandchildren's legitimacy and to avoid testamentary complications. They had long spoken of one another as husband and wife.

9. Stephen Joyce made the announcement about the letters' destruction in June 1988 at the Eleventh Annual International James Joyce Symposium at Venice, during a panel on biographies of Joyce and his family organized by Shloss. He had also, he told the assembled scholars, complied with Samuel Beckett's request that he destroy a telegram, a letter, and a postcard that Beckett had sent to Lucia Joyce. See Carol Loeb Shloss, *Lucia Joyce: To Dance in the Wake* (New York: Farrar, Straus and Giroux, 2003), 28; and Morris Béja, "'A Symposium All His Own': The International James Joyce Foundation and Its Symposium," *Joyce Studies Annual 2001*, ed. Thomas F. Staley (Austin: University of Texas Press, 2001), 139.

10. Caryn James, "The Fate of Joyce Family Letters Causes Angry Literary Debate," *New York Times* (Aug. 15, 1988).

By the time Carol Shloss began looking into the nature of Lucia Joyce's life in 1988, researching what would become *Lucia Joyce: To Dance in the Wake*, the field of scholarly inquiry was already warped by power plays, conflicting principles, unspoken assumptions about the boundaries between public and private life, and the possible uses of copyright ownership in setting these boundaries.

Historical Underpinnings of the Joyce Estate's Positions

According to his grandson, James Joyce has been abused "more than... any literary figure in this century."[11] "Where do you draw the line?" Stephen Joyce asked in 1988. "Do you have any right to privacy?"[12] His questions pointed, however unwittingly, to privacy's historical contingency—to the fact that it has been construed differently over time. Private life, as Antoine Prost insists, "is first of all the history of its definition... something that has evolved primarily in the last century."[13] And if privacy as an idea has emerged in relation to changing mores, shifting social patterns, and distinctions of class, the conception of privacy's invasion as a tort—that is, as a legally remediable injury—has evolved even more recently. If we look at Stephen Joyce's position not as an abstract, self-evident assertion of inalienable rights but as a historically situated claim, we can think more clearly about Western culture's assumptions about the nature of reputation and the social and legal practices that have arisen to protect it.

Were we able to visit the turn-of-the-twentieth-century living and working conditions in either Europe or the United States, we would immediately recognize the complexity of acquiring and organizing a private life. The family privacy that Stephen Joyce imagines to have been violated belongs, first of all, to a bourgeois family whose ability to enclose itself and to keep secrets would have differed markedly from that of both similar families in the more distant past and contemporary families in more fragile economic circumstances. The bourgeois family's claim to have a "reputation" that has purportedly been harmed sets it apart from peasant and landless families; the families of workers in factories, mines, and railroad yards; and even those of salaried workers in stores and offices. And it is a concept of family very different from that known to penniless artists

---

11. Lisa Mundy, "The Wars of the Joyces," *Washington Post* (July 10, 1988): 101.

12. James, "The Fate of Joyce Family Letters."

13. Antoine Prost, "Public and Private Spheres in France," in *A History of Private Life: Riddles of Identity in Modern Times*, ed. Antoine Prost and Gérard Vincent (Cambridge, MA: Harvard University Press, 1991), 3.

whose lack of resources led them to improvise living arrangements that precluded bourgeois niceties.

The young James Joyce, struggling to make a living for himself, his lover, and their baby son, Giorgio, in Trieste comes to mind; for Joyce was not then a world-famous modernist writer but an Irish immigrant in Europe, teaching English as a second language to Italians, and he was poor. As did many others in his situation, he invited his brother to join them in their cramped lodgings; Stanislaus and James Joyce combined financial resources until an even more boisterous, overcrowded (and un-private) arrangement presented itself. In 1906, their friends the Francini-Brunis invited all of them, Stanislaus included, to live together. Two husbands, two wives, three children, and a bachelor sharing a rented space precluded singular intimacies. For Nora, this was welcome: she was lonely when left alone with an infant during the day and appreciated Clothilde Francini-Bruni's company.[14] But for Joyce, who needed to work in the home as if he were a self-employed fan maker or a seamstress, this housing arrangement barred the practice of his art. He could not concentrate. In July, he moved out and took Nora and Giorgio to Rome, where he faced a series of rented rooms, plaintive companions, and evictions. In December, he described his situation as "no pen, no ink, no table, no room, no time, no quiet."[15]

Like most of the urban poor, Joyce found that space in and of itself set the parameters of individual and family privacy. He was also living against the grain of industrial and managerial history, for the home as a male workplace had, by the early 1900s, been largely replaced by factories and offices. At a time when most other men went to public spaces to earn money, understanding "the private" as what one left behind in order to labor, Joyce wrote, or tried to write, at home. That unity of domicile and workplace denied him the kind of privacy that depended on a more specialized, differentiated sense of space. The common distinctions between public and domestic behavioral norms were also obscured for him.[16] Unlike those who could divide their impersonal, contractual bearing as workers from their intimate behavior with friends, lovers, and family, Joyce lived the conflation of business and kinship. The young writer's problem would not have been that he had secrets to hide or a reputation to uphold but that, in the absence of private space, secrecy and concealment would barely have been possible. Had someone assaulted his self-esteem or that of his family; had he felt injured or shamed; had

14. See Shloss, *Lucia Joyce: To Dance in the Wake*, 44.
15. James Joyce to Stanislaus Joyce, Dec. 7, 1906, in *Letters of James Joyce*, ed. Richard Ellmann (New York: Viking, 1966), 2:202.
16. Prost, "Public and Private Spheres," 9.

someone tried to "invade" whatever privacy he did have, he might have found himself hurling insults or lifting a fist to a jaw, but he would also have discovered his sense of damage to be beneath the notice of most social structures and certainly beneath the notice of the law. The young James Joyce, the man who wrote the erotic letters that his grandson later found so offensively revealed by publication, would have had scant resources for protest, since his obscure poverty meant that he had no reputation that society had a stake in defending.

Reputation, then, was not something that the law concerned itself with unless the person involved was of upper-class standing. Had anyone discovered Joyce's erotic letters to Nora in his youth, we can imagine raised eyebrows, a sense of titillated amusement, or possibly moral indignation, but not the activation of a social or legal mechanism for the redress of feelings. Stephen Joyce's sense of outrage at privacy's violation belongs neither to the young James Joyce's class position nor to our own twenty-first-century worries about privacy, which tend to be about surveillance and civil liberties or about sex, reproduction, and choices of intimate partners. The grandson speaks, rather, in the voice of what Lawrence Friedman calls the "Victorian compromise," a legal culture (i.e., a system not just of laws but of ideas, attitudes, and values that people hold about the legal system) that is historically situated in the nineteenth century.

Friedman describes the Victorian compromise as "a kind of double standard" whereby vice—and particularly the sexual misconduct of elites—was officially condemned but unofficially tolerated as long as it was kept discreet.[17] Its underlying axiom was that the community as a whole stood to suffer when the reputations of prominent individuals were damaged. When we look back, we can see that the legal practices that arose to shield the reputations of prosperous or influential Victorians grew out of an implicit acknowledgment that society itself could be destabilized if those most responsible for upholding its institutions were to suffer humiliation. Thus, it was more important for a judge or senator to retain a reputation for decency and good moral character than for a factory worker, a shop girl, or an ad canvasser to do so. This was not simply because status made a person more morally valuable or able to "afford" protection but because it was presumed that a person of high standing carried responsibilities that affected many people beyond himself.[18]

17. Lawrence M. Friedman, *Guarding Life's Dark Secrets: Legal and Social Controls over Reputation, Propriety, and Privacy* (Stanford, CA: Stanford University Press, 2007), 66. Further references cited in the text as *GL*.

18. "If you insult the king, you not only hurt the king's 'personal interests,' you also damage...the social status with which society has invested the role of kingship" (*GL*, 49).

Friedman's use of the term *compromise* speaks not only to this distinction bet-ween classes of people—a distinction in which only those of rank counted—but also to a negotiation between real virtue and the constructed but false appearance of virtue. There was a moral code, a template or pattern of expected behavior, and then there was how people actually behaved (*GL*, 34). The "compromise"—pro-tecting certain people who were *not* innocent, people who were the authors of their own regrettable behavior—tried to bridge this gap between seeming and being. To the extent that the law served only selectively as a cover-up or shield for misconduct, it also served the interests of hierarchy, for it granted the right to keep secrets, to conceal transgressions, only to those with enough prestige to tear the social fabric if they were brought low.

In the many times that Stephen Joyce has decried the invasion of "Joyce family privacy," he has seemingly felt that James Joyce, by virtue of his eventual fame, belonged at the pinnacle of this hierarchy. He has also, by his very insistence upon privacy, seemed to presuppose a guilty secret. This rage for secrecy, too, he inherits from the Victorian compromise, at whose heart was a portrait of reputation as depending less on what people know about one than on what they do not know (*GL*, 168). Skeletons—and, again, these often entailed sexual transgression—re-quired secrecy. Presumably, Stephen Joyce felt that James Joyce's 1909 letters to Nora, although written during his obscure years, constituted such a transgression and required hiding in order to maintain both the reputation and the elite status that Joyce's writing had subsequently won him. It was not so much that the grandson objected to his grandparents' sexual behavior or to their having written the letters as that he valued the appearance of conforming to dominant social norms. Hovering over all of this are questions to which we will return—questions about whose reputation, and whose privacy, truly hung in the balance. Could James Joyce's posthumous reputation possibly be of interest to the law when he could no longer suffer from diminution in his standing? And would even the Victorians have allowed that the privacy and reputation of the living might be marred by revelations about the century-old sexual lives of the dead?

These questions and principles (if the presumption of the right to keep secrets can be called a principle) interest us partly because contemporary concerns about privacy have shifted so much. Privacy is still an important value, but its meaning has changed. As Western culture has moved generally toward democratization, it has felt a diminished imperative to uphold the good name of elites. In addition, it is arguably less concerned with "regime[s] of silence and darkness...regime[s] of taboos and cover-ups" (*GL*, 20) because many of the behaviors that were formerly considered shameful or illegal have been decriminalized. The legal culture of the

Victorians, at least surrounding privacy, was slowly dismantled—first by those who were repelled by its hypocrisy and implicit tolerance of "sin," and later by those who were simply more open to the varieties of human choices about sexual behavior.

By the time that Stephen Joyce began to protest the publication of his grandfather's fantasies about his grandmother, few people would have seen the need to shield those visionary desires since they were no longer considered scandalous. One irony of this is, of course, that James Joyce's writing, particularly in *Ulysses*, had exposed and even contributed to this shift toward a more open-minded set of public mores. And a further irony is that the grandson has seemed more interested in control than in substance, since the content of his protests about the Joyce family's privacy soon shifted from outrage over the *Selected Letters* to trying to manage the image of his aunt Lucia, as if any scholarly interest in his ancestors was akin to the aggressive and sensational intrusions of the media into the lives of celebrities.

Such cases, often involving the unregulated use of personal photographs to promote a product or the publication of unflattering gossip without consent, had led legal culture out of its nineteenth-century assumptions about rights of secrecy for the few to a more considered discussion of the meaning of privacy in the modern era.[19] Those later meanings were also the flourishing of a legal discourse on privacy rights that had taken root, in the United States at least, during the late nineteenth century. In 1890, Samuel Warren and Louis Brandeis, who had gone to Harvard Law School together, wrote a groundbreaking article on privacy for the *Harvard Law Review*. In researching their essay, they learned that U.S. law contained no clear definition of *privacy*. They found references to the notion that people had a "right to be let alone," to the relationship between privacy and liberty in the face of government encroachments, and to common-law ideas about not trespassing on other people's land—but there was no formal conception of privacy torts.[20] Warren and Brandeis argued that there should be such laws so that people could seek justice, especially against an unbridled press. "The press is overstepping in every direction the obvious bounds of propriety and of decency," they wrote. "Gossip is no longer the resource of the idle and of the vicious, but has become a

<hr/>

19. See, for example, *Pollard v. Photographic Co.*, 40 Ch. Div. 345 (Ch. Div. 1888); *Manola v. Stevens & Myers*, N.Y. Times, June 21, 1890, at 2 (N.Y. Sup. Ct. June 20, 1890); *Mackenzie v. Soden Mineral Springs Co.*, 18 N.Y.S. 240 (N.Y. Sup. Ct. 1891); and *Marks v. Jaffa*, 26 N.Y.S. 908 (N.Y. City Super. Ct. 1893), cited in Gini Graham Scott, *Mind Your Own Business: The Battle for Personal Privacy* (New York: Insight, 1995), 39, 41.

20. Samuel D. Warren and Louis D. Brandeis, "The Right to Privacy," *Harvard Law Review* 4 (1890): 193. Further references cited in the text as "RP."

trade, which is pursued with industry as well as effrontery. To satisfy a prurient taste the details of sexual relations are spread broadcast in the columns of the daily papers" ("RP," 196). Because the modern world was increasingly complex, people needed a "retreat from the world" through solitude and privacy. They needed to determine the degree to which their thoughts, feelings, and emotions—their "inviolate personality"—were broadcast to others ("RP," 205).

Warren and Brandeis's essay marked the beginning of a move in U.S. court decisions and legislation to recognize privacy rights. The authors anticipated growing concern about government surveillance and search and seizure. New technologies permitted access to information without anyone's having physically to enter private space. When the 1928 *Olmstead v. United States* decided the extent to which a telephone wiretap was a kind of warrantless search, Justice Brandeis, now on the Supreme Court, argued that the secret interception of any communication by wiretapping, even without the physical trespass of property, was illegal.[21] In his view, still other types of privacy protection were needed to defend people from government snooping.[22] Although Brandeis was in the minority in the *Olmstead* decision, his views on privacy were eventually taken up by lawmakers and the courts. Moving from issues arising from Fourth Amendment rights based on the idea that individuals should be secure in their homes, the law next developed an interest in individuals' freedom to make fundamental choices about their practice of religion, the education of their children, their choice of life partner, and the fate of their own body in reproduction and dying.

None of these issues appeared to concern Stephen Joyce, and understandably so. For the legal culture that addressed rights of privacy in the contemporary era was interested solely in the privacy of living people, whose ability to pursue active, self-actualizing lives had been, or might be, damaged by interference of one kind or another. Even nineteenth-century law protected only the reputations of prominent *living* people lest society be destabilized by their humiliation. But James, Nora, and Lucia Joyce were dead, and thus unable to suffer embarrassment, when Stephen Joyce began to ramp up his complaints about the invasion of privacy. No one was interfering with his personal ability to construct a valuable, self-determined life, to remain in solitude or seclusion, or to withhold embarrassing private facts about *himself*. In light of the history of the evolving legal culture outlined here, Stephen Joyce's grievance seems to have been powered by a Victorian

21. For Justice Brandeis's dissenting opinion in the case, see *Olmstead et al. v. United States* 277 U.S. 438, 471 (1928).
22. Scott, *Mind Your Own Business*, 44.

theory of reputation as a kind of intangible property, coupled with the conviction that he owned the property right in his aunt's and grandparents' reputations after their deaths. Those reputations he would defend by using the intellectual property rights that he held as the latest beneficiary of James Joyce's literary estate. Through copyright rather than privacy law, he would attempt to control the shape of historical remembrance and challenge scholars like Ellmann, Maddox, and Shloss.[23]

The Social Value of Scholarship about Privacy

The plaintiff's view in *Shloss v. the Estate of James Joyce* also involved questions of privacy, but seen from another perspective. Where Stephen Joyce participated in something like the Victorian "regime of taboos and cover-ups" described by Friedman (*GL*, 20), Shloss's biographical work sought to realign the very attitudes that seemingly triggered the grandson's sense of shame. Although the suit was ostensibly about determining the parameters of fair use, it was catalyzed by the Joyce estate's attempts to shut down *all* language about certain subjects that it wanted kept in silence and darkness and by Shloss's resistance to that program of private censorship.

By the mid-1980s, the estate was no longer focused on the "dirty" letters of 1909 but on the subject of Joyce's daughter, Lucia. It had shifted its attention from wanting to conceal the sexual intimacy between life partners to the "shame" of their child's mental illness. Recall that, when Stephen Joyce announced in 1988 that he had destroyed his aunt's letters to him, he justified his actions by saying she had not been a writer.[24] This claim was untrue even by strictly literary notions of writ-

---

23. Stephen Joyce's deployment of copyright to enforce privacy had some precedent and colorability in law. In their 1890 article, Warren and Brandeis had pointed to copyright's compatibility with the common law's "secur[ing] to each individual the right of determining, ordinarily, to what extent his thoughts, sentiments, and emotions shall be communicated to others" ("RP," 198). Copyright's financial incentive to publish work, that is, dovetailed with the common law's guarantee that publication not be compelled—that unpublished works belonged absolutely to a private sphere. This argument played an important role in a series of federal court decisions during the 1980s that categorically denied the fair use of unpublished works. However, as Mark Fowler's chapter in the present volume shows, both judges and lawmakers subsequently softened that hard line; since 1992, the final sentence of 17 U.S.C. § 107 has read, "The fact that a work is unpublished shall not itself bar a finding of fair use if such finding is made upon consideration of all the [fair use] factors." In its claim of copyright misuse, the complaint in *Shloss v. the Estate of James Joyce* argued not that copyright and privacy were discontiguous but that the estate had attempted to redraw the border between them in ways that were unsupported by law.

24. James, "The Fate of Joyce Family Letters."

erliness—Lucia had written poems and a novel—but it did generally describe the way in which the literary world perceived her. She was unknown and she was "mad." Such an assessment ignored the other parts of social history to which she did belong, including the history of pariahs—those who have been outcast from society (often by being "kept in private") in the very way that her nephew attempted to effect through a restrictive use of copyright.

According to Stephen Joyce, Lucia's position was self-evidently to be concealed. As the daughter of an educated man of a certain era, but also as someone who had forfeited full rights to self-determination, she belonged in the home and in the shelter it provided from public view. She was, so to speak, the property of her family. According to Shloss, this clandestine status was not necessarily good. She thought it imperative to question boundaries that had previously hidden violent or regrettable or shameful behavior from public discourse. It was equally important to show the connection between forms of institutional and cultural power and problems that appeared in the past to be merely private, particular, or pathological.[25] Indeed, one cannot even address questions of possible injustices unless private misfortunes are revealed to be part of a collective tendency. Yet, for all that individual experiences take on social importance when they are shown to participate in collective practices, these practices can only be discerned through the scrutiny of single cases.

The attitudes that guided Shloss's scholarship also had a history; like the right to privacy, they arose at a particular cultural moment—in this case, in response to feminist critiques of both social practices and biographical narratives that confined women's lives solely to the private realm. Shloss was also influenced by political philosophers who found it imperative to consider when, and in what manner, private matters should assume political dimensions. Her touchstones were the work of Virginia Woolf and the political philosophy of Hannah Arendt.

To Virginia Woolf, who was James Joyce's exact contemporary, the privacy that seemed so self-evident a good to Stephen Joyce was anathema. She spent a long writing career considering the insidious ways that compulsory privacy could harm women. In both her novels and her nonfiction essays, Woolf exposed the private homes of Victorians and Edwardians as sites of unspeakable and dreary isolation from activity, thought, and the world of policy and effective achievement. Only with the passage of the Sex Disqualification (Removal) Act in 1919, she pointed out, were the professions opened to women in England, and only at that point, at

25. See Patricia Boling, *Privacy and the Politics of Intimate Life* (Ithaca, NY: Cornell University Press, 1996), 73.

the moment when they were free to earn money, could "the daughters of educated men" begin to assume a voice in their own fates or in that of the nation. "The door of the private house was [then] thrown open," she wrote in *Three Guineas* (1938). "In every purse there was, or might be, one bright new sixpence in whose light every thought, every sight, every action looked different."[26] No longer were women bound to acquiesce in the opinions of their fathers, brothers, husbands, or nephews. They might be free, despite the enormous differences in their class status, to experience and criticize the world from their own vantage points.

Yet, as *Three Guineas* also attests, that viewpoint would long be colored by the discomfitures of enforced privacy. Not only did it account for the isolation and acquiescence of the women who had heretofore been financially dependent, but privacy also engendered a perspective on all that they had been excluded from in the public world. Woolf called the institutions of that world "the procession":

> There they go, our brothers who have been educated at public schools and universities, mounting those steps, passing in and out of those doors, ascending those pulpits, preaching, teaching, administering justice, practicing medicine, transacting business, making money.... Great-grandfathers, fathers, uncles—they all went that way, wearing their gowns, wearing their wigs, some with ribbons across their breast, others without. One was a bishop. Another a judge. One was an admiral. Another a general. One was a professor. Another a doctor. (*TG*, 70–71).

Women, meanwhile—"We who have looked so long at the pageant in books or from a curtained window" (*TG*, 74)—had reason to object to the so-called civilization that these institutions had produced. Writing during the run-up to World War II, Woolf articulated those scruples in a harshly contemporary manner. She equated the voices of Hitler and Mussolini abroad with the voices of "dictators" at home. England's domestic dictators, she added, were the practices and institutions that had excluded women and, in seeming to protect them in the home, had left them without recourse to the law, financial independence, wealth, education, or independent judgment. That dictator was "raising his ugly head, spitting his poison...in the heart of England," and the struggle against "him" had worn down the British woman's strength and "exhaust[ed] her spirit" (*TG*, 62). Why fight dictators who speak German or Italian, Woolf asked, when such "ugly animals" speak English as well?

26. Virginia Woolf, *Three Guineas* (London: Hogarth, 1986), 19. Further references cited in the text as *TG*.

The primary consequence of Woolf's writing for Shloss and other feminist biographers was the conviction that privacy for women of, say, Lucia Joyce's generation had not been an unambiguous benefit. Its particular consequence for Shloss was an understanding of the Joyce estate's private censorship of Lucia's life as extending what Woolf called the very "cruelty... poverty... hypocrisy... immorality... inanity" that had for so long characterized women's lives. But because Lucia's private experiences were unsettling, such restrictions were complicated. One might argue that mental health problems like Lucia's uniquely deserved shielding by the family. Or one might wonder if the family itself was the originary site of those troubles. How should this distinction be made? Part of Shloss's answer lay in considering Lucia's status within the Joyce family. After Lucia's death in 1982, no one would be interrupting the privacy of a living sufferer but, instead, inquiring into the historical record of suffering; and Lucia's was, ironically, a kind of suffering that had partly occurred in public institutions.

Lucia lived most of her life not under the protection of her relatives but in a sanitarium and under the legal guardianship of two Quakers, Harriet Shaw Weaver and (later) Jane Lidderdale. At first, Weaver, who was also Joyce's literary executor, shared Stephen Joyce's attitude about keeping knowledge of Lucia's emotional instabilities quiet. She told Stuart Gilbert, who was then editing the first collection of James Joyce's letters, that she had worked with two principles in mind when selecting which letters to allow him to publish: "to avoid hurting anyone's feelings and to protect the Joyce family's privacy."[27] But she later underwent a change of heart. She wrote again to Gilbert, saying, "And perhaps some of the passages about Lucia that I had deleted or suggested deleting, might also be retained as the fact of her illness seems to be widely known now and they throw light on Mr. Joyce's very great affection and solicitude for her."[28] It was also the case that Weaver had come to love Lucia herself and that her personal feelings were contained within larger principles. Weaver told Jane Lidderdale that "she was opposed to censorship and to inviting piracy by suppression."[29]

Had Stephen Joyce or even his father, Giorgio, been involved in Lucia's care, and had she lived out her final years shielded by her family, one might have concluded that her brother and nephew had invoked privacy in the name of tenderness or

27. Jane Lidderdale and Mary Nicholson, *Dear Miss Weaver: Harriet Shaw Weaver, 1876–1961* (London: Faber and Faber, 1970), 420.

28. Stuart Gilbert, "A Note on the Editing," in *Letters of James Joyce*, ed. Stuart Gilbert (New York: Viking, 1957), 1:40.

29. Jane Lidderdale, interviews by Brenda Maddox, June 22, 1987, and Jan. 1, 1988, quoted in Maddox, *Nora*, 438.

intimacy. But since Lucia, in later life, seems to have awakened neither of these responses in her relatives, her nephew likely had other reasons for drawing the cloak of family privacy about her—including, perhaps, the desire to shield the family from charges that it had neglected her. These circumstances contributed to Shloss's conviction that Lucia's story belonged out in the open—in the polis, if you will—rather than mewed up in the private world of domestic lore.

In thinking about how the life of James Joyce's daughter could become part of the collective discourse and debate, Shloss turned to Hannah Arendt's 1958 *The Human Condition*. There, Arendt was concerned about identifying the activities that belonged in either the public or private sphere; about the transition from one sphere to another so that private misfortunes could become claims that are politically negotiable; and about writing as a mode of public action that is connected to responsibility for the world, citizenship, and potential political deliberation. Arendt's writing had been primarily concerned with the fate of Jews in Europe and with the moment when religion and ethnicity became deadly, but for Shloss it also underscored the political importance of various life situations typically regarded as trivial or particularistic. Rather than see Lucia's circumstance as pre-political, as requiring the darkness of the household, Shloss came to see it as a chapter in the history of medicine and as exemplifying the fate of many other young women who had been labeled "mad" by an emerging and still-fragmented professional community.

Just as Arendt had struggled to understand when the transition from private to public became more than a matter of compunction, so Shloss sought to determine when closely held confidences needed to yield to public dialogue. In hiding the content of individual or family secrets from the public gaze, the claim of privacy also impairs our ability to study the historical and political ramifications of what it hides. In one context, religion, for example, might be an intimate, personal choice; in another, it might account for abysmal national policies that need, beyond doubt, to be engaged. In one context, the "fact" of a woman's emotional instability might be confined to the few people involved in her care; in another, it might provide a chapter in the history of women's creativity and its (mis)perception.

All of these influences, questions, and convictions shaped the debate about Lucia Joyce that culminated in *Shloss v. the Estate of James Joyce*. One party in the case believed that to own copyright was de facto to own an absolute dominion over privacy and reputation; the other, that privacy was itself a subject—perhaps the central subject—of investigation. One party believed that boundaries should be maintained around whatever families want to keep secret; the other, that biography can offer a history of exclusion itself. Virginia Woolf had valued biography for that very reason, claiming that, along with history, biography was "the only evidence available to an outsider" (*TG*, 89). Not only could it provide stories that had previously been omitted from our common heritage, but it could also bring the excluded into symbolic community.

The Confluence of Copyright Law and Social Attitudes toward Privacy

The fundamental questions in *Shloss v. the Estate of James Joyce*, then, were these: In whose service should protected language be used? Should individual rights-holders' proprietary and privacy claims give way at some point to the greater social importance of exposing the damage caused by compulsory privacy?

It seemed to Shloss and her advocates[30] in the suit that the Joyce estate's sole beneficiary had attempted to misuse copyright ownership to enforce a personal view of the past—to engineer the "concert hall" of modernism's history according to his own scrupulous design. To the other would-be architects of that resonant historical space, he attributed only the motive of "greed," as if scholarship that made transformative use of its sources was nothing more than a rival firm in a bidding war. For his adversaries, however, considerations of revenue and reputation were secondary to an interest in the social function of the law. Although copyright secures financial incentives for creative individuals, its raison d'être in the Anglo-American tradition is the provision of shared benefits: "for the Encouragement of Learning" (United Kingdom); "to promote the Progress of Science and the useful Arts" (United States).[31] For Shloss, the ultimate questions in the case went beyond copyright law, but they shared with that law a devotion to the dynamism and openness of the social world. What would be the broader consequences of removing certain stories from public accountability, deliberation, and control? What social damage would ensue if copyright claims could be used selectively to remove knowledge from the realm of collective responsibility and possible action? What other stories would remain, perforce, untold?

As it turned out, a settlement agreement precluded a full adjudication of both the primary question of fair use and the subsidiary claims of unclean hands and

---

30. These were Stanford Law School's Center for Internet and Society and the law firms Doerner, Saunders, Daniel & Anderson, L.L.P. (Tulsa, Oklahoma); Howard Rice Nemerovski Canady Falk & Rabkin, P.C. (San Francisco); and Keker & Van Nest, L.L.P. (San Francisco).

31. Statute of Anne, 1710, 8 Anne, c. 19 (Eng.); U.S. Constitution (art. I, § 8).

copyright misuse.[32] Shloss was granted the right to create a website containing all of the deleted language from *Lucia Joyce: To Dance in the Wake* and to use the same material in any printed reissue of the book.[33] A few dead spots in the history of modernism, medicine, and privacy were quickened. Since no resounding legal precedent was established in *Shloss v. the Estate of James Joyce*, the plaintiff remained free to make her own judgment. She understood herself to have acted at a particular moment in the history of privacy, a moment when women had emerged from "private houses" to engage in dialogue with the past; it was a moment, given the immense scope of all of written history, which was relatively new. Ironically, at the point when women could write of their own exclusions from the historical world, the abuse of copyright in the name of privacy emerged as an instrument of continued silence. Shloss decided that aggressive responses to possible humiliation, cloaked in the language of supposed intimacy, constituted the real shame.

32. Although the case did not go to a final judgment and thereby produce a comprehensive decision, it did yield two published judicial opinions to which future courts may look for guidance in similar cases. In rejecting the estate's motion to dismiss and most of its motion to strike, the first opinion, *Shloss v. Sweeney*, 515 F. Supp. 2d 1068 (N.D. Cal. 2007), allowed that the facts in the case might indeed give rise to a finding of copyright misuse by the estate. The second, *Shloss v. Sweeney*, 515 F. Supp. 2d 1083 (N.D. Cal. 2007), declared the plaintiff to be the "prevailing party" under the Copyright Act (17 U.S.C. § 505), entitling her to have her attorneys' fees paid by the estate. (Those fees, in the amount of $240,000, were paid in September 2009 pursuant to settlement.) For additional discussion of the case's legal details and ramifications by one of the plaintiff's attorneys, see Robert Spoo, "Archival Foreclosure: A Scholar's Lawsuit against the Estate of James Joyce," *American Archivist* 71 (2008): 544–551; and Spoo, "Litigating the Right to Be a Scholar," in *Joyce Studies Annual 2008*, ed. Philip Sicker and Moshe Gold (Bronx, NY: Fordham University Press, 2008), 12–21.

33. See http://www.lucia-the-authors-cut.info.

PART SIX

Calving the Wind

11 Beyond the Grave

Continuing Life through Great Works
Stanford G. Gann Jr.

Who was Gertrude Stein? How did she impact the lives of those who were famous and those who were not? Was she an American or a Parisian or both? As difficult as such questions are, we at least know where to begin looking for answers: in accounts by contemporaries who knew her or read her work; in materials that illuminate the world that formed her and the world in which she wrote; and, above all, in the published and unpublished works she left behind. But what materials and criteria should we consult in asking, more than a half-century after Stein's death, whether she would allow someone to use—or, as some might characterize it, to manipulate—her works? How can anyone presume to know how a long-deceased writer might respond to a request for the right to utilize her works or the facts of her life, especially when that writer was as unique as Gertrude Stein? The simple and truthful answer is that one cannot know for certain nor can one expect to get it right all of the time. Recognizing the limits of certainty, I suggest, ought to free a literary executor to take other facts into consideration, chief among them that access to a great body of work might gain it appreciation by a greater audience in perpetuity.

Since we cannot know what Gertrude Stein might have done if she were able to consider new requests for the rights to publish, perform, or adapt her works, my approach as the literary executor of her estate is to attempt to honor the spirit of the person and the works as I understand them. That spirit includes notions of character, context, and appeal, and honoring it requires a thoughtful balancing of diverse interests. The "character" to which I refer is the author's, as it is revealed both in her works and by those who knew and wrote about her. "Appeal," in my view, is limited to the work itself and its ability to reach traditional audiences and beyond. (Of course, audiences traditional for one author may be nontraditional for another.) "Context," the new work or situation in which an existing work is to be deployed and given new meaning, can often be the decisive consideration, as I will explain below.

Requests to republish or perform Stein's work might seem to be the easiest to consider. However, the contexts of such use can often alter even verbatim reproductions or performances of the work in ways that are less than accurate or flattering—and in ways that are creative and transformative. Thus, the context intended for a proposed work is often the criterion, over and above Stein's character or the appeal of her work, that most guides my assessment. At the same time, the character of an author should inform one's sense of the contexts in which her work might appropriately be used or reproduced. In my judgment, Gertrude Stein's avant-garde lifestyle and tastes should expand rather than contract the range of her work's permissible uses.

Barring extraordinary circumstances, the express intentions of the author or creator, if they can be construed, say, from a last will and testament, must be respected. Where the creator's wishes are ambiguous or uncertain, an appealing secondary use, performance, or adaptation—one that will acquaint new readers or audiences with the original works—can weigh against or even override one's speculations as to the author's desires. A literary executor must consider not only the privacy of an author and her circle, but also the accessibility and longevity of her works. And there are other important considerations. After an author's demise, the rights in her creations pass, like all assets, to her heirs, whose interests as rights-holders must be respected and harmonized with the apparent desires of the author, as well as with the nature of the work, if possible. In the wake of the author's death, concerns for her privacy should play a lesser role, and concerns for the needs, preferences, and aspirations of the living a greater one.

It is an honor and privilege to serve as a literary executor over anyone's life works. In a sense, one follows the course of the works in assessing a request for permission. One starts by considering the authorial source and then factors in other interests—those of the heirs, those of the users, and those of the works themselves. Yes, a clearly expressed direction or limitation in a will is invaluable when considering requests. But limits that seem reasonable to one generation may prove undesirable, even counterproductive, to the next. The *absence* of an author's express intentions, then, can be enormously valuable. Such an absence tacitly recognizes that future generations will find creative, unforeseen ways to utilize great works of the past and to give them new life.

12 Mens Sine Affectu

Mary de Rachewiltz

No wind is the king's wind.
Let every cow keep her calf.

—Ezra Pound, Canto IV.16

I can but offer a few random, disjointed thoughts on a topic I never was schooled in and that never held my interest for very long because I felt legally powerless. When Paul Saint-Amour asked me to contribute to *Modernism and Copyright* and to provide a chapter title, the first that came to mind was "Mens sine affectu."[1] The quotation is from the British political theorist Algernon Sidney's *Discourses Concerning Government* (1698), although I come to it by way of John Adams's 1770 defense of the British soldiers involved in the Boston massacre. Adams concluded his speech by invoking Sidney, who,

> from his earliest infancy, sought a tranquil retirement under the shadow of the tree of liberty with his tongue, his pen, and his sword. "The law, (says he), no passion can disturb. 'Tis void of desire and fear, lust and anger. 'Tis

Unless otherwise indicated, the following notes were added by the editor; in some cases, the sources indicated may not be precisely those consulted or recollected by the author while preparing the chapter.

1. Ezra Pound, *The Cantos* (New York: New Directions, 1995), LXII.343. This edition is hereafter cited in the text with the Canto and page number(s).

mens sine affectu; written reason; retaining some measure of the divine perfection."[2]

Contrary to accepted opinion, Cantos LXII–LXXI, the *Adams Cantos,* are to my mind the mandrel, the axial center that holds Pound's epic together. They open with the words of a grandson: "*Acquit of evil intention…/ to correct it with cheerfulness*" (LXII.341). For the rest of the decade, it is John Adams speaking, with the framed motto to underline Pound's message

| JOHN ADAMS |
| FOR PEACE |
| 1800 |

and the hymn to Zeus at the end (LXXI.418). From then on, the plan for *The Cantos* was to continue with a "serene and philosophical heaven…more subtle than air."[3]

In 1939, as soon as Pound had completed the manuscript for the *Chinese History* and *Adams Cantos,* LII–LXXI, he returned to America, at his own expense, on what we might call his own "peace mission." Contrary to what had occurred in Rome in 1933, in Washington the poet was not granted an audience. Senator Borah said: "am sure I don't know what a man like you / would find to *do* here" (LXXXIV.557; emphasis in original).

So he returned to Italy. War broke out. He invaded the air and was imprisoned for it. Yet the poem continued, and in the first of the *Pisan Cantos* he stated: "free speech without free radio speech is as zero" (LXXIV.446). And at the end of LXXXIV, we find:

> John Adams, the Brothers Adam
> > there is our norm of spirit
> …
> > whereto we may pay our
> > > homage (560)

American readers should not forget that, during the Vietnam War, those who spoke out against it, even outside the confines of the States, were not called

---

2. John Adams, *The Works of John Adams, Second President of the United States: With a Life of the Author, Notes and Illustrations,* ed. Charles Francis Adams (Boston: Little, Brown, 1850–1856), 1:114.

3. Ezra Pound, *I Cantos,* trans. Mary de Rachewiltz (Milan: Mondadori, 1985), 1566.

"traitors,"[4] nor were those who did not like a certain president punished when they clamored for his impeachment. As for Pound's much discredited "economic" ideas, every day they prove themselves right. Dag Hammarskjöld did call him "seer" and "prophet" when enlisted to obtain a fair trial.[5]

Canto XIII had already introduced the concepts of "filiality," "order," "compassion," "brotherly deference," and "music fit for the Odes" (XIII.58–60). And yet a legalized tyranny still throws its shadow across two worlds. Until psychiatry and the American legal system put an end to their *escamotage*, cavils, evasions, stratagems and give Pound a fair trial, there is no hope for Pound's own instructions and wishes, also in matters of copyright, to be carried out.

Robert Spoo has mentioned *le droit moral* as largely unrecognized by American law, and in his contribution to the present volume he highlights the main passages in Pound's many articles on the subject.[6] He has studied Pound's prose thoroughly and knows the rules. Authors are entitled to protection for their intellectual labors, to receive royalties and pass them on to their descendants. Like John Adams, Spoo is a lawyer and must speak of statutes. Whereas for me, Pound wrote *laws*. I know it's bad form to speak of oneself, and Pound warned against the use of "I," yet hard as I try to disentangle my self, there are still a few details that might reveal the pattern in the carpet.

From my childhood onward, Pound tried to teach me the "family profession." To set an example, he translated into English what I had been requested to write in Tyrolese Italian about "The Beauties of the Tyrol" and sent it to Faber with the request that the contract be made with "the authoress to whom I cheerfully deed over translation fees as encouragement." The unpublished correspondence between him and T. S. Eliot and Christopher Morley on this subject is hilarious.

During our 1941–1943 isolation in Sant'Ambrogio, we started to translate *The Cantos* into Italian. I was totally unprepared, yet was repeatedly told I had to *learn* rather than understand. Questions had to be pertinent, yet were usually answered vaguely, like "some bloomin' nymph." Thus, "Let every cow keep her calf" (IV.16) elicited a mere "refers to copyright."[7] Yet in real life I knew very well that after about three weeks the calf is weaned and, depending on its sex, destined for the

---

4. Author's note: The reason, I am told, is that America had not officially declared war on Vietnam (courtesy Richard Sieburth).

5. See Dag Hammarskjöld, "The World of Modern Art," *Bulletin of the Museum of Modern Art* 22 (1954): 9.

6. See Robert Spoo, "Copyright Protectionism and Its Discontents: The Case of James Joyce's *Ulysses* in America," *Yale Law Journal* 108 (1998): 633–665.

7. Author's note: For an explanation of the line "Let every cow keep her calf," see Richard Taylor, "Editing the Variorum *Cantos:* Process and Policy," *Paideuma* 31 (2002): 333.

slaughterhouse or for reproduction. The line still makes me strangely uneasy because of my love for cows. Though I have never owned a cow myself, I like the myths, the ancient symbols of sacred cows. (One of our contemporary horrors has been the slaughtering of thousands of supposed "mad cows." It will here sound out of context, yet I must mention it and jump *in medias res*.) As of today, a still unpunished infringement of copyright was Pasolini's use of a long passage from Canto XCIX in his film *Salò, or; The 120 Days of Sodom*. My personal protest went unheeded by the Pasolini estate. It is ironic however, perhaps fair, that the documentary of Pasolini interviewing Pound has contributed to the popularity not only of Pasolini but also of Pound. The younger poet belatedly paid homage to the older: "Peace comes of good manners" (XCIX.718).

During the St. Elisabeths years, the instructions were about *form*, formatting, printing, translating, circulating. Giovanni Scheiwiller had published *Confucius, Digest of the Analects* and the anthology *Profile*, before World War II. Because his son Vanni was continuing the family profession and had defied political prejudice by publishing *Lavoro e Usura* in 1954,[8] Pound entrusted the publication of his new volume of cantos, *Rock-Drill*, to him. At risk of losing copyright, for the sake of good printing he trusted and trained the younger generation. His Italian, French, and Swedish publishers were all in their twenties. Pound's work needed translations and he followed them closely, especially into German and Italian. I like to call *The Cantos* "the American epic"—a greater gift can no poet make to his country—though I know that his message has universal value.

That I was, according to Pound's wishes, to act as literary executor I had interpreted as having the responsibility for protecting Pound's work, his property, his ideas and reputation, his "cultural unit." Respect for privacy should not entail disregard for the author's instructions and provisions. When, in 1966, Yale promised to establish a Center for the Study of Ezra Pound and His Contemporaries and a friend supplied the funds to acquire the Pound Archive, its "ownership" was disputed and I was forced to engage a lawyer. I turned to Thurman Arnold because he had managed to get Pound released from St. Elisabeths, however unsatisfactory the conditions.

Judge Arnold decided I had some say in the matter as "joint partner." I did not object to the joint partnership; after all, we had been partners when buying a sheep or a beehive. The main idea was to keep the cultural unit, i.e., his archive and

8. Ezra Pound, *Confucius, Digest of the Analects* (Milan: Giovanni Scheiwiller, private printing, 1937); Pound, *Profile: An Anthology* (Milan: Giovanni Scheiwiller, private printing, 1932); and Pound, *Lavoro e Usura* (Milan: All'insegna del pesce d'oro, 1954).

library, safe and together. At that time, some funds might also have made life easier for my parents, in fact for all of us, since Pound was ill and worried.

One need not rehash that story. Donald Gallup has given some account in his *Pigeons on the Granite*.⁹ I spent time translating contemporaries of Pound and writing *Discretions*, being well aware of "the dangerous power of discretion,"¹⁰ i.e., as Cicero said, "by law hide neither truth in favor or in disfavor." The book was published in 1971 with a few excisions by the editors for fear of libel.¹¹

When the time came to settle Pound's estate, the argument was: "If a madman throws his golden watch from the window, his wife has a right to demand it back." As "literary agent for Europe," I had a right to a generous "rake-off," as an attorney called my 25 percent, and my mother was provided for.

In 1948, Olga Rudge had published *"If This Be Treason…"* at her own expense, in an attempt to call attention to Pound's predicament.¹² She was severely criticized for it. As soon as the Pound Archive in the Beinecke Library was opened, I set about obtaining permission from the trustees of the Pound estate to edit the radio speeches. Pound had wanted a hundred published. Only the most vituperative and damaging parts of the speeches were continually quoted out of context or, even worse, used by maniacs to further their own interests. *Ezra Pound Speaking* was edited by Leonard W. Doob and published by Greenwood Press in its Contributions to American Studies series in 1978. Just as my time and energy, let alone emotions, had been tenfold, the work was even more criticized than *"If This Be Treason…"* Both our attempts were perhaps historically untimely and achieved the wrong results.

Thanks to *Discretions*, I had been awarded a Radcliffe Fellowship that enabled me to return to the translation of *The Cantos* while the trustees were attending to contracts, etc. "There is no rogue in this play," said Pound somewhere,¹³ and, in Canto LXXXVII, "There is no such play for a goat" (594)—whatever the meaning. I was able to live in Cambridge, on Brattle Street, visit the Harvard Law School Library as well as the tomb of Pound's grandmother Mary Weston in Hopkinton and the Adams residence in Quincy.

9. Donald Clifford Gallup, *Pigeons on the Granite: Memoirs of a Yale Librarian* (New Haven, CT: Yale University Press, 1998).

10. Sir James Mackintosh, "A Discourse on the Law of Nature and Nations" (1799), rpt. in *The Miscellaneous Works of the Right Honourable Sir James Mackintosh* (London: Longman, Brown, Green, and Longmans, 1846), 1:381.

11. Mary de Rachewiltz, *Discretions* (Boston: Little, Brown, 1971).

12. Ezra Pound, *"If This Be Treason…"* (Siena, Italy: printed for Olga Rudge by Tip. Nuova, 1948).

13. Quoted in de Rachewiltz, *Discretions*, 188.

Occasionally, I passed the building with the name of Judge Pound on it—Homer Pound had addressed him as "cousin"—and I visited the Wadsworth Athenaeum and Longfellow House. Pedestrian research, it felt like

> Here from the beginning, we have been here
> from the beginning (CXII.804)

If we consider that scholars are still debating whether Pietro Pomponazzi wanted his *De Fato* published or to circulate in manuscript—as was still customary in early 1500—and that Pound himself questioned the various readings of Cavalcanti's "Donna mi prega," who will decide between right and wrong text, who is able to interpret the antinomies, the "double language"?[14]

In Canto LIII we read "to catechumen alone" (272), and in Canto XCVI there is a footnote stating the right to address people with "*special interests and whose curiosity reaches into greater detail*" (679). What is absolutely clear is that the poet demanded just distribution and communication, honesty of mind and sincerity, and strove to enhance awareness in his readers. Although he occasionally fired off angry letters to publishers like Mondadori or even to his friends T. S. Eliot and J. Laughlin, it was not about percentage but about shabby printing. He was dead against all forms of monopoly.

But I can't help feeling genetically responsible for Pound's palimpsest as well as for his descendants because I know he cared. He wanted us to establish a homestead, plant trees, and protect the endangered green world. It may entail parting with some tangible property. Some of Pound's manuscripts, early and late, are veritable artworks, telling a story of their own like old parchments or brittle fabric. Pound was an advocate of facsimiles, went to great trouble to have "plates," i.e., photocopies, of Cavalcanti manuscripts and Vivaldi concerts. One of his lasting disappointments was the failure of Harvard University Press to produce an edition of *The Confucian Odes* with the music. His last definition of *The Cantos* was: it's *music*.[15]

Now that "artificial intelligence" offers so many new possibilities of reproducing and making a poet's striving and intentions public, perhaps it's time also to formulate new copyright statutes for facsimiles: "The shrine seen and not seen" (CX.801). No Lasa marble columns stand as yet on top of our mountain and "stone

14. See Ezra Pound, *Ezra Pound Speaking: Radio Speeches of World War II*, ed. Leonard W. Doob (Westport, CT: Greenwood, 1978), 349.

15. See Pound, "Breaking the Silence: The Interview of Vanni Ronsisvalle and Pier Paolo Pasolini with Ezra Pound in 1968," trans. David Anderson, *Paideuma* 10 (1981): 331–345.

eyes" no longer look seaward (LXXIV.455), yet in one of the last, as yet unpublished holograph fragments Pound reaffirms and capitalizes: "MA LA BELLEZZA ESISTE," i.e.,

> But the beauty exists...
> as toward a bridge over worlds.

(Only the second line has appeared in print; see Notes for CXVII et seq., 823).

> Let the wind speak (CXX.822)

> No wind is the king's (IV.16)

PART SEVEN

Modernism after Modernism after Modernism

13 "It's Good to Be Primitive"

African Allusion and the Modernist Fetish of Authenticity

Joseph R. Slaughter

---

if you will go to a certain place and there digge, you will find traces of a civilization with such and such characteristics.

—Ezra Pound, paraphrasing Leo Frobenius, in *Guide to Kulchur*

What has been done here cannot possibly be denied. It cannot by any stretch of the imagination be explained or excused as the sort of utilisation of literary source-material that characterises much of the work of Joyce, Eliot, Pound and other writers. It is no act of homage to Graham Greene, and it is assuredly not a coincidence. It is simple and straightforward plagiarism.

—Robert McDonald, "*Bound to Violence*: A Case of Plagiarism"

A hole in the head and a broken neck: these are the contradictory findings of an informal literary autopsy on a colonial corpse in Malian writer Yambo Ouologuem's 1968 novel *Le Devoir de violence*. The discrepancy between a gunshot to the forehead and a twisted neck creates a textual enigma that might, at first glance, appear to be a simple and straightforward problem of translation. But it is also a problem of allusion, and one that had nearly fatal consequences for this Francophone novel in which a character dies twice in English while he dies only once in French. The double death occurs in a scene in which two henchmen of an African chief (Saif ben Isaac al-Heit) execute a colonial French governor in the Sahel. By a quirk of the historical present tense, death comes to the Saif's arch-rival differently for readers of the two English translations, Ralph Manheim's *Bound to Violence* (1971) and Christopher Wise's "The Duty of Violence" (2008). The following takes place between midnight and 1 A.M., July 14, 1913:

> For awhile [*sic*] now, [Governor Vandame] had been moving closer and closer to the rock where his pistol lay. Kratonga had noticed it, and Wampoulo too, no doubt. Suddenly, he pivoted and plunged head first for the rock to grab the gun. He picked it up, aimed it at the two men, and pressed the trigger—he pressed it again, three times in a row. Then his hand went limp and dropped to his side....
>
> A hyena, far off in the bush, let loose a deafening howl. Vandame remained in the shadows, sweating profusely....
>
> The governor stepped from the shadows, fully cognizant of what awaited him. "We can forget about all this, if you like," he said without much conviction.
>
> . . .
>
> "I just adore you, Vandame. You are the picture of the righteous colonizer.... I tell you what. We're going to play William Tell.... Pick up your report about His Royal Highness [the Saif].... Roll it into a ball, Vandame. Put it on top of your head, captain."
>
> . . .
>
> Kratonga ground his teeth. The barrel of his automatic pistol precisely marked its target. Kratonga held the pistol at arm's length and took careful aim.
>
> The pistol emitted a dry crackling sound, muted by the crashing of the waterfall. Vandame frantically jumped up, as [the report] burst into flames. Kratonga blew out the fire and then placed the barrel against Vandame's head. He steadied his aim. The pistol rang out in the night. A small hole appeared on the forehead of the governor, near his right eyebrow, along his nasal canal. He partially opened his eyes, as blood flowed from his head to the ground. He stepped forward to lift himself up, as if he wished to flee the scene. Then he softly slouched to the ground, stiffening for an instant and slobbering on the sand. At last, he collapsed on his belly. His feet scraped against the rock, as a rumbling of his bowels could be heard, a gurgling sound that escaped from his throat. Then his lungs let loose a long, uneven death rattle. He was a righteous man.[1]

1. Yambo Ouologuem, "The Duty of Violence," trans. Christopher Wise, in *The Yambo Ouologuem Reader*, ed. Christopher Wise (Trenton, NJ: Africa World Press, 2008), 132–135.

This translation by Christopher Wise is a rather literal rendition of Ouologuem's French; it maintains the plot and the prosaic details of the original passage, and it carries in English the apparent Homeric allusions of the French version that comprise the graphic death sentences of Vandame's Iliadic end. But is *The Iliad* really the object of allusion in Wise's translation? To which text(s) does it point? Does the English passage simply index a corresponding French passage in Ouologuem's novel, or does it directly invoke similar passages in Homer? If the latter, then which Homer? Leconte de Lisle's *L'Iliade* (1850), or Mario Meunier's *Iliade* (1943), or some other modern French translation of the classical Greek epic? Or, does the English translation (directly or indirectly) refer to an English translation of *The Iliad*? or to the Greek text? or to a Platonic ideal of Homer? In short, does the passage allude to an idea (which is not susceptible of copyright) or to a particular form of expression of an idea (which can be protected by law)? However critics answer such literary questions (and from a legal and economic perspective, such answers might be material), readers who recognize Homer in Ouologuem's novel are unlikely to call this intertextual liaison plagiarism. And yet, *Le Devoir de violence*—awarded the 1969 Prix Renaudot for outstanding original novel in French—is today mostly remembered for the plagiarism and copyright scandal that erupted in 1972 after Heinemann published Manheim's English translation of *Bound to Violence* and Robert McDonald detected in it an extended passage from Greene's 1934 novel *It's a Battlefield*.[2]

The elusiveness of allusion in this scene raises larger questions about the contingency of intertextuality, and *l'affaire Ouologuem* offers rich material for examining how the lines between closely related forms of intertextuality—allusion, quotation, translation, parody, and plagiarism (among others)—were inflected by the postcolonial politics and racial dynamics of metropolitan France in the late modernist period (dynamics that are, I think, characteristic of Euro-modernity generally). Indeed, the ways in which the literary industry adjudicated matters of intertextuality in this case are instructive for thinking about the transnational, transcultural, and translinguistic condition (and entanglements) of a

---

2. That McDonald discovered the plagiarism in translation (and in English) is a particularly interesting aspect of this case—especially since the text that was copied into the original (French) *Le Devoir de violence* was not Greene's (English) novel itself but its French translation, which was then translated back into English by Manheim. The copyright matter was apparently settled "in-house," since Heinemann handled the rights for both Greene's novel and the English translation of Ouologuem's. I should note that *Le Devoir de violence* is filled with appropriations from (among many others) Guy de Maupassant, Ian Fleming, Alain Robbe-Grillet, Camara Laye, Georges Bataille, Victor Hugo, Emile Zola, Proust, and Baudelaire.

Euro-modernity that has historically pretended to be self-styled and self-contained, even as it has devoured other (non)modernities and claimed an expanding monopoly on modern intellectual property.

The beginning of the modernist era can be marked by two simultaneous major property grabs: the distribution among European powers of African land and resources, formalized in the General Act of the Conference of the Treaty of Berlin (1885), and the legal consolidation of predominantly European intellectual property at the international level with the Berne Convention for the Protection of Literary and Artistic Works (1886), which effectively partitioned (or redlined) "world literary space"[3] between those who own culture and those who don't—between, that is, the autonomous intellectual-property-owning peoples of the global North and the dependent, mostly intellectual-property-less peoples of the global South. According to this (largely racialized) model, Africa and other non-Western locations have a store of raw intellectual and cultural resources, but the West possesses the modern technology to process and propertize those unrefined materials—to personalize and privatize the cultural commons.

Paris in 1968 was not just the scene of student revolts; it was also the hothouse for a "revolution in poetic language" that brought both the death of the author and the birth of *intertextualité* (in Julia Kristeva's 1967 neologism)—the recognition that every text is, as Roland Barthes wrote, "the text-between of another text."[4] The specific "relationship of co-presence between two texts" is notoriously difficult to determine, but, to put it bluntly, over the stretch of long modernism, the "problem" of plagiarism has often been a problem of the color line.[5] Early critical condemnations of Ouologuem's novel drew on older modernist assumptions about authorship and textuality that underwrote the territorial expansion of international intellectual property law and facilitated modern European art's wholesale appropriation of "primitive" cultural production. However, just as "the inevitability of

---

3. Pascale Casanova, *The World Republic of Letters*, trans. M. B. DeBevoise (Cambridge, MA: Harvard University Press, 2004), 43.

4. Julia Kristeva, *Revolution in Poetic Language*, trans. Margaret Waller (New York: Columbia University Press, 1984), 59; Roland Barthes, "From Work to Text," in *Image/Music/Text*, trans. Stephen Heath (New York: Noonday, 1977), 160.

5. Gérard Genette, *Paratexts: Thresholds of Interpretation*, trans. Jane E. Lewin (Cambridge: Cambridge University Press, 1997), 1. Roger Little traces the colonial roots of plagiarism charges against black authors to the earliest African writing in the eighteenth century. Little, "Reflections on a Triangular Trade in Borrowing and Stealing: Textual Exploitation in a Selection of African, Caribbean, and European Writers in French," *Research in African Literatures* 71 (2006): 18.

allusion's misfiring"[6] in modernist poetry poses problems for the New Critical estimation of a poem's formal integrity and internal coherence, the radical inter-textuality of Ouologuem's novel punctures a pair of cultural essentialist (read: rac-ist and racialist) corollaries at the heart of modernism and copyright: metropolitan pretensions about the integrity of French (or, more broadly, Western) literary culture and the equally problematic presumptions about the racial coherence and radical alterity of African literary production.[7]

"The Savage Novel That Won the Prix Renaudot in Paris"[8]

Le Devoir de violence tells the epic story of a fictional African empire called Nakem, from its precolonial beginnings in 1202 to the verge of its nominal integration into "postcolonial" France with the election of deputies to the national assembly in 1947. The novel traces the political intrigues of Nakem's dynastic rulers (the Saifs) and what the narrator describes as "the bloody adventure of the niggertrash [*négraille*]"—a word Aimé Césaire coined in *Cahier d'un retour au pays natal* (1939) to characterize the degraded black masses and that Christopher Wise trans-lates, from Ouologuem's novel, as "black-rabble."[9] In the fictional empire of Nakem, the *négraille* are subjected to interminable violence, sexual degradation, and exploitation, first by native African "notables" (the Saifs) and later with the foreign aid of Arab slave traders, Catholic missionaries, and French colonial offi-cers. In a sense, *Le Devoir de violence* offers a prehistory of Césaire's *négraille*, only without the existential redemption of *négritude*—without, in other words, Césaire's famous racialist embrace in *Cahier*: "J'accepte...j'accepte...entièrement, sans réserve."[10] Indeed, Ouologuem's cynical vision of eternal degradation mounts a frontal assault on what the novel's narrator calls the "Black romanticism" of

6. Kevin J. H. Dettmar, "The Illusion of Modernist Allusion and the Politics of Postmodern Plagiarism," in *Perspectives on Plagiarism and Intellectual Property in a Postmodern World*, ed. Lise Buranen and Alice M. Roy (Albany: State University of New York Press, 1999), 101.

7. The New Critical creed about the internal coherence of a poem seems related to the cultural nationalist ideology that pervades the modernist period.

8. This is from the blurb on the back of the Heinemann edition of *Bound to Violence*.

9. Yambo Ouologuem, *Bound to Violence*, trans. Ralph Manheim (London: Heinemann, 1971), 3. All subsequent citations of *Bound to Violence* are to the Manheim translation and are given parenthetically in the text as *BtV* with page or (where appropriate) line numbers.

10. Aimé Césaire, *Notebook of a Return to My Native Land/Cahier d'un retour au pays natal*, ed. Timothy Mathews and Michael Worton, trans. Mireille Rosello and Annie Pritchard (Newcastle upon Tyne: Bloodaxe, 1995), 120.

"dreamers of African unity" (*BtV*, 8, 5), like Césaire, Léon Damas, and Léopold Sédar Senghor, as well as of the German explorer and archaeologist Leo Frobenius, upon whose speculative ethnological foundations those romantic dreamers erected the edifice of *négritude*. (As we shall see, Ouologuem lampoons Frobenius in the figure of the gullible salvage ethnographer Fritz Shrobenius.)

Le Devoir de violence was hailed in *Le Monde* in 1968 as "le premier roman afric-ain digne de ce nom" ("the first African novel worthy of the name"); the American press greeted its English translation with an equally extravagant sobriquet: "the first truly African novel."[11] These essentialist epithets largely set the terms of early criticism, which consistently focused on the novel's ethnocultural "authenticity" or, more exactly, its Africanicity. For many readers, Yambo Ouologuem embodied the "hopes" and "promise" of an entire race; his novel represented "a genuine impulse emanating from an individual talent and lending expression to the his-torico-ethnic heartbeat of a misunderstood continent," in the stirring words of Eric Sellin, echoing T. S. Eliot's vision of the embeddedness of "the individual talent" within a cultural tradition.[12] *Le Monde* had lauded such an enduring ethnic essence (uncontaminated by imperialism) at the novel's publication: "Six years in France, months of teaching at the lycée de Charenton, preparation for a diploma in English studies—successfully passed—then the *agrégation de lettres*, none of this has altered his authentically African vision [*vision authentiquement afric-aine*]."[13] Ouologuem was quickly enrolled as part of a new wave of modern African writers who seemed to reject the realism and romantic nationalism of the first generation.[14] The novel was especially praised for "delivering the final death-blow to Senghorian *négritude*,... clearing the way for a more honest literature divested of the sickly longing for a false African past."[15] However, even as its iconoclasm was praised as "inevitable and salutary" (in Wole Soyinka's words), some critics feared that, in its rebuttal of Senghorian mythopoetics, the novel may have gone too far, pandering to Western prejudice by exaggerating and exacerbating the dominant culture's images of savage and primitive Africa.[16]

11. Matthieu Galey, "Un grand roman Africain," *Le Monde* (Oct. 12, 1968): ii, cited in "Something *New* Out of Africa?" *Times Literary Supplement* (May 5, 1972): 525.

12. Eric Sellin, "The Unknown Voice of Yambo Ouologuem," *Yale French Studies* 53 (1976): 139.

13. Philippe Decraene, "Un Nègre à part entière," *Le Monde* (Oct. 12, 1968): i.

14. Abiola Irele, "A New Mood in the African Novel," *West Africa* (Sept. 20, 1969): 1113–1115.

15. Christopher Wise, "Introduction: A Voice from Bandiagara," in *Yambo Ouologuem: Postcolonial Writer, Islamic Militant*, ed. Christopher Wise (Boulder, CO: Rienner, 1999), 10.

16. Wole Soyinka, *Myth, Literature and the African World* (Cambridge: Cambridge University Press, 1976), 100. See J. Mbelolo ya Mpiku, "From One Mystification to Another: 'Négritude' and 'Négraille' in *Le Devoir de violence*," in Wise, *Yambo Ouologuem*.

The symbolic death-blow delivered in the colonial governor's murder scene seems less directed to *négritude* than to its popular French companion *négrophilie*, the exoticist enthusiasm for black "primitive" cultural expression that spurred the modernist rejuvenation of European arts in the early twentieth century. The novel travesties negrophilia's dark side in a series of colonial officials who fetishize African culture, difference, and their imperial domination through predatory sexual encounters with black bodies. The gritty "pornographic excess" of such scenes propels the novel's scattershot sarcasm, undercutting a romanticized vision of African society while also indicting a European anthropological gaze for its negrophilic fascination with the so-called primitive libido and black essence.[17] Ironically, although the excessive (and formulaic) violence of Vandame's murder is traceable to the founding text of Western civilization and imperialism, its Homeric echoes went largely unheard by readers listening for the authentic savage strains of prehistoric Africa.

While the gory scene repeats particular Homeric formulas, the opening lines of the novel appear to be composed according to traditional African (and Islamic) oral formulaic principles:

> Our eyes drink the brightness of the sun and, overcome, marvel at their tears. *Mashallah! wa bismillah!*... To recount the bloody adventure of the niggertrash... there would be no need to go back beyond the present century; but the true history of the Blacks begins much earlier, with the Saifs, in the year 1202 of our era. (*BtV*, 3)[18]

However, the appearance of an oral introduction is somewhat misleading, since these lines adapt the opening words of André Schwarz-Bart's Goncourt Prize–winning epic of the Jews, *Le Dernier des justes* (1959): "Our eyes register the light of dead stars. A biography of my friend Ernie could easily be set in the second quarter of the twentieth century, but the true history of Ernie Levy begins much earlier, toward the year 1000 of our era."[19] Evidence of this "imitation" was a blow to

---

17. Eleni Coundouriotis, *Claiming History: Colonialism, Ethnography, and the Novel* (New York: Columbia University Press, 1999), 138. This "ethnological" attitude persisted in many of Ouologuem's interviews. Thus, for instance, he was asked to respond to the following observation: "In the West, we have our own ideas about black sexuality. We believe that it has retained a spontaneity that the whites have lost." Ouologuem, "An Interview with Yambo Ouologuem," *Journal of the New African Literature and the Arts* 9–10 (1971): 136.

18. On Ouologuem's debt to African oral histories and Arabic epics, see Christopher Wise, "Qur'anic Hermeneutics, Sufism, and *Le Devoir de violence*: Yambo Ouologuem as Marabout Novelist," in Wise, *Yambo Ouologuem*, 175–195.

19. André Schwarz-Bart, *The Last of the Just*, trans. Stephen Becker (New York: Atheneum, 1960), 3.

wistful Western liberals longing for an authentic African essence that had somehow survived the cultural and intellectual ravages of the slave trade, colonialism, and postcolonial socialization. If *Le Devoir de violence* was simply "an African *Dernier des Justes*" (as Eric Sellin lamented in his exposé), and if it was Graham Greene who was apparently "capable of effortlessly conveying [Africa's] traditional rhythms" (as the *Times Literary Supplement* teased), then the novel was "not fundamentally autochthonous in its rhythms and in its genesis" and, therefore, this "first truly African novel" was "not the first real African novel"![20]

Authenticity is a question of framing—of delimiting a hypothetical field of resemblances and expectations within which the object is judged, e.g., the "African novel," "African vision," postcolonial literature, or "véritable roman nègre," in the phrase that introduced a metropolitan reading public to René Maran's Goncourt Prize–winning Francophone novel, *Batouala* (1921). Before the plagiarism scandal, critics generally framed Ouologuem's novel according to the biographical clues printed on the book's back cover, emphasizing his extraordinary intellectual credentials to heighten the apparent contrast between his staid European education and his wild African vision: "Né en 1940 au Mali. Admissible à l'École normale supérieure. Licencié ès Lettres. Licencié en Philosophie. Diplôme d'Études supérieures d'Anglais. Prépare une thèse de doctorat de Sociologie." Ouologuem was caught between the discourses (or cults) of authenticity and originality, racked between the poles of (African) tradition and (French) individual talent. Theoretically, these are not opposed principles; however, within what James Clifford calls the "art-culture authenticity system" that processes and packages (i.e., cleanses and authenticates) African and other "ethnic" artifacts for admission into the cultural institutions of Euro-modernity, the kind of racialized authenticity promoted for African writers is very different from the monadic version of existential self-authenticity comprehended by authorial originality.[21] Despite having "the whole of the literature of Europe from Homer" at his disposal (as Eliot urged),[22] the de facto redlining of world literary property seems to have meant that Ouologuem's being Malian struck his reviewers more sharply than the fact that he was a *normalien*.

20. Eric Sellin, "Ouologuem's Blueprint for *Le Devoir de violence*," *Research in African Literatures* 2 (1971): 118, 120; "Something *New* Out of Africa?" *Times Literary Supplement* (May 5, 1972): 525.

21. James Clifford, *The Predicament of Culture: Twentieth-century Ethnography, Literature, and Art* (Cambridge, MA: Harvard University Press, 1988), 235.

22. T. S. Eliot, "Tradition and the Individual Talent" (1919), rpt. in *Selected Prose of T. S. Eliot*, ed. Frank Kermode (New York: Harcourt Brace Jovanovich, 1975), 38.

"Out of Place, Out of Style, and Out of Character";[23] or, Whatever Happened to Homer?

As I noted, 2008 was not the first time Vandame died in English, nor was an execution-style head shot the first cause of death in the original translation of *Bound to Violence*, in which Ouologuem apparently had a hand. Manheim's translation tells a different story. The following takes place (again) between midnight and 1 A.M., July 14, 1913:

> For some moments he [Governor Vandame] had been moving imperceptibly closer to the automatic. Kratonga had noticed, and so had Wampoulo no doubt. Suddenly Vandame pivoted, plunged head-first at the rock, and seized the weapon. He aimed it at the two men and, in the awful daring of a moment's surrender, pulled the trigger, 5 pulled it again, three times in succession. Then blood shook his heart; his hands slowed down and stopped....
>
> From far off in the bush the muffled plaint of a hyena was heard. There was no end, only addition: Vandame was sweating profusely....
>
> The governor turned around and, dying in his own death, whis- 10 pered: "You're taking a terrible risk."
>
> ...
>
> "I love you, Vandame. You're the righteous man of colo-nialism.... You're okay, pal. We're going to play William Tell.... Pick 15 up your report about His Royal Magnificence [the Saif].... Roll it into a ball, Vandame. Put it on your head, Major."
>
> ...
>
> Kratonga ground his teeth. The barrel of the automatic describing diminishing circles. Kratonga held it at arm's length and took metic- 20 ulous aim.
>
> The automatic gave a dry cough, muffled by the roaring of the waterfall. Vandame jerked convulsively and the report burst into flames. Wampoulo extinguished the blaze and replaced the report on the governor's head. Again Kratonga took aim. "Oh, Governor," he 25 gasped. "I had such an awful dream. I dreamed about me. I thought some Whites were chasing me, and I couldn't run, and my neck was— oh, it was all covered with blood. Oh-h, I can't go on."

23. James Olney, *Tell Me Africa: An Approach to African Literature* (Princeton, NJ: Princeton University Press, 1973), 204n4.

Vandame was seized with a panic terror, unreasoning, instinctive. "Not a soul need know what's happened to us," Kratonga wailed. And his dry, passionate talk commanded attention.

For some time Vandame had not heard Wampoulo moving and had begun to wonder what he was doing.

When he sensed danger, he groped at shapes and ran because he could not stop for death. Suddenly Wampoulo clasped his shoulders and shook them so frantically that Vandame's neck swung and broke.

Quicker than speech, his arms waltzed above him, then rowed him softlier home, to the Artful Creator.

Blood spurted from the nape of his neck like reluctant rubies grasped by a beetle. His eyeballs like frightened beads, Vandame drank a dewdrop from a blade of grass. He was a righteous man. (*BtV*, 112–115)

In England in 1971, Vandame was shaken to death, not shot as he was in France in 1968 and in the United States in 2008.[24] The discrepant modes of death are probably not the most interesting or significant differences between the two scenes. From the perspective of plot and theme, the alterations in English are rather inconsequential. More striking are the manner and extent of the embellishments, which would appear to violate the identity, or even the dignity, of the original text—what John Crowe Ransom referred to as "the living integrity" of a literary work.[25] Manheim's translation no longer invokes Homer, and its relationship to the original French text (represented in this chapter by Wise's literal translation) is unclear. What is gained in translation might seem scandalous (as Lawrence Venuti characterizes these sorts of things), if as readers we hold the idea (or expectation) that translation "produces an exact copy of the form and content of the underlying work. A translation is not regarded as an independent text . . . [even when] linguistic and literary differences which are specific to the translating culture . . . are added to the foreign text to make it intelligible in that culture."[26] The French and English

24. The multiple versions of this scene raise interesting questions about the temporality of literature and of criticism. When is the literary present? Are all literary presents, across all translations of the same text, the same? synchronous? When is the critical present? Where and how is Vandame currently dying, in the progressive tense? Which of these texts should be given priority, in terms of both authority and precedence?

25. John Crowe Ransom, "Criticism, Inc." (1938), rpt. in *Praising It New: The Best of the New Criticism*, ed. Garrick Davis and William Logan (Athens: Ohio University Press, 2008), 61.

26. Lawrence Venuti, *The Scandals of Translation: Towards an Ethics of Difference* (New York: Routledge, 1998), 51.

cultures of violence and imperialism are not so very different that a gunshot at home would be better understood as a neck wringing abroad; and in any case, the smoking gun remains in Manheim's translation, even if its narrative significance has changed.

Triangulated with the French original and the more recent American edition, Manheim's text appears to be what contemporary intellectual property law refers to suggestively as an "unfaithful translation" (*une traduction infidèle*).[27] The international right not to have one's writing adulterated in such fashion is one of the moral rights (taken from the French *droit moral*) that attach to authors, including the right to be identified as the creator of a work and to "object to any distortion, mutilation or other modification of, or other derogatory action in relation to, the said work," in the language of the current Berne Convention.[28] The moral rights clause, protecting an author's rights of "paternity" and integrity (among others), imagines a stable text that remains uncompromised even by the kinds of changes that translators often make to domesticate it in a target language. Although the mere act of translation tends to excite "fear[s] of inauthenticity, distortion, [and] contamination," those fears are compounded here by the fact that Ouologuem himself apparently introduced these textual impurities specifically for an English-reading audience.[29] If, as Venuti writes, "the very function of translating is assimilation," then common "translation practices…[that] routinely aim…for their own concealment" resemble the "illicit" activities we ordinarily associate with plagiarism, since the ostensible goal of the plagiarist, like that of the self-effacing translator, is to displace text without seeming, or being seen, to displace text.[30] Ouologuem's literary infidelity to himself makes it possible to see how fine are the (color) lines between translation, allusion, and plagiarism.

As readers familiar with American and modernist canons will have noticed, errant fragments of famous poetry written in English have wandered into the Manheim translation; specifically, Homer has been displaced by T. S. Eliot and Emily Dickinson. Thus, the narrator's description of Vandame's desperate escape attempt—"He aimed it at the two men and, in the awful daring of a moment's

27. See Pierre Monnet, *Dictionnaire pratique de propriété littéraire* (Paris: Cercle de la Librairie, 1962), 256–260.

28. Berne Convention for the Protection of Literary and Artistic Works, 1971 Paris text, art. 6bis. The article adopting *le droit moral* as an international legal norm was added to the convention in the 1928 revision.

29. Venuti, *Scandals of Translation*, 31.

30. Ibid., 11, 31. On translation as a "legal form of plagiarism," see Emily Apter, "What Is Yours, Ours, and Mine: Authorial Ownership and the Creative Commons," *October* 126 (2008): 102.

surrender, pulled the trigger.... Then blood shook his heart" (*BtV* excerpt, ll. 4–6)—recalls "What the Thunder Said" in Eliot's *The Waste Land*:

> *Datta:* what have we given?
> My friend, blood shaking my heart
> The awful daring of a moment's surrender
> Which an age of prudence can never retract[31]

And the sultry atmosphere announcing the governor's doom—"From far off in the bush the muffled plaint of a hyena was heard. There was no end, only addition: Vandame was sweating profusely" (*BtV* extract, ll. 8–9)—has a whiff of the air of "The Dry Salvages" from Eliot's *Four Quartets*: "There is no end, but addition: the trailing / Consequence of further days and hours."[32] Vandame, who "ran because he could not stop for death" (*BtV* extract, ll. 33–34), is inevitably overtaken like Dickinson's speaker: "Because I could not stop for Death, / He kindly stopped for me" (#712).[33] Finally, the old Homeric register of Vandame's Iliadic death is now related in terms of Dickinson's account of a little bird's ordinary odyssey:

> Suddenly Wampoulo clasped his shoulders and shook them so frantically that Vandame's neck swung and broke.
>
> Quicker than speech, his arms waltzed above him, then rowed him softlier home, to the Artful Creator.
>
> Blood spurted from the nape of his neck like reluctant rubies grasped by a beetle. His eyeballs like frightened beads, Vandame drank a dewdrop from a blade of grass. He was a righteous man. (*BtV* extract, ll. 34–40)

> A Bird came down the walk:
>
> . . .
>
> And then he drank a dew
> From a convenient grass,
> And then hopped sidewise to the wall
> To let a beetle pass.
>
> He glanced with rapid eyes
> That hurried all abroad,—

31. T. S. Eliot, *The Waste Land* (1922), rpt. in *Collected Poems: 1909–1962* (New York: Harcourt, Brace and World, 1963), 68, ll. 402–405.

32. T. S. Eliot, "The Dry Salvages" (1941), rpt. ibid., 193.

33. Emily Dickinson, "Because I could not stop for Death" (1863), rpt. in *The Complete Poems of Emily Dickinson*, ed. Thomas H. Johnson (Boston: Little, Brown, 1961), 350.

They looked like frightened beads, I thought
He stirred his velvet head

Like one in danger; cautious,
I offered him a crumb,
And he unrolled his feathers
And rowed him softer home[34]

For literary English readers, these "borrowings" or "apparent allusions" (as Charles Larson and James Olney first called some of them) are not particularly difficult to discern; they are hardly hidden, and they leap out in a comparative reading of the texts.[35] So, what sort of literary (property) units are these itinerant fragments that showed up for the English translation?

The invocation of Eliot, especially of *The Waste Land* (that "tissue of allusions and half-allusions," as Cleanth Brooks described it), suggests that these are ordinary allusions of the modernist sort that Eliot himself is often credited with having "elevated to the status of a master trope in modernist fiction and verse."[36] Allusions perform a wide range of functions, but their work is culturally contingent and sociohistorically determined; that is, if "allusions are assumed to mean something," their meaning ostensibly depends upon recognition by a reader, which implies a whole set of literary and social relations in which "the reader must share a tradition with the author."[37] The practice of allusion is implicitly, if not explicitly, discriminative, separating those "in the know" from those who don't know, freeholders and leaseholders of literary property from trespassers and squatters.

Much has been written about the messy practice of modernist allusion and its complicated relation to what Andreas Huyssen famously called modernism's "anxiety of contamination"; for example, the footnotes Eliot provided to *The Waste Land* have been read variously as a formal symptom of contamination anxiety and as a "signal that the modern age has lamentably lost a common literary culture and tradition."[38] Typically, we talk about allusions working when readers recall the

34. Emily Dickinson, #328 ("A Bird came down the walk," ca. 1862), rpt. ibid., 156.
35. Charles R. Larson, *The Novel in the Third World* (Washington, DC: INSCAPE, 1976), 54; Olney, *Tell Me Africa*, 234. There are other rogue verses that do not appear in the original French, including more scraps recycled from Eliot: "Sweeney Agonistes" ("You're taking a terrible risk") and "A Song for Simeon" ("dying in his own death"). There are likely other unidentified fragments.
36. Cleanth Brooks, *The Well Wrought Urn: Studies in the Structure of Poetry* (New York: Houghton Mifflin Harcourt, 1956), 107; Dettmar, "The Illusion of Modernist Allusion," 99.
37. Gregory Machacek, "Allusion," *PMLA* 122 (2007): 530, 526.
38. Andreas Huyssen, *After the Great Divide: Modernism, Mass Culture, Postmodernism* (Bloomington: Indiana University Press, 1986), ix; Machacek, "Allusion," 531.

texts they invoke, closing "the circle of Tradition."[39] In such cases, allusions activate in readers' minds a memory of associated ideas, events, persons, or themes from literature past.[40] According to this mnemonic model of allusive reference, it is not so much the language of the text that is re-cited (or re-sited); rather, an allusion invokes the ideas evoked by the original phrasing—the connotations associated in the readers' literary experience with those words in their original context. If this is the case, then the particular expressive form of an allusion (its phrasing) is merely the most convenient vehicle for its tenor—for the train of its associated ideas.

Interestingly, early objections to Ouologuem's textual practices were more about the fitness of his appropriations than the quantity or duplicity of the imitations; references to writers like Eliot and Dickinson, it was said, "make little sense."[41] This was the complaint about Ouologuem's transplantation of "a rather sedate scene in an English communist's stronghold" to "the primitive scene" of Africa, where, in Robert McDonald's judgment, it had been "rammed in regardless of the fact that it does not fit into the altered context."[42] It was not so much the form of Greene's expression that seemed "ill-suited to the context into which it ha[d] been press-ganged"; rather, the ideas and themes clinging to Greene's prose struck McDonald and others as "noticeably out of place"—that is, the contents of the form seemed inauthentic, in an ethnocultural sense, and improper, in a historical and ideological sense. According to these judgments, *Bound to Violence* is out of modernist bounds; Ouologuem's intertextual practices are qualitatively (if not quantitatively) different from modernist allusion, from what "Joyce, Eliot, Pound and other writers" did. Indeed, Ouologuem is accused of being not just a bad writer and mimic man but, worse, a bad plagiarist—a clumsy craftsman with "not nearly enough care or skill" to accomplish "relevant adaptation."[43]

If the perceived "poverty of the borrowings" (as Larson characterized Ouologuem's practice)[44] jeopardizes their status as legitimate allusions, the

---

39. Dettmar, "The Illusion of Modernist Allusion," 100.

40. Dettmar offers the example of Eliot's allusion to Edmund Spenser's "Prothalamion," which, he suggests, for the "reader who recognizes the line" heightens the ironic conflation of love and sex in *The Waste Land*. Ibid.

41. Olney, *Tell Me Africa*, 234n19.

42. Tim Devlin, "Echoes of Graham Greene Halt Prizewinning Book," *Times* (London) (May 5, 1972): 1; Robert McDonald, "*Bound to Violence*: A Case of Plagiarism," *Transition* 41 (1972): 67.

43. McDonald, "*Bound to Violence*," 66–67. There's a certain irony in McDonald's charges of inauthenticity because his own account of the scenes from *Bound to Violence* are inaccurate. His sense of inauthenticity derives, at least partially, from his Orientalist expectations about Africa: for instance, he transports the Sahel to the dark Conradian "jungle" of Africa and finds Ouologuem's realist description of it wanting (64).

44. Larson, *The Novel in the Third World*, 59.

following bits of smuggled text break the illusion of allusion altogether. The literary memory that recalled these past passages was not human; it was digital, specifically Google Books.

Ouologuem, *Bound to Violence*	Frank Norris, *McTeague*[45]
Again Kratonga took aim. "Oh, Governor," he gasped. "I had such an awful dream. I dreamed about me. I thought some Whites were chasing me, and I couldn't run, and my neck was—oh, it was all covered with blood. Oh-h, I can't go on." Vandame was seized with a panic terror, unreasoning, instinctive.	"Oh, Mac," gasped his wife, "I had such an awful dream. I dreamed about Maria. I thought she was chasing me, and I couldn't run, and her throat was—Oh, she was all covered with blood. Oh-h, I am so frightened!" (331) Then suddenly Trina was seized with a panic terror, unreasoned, instinctive. (266)
"Not a soul need know what's happened to us," Kratonga wailed. And his dry, passionate talk commanded attention. For some time Vandame had not heard Wampoulo moving and had begun to wonder what he was doing. (ll. 24–32)	"Not a soul need know what's happened to us," she said to her husband. (268) She had not heard McTeague moving about for some time and had begun to wonder what he was doing. (268)

These textual units, not in the French original, are also not the sort that would likely trigger particular associations in the reader's mind; they are banal and forgettable, even for avid fans of Frank Norris's classic novel of lust, greed, and murder in late nineteenth-century San Francisco. And yet their presence in the translated text is no accident; their assimilation required work: small modifications of the Norris passages and minor adjustments to the murder plot. The masked appearances of *McTeague* in *Bound to Violence* seem inadequate as allusions, but their substitution for perfectly adequate phrases in the French text complicates the easy judgment that a plagiarist is "not an author" because "he lacks the talent to become one."[46]

45. Frank Norris, *McTeague: A Story of San Francisco* (New York: Doubleday, Page, 1914).
46. Marilyn Randall, *Pragmatic Plagiarism: Authorship, Profit, and Power* (Toronto: University of Toronto Press, 2001), 17.

There may be some tenuous logic to this textual promiscuity, a thematic correspondence that hooks up the two novels; in place of Homer, the converted *McTeague* passages invoke a sense of the beastliness of human nature associated with Norris's naturalism, which, some say, was itself too indebted to Zola. *McTeague* is a good early modernist study of man's primal passions that anticipates Freud's version of the repressive hypothesis elaborated in *Civilization and Its Discontents*: just below the placid, studied surface of civilized man lurk the basest instincts, which may escape savagely (as in the violent rages of Norris's dentist) or may be liberated artistically (as in the contrived creative expressions of "modernist primitivism" that came into vogue with French negrophilia).[47] As plausible as such a reading is (and a similar argument could account for the presence of Graham Greene's novel), it requires us to accept one or two improbable assumptions: either the reader could be expected to recognize Norris's novel as the source of the translation (which the critical record refutes), or the naturalist overtones of modernist primitivism are carried even in the imported language of these extraordinarily ordinary sentences.

Like some of the violence in the text, the shotgun spray of Ouologuem's "allusions" seems almost gratuitous—an excessive spillage of canonical blood to accompany the excessive spillage of colonial blood. We can forge a meaning from this effect, in good New Critical fashion, by making the text's appropriative form match its themes, if not in content then in performance—as, for instance, an anti-imperialist assault on the Western literary industry and "European assumptions about writing and creating," as many postcolonial salvage critics have done.[48] Such

47. James Clifford, "Negrophilia: 1933, February," in *A New History of French Literature*, ed. Denis Hollier et al. (Cambridge, MA: Harvard University Press, 1989), 901. See also Bernard Gendron, "Fetishes and Motorcars: Negrophilia in French Modernism," *Cultural Studies* 4 (1990): 141–155; Petrine Archer-Shaw, *Negrophilia: Avant-Garde Paris and Black Culture in the 1920s* (London: Thames and Hudson, 2000).

48. Christopher L. Miller, *Blank Darkness: Africanist Discourse in French* (Chicago: University of Chicago Press, 1985), 219. Richard Serrano, who leverages the novel to indict postcolonial criticism for its "insistence on reading only for 'authenticity,'" concludes straight-facedly that "the inauthenticity of Yambo Ouologuem's *Le Devoir de violence* ... renders it an authentic African text." Richard Serrano, *Against the Postcolonial: "Francophone" Writers at the Ends of French Empire: After the Empire* (Lanham, MD: Lexington, 2005), 35. In the name of debunking postcolonialism, Serrano conducts an eloquent postcolonial reading of the novel; he supports his confused indictment by citing critics who are, or were at the time, cultural nativists, writing before the advent of postcolonialism as a mode of reading, and they represent the sorts of essentialist thinking that good postcolonial work (and Ouologuem's novel itself) undoes. In order to characterize postcolonialism as obsessed with "authenticity," Serrano strategically distorts (or ignores) critiques by Seth Wolitz, Christopher Miller, Christiane Chaulet-Achour, Abiola Irele, Biodun Jeyifo, Graham Huggan, and K. Anthony Appiah.

readings seek to maintain the integrity, identity, and authenticity of the novel by coordinating Ouologuem's medium and message. In this vein, the conversion of *The Waste Land* into a recycling center for postcolonial scrapbooking may seem rather canny to many readers today; it pushes the limits of authorship, flouts the authority of the dominant literary institutions, and reintroduces excess, free play, and the principle of waste into the semantic economy of "a world where," as Foucault wrote, "one is thrifty not only with one's resources and riches but also with one's discourses and their significations."[49] However, such readings largely ignore the fact that some blocks of wayward text in *Bound to Violence* have an anti-allusive quality that doesn't openly invite readers to make something thematic of Ouologuem's illicit textual relations with other authors.

"[O]nly the text can tell us whether an allusion exists," Allan Pasco tells us, but typically, the discovery of textual co-presence is enough to bring back, with a vengeance, the author and authorial intention (theoretically banished with New Criticism and undone entirely with poststructuralism).[50] The presence of Norris's frontier American dentist in Ouologuem's colonial West Africa may expose the raw nerves of our assumptions about literary property and propriety, but it also reveals the arbitrariness of the boundary between allusion and plagiarism. Allusion, like translation, is a close cousin of plagiarism; indeed, it tends to drift toward plagiarism. Unlike translation, allusion *becomes* plagiarism only when references to source texts are not readily apparent to readers.[51] Small fragments of text immediately recognized are rarely regarded as plagiarism. Allusion, it seems, is impossible and plagiarism only possible when writer and reader do not share a common text—either narrowly (a particular text) or broadly (an entire cultural canon). Ouologuem was blamed for his recitations because, despite centuries of colonial history, early readers prejudicially assumed that a redlined African author would not (or could not or should not) borrow from the bank of Western literature in an "authentic African novel."

The distinction between allusion and plagiarism can be parsed in terms of the idea/expression dichotomy enshrined in copyright law; this may shed some light on modernist appropriative practices and the ways in which the (international) inter-

---

49. Michel Foucault, "What Is an Author?" (1969), rpt. in *The Foucault Reader*, ed. Paul Rabinow (New York: Pantheon, 1984), 118.

50. Allan H. Pasco, *Allusion: A Literary Graft* (Charlottesville, VA: Rookwood, 2002), 17.

51. For instance, as readers get further and further from T. S. Eliot's setting and season, his unmarked allusions drift closer and closer to plagiarism. Dettmar suggests that readers who do not initially recognize Spenser in Eliot's poem will likely conclude, upon discovering it, that Eliot plagiarized. Dettmar, "The Illusion of Modernist Allusion," 101.

textual color line is anxiously policed in the modernist period. Copyright protects the form of expression, but it does little for ideas, themes, and plots. If plagiarism reproduces an "external text" within "the text in hand" and "attempts to prevent the reader from seeing their identity and bringing them together," allusion prompts the literary memory to recall the external text and to activate its associated ideas, themes, and meanings.[52] When we respond to snippets of text as allusions, we tend to weigh the (unprotected) ideas and themes that they index more heavily than we do the (protected) form of expression—that is, perhaps surprisingly for literary studies, we treat the form of expression as merely the inevitable and incidental vehicle for an idea. When we weigh the form of expression over the idea (as copyright law does), we tend to read the presence of one text in another as plagiarism—in which case, the hijacked vehicle seems to be carrying no ideas at all or only stolen goods.

After the "revelations" of Ouologuem's debt to Schwarz-Bart and Greene, scandalized critics seemed to view *Le Devoir de violence* as a kind of semantic wasteland, a contaminated scrapyard filled with the rusting, hollowed hulks of modernist masterpieces—"the dead carcasses of words," as Ouologuem's narrator describes a *négraille*'s first encounter with Paris and with French literature (*BtV*, 137); all that remains of Eliot, Dickinson, Greene, and others are the shells of their texts emptied of their once-vital contents.

I propose that we think about the anti-allusive effect of Ouologuem's appropriative practices in the formalist terms of the idea/expression dichotomy. Following the logic of copyright law, Ouologuem's recitations split the form of expression from the idea, stripping the appropriated language down to its bones, to its most basic formal elements—just words on a page. The form of expression is isolated from its cultural and historical context to become pure linguistic form, unburdened by the weight of its traditionally associated ideas and themes. This formal separation is a kind of ethnic cleansing of language (and of the Euro-modernist canon)—a mode of abstraction that is, as we shall see, characteristic of Euro-modernism's own appropriative encounters with its (ethnic) others.

A Brief Note on Time

Temporal matters keep cropping up in this analysis. Copyright and plagiarism prohibitions can be distinguished in terms of time: whereas copyright law gives the holder a limited monopoly on literary property, ethical codes against

---

52. Pasco, *Allusion*, 15.

plagiarism are indifferent to questions of time—to how much time has passed since the words and ideas were originally penned. Thus, copyright infringement is a material crime against property and profitability—against an individual; plagiarism is a moral offense against the (academic) codes of proper literary conduct—against an institution. Because of the time limit on authorial ownership, the writings of Dickinson and Norris (but not Eliot and Greene) had lapsed into the public domain by the time Ouologuem conscripted them. The mode of some of Ouologuem's appropriations (his use of Norris, for example) means that they would almost certainly have a delayed effect on the novel and our interpretations. This effect, which partly registers the reading labor involved in identifying source material, reflects the half-life of many literary allusions, which, like Eliot's use of Spenser, drift toward plagiarism with the receding frame of cultural reference. In these cases, the forms of expression seem more durable than the ideas they once carried. The problem of literary time zones is reframed in the final section of this chapter as I turn from copyright and plagiarism to examine other forms of cultural and intellectual property appropriation in the encounter between the "modern" and the "primitive." Indeed, that encounter is often characterized as a conflict between, on one hand, the timelessness (and unchanging durability) of the primitive and, on the other, the transience of the modern and its relentless demands to give old forms new ideas.

Authenticity Marks; or, Translation "à la Nègre"

The critical obsession with the authenticity of Ouologuem's novel is surprising if we consider its rough treatment of a connoisseur of African authenticity, Leo Frobenius, and of his relentless pursuit of artifactual evidence of "the splendour of harmonious and well-formed civilizations" in black Africa.[53] *Le Devoir de violence* repeats Frobenius's famous exclamation that Césaire had cited affirmatively in *Discours sur le colonialisme* (1950): "Civilisés jusqu'à la moelle des os!"[54] However, the novel gives it a characteristically subversive twist:

> [T]hese people are disciplined and civilized to the marrow!...It was only
> when white imperialism infiltrated the country with its colonial violence

53. This sentence from Frobenius is cited and translated in W. E. B. Du Bois, *An Inquiry into the Part Which Africa Has Played in World History*, 8th ed. (New York: International Publishers, 1965), 79.

54. Leo Frobenius, *Histoire de la civilisation Africaine*, 4th ed., trans. H. Back and E. Ermont (Paris: Gallimard, 1936), 14–15.

and materialism that this highly civilized people fell abruptly into a state of savagery, that accusations of cannibalism, of primitivism, were raised, when on the contrary—witness the splendor of its art—the true face of Africa is the grandiose empires of the Middle Ages, a society marked by wisdom, beauty, prosperity, order, nonviolence, and humanism. (*BtV*, 94)

Ouologuem doesn't just lampoon Frobenius, he profanes the sacred text of *négritude:* chapter 2 of Frobenius's *Kulturgeschichte Afrikas* (1933), which Senghor claimed he, Césaire, and Damas immediately "knew by heart" in its 1936 French translation, "Que signifie pour nous l'Afrique?"[55] Frobenius's burlesqued text is ultimately only a lever for Ouologuem's satirical attack on the pretensions of both *négritude* and *négrophilie*.

In *Bound to Violence*, Frobenius's words appear as the direct speech of Fritz Shrobenius, a German ethnologist-errant who, with his wife and daughter, wanders into Nakem in July 1910 seeking to buy "old wood...and a carload of native masks" (*BtV*, 85). Ouologuem's is a fairly obvious (if not fully faithful) reproduction of Frobenius's text, with his words safely protected behind quotation marks and attributed to the Shrobenius avatar. Shrobenius's intoxicating vision of the "Nakem ethnos" is the product of a relay of displacements: his African fantasy is stoked by "the words of informants sent by Saif"; by Saif's son, Madoubo, who "spouted myths for a whole week"; and by Saif himself, who "made up stories and the interpreter translated, Madoubo repeated in French, refining on the subtleties to the delight of Shrobenius" (*BtV*, 86–87). Shrobenius's Africa is mediated through interpreters and translators in at least three languages, and Frobenius's magisterial disquisitions on the "magico-religious, cosmological, and mythical symbolism" of African art and life (the "pure art" of "African life") are rendered ridiculous by their *détournement* into Ouologuem's ultra-violent African dystopia (*BtV*, 95, 87). In other words, the artless life of the *négraille* contrasts sharply with the mystifications of Shrobenius's glorious African cosmology. Indeed, Shrobenius delivers Frobenius's famous pronouncement immediately after one of Saif's *négraille* servants brutally murders his own wife when she catches him masturbating while peeping on Frobenius's daughter making passionate love to Saif's son. This is the scene that Soyinka hailed as "a levelling down of the Aryan myth";[56] but it also levels down the *négritude* myth (and snipes at Senghor), since the mutual "appeal of the exotic" excites equally the young blood of the white woman and the black prince.

---

55. Léopold Sédar Senghor, "The Lessons of Leo Frobenius," in *Leo Frobenius: An Anthology*, ed. Eike Haberland (Wiesbaden, Germany: Steiner, 1973), vii.
56. Soyinka, *Myth, Literature and the African World*, 102.

The scene preceding Shrobenius's negrophilic affirmation foregrounds precisely the kinds of living evidence that Shrobenius must ignore to declare Africans civilized to the marrow. Unbeknown to Shrobenius, his pronouncement results directly from this sequence of erotic-violent events, since to redeem the splendor of his civilization in the ethnologist's eyes, Saif takes out his anger on art:

> [S]hrewd ideologist that he was, [Saif] raised (to avenge himself for the scandal created by the murder of Awa) the prices on the Negro art exchange, cooking up...a stew of pure symbolic religious art [and]...peddled it to the curiosity seekers, tourists, foreigners, sociologists, and anthropology-minded colonials who flocked to Nakem....henceforth Negro art [*l'art nègre*] was baptized "aesthetic" and hawked in the imaginary universe of "vitalizing exchanges." (*BtV*, 93–94)[57]

Not only are Shrobenius's myths fabricated from trumped-up stories strategically supplied by Saif and his planted native informants; the ritual artifacts presented as "Shrobeniusological" evidence are themselves fakes:

> Saif—and the practice is still current—had slapdash copies [of African masks] buried by the hundredweight, or sunk into ponds, lakes, marshes, and mud holes, to be exhumed later on and sold at exorbitant prices to unsuspecting curio hunters. These three-year-old masks were said to be *charged with the weight of four centuries of civilization.* (*BtV*, 87, 95–96; my emphasis)

Shrobenius and Saif, "concierges de la négritude,"[58] are a symbiotic matched set; Shrobenius, "shrewd anthropologist that he was,...sold more than thirteen hundred pieces...to the following purveyors of funds: the Musée de l'Homme in Paris, the museums of London, Basel, Munich, Hamburg, and New York" (*BtV*, 95). Between the two of them, "Negro art [*l'art nègre*] found its patent of nobility in the folklore of mercantile intellectualism" (*BtV*, 94, 110). In *Le Devoir de violence*, Shrobenius is the founder and primary supplier of European *négrophilie*, the source of a stream (both intellectual and artifactual) that ultimately feeds the *négritude* of the 1930s, but that prehistoric stream is already contaminated by modernism.

The French term *art nègre* is out of place in Ouologuem's critique because, like the Musée de l'Homme, it is anachronistic, dating (proleptically) from the interwar

57. The French is from Yambo Ouologuem, *Le Devoir de violence: Roman* (Paris: Seuil, 1968), 111.

58. Yambo Ouologuem, *Lettre à la France nègre*, ed. Pierre Bisiou (Paris: Serpent à Plumes, 2003), 213.

era of high modernist *négrophilie*, when it paid to be primitive—when it was "good to be primitive, indeed, but unpardonable to be simple," as Ouologuem later quipped.[59] The commercial phenomenon of the *vogue nègre* that swept over Paris between the two world wars recoded the primitive as a symbol of "liberation and spontaneity"—a kind of fetish for the reenchantment of modernity.[60] Ouologuem depicts the transformation of old African wood into modern *art nègre* as the instantaneous effect of Saif's vindictive inflation of the prices on Negro art, but the literal and figural journey of African art from field to museum is more circuitous.

The term *art nègre* was consecrated in 1912 and popularized by the influential Parisian art dealer Paul Guillaume, who made his name trading in African artifacts (collected through his work at a Conradian rubber tire company) before becoming a leading patron and promoter of modern art—the "Novo Pilota" of modernism, as Modigliani dubbed him in his "primitivist" portrait of the collector. The Musée de l'Homme became the institutional home of *art nègre* in 1937, after it inherited the space and collection of the former Musée d'Ethnographie du Trocadéro, the very museum in which Picasso is said to have "discovered" African art (before it was "art") around 1906.[61] At about the time that Picasso made that now-legendary wrong turn into the Trocadéro's Africa room, which eventually detourned African artifacts into modernist fetishes and launched the primitivist revolution in modern European art, Frobenius was canvassing the "customs and thoughts of the primitive races" of French West Africa, including Ouologuem's Mali, and amassing (in his words) "as many things as possible for as little money as possible" for the Museum für Völkerkunde in Hamburg.[62]

As Dennis Duerden has observed, Picasso's "discovery" entailed the "appropriation of an object that *became known* as 'the African mask'" (my emphasis).[63] The process by which ethnological artifacts became the quintessential *objets d'art* of Africa in Europe involved broad conceptual and categorical changes to European

59. Yambo Ouologuem [Utto Rodolph, pseud.], *Les Milles et une bibles du sexe* (Paris: Dauphin, 1969), Avertissement; my translation.

60. Clifford, "Negrophilia," 901. See also Clifford, *Predicament of Culture*, 137.

61. For Picasso's account of this discovery, see André Malraux, *Picasso's Mask*, trans. June Guicharnaud and Jacques Guicharnaud (New York: Da Capo, 1995), 10–11.

62. Cited in Suzanne Marchand, "Leo Frobenius and the Revolt against the West," *Journal of Contemporary History* 32 (1997): 160. See Leo Frobenius, *The Voice of Africa*, trans. Rudolf Blind (London: Hutchinson, 1913), 2:651; Leo Frobenius and A. H. Keane, *The Childhood of Man: A Popular Account of the Lives, Customs and Thoughts of the Primitive Races* (London: Seeley, 1909).

63. Dennis Duerden, "The 'Discovery' of the African Mask," *Research in African Literatures* 31 (2000): 30.

institutional assumptions about realism and representation; it also entailed, as Shelly Errington has shown, certain material and mystical modifications to the objects themselves.[64] We can see the dynamics of that figurative transformation if, alongside Ouologuem's account of Shrobenius's prospecting, we read Frobenius's own report of the (unscrupulous) means by which he acquired the head of Olokun in Ife in 1910:

> Before us stood a head of marvellous beauty, wonderfully cast in antique bronze...the Olokun, Atlantic Africa's Poseidon.... The purchase-money had been accepted, and, therefore, the head...had become our property; all that they wanted was to make a sacrifice to it next day, and "unsanctify it."... The head belonged to the Oni... [who] agreed that I was to retain [it], but also, in exchange, that he was to have an exact copy.... I explained that a [galvanic] replica indistinguishable from the original could be made.... I specially insisted on the need of a formal agreement to be drawn up in the presence of us all to the effect that the original was to be our own and its counterpart the property of the Oni. Bida confessed later on that, to save himself a little trouble..., he had translated the other way round in the real "negro" fashion.[65]

Not long after this episode, in an informal colonial British court, Frobenius was accused of being a "trafficker in illicit goods."[66]

By his own account of headhunting, Frobenius is anxious about appearances, property rights, and counterfeiting. The head of Olokun is purchased "according to the good custom obtaining in Yorubaland," but the monetary exchange does not complete the transaction nor the conversion of the artifact into art; the head must be "unsanctified"—that is, literally or symbolically decommissioned from the world of spiritual work, freed from its social symbolical context—to become

64. See Shelly Errington, *The Death of Authentic Primitive Art and Other Tales of Progress* (Berkeley: University of California Press, 1998); and Errington, "What Became Authentic Primitive Art?" *Cultural Anthropology* 9 (1994): 201–226.

65. Frobenius, *Voice of Africa*, 1:98–103. For an analysis of this "scene" and discussions of some of the methodological and ethical problems with Frobenius's archaeology and ethnography, see J. M. Ita, "Frobenius in West African History," *Journal of African History* 13 (1972); Janheinz Jahn, *Leo Frobenius: The Demonic Child* (Austin: African and Afro-American Studies and Research Center, University of Texas, 1974).

66. Jahn, *Leo Frobenius*, 11. See also Soyinka's account of his own madcap adventures to rediscover and reappropriate the head of Olokun: Wole Soyinka, *You Must Set Forth at Dawn: A Memoir* (New York: Random House, 2006), 187–221. Interestingly, the British officer who charged Frobenius, Charles Partridge, is likely one of the sources for the character of the district commissioner at the end of Chinua Achebe's *Things Fall Apart*.

transferable. The Oni's willingness to relinquish the head is finally bought not with money but with a fraudulent promise to make a copy to replace the piece. (The false promise and the galvanic copy are both "unfaithful translations.") Ouologuem's novel insinuates that objects like the head of Olokun that Frobenius acquired may already have been inauthentic "tourist art"[67] (airport art before airports); nonetheless, the act of appropriation itself consecrates the exchange value of the object and converts the ethnic artifact from common cultural heritage into personal intellectual property—from whose derivative rights, *Bound to Violence* insists, Frobenius profited handsomely, "collect[ing] rental, reproduction, and exhibition fees" in Europe (*BtV*, 95). The texts of Frobenius and Shrobenius remind us that the invention and liberation of "authentic primitive art" are bound up, from the very beginning, with modern forms of mechanical reproduction and the market logic of property creation and exchange; and, of course, these are precisely the aura-degrading entanglements that must be disavowed for ethnic artifacts to enter modernity as authentic.

The decommissioning process that removes the traditional object from the mundane world of work and spiritual demands of functionality, preparing it for exportation, also prepares it for the supposedly nonlaboring realm of the aesthetic; the future art object is desanctified in one sign system and resanctified in another.[68] The working African artifact is defetishized (in the popular anthropological sense) to be refetishized (in the technical Marxist sense) as, ironically, a "work" of art— that is, as a commodity wholly alienated from the labor of its production. And yet, of course, the value of primitive ethnic art depends upon its "authenticity," upon the prospective buyer's sense that the object was "made by people for their own use rather than for the market."[69] In this sense, the authentic (as the early reviewers and promoters of Ouologuem's novel insisted) is precisely that which was not made for our prurient consumption, and so it must be expertly authenticated; it must be "marked," ideally with a certificate of authenticity, which, in the case of the African mask, guarantees that the thing has been danced.[70] In other words, the

67. In his reading of the novel, Appiah calls these "neotraditional objects." K. Anthony Appiah, *In My Father's House: Africa in the Philosophy of Culture* (New York: Oxford University Press, 1992), 148.

68. This process resembles the intertextual transaction that Julia Kristeva defined as the "transposition of one (or several) sign system(s) into another." Kristeva, *Revolution in Poetic Language*, 59.

69. Errington, *Death of Authentic Primitive Art*, 137.

70. Contemporary intellectual property law refers to these guarantees, particularly with regard to the artworks of indigenous peoples and their knowledge, as "trustmarks" or "authenticity marks." For an overview of the law, see Bernard O'Connor, *The Law of Geographical Indications* (London: Cameron May, 2004).

authentic must have a history, but a history of a particular, generic sort—a history of being untouched by history.

In addition to the symbolic translations that facilitated the conversion of traditional ethnic artifacts into modern aesthetic objects, their complete transformation usually involved a number of specific material refinements that made them more durable, more portable, and more commodifiable. "It was standard practice among art dealers in the 1920s," writes Errington, "to strip African artifacts of their soft and fibrous parts, rendering them starkly 'modern' looking."[71] The process of abstraction that took anthropological items out of the world and into the gallery denuded the traditional object of its ephemera (its "superficial decoration" and symbolic burden), reducing it—like Ouologuem's decontextualizing appropriations—to its most basic form, its sculptural or "plastic qualities," in Paul Guillaume and Thomas Munro's approving phrase.[72] In terms of the idea/expression distinction that underpins modern copyright law, abstraction relieves the expressive form of its ideational content, making old forms available to carry new ideas.

For primitive art to become primitivism (and thus available for resignification by cubists, fauvists, expressionists, and surrealists), "the Other needed to be evacuated from the scene of the modern so that it could enter the institutions of high art," observes Simon Gikandi.[73] Abstraction alone, however, cannot accomplish this evacuation of the ethnic other, cannot unscramble Africa from the object; in fact, it is only one part of a twofold (ethnic) cleansing performed to process artifacts for entry into modernity. The primitive object can be authenticated only if it bears no "traces of that culture's contact with other cultures," especially not the traces of "colonialism that enabled such works to make their way into Western markets."[74] This is a curious manifestation of contamination anxiety, because to become modernist, the primitive object must be rid of all signs of modernism. In other words, primitive objects had to be both abstracted and decontaminated, streamlined to their durable parts and purified of colonialism's contaminants. Abstraction simplified the object to become pure modernist form, and decontamination cleared away any imperial impurities that might intimate that the object was already a modernist form. With this final step in the transformation of African

71. Errington, "What Became Authentic Primitive Art?" 204. Errington argues that the frame accomplished the same effects for European art during the Renaissance.

72. Paul Guillaume and Thomas Munro, *Primitive Negro Sculpture* (New York: Harcourt Brace, 1926), 37, 45.

73. Simon Gikandi, "Picasso, Africa, and the Schemata of Difference," *Modernism/Modernity* 10 (2003): 457.

74. Rosemary J. Coombe, *The Cultural Life of Intellectual Properties: Authorship, Appropriation, and the Law* (Durham, NC: Duke University Press, 1998), 218.

artifacts into *art nègre*, the primitive was eliminated from modernist primitivism; African "craftsmen" were turned into "nègres"—the ghost painters and ghost sculptors of famous Euro-modernist artists who appropriated the forms of African expression stripped of their associated ideas.[75]

The simplification of the social object to its abstract formal elements (in order to reveal "its own internal logic," the "harmony of its parts," its rhythms and "plastic themes")[76] resembles the New Critical abstraction of the poem from its author and history, but it also resembles Yambo Ouologuem's anti-allusive practices. Like the modifications made to the body of an artifactual object that separate the form from its original (and originating) ideas—from "the fog of associations" (in Guillaume and Munro's words)—Ouologuem's literary appropriations dissociated old forms of expression from their social, cultural, and historical causes (and effects).[77] Ouologuem's practices "unsanctified" the modernists' forms of expression, putting their language back to work, giving it new ideas to carry, making it labor anew in another context. If allusion keeps up the appearance of cultural continuity and tradition, plagiarism (especially when carried out through illicit translinguistic and transnational practices like Ouologuem's) works behind the scenes, below the allusive surface, at the subterranean roots of literature, where the messy intertextual transactions that have entangled cultural traditions for centuries belie the superficial ethnic "authenticity" of the text. Recognizing the deep extra-African entanglements of *Le Devoir de violence* and its translations ought to disabuse us of the still-prevalent parochial expectation (and ideological delusion) that "the African novel" be somehow completely (that is, ethnically) distinct from the non-African novel.

Le Devoir de violence insists that Euro-modernity was underwritten by Africa; indeed, in intellectual property terms, Ouologuem's novel suggests that the international relations between Africa and Europe have (for better and worse) been intertextual for a very long time, although they have often consisted of illicit trafficking in unfaithful translations, mystifying allusions, unacknowledged appropriations, and bootlegged (and leg-ironed) goods. If the beginning

---

75. In an essay that is often taken to be a "confession" of his modus operandi, "Lettre aux pisse-copie nègres d'écrivains célèbres" ("Letter to the copy-pissing slaves/ghostwriters of famous writers"), Ouologuem exploited the polysemic French word *nègre*—that through a chain of substitutions links "black" to "slave" to "nigger" to "Negro" to "ghostwriter"—in order to conduct a fierce critique of the postcolonial racism of Gaullist France, the French literary industrial complex, and the links between the two that imposed a "law of [black] silence." Ouologuem, *Lettre à la France nègre*, 183, 185.

76. Guillaume and Munro, *Primitive Negro Sculpture*, 33, 45, 41.

77. Ibid., 45.

of the Euro-modernist era is marked by the legalized appropriation of intellectual and material resources from Africa (and other non-Western cultures and
countries), the end might be marked by the World Trade Organization's
protectionist legislation—particularly the Agreement on Trade-Related Aspects
of Intellectual Property Rights—which has consolidated intellectual property
monopolies and formalized the advantageous terms for the information societies of the global North to sell back to the information-raided societies of the
global South their own processed (read: ethnically cleansed) knowledge and
patrimony—the very resources that sustained Euro-modernity.[78] Copyright
protects that which is "original" and, by extension, "authentic." But when the
law's idea/expression logic is applied to the content and composition of
Ouologuem's novel, the categories of originality and authenticity lose their
meaning. If the authentic is that which supposedly remains untouched—especially by modernity, which greedily appropriates everything that appears as yet
untouched by modernity—then Ouologuem's novel reminds us that everything
is already touched, miscegenated, contaminated, counterfeited, and compromised by the institutional power structures that *originated* it and the abstraction
processes that *authenticated* it.[79] The implication of Ouologuem's *art nègre* scenario is that the "primitive" cultural objects that sparked the modernist intellectual revolution were likely fakes: new wood in old forms. *Le Devoir de violence*
proposes that at the bottom of modernism may be a black-market primitivism.

78. The beginning of the end of modernism would be the United Nations' Declaration
on the Granting of Independence to Colonial Countries and Peoples (1960), which recognized all peoples' rights to their own human and natural resources. The current neo-
imperial intellectual property regime has received much criticism for its patent guarantees,
which have been exploited (especially by multinational pharmaceutical companies) to privatize common indigenous knowledge. See Vandana Shiva, *Protect or Plunder? Understanding
Intellectual Property Rights* (London: Zed, 2001). We should extend the patent critique to the
still-dominant Eurocentric models of modernism and world literature.

79. It is a common modernist lament that the primitive is disappearing under the
weight of modernity. But the primitive is not disappearing because of modernity—or,
rather, it *is* disappearing because of modernity, but only because modernity brought it into
being in the first place *as* that which disappears under modernity's weight.

14 Solomon's Bluff

Virtual Property and the Aesthetics of Modern Worldmaking

Eric Hayot and Edward Wesp

A fictional world, Ruth Ronen tells us, is "constructed as a world having its own distinct ontological position, and as a world presenting a self-sufficient system of structures and relations." This self-sufficiency differentiates fictional worlds from the "possible" worlds of the logician-philosophers, these latter sharing neither the "ontological autonomy" nor the "independent modal structure" of the fully fictional world, which sheds its responsibility to the actual through the series of material, linguistic, and social devices that allow us to recognize it as a fiction. Ronen concludes: "fictional facts do not relate *what could have or could not have occurred in actuality, but rather, what did occur and what could have occurred in fiction.*"[1]

True statements about the rules that govern our most prominent imaginary modes are harder to make than they seem. Hence the hiccupping start of Ronen's first sentence: the fictional world is constructed, she writes, before assigning it any properties, "as a world," and also, before adjoining a second property to the first, "as a world": a fictional world is "constructed *as a world* having its own distinct ontological position, and *as a world* presenting a self-sufficient system of

1. Ruth Ronen, *Possible Worlds in Literary Theory* (Cambridge: Cambridge University Press, 1994), 8–9. On possible worlds, see John Divers, *Possible Worlds* (London: Routledge, 2002); and Lubomir Dolezel, *Heterocosmica: Fiction and Possible Worlds* (Baltimore, MD: Johns Hopkins University Press, 1998).

structures and relations." This type of world constructed "as a world," this world made in the image of a world, of worldliness, differentiates itself from the possible worlds of philosophy both in substance and in style. The first (and second!) thing one says about fictional worlds: that they are constructed *as worlds*, which is why whatever those fictional worlds do they do first of all by bringing to bear on their narratives the principles that govern the realm of the possible within them, that make them fictional *worlds* and not just *possible* instances of this world. Hence, in some fictions, warp drives, but no stately pleasure domes decreed; or decrees of domes, and no warp drives. In the difference between these choices, in the degree to which such choices mark, by agreement and by habit, the form proper to a coherent and recognizable world shape, all of which come down to our definition of a totality, the fictional world *worlds itself* (*fait monde*, as the French say).[2] It worlds itself into being.

From the earliest fictional apprehension of the modern condition—we are speaking here of Miguel de Cervantes' *Don Quijote*—the world-organizing, world-creating impulse of the novel has taken as one of its subjects its own self-production as a world. (So Ronen's sentence mirrors the fate of the novel itself.) This not only because the contrast between *Don Quijote*'s eponymous, zany jouster and its hoi polloi shows us identical phenomenological inputs producing radically different interpretations (windmill or giant, inn or castle?),[3] but also because the ten-year gap between the novel's two volumes saw the publication of a competing second volume of the Quijote story, Alonso Fernández de Avellaneda's "false" *Quijote* of 1614. A year later, in Cervantes' second volume, many of the minor characters have read both prequels, and the encounters between Sancho, his Don, and these strangers offer our heroes an occasion to rectify the "lies" of the Avellaneda version, as Sancho does in a conversation with Don Gerònimo: "The Sancho and the Don Quijote in that book have got to be different people from the ones in [the Cervantes book], because the ones in *his* book are us: my master is brave, and wise, and madly in love, and I'm just a plain fellow with a good sense of humor, and no

---

2. See, for instance, Deleuze: "Becoming everybody/everything [*tout le monde*] is to world [*faire monde*], to make a world [*faire un monde*]" (*The Fold: Leibniz and the Baroque*, trans. Tom Conley [Minneapolis: University of Minnesota Press, 1993], 280). On the use of the verb "to world" in English, see Djelal Kadir, "To World, to Globalize: Comparative Literature's Crossroads," *Comparative Literature Studies* 41 (2004): 1–9.

3. The novel gives us a world that can be seen in two ways; it is also a document that exemplifies the possibilities of seeing the actual world in two ways. On the relationship between exemplification and worldmaking, see Nelson Goodman (from whom we have borrowed the delightful phrase "zany jouster"), *Ways of Worldmaking* (Indianapolis, IN: Hackett, 1978), 104n10.

glutton and no drunkard."[4] Only the most unaware of readers will fail to connect Sancho's assertion of the power of subjective self-recognition to Cervantes' own real-world claim to the right to decide the true character of his invented personas. This fact is not lost on Sancho's master, who follows his squire's comment with this judgment: "if it were possible, it ought to be made illegal for anyone but [the original author] to write about the great Don Quijote and his doings, just the way that Alexander ordered that no one but Apelles might dare paint his portrait."[5] In this sentence of Don Quijote's, we glimpse an early apprehension of the relation between fictional worldmaking and the history of copyright.

Beyond Representation: Property in Virtual Worlds

Every world prompts a mythology, every mythology its own world. The accretion of narratives, the addition of new major and minor characters, are acts of world extension; what we call a "world" is the name of a particular kind of invitation to extend, to alter, or otherwise to fill in the interior of a unifying frame. This is no accident, Jean-Luc Nancy writes: "a world perhaps always, at least potentially, shares the unity proper to the work of art," since each is defined by a set of "inner resonances" that leave their trace on all of its objects and events (what we call a "style").[6] Like the work of art, a world is an enclosure, a "totality of meaning," and also, on its inside, an infinite opening toward the possibility of other making. Their similarity on this point may well be a function, as Nancy notes, of a reciprocity that is "constitutive of both": the similarity between worlds and artworks would be, in such a conception, primary rather than coincidental.[7] A world, like a work

---

4. Miguel de Cervantes, *Don Quijote*, trans. Burton Raffel, ed. Diana de Armas Wilson (New York: Norton, 1999), 674.

5. Ibid. The situation is a bit more complicated: Don Quijote gives the original author's name as "Sidi Hamid," whose notebooks the novel's major external narrator ("I, your second author"; 49) claims to have had translated from Arabic after finding them in a marketplace in Toledo; the novel's first eight chapters are narrated by the "second author," who mentions multiple written sources for his information; beginning with the ninth chapter, the tale is mostly derived from the second author's transcription of the Sidi Hamid Benengeli notebooks, which have been translated for him by a Moor.

6. Jean-Luc Nancy, *The Creation of the World; or, Globalization*, trans. François Raffoule and David Pettigrew (Albany: State University of New York Press, 2007), 42.

7. Ibid., 41, 42. About Nancy's phrase "a world is a totality of meaning": here, too, we can play at dialogism. Perhaps the reciprocity between "world" and "totality" is constitutive of both, but it is possible to imagine that this reciprocal relation between world and totality belongs particularly to modern conceptions of worlds and worldliness. Nancy's claims would have to be adjusted to account for that contingency.

of art, like a totality (and these two each like the others), is a framework, first of all, for the production of new meanings and, second, for the reproduction, reaffirmation, and renewal of old ones.

The advent of contemporary virtual worlds, made possible by enormous leaps forward in digital processing power and the reach of wired and wireless networks, is a sociohistorical phenomenon whose effects on the history of aesthetics and culture have been neither fully decided nor fully understood. Like Avellaneda's, most such worlds—the worlds of online and stand-alone video games and other virtual spaces—are parasitic, usually borrowing heavily from the generic field of fantasy literature and leavening their pseudo-medieval geographies and technoscapes with heavy doses of swordplay and magic. The narratives they organize draw from ancient and contemporary myth, romance, and the bildungsroman; they are appreciated largely though not exclusively by young men, perhaps because, at least representationally, they tend toward the kind of "reactionary nostalgia for Christianity and the medieval world" popularized by the novels of J. R. R. Tolkien, among others.[8]

Edward Castronova was among the first scholars to understand that the traditional representational content of fantasy worlds was only a single feature—and perhaps not the most important one—of the online virtual worlds that borrowed from them. His economic analyses of the behavior of the players of the online game *EverQuest* demonstrated that, whatever the players *seem* to be doing in the game's virtual world, Norrath, what they *are* doing at an economic level is something quite different.[9] All the treasure hunting, monster killing, and crafting

8. Fredric Jameson, *Archaeologies of the Future: The Desire Called Utopia and Other Science Fictions* (London: Verso, 2005), 67. Nick Yee's studies suggest that about 70 percent of the participants in the major online virtual game worlds are men; participants in the most important non-game virtual world, *Second Life*, tend to be more evenly split between the sexes and to skew older (mean age 41.14 in a 2006 study, versus a mean of 29.78 for *World of Warcraft*). See Nick Yee, "The Blurring of Work and Play," *Daedalus Project*, posted July 9, 2004, http://www.nickyee.com/daedalus/archives/000819.php; Yee, "The Labor of Fun: How Video Games Blur the Boundaries of Work and Play," *Games and Culture* 1 (2006): 68–71; Yee, "The Demographics, Motivations and Derived Experiences of Users of Massively-Multiuser Online Graphical Environments," *Presence: Teleoperators and Virtual Environments* 15 (2006): 309–329. For the most recent figures, see Nicolas Ducheneaut and Nicholas Yee, "Avatar Survey: Age," *PlayOn: Exploring the Social Dimensions of Virtual Worlds* (blog), http://blogs.parc.com/playon/archives/2008/07/avatar_survey_a.html; and "Avatar Survey: Gender Demographics," *PlayOn: Exploring the Social Dimensions of Virtual Worlds* (blog), http://blogs.parc.com/playon/archives/2008/07/avatar_survey_d.html.

9. The crucial first essay was Edward Castronova, "Virtual Worlds: A First-Hand Account of Market and Society on the Cyberian Frontier," CESifo Working Paper series, no. 618 (2001), available at SSRN: http://ssrn.com/abstract=415043. Castronova has since extended his analyses: "The Price of 'Man' and 'Woman': A Hedonic Pricing Model of Avatar

that the players engage in may have the representational form of medieval-style fantasy fiction, but the economy the game generates operates according to real-world rules, especially once players begin trading their virtual items (including their avatars) for real-world money. Castronova's analyses of the market for virtual goods led to his discovery that the per capita GNP of Norrath made it, in 2001, roughly the seventy-seventh richest country in the world, ranking it somewhere around Russia (and above both India and China). This constituted a major step forward in the study of virtual worlds not because the economic calculus justified the claim that such worlds ought to be taken seriously (about as seriously, say, as Russia), but because of how clearly it demonstrated that purely representational or narrative studies of virtual worlds cannot alone account for their sociohistorical and cultural impact on the meaning of contemporary life.

Here, once again, *Don Quijote* feels spookily ahead of its time. Its representation of the novel's own troubled relation to the idea of intellectual property suggests how intimate the interference has been between the novel's status as a particular kind of legal object and its own acts of representation, between the spatial and temporal horizons of the novel's appearance in this world and the spatial and temporal horizons of its imaginary ones.[10] The difference in the twenty-first century is that in virtual worlds the ownership of goods inside the fictional world is not *represented* but *actual.* Unlike fictional objects, which can only produce via sympathetic identification the *feelings* that one might bring to bear on them (Proust's madeleine, or Hester's scarlet A), virtual goods exist in material form, appearing at the intersection between a collection of zeros and ones that encode their existence and another set of zeros and ones that encode the set of

---

Attributes in a Synthetic World," CESifo Working Paper series, no. 957 (2003), available at SSRN: http://ssrn.com/abstract=294828; "On Virtual Economies," *Game Studies* 3 (2003), http://www.gamestudies.org/0302/castronova; "The Right to Play," *New York Law School Law Review* 49 (2004): 185–210; and *Synthetic Worlds: The Business and Culture of Online Games* (Chicago: University of Chicago Press, 2006).

10. That said, we witness also the degree to which the articulation of intellectual property *within* the diegetic space differs substantially from the argument about intellectual property that opposes Cervantes to Avellaneda. Don Quijote imagines adjudicating the competing claims to his representation on the basis of representational fidelity, just as only Apelles could paint Alexander's portrait because he was the most accurate portraitist. From Don Quijote's perspective, the property Avellaneda has stolen or misused is the accurate representation of Don Quijote's own "life"—whose meaning and value belong, first of all, to him as its property-holder (what the continental tradition of *le droit moral* would call the "right of personality")—and not Cervantes' right to profit from his inventive labor by obtaining legal protection for its imitation or reproduction.

rules that determines their properties and uses.[11] That virtual goods can be traded, bought and sold, given away, conceived as a reward for labor, destroyed or otherwise disposed of; that they operate in economies that allow for the social recognition of loss and theft—all these take us some distance from the quixotic imaginaries of the modern novel which, no matter how compellingly it *imagines* property relations (think of *Jarndyce v. Jarndyce*), fails to *enact* them.

The question is, how far exactly? And what does this distance matter for thinking about our literary past and our multimedia present? If you walk away with only two things from this chapter, they should be, first, the idea that the advent of virtual worlds is producing in contemporary society a significantly new kind of relationship between property and the cultural imagination; and, second, a sense of the degree to which the innovative potential of this new form has largely been ignored in favor of the reproduction of the most conventional forms of property relations. What follows lays out the shape of that new relationship and reviews its legal and cultural history. We will argue that its development is significant as an event in the historical conception of property and property rights, whose redirection of the common and shared toward the private and restricted has profoundly shaped the modern history of invention, originality, and the work of art. We will close by locating virtual worlds within the history of modern fictional worldmaking and, via a brief detour through the work of two unusually world-creative modernists, will show how modernist fiction might cue virtual worlds to expand the range of their representational structure and function, in whose light modernism itself might once again be made new.

Virtual Property: Parasite or Symbiote?

Virtual worlds' construction of "a self-sufficient system of structures and relations" actualizes for the first time in the history of fictional worlds, we are suggesting, the network of relations between people and objects governed by the social and legal category known as "property." This is obviously true in a wildly popular computer game like *The Sims*, whose suburban paradise mirrors the idealized

---

11. This is not to diminish the importance of the history of the representation of objects (and their status as things), whose innovative remakings in the work of a Henry James or Georges Perec trace the histories of life among the commodities. But these never amount to direct ownership. Though the back pages of our *SkyMall* catalog offer us the chance to own a copy of Gandalf's sword or of the One Ring, that such objects are indiscriminately sold suggests an awareness of the fact they are replicas: they are One Rings that are not the One.

adventures of American middle-class consumerism and revolves entirely around the purchase and arrangement of virtual home goods.[12] But it is also true in the popular genre of fantasy role-playing games, whose narrative progress requires the player to accumulate a wide variety of virtual goods to clothe, ornament, and protect the player's avatar, increase its knowledge or skills, function as tools of its play and labor, and testify to its accomplishments. In these virtual worlds, to refuse to treat such goods as a form of property is to refuse to play the game.

Whether virtual goods in such games are *really* property might have remained a question for particularly masochistic philosophers had it not been for the advent in the early years of the twenty-first century of online virtual worlds. Unlike offline games, in which the player's relation to property is mediated exclusively through exchanges with nonhuman objects (programmed shopkeepers, for instance), online worlds allow players to mediate their property relations with other human beings. Though such exchanges can occur purely within the framework of the virtual world (exchanging a pile of gold, say, for a book or a horse), players can also exchange their goods for real money; substantial auction sites exist to allow them to do so. While real-money transactions do not necessarily confirm a virtual object's ability to function as property, they testify to players' capacity to conceive as property a sword that will never leave the digital fictional world that grants it its significance, or an article of clothing wearable only by a digital avatar in *Second Life*. These instances of cross-world transaction do not so much make the property relations real—virtual commodities are no less hieroglyphic than real ones— as they reveal that the property has been "real" from the moment it came into being, that the system of representational, social, economic, and physical rules that would allow a given thing to be recognized as property was encoded into its existence from the moment of its creation.[13]

12. The array of virtual goods in *The Sims* is extensive to a degree that seems to have overwhelmed even the game's marketers, whose follow-up editions to the game began by offering new content under a variety of titles—*Livin' Large, Bon Voyage, Open for Business*—but have devolved into labeling everything a kind of "stuff." Hence, *Family Fun Stuff, Teen Style Stuff, Celebration Stuff, Glamour Life Stuff, Kitchen & Bath Interior Design Stuff, IKEA Stuff, H&M Fashion Stuff,* and so on (these last two instances are real-virtual cross-marketing, in which players can own in virtual space models or copies of the things they own—or desire—outside it, and vice versa).

13. One ramification of this argument is that virtual property does not in any important ontological sense differ from real property; the quiddity of property dwells not in its materiality but in its being the subject of a social agreement to recognize the possibility of its exchange. In advance of such an agreement, any new system can produce a forceful social drive toward considering new object A as property if it surrounds that object with the phenomenological and social cues that allow it to be recognized as "like" other kinds of property (think of virtual couches in *The Sims*). This initial step allows an object to be treated

The nature of the law, in which advances must occur in relation to established precedents, means that legal arguments about the status of virtual goods have borrowed extensively from the history of intellectual property rights and particularly from the latter's successful reorientation of the concept of the property-bearing object. Greg Lastowka and Dan Hunter, for instance, preface their more general case for the development of virtual property rights by noting that "the development of Western property laws and property systems over the last 200 years has been characterized by a shift from the tangible to the intangible," and suggest that property rights "have from their inception been invoked to protect intangible interests."[14] Advocates of virtual property rights tend accordingly to narrate the inclusion of virtual goods under the property regime as an effect of a long-standing expansion of the range of things covered by the word *property*. From this perspective, digital objects produced in virtual worlds are simply another step forward in the history of the legal recognition of intangibility, and their placement inside the ambit of the law simply a matter of recognizing the ontological category to which such objects already belong.[15]

Legal arguments that aim to recognize virtual goods as property have also been at least partially subtended by arguments that draw on the classically Lockean relationships among property, transformation, and labor.[16] Users' efforts within the virtual world call virtual objects into being, they say, transforming the virtual world's "state of nature" as set up by its designers; just as the untilled field becomes property by virtue of the labor invested in it, so the virtual good becomes property

---

like property, to simulate being property. To call virtual property "property" means emphasizing the ways in which it shares with real property a basis in social practice. So, while the differences that allow us to distinguish between real and virtual property do not disqualify virtual property claims, it does not follow that these differences are without meaning or effect. The claim that a virtual couch *is* property may be correct, but it remains a minority opinion (as evinced, for example, by the incredulity with which virtual property is most often described in the mainstream press). And if property draws its power from collective agreement, virtual property remains provisional as long as its owner cannot count on the next person agreeing that their virtual couch is really property, a problem we need hardly worry over in regard to the furniture in our living rooms.

14. Greg Lastowka and Dan Hunter, "The Laws of Virtual Worlds," *California Law Review* 92 (2004): 40–41.

15. Among other things, this line of argument reveals that the complex material status of the digital object—which is not, strictly speaking, intangible—is ignored, since there is no direct precedent for it. This suggests that the resolution of the legal claims regarding virtual property may unwittingly carry along with it a particularly limiting "solution" to the problem of digital objecthood.

16. On this tendency among players of multiplayer online games, see Yee, "The Blurring of Work and Play"; and Yee, "The Labor of Fun."

insofar as it results from the user's work in the virtual world that provides it.[17] Provoked by arguments like these, game players and virtual-world theorists have wondered, for instance, whether the corporate owner of a given virtual world would have the right to terminate the existence of that world, given that such an event would in effect cause all the world's users to lose the value of the property they held within it. And in at least one case, a user of a virtual world sued the creator of that world to receive compensation for the loss of his virtual goods on the ground that the world created the conditions under which they were stolen.[18]

For the corporate owners of virtual worlds, however, that kind of argument founders on the following conundrum: the creator of the virtual world that allowed for the possibility that those goods might be stolen also established the conditions under which they were created and through which they acquire social meaning and economic value. That is, the status of virtual goods *as property* is determined by their enclosure within a fictional world operating as a "totality," that is, as a (more or less) self-sufficient system of rules, representations, and other forms of political, social, and economic constraints that allow for property relations to develop in the first place. And likewise, as Steven Horowitz has argued, for the Lockean claim to "labor-desert," which comes up fairly strongly against corporate claims to have effectively *created* the commons. An item one earns by "defeating a virtual foe that carries it" does not obviate the fact that the game's creators "have created both the foe and its item," Horowitz writes, and he notes that, as a result of the totality of virtual creation, there is effectively no public space (no unowned, deserted land) in virtual worlds at all.[19] The virtually natural, common world that users seem to face is anything but: their transformative labor—by which Locke's laborer earns property claims in the real world—is always preceded by that of the world's designers, at least in the real-world legal context, where they compete on level terms with the users of their world for the right to own and dispose of the fruits of their work.

17. The Lockean approach to virtual property claims is widely recognized by legal scholars on the issue. Lastowka and Hunter address it (see their "Laws of Virtual Worlds") as do valuable survey articles such as Steven J. Horowitz, "Competing Lockean Claims to Virtual Property," *Harvard Journal of Law and Technology* 20 (2007): 443–458; and Katie Hollstrom, "Legal Conceptions of Virtual Property: Should Virtual Property Be Afforded the Same Rights as Its Real-World Counter-Part?" *Law and Society Journal at the University of California, Santa Barbara* 7 (2007–2008): 59–68.

18. For more information on the first of such lawsuits, filed in Chinese courts starting in 2003, see the unsigned articles "Lawsuit Fires Up in Case of Vanishing Virtual Weapons," *China Daily* (Nov. 20, 2003); and "Cyber Property Suit Accepted," *Xinhuanet* (Apr. 28, 2004).

19. Horowitz, "Competing Lockean Claims," 12.

These arguments, which we find convincing, suggest that virtual property, if it exists, must be thought of as a *kind of* property that exists within, is made possible by, and is rightly understood as part of and as inseparable from a work that is itself a piece of intellectual property.[20] In this, virtual property resembles the "pleats of matter" Deleuze ascribes to Leibniz's baroque universe, in which "an organic fold always ensues from another fold, at least on the inside from a same type of organization," in a movement that "is always determined from the outside [the "real" world] . . . but unified from the inside [as a "virtual" world of its own]."[21] The virtual world establishes a situation of temporally limited scarcity that creates an economy and a property regime: Blizzard Entertainment holds a copyright for *World of Warcraft*, a piece of software that creates, when interpreted by the proper hardware, a virtual world within which players can own and exchange virtual goods. The social meaning and economic value of such goods rest entirely on their contingent relation to *World of Warcraft*, both materially (since they reside on servers owned by Blizzard and must be interpreted by the company's software in order to "be") and ideally (since they have value only in relation to their function inside that world; you can't use a digital shovel from *World of Warcraft* to dig a hole in *Second Life*). From this position, virtual-world designers have gone on to insist that all virtual goods produced inside their worlds effectively belong to them, and not to the world's users or players.[22] That's why the

20. The word *within* here should not be taken too literally. The topology of nested property forms is complex; though here the impression one has is of a sphere enclosed inside another sphere, the intellectual property functioning as a kind of world of worlds inside which smaller units operate, the transactions that allow owners of objects inside the inner sphere to exchange their goods for money that is ontologically equivalent to the outer sphere (imagine, for instance, that someone could become wealthy enough by selling virtual objects to purchase the copyright to the world in which he or she acquired those objects) effectively perforate the sphere from within.

21. Gilles Deleuze, *The Fold: Leibniz and the Baroque*, trans. Tom Conley (Minneapolis: University of Minnesota Press, 1993), 12.

22. *Second Life* is a notable exception here; it allows players to copyright and sell in and out of the game world the products they invent with the tools the makers of *Second Life* have given them. Accordingly, the first major copyright disputes regarding goods within *Second Life* involved disputes between residents of the virtual world. In both cases—*Alderman v. John Doe, aka Volkov Catteneo*, and *Eros, LLC et al. v. Thomas Simon, aka Rase Kenzo*—producers of virtual products charged others with illegally duplicating and selling their copyrighted goods.

While Linden Labs (which operates *Second Life*) was not directly involved with the disputes, the complexities of virtual property reveal themselves in the plaintiffs' complaints that Linden's software failed to restrict the duplication of the items in question. Furthermore, Kevin Alderman was forced to file his suit against an unidentified John Doe, because Linden Labs would not reveal the name of the person behind the copyright-infringing avatar Volkov Catteneo. The interested parties discovered that Linden had created the tools by

battle lines were drawn where they were in one of the earliest legal struggles over the ownership of virtual objects, when in 2001 Sony Online Entertainment convinced the online auction sites eBay and Yahoo! Auctions to ban the trading of items discovered or created by players within the virtual world of *EverQuest* by prevailing on them to honor their policies prohibiting the auction of items that violate intellectual property law.[23]

The parasitic or subordinate relationship that structures the existence of virtual goods has been the subject of some consideration in the legal literature. Lastowka and Hunter, for instance, wonder if the legal status of an individual in a virtual world is akin to that of someone who rents a hotel room, with that person having rights of private use but not private ownership. But the list of ways in which virtual goods aren't like hotel rooms is long. The situation would be simpler if this were not the case, just as it would be simpler if virtual goods were just like intellectual property. Our task is not, however, to make things easy, but to make virtual goods legible to the law, to literary criticism, and to philosophy *as they are*, not to transform them into the perfect analogues of a property or an object form we already know. Even if one grants that virtual property resembles

---

which players could make their own copyrightable products, but had also created a powerful veil of anonymity for those who violated those rights.

While these cases reveal the inevitable complexities of virtual property, *Second Life*'s greatest innovation may well be its owners' intentional disinterest from the property claims of the products that circulate within its virtual domain. Despite this innovation, and despite frequent discussions of *Second Life* in the mainstream media, it remains a fairly unpopular world, and its model has not exerted any appreciable influence on the virtual worlds that have followed it.

23. Additionally, Sony claimed that the sales were a violation of the end-user license agreement (EULA) agreed to by each player every time he logs on to an *EverQuest* server. Whether or not these EULAs may be able to quash players' legal claims to own their virtual property (an open question currently), that power doesn't diminish the provocative questions raised by this intersection of competing forms of intangible property. For a review of the role played by EULAs in this context, see Kevin Edward Deenihan, "Leave Those Orcs Alone: Property Rights in Virtual Worlds," Working Paper series (2008), http://ssrn.com/abstract=1113402.

The case *Bragg v. Linden* yielded an intriguing test of users' ability to shrug off the limitations of a EULA despite their agreement to its terms. The judge in the case, Eduardo C. Robreno, determined that the insistence upon arbitration imposed by the *Second Life* Terms of Service constituted an unconscionable agreement and dismissed Linden's motion to compel arbitration. While the implication for the case at hand was simply to allow Bragg's case to move forward in court (it was later settled out of court), the broader implication of the decision is that Judge Robreno's rationale for deeming the *Second Life* agreement unconscionable seemed potentially to apply widely to the take-it-or-leave-it nature of EULAs overall. For more on the implications of *Bragg*, see Candidus Dougherty, "*Bragg v. Linden*: Virtual Property Rights Litigation," *E-Commerce Law and Policy* 9 (2007), http://papers.ssrn.com/sol3/papers.cfm?abstract_id=1092284 (accessed May 9, 2010).

intellectual property in some ways—that the ownership I should have over a digital avatar whose various statistics constitute an embodiment of my life experience in the game world ought to resemble, say, my ownership over the exciting story of my discovery of the North Pole—the relation between my avatar (virtual property) and its world (intellectual property) is substantially different from the one obtaining between my life and the North Pole, and not just because the North Pole doesn't belong to anybody in particular.[24]

The present legal situation makes even that limited form of nuance difficult to sustain. The legal struggle over virtual property offers little room for compromise: from one side, there is an insistence that the primary act of creation effectively subsumes all other activity in the world's ambit, and thus that users have no property rights except those granted by the world-holder; from the other comes the demand that the user's labor gives him an absolute right to dispose of that property as he or she sees fit, including the right to sell it to someone else for goods or cash that are useful and valid outside the virtual world's boundary. From the world-holders' perspective, the claim of total ownership over their intellectual property means that the users' apparent property does not exist (and thus that the right to intellectual property includes the right to all derivative objects created under its structural or representational aegis). But users do not want to accept a system that leaves them no claim to the products of their experience and labor and no sense that their work and play in the virtual world could translate into meaningful currency (cultural or actual) outside of it, and they argue, quite rightly, that their presence in the virtual world is required for property relations to develop at all.[25]

24. The government of Russia notwithstanding: in August 2007, a Russian submarine planted a flag in the ocean seabed 14,000 feet under the North Pole in order to symbolize that nation's claim to the oil and gas resources in the region. See Adrian Blomfield, "Russian Submarine Plants Flag at North Pole," *Daily Telegraph* (Aug. 3, 2007).

25. At first glance, there may seem to be a useful parallel here between fan fiction and the creation of virtual property within virtual worlds, since both are derivative entities in intellectual property terms, and both develop or extend the primary text, rather than competing with it. But fan fiction is by its very nature transgressive, both of the formal boundaries of the "primary" text and of the well-established frameworks for the fair use of copyrighted material (since the only legal fan fiction, at least technically, is that which never enters into the public realm). But there is nothing transgressive about the generation of virtual goods within virtual worlds, since those worlds are intended precisely to be occasions for the generation of virtual goods. Henry Jenkins argues that contemporary fan fiction largely parallels older storytelling traditions, with the difference that fan fiction draws from privately rather than commonly held cultural source material. In light of our discussion here, it is worth asking whether fan fiction's transgression of copyright restrictions is simply overcoming an obstacle to the reexpression of folk narrative or whether the pleasures of fan fiction are derived in part (that is, not accidentally) from the transgression of copyright.

The contradiction between the virtual worlds' intense invitation to create and the refusal of corporate designers to acknowledge the results of that invitation makes the situation of contemporary virtual worlds perplexing and a bit tragic. Virtual worlds promise users a world awaiting and only completed by their efforts, and reward those efforts most consistently with virtual objects. The energies by which the players transform the resting "natural" world, the time and energy that in turn make these objects feel so real and so justly deserved, so *owned*—all of this is exactly what the world designers intend and is exactly why players are drawn to these virtual worlds. Who could blame them for wanting recognition of this structure as property-justifying labor, especially when the worlds expressly encourage these objects to be bought and sold within the game? And yet this powerful reality effect is abruptly suspended at the moment that corporations act to strip players of all but their most representational or purely virtual claims to property.

This could be viewed as a desultory result of property reasserting itself against the apparent novelty of the virtual-world form; as we move into the virtual, we find that the land there, too, was already enclosed. In such a view, the alluring novelty of virtual worlds is an *ignis fatuus*, a false promise of escape from the real world in which the raw material of cultural fiction is already owned. Such a view stems quite naturally from the normative history of intellectual property law and particularly from the history of the relation between creative genius and property that marks the boundary between acts of creation that qualify as "original" (and thus qualify for copyright protection) and those that do not. In the history of those norms, recombination always lies on the dark side of the property boundary and creation on the bright side—though one might also simply say that the boundary between those two acts is the dialectical counterpart of the decisions made by property law, that "recombine" and "create" have no meaning today outside of the framework that makes one imaginative act worthy of property protection and another not.

The hard line on virtual objects taken by a number of corporate copyright owners thus argues that no amount of effort or imagination spent acquiring a virtual shovel can ever amount to anything but recombination, the confirmation of a process that the world designers have put into place. Each object in the virtual world is, from this perspective, merely the outcome of a copyrightable system designed to generate just such outputs; what counts as property is the system, not its outputs. But users of virtual worlds express a similarly constricted imagination of property when they argue that their invested labor effectively gives them the right to transfer virtual objects to other people—not from avatar to avatar, but from person to person, which means real-world transactions, which is, after all, where the question of whether something is property becomes of interest to the law. (In this sense, the real world is the law's home world; like property relations, the arrival of "legal" issues inside a virtual world perforates the worldly self-enclosure that would keep the two systems from interacting.) Though analogies will be imperfect here, it's as though the designers, having rented out a bunch of shovels, claimed all possible outcomes of shoveling as their own; or as though shovelers, having bothered to rent the shovels, claimed that the holes they dug had nothing to do with the labor that created the shovels in the first place. The evidently collaborative relationship between designers and players is disguised by this struggle over exclusive, individual ownership, which participates in a larger cultural aversion to conceptions of creativity and property that do not finally rely on solitary, novel genesis.

Against this aversion, we might find an opening in a number of aesthetic precedents. Among these are contemporary debates over authorship and originality raised by sampling in popular music. These, too, produce an apparent mismatch between the authorial status of "producers" like Danger Mouse and the "artists" whose work they (re)work. But there does seem to be room, at least in the popular imagination, for the quality of a particular instance of remixing to rise to the state of independence that we call "art."[26] Another analogy, imperfect but instructive, comes from an earlier chapter in the history of copyright: the print culture's sampling form known as the cento, or mosaic, poem. Poems stitched together from popular and classic literature, these works could claim no originality but the selection and arrangement of the preexisting material. That these works gained copyright status may or may not offer another avenue to argue the legal disposition of virtual goods in contemporary courts, but their example helps distill some of the convoluted elements of virtual property in the history of copyright as a cultural fact. The cento form identifies and validates a relationship among author, work, and previously authored cultural material in ways that inspire a reorientation of the virtual property debate. As Paul Saint-Amour has noted, "[T]he cento did not demand a discrete identity of its own, suggesting instead that the literary object is the sum of its maker's readerly acts of consumption just as the maker's identity is at once constituted and eclipsed by those acts of reading."[27]

<hr />

26. Evidence of this can be found in the positive reviews of *The Grey Album* that appeared in major newspapers and magazines upon its release, which addressed the success of Danger Mouse's combination of music from the Beatles and Jay-Z, rather than re-reviewing the "original" work. On *The Grey Album*, see Davis Schneiderman, "Everybody's Got Something to Hide Except for Me and My Lawsuit: William S. Burroughs, DJ Danger Mouse, and the Politics of 'Grey Tuesday,'" *Plagiary* 1 (2006): 191–206.

27. Paul K. Saint-Amour, *The Copywrights: Intellectual Property and the Literary Imagination* (Ithaca, NY: Cornell University Press, 2003), 42.

How might the cento model for us a way out of the antagonism that currently structures debates on virtual property? First, by reminding us that the demand for "discrete identity" is at the heart of property conflicts; and second, and more speculatively, by urging us to think of the user's activity in the virtual world as like, in some ways, the work of putting together a collection. This has the advantage of seeing through the useful *representational* fiction that differentiates between a user's avatar and her objects, reminding us that, at the material level, as a matrix for the recording and filtering of experience, the avatar is just as much a created good as the objects are (just as, in Locke, one's first property relation is to one's own will). If we set aside, at least temporarily, this identificatory anthropomorphization, we can imagine the avatar and its accretions of hard-won possessions as a patchwork representation of some of the systemic possibilities of the virtual world it inhabits, a work whose meaning and value depend precisely on its not needing a discrete identity of its own, even as it makes visible the user's experience of the world *whose specific details can be predicted but not determined in advance:* a kind of virtual erudition, or a world-particular cabinet of curiosities.[28] The user (or inhabitant) of the virtual world might "own" this arrangement without having to insist on untenable claims of purely original creation and without needing to undermine the creatively original status of the copyrighted world itself. For such a procedure, one model comes from Margaret Jane Radin, who suggests that the use of any property directed toward the embodiment of personhood ought to grant the user limited property rights in that property—regardless of who owns it in the strict legal sense.[29] The opportunity to rethink the implications of intellectual property will not be taken up by all parties or in all arenas. In fact, the case of virtual property, which is so much like and unlike other, earlier forms, serves as a reminder of the uneven history of copyright's intersection with works of cultural imagination. Don Quijote's Alexandrian restriction, Joyce's rewriting of *The Odyssey*, the indeterminate implications of contemporary virtual worlds— together, these make a cento patchwork of the history of the imagination and its

28. A metaphor made apter, perhaps, by the fact that much of the esoterica collected in virtual fantasy worlds would be right at home in those early modern proto-museums.

29. See Margaret Jane Radin, *Reinterpreting Property* (Chicago: University of Chicago Press, 1993), especially the chapters "Property and Personhood" and "Residential Rent Control." Radin proposes revising the current legal theories of property via the recognition that personhood develops at least partly through a relation to things (one's person is tied up, that is, more in one's own couch than in a copy of that same couch at the furniture store). Tenants have limited property rights, Radin argues, in the homes they rent from landlords (whose interest in the property they rent is not personal but "fungible") by virtue of just such an assumed relation (though the law has tended to justify those rights on the basis of the right to privacy, and not property law).

belongings, one that directs our attention to the relentless interactions between the legal status of the worldly imaginary and its mimetic and aesthetic histories.

Modernism and the Virtual Aesthetic

In its current configuration, and in the face of the seemingly natural antagonism between the designers of virtual worlds and their users, it seems likely that the history of virtual property will confirm the long drift of property law toward what Hardt and Negri call the "expropriation of the common."[30] That drift suggests how closely contemporary virtual worlds hew to the aesthetic line traced by the history of modern realism, whose texts and works of art tend to confirm the worldly imaginary that organizes the social spheres within which they emerge. Beneath the virtual's magical trappings and suits of armor (which direct us toward fantasy or the romance) lies a property regime and a system for the production and dissemination of embodied value that resembles in almost every respect the one that dominates the actual economy of the planet. The virtual system not only resembles but affirms the actual system, since the appearance of modern property relations inside virtual worlds appears to test, and confirm, the universal applicability of our deepest structural ideologies: "it may be that, in the West at least, we are simply incapable of imagining a new world without property," as Lastowka and Hunter put it.[31] Though we generally imagine virtual worlds as a set of "fantasy" spaces motivated primarily by the aesthetic history of the romance, then, the perspective organized by property suggests that they are also enactments of a profoundly economistic form of realism. The "escape" provided by virtual worlds turns out to be an exit only from life experience and human history, with its already-determined distributions of property and value, and an entry into a tabula rasa of labor that is in effect a perfected but unrevised version of the regime of

30. Michael Hardt and Antonio Negri, *Multitude: War and Democracy in the Age of Empire* (New York: Penguin, 2004), 150.

31. Lastowka and Hunter, "Laws of Virtual Worlds," 34. The appearance of real property (rather than just represented property) also breaks what game designer Richard Bartle calls (following Johan Huizenga) "the magic circle" between labor and play. "You can't have commodification and a hero's journey," he writes, since the very appearance of property rewrites, preposterously, the meaning of the activity that produces it: if the result of user activity is property, then the activity is labor; if the result is rather an imaginary thing, like any of the objects that harmlessly inhabit the fictive worlds of film and literature, then the users have been playing all along. See Richard A. Bartle, "Pitfalls of Virtual Property" (Durham, NC: Themis Group, 2004), 1, 16. This white paper is available at http://www.themis-group.com/uploads/Pitfalls%20of%20Virtual%20Property.pdf (accessed May 9, 2010).

ownership we already have.[32] Here, we may recall Lukács's critique of Zola in his essay on narration and description: the latter's minute descriptions of the system of objects that surrounded the inhabitants of late nineteenth-century France simply *reproduced* the logic of the socioeconomic system it represented, Lukács complained, partly because the intensity of its descriptions concealed the fact that the social system itself never became visible.[33] Most contemporary virtual worlds, one might say, conceal the realism of their system of objects under the fantastical armature of their medieval world picture and the kinesthetic pleasures of immersive game playing.

The history of modern aesthetics, particularly narrative aesthetics, is at least partly a history of orientation toward the questions of the world: of what makes or shapes a world; which of its capacities can be erased, expanded, or transformed; of its capacity for change as a world, of its openings to possibility, of its intentions, whether mythological or scientific; and, finally, of its singularity or multiplicity and of the possibility of its negation. Realist works in this tradition have tended toward the confirmation or affirmation of the world—not of the world's particular state of affairs, but of the world *as* world, of the dominant ideology of the world as such that obtains in the cultural context from which the work emerges (to be "realist" in worldly terms in 1600 is thus different than to be "realist" today, since notions of what the world is have changed). This is the general modality to which most of the new virtual worlds—and all of the truly popular ones—belong, since they tend very strongly to reproduce in their own world space the assumptions regarding property, labor, and value that obtain in the world we already know (even as they occasionally clothe those assumptions in romantic garb—a fact which cannot be dismissed purely as superstructural). That decision aligns them,

32. Here, it is worth distinguishing between stand-alone, single-player virtual worlds of the video-game type, in which property relations are in some sense exemplified without being enacted, and the online, multiplayer virtual worlds in which those relations are both exemplified and enacted. In the former, the property regime tends to be, from the perspective of the world's digital inhabitants, profoundly "unfair," since it is entirely devoted to the narrative progress and productive development of the game player. In the online worlds, however, equal opportunity prevails, at least partly because users demand it, insisting that each entrant into the virtual world be granted the same chances at advancement as any other. In these worlds, real-world distortions of equal access to property, such as genetic, parental, or financial inheritance, are substantially diminished, if not entirely eliminated. For a longer discussion of the ideological implications of that fact, see Eric Hayot and Edward Wesp, "Reading Game/Text: *EverQuest*, Alienation, and Digital Communities," *Postmodern Culture* 14 (2004), http://pmc.iath.virginia.edu/text-only/issue.104/14.2hayot_wesp.txt.

33. See Georg Lukács, "Narrate or Describe?" in his *"Writer and Critic" and Other Essays*, trans. Arthur D. Kahn (New York: Grosset and Dunlap, 1978).

in the final analysis, with the aesthetic trajectory of world-affirming realism that dawns in *Don Quijote*, which is a novel, after all, about a fantastical world imagined by its romance-addled protagonist that results, at the end of 126 chapters, in little more than a cascade of regrets and a mouthful of broken teeth.

In the extended history of worldmaking, whose realistic and romantic habits are outlined in the gap between Cervantes and Blizzard Entertainment, what place is there for the aesthetic specificities of modernism? The governing subject of this volume must—if we are to be true to it—reveal itself in these final pages as the endpoint (and thus the origin) of this essay's meditation on the history of modern and virtual worldmaking and on the role of property in these second-natured worlds, whose actually existing creators so rarely gift their users with the rights of unencumbered property holding. Here, one might begin by noting that modernism's stylistic, affective, symbolic, and political challenges to both realism and romanticism have, since the middle of the nineteenth century, constituted a third major modality of aesthetic worldmaking inside the history of modernity.[34] If this is so, then the worldmaking habits of modernist works may well offer some opportunities to think past the impasse created by the baleful combination of realism and romanticism that governs the appearance of virtual property today—especially since the general effort of modernist worldmaking has been to undermine or dismantle the philosophical and aesthetic satisfactions of its realist counterpart (while remaining largely impotent regarding its economic, political, and legal ones).

We will close this chapter, therefore, by finding two potential openings beyond the virtual impasse in the examples provided by the work of Fernando Pessoa and Jorge Luis Borges, two exemplary literary modernists whose acts of fictional worldmaking continually confound the self-sufficient boundary between worlds and their outsides. These authors open for us a language and a tradition within which to think the strange, doubled-over property status of virtual objects and the avatars that own them, both of which rely so heavily for their existence on the intellectual property regime that is their framing sine qua non. Neither Borges nor Pessoa, working in nonvirtual media, can enact the property relations and property worlds they imagine. But what they imagine is more ambitious and more challenging to contemporary thought than what we get in the virtual worlds we have now. It is insofar as they provide *imaginary* solutions to the legal-aesthetic

---

34. Realism, romanticism, and modernism, in short, together form a system of worldmaking relations that shapes the aesthetic history of modernity. A full elaboration of this literary historical claim will appear in Eric Hayot's forthcoming *The Ends of the World: An Essay on Literature.*

impasse we have outlined here—solutions whose actually existing status can be verified, to be sure, by the ability of any number of people on the planet to read, and think about, the works in which they appear—that these two authors can consummate this essay and point us toward new directions in the study of virtual property and virtual worlds.

Pessoa is best known for his development of full-blown heteronyms—Alberto Caeiro, Ricardo Reis, Álvaro de Campos—under whose names he published collections of poetry, articles, and critical commentaries, and for whom he developed separate biographies, literary styles, and astrological charts. (He was disposed, Darlene Sadlier writes, "from his childhood onward to a kind of literary ventriloquism.")[35] Though Pessoa sometimes wrote parodies, sometimes even parodies of parody itself (the essay "La France en 1950—par un Japonais," signed by Jean Seul de Méluret, includes the traveler's observation that, in the hexagon, "animal sperm as a beverage has fallen out of fashion"),[36] most of his life's work appears under the sign of a coruscating sincerity; the major heteronyms are not pseudonyms, not forms of concealment or irony, but things whose projective and imaginative force makes them more than characters, if less than people. Call them avatars. The relation between Pessoa and the work of his various invented personas thus resembles, at least provisionally, the one between intellectual and virtual property in contemporary virtual worlds, the former serving as a sort of primary pretext or framing totality, the latter as the most visible and tactile expression of that totality, its raison d'être and its most compelling substantive outcome.

To be sure, the demands of copyright and of literary scholarship have returned Pessoa's virtual works to a single legal and historical home, just as the mysteries involving American poet Kent Johnson's turn as the Hiroshima survivor Araki Yasusada in the late 1990s seemed to be undone, at the moment of the distribution of profits and rights of reproduction, by the appearance of Johnson's own name on the copyright page of Yasusada's published notebooks.[37] But the facts that

35. Darlene J. Sadlier, *An Introduction to Fernando Pessoa: Modernism and the Paradoxes of Authorship* (Gainesville: University of Florida Press, 1998), 4.

36. Fernando Pessoa, *The Selected Prose of Fernando Pessoa*, trans. and ed. Richard Zenith (New York: Grove, 2001), 233.

37. See Araki Yasusada [Kent Johnson], *Doubled Flowering: From the Notebooks of Araki Yasusada* (New York: Roof, 1997). "The limit of the truth," writes Irene Ramalho Santos, "is that Pessoa is the *only one that there is.*" Santos, *Atlantic Poets: Fernando Pessoa's Turn in Anglo-American Modernism* (Hanover, NH: University Press of New England, 2003), 16. Pessoa's translator Richard Zenith called his edition of Pessoa's selected poems in English *Fernando Pessoa & Co.*, the "& Co." an attempt to resist the necessities of attribution. John Fuegi's notorious *Brecht and Company* made the same maneuver, though since in Fuegi's case the "company" included actual persons, the title directed readers toward an authorial scandal.

during Pessoa's lifetime he published so little of this work, that he planned with meticulous care the publication order of his various literary productions (this book by de Campos to appear only after this one by Reis, and so on), that he sometimes wrote of "Fernando Pessoa" as one heteronym among others and on at least one occasion carried on an extended conversation with two friends *as* Álvaro de Campos, and, giving hope to those who dream that history is the mother of truth, that *pessoa* is also the Portuguese word for "person"—all these demonstrate a depth of commitment and care in Pessoa's play with the norms of property, copyright, and the work of art that require us to take seriously his attempt to expose their limits and imagine their alternatives.[38]

Likewise for the improbable death notice that is Jorge Luis Borges's short story "Pierre Menard, Author of the *Quixote*." There, the author's defense of his friend Menard, whose greatest literary work is an exact sentence-by-sentence rewriting of the Cervantes novel, allows Borges to suggest that even total textual identity does not obviate the prospect of originality. In "Pierre Menard," as in Pessoa, we see the kind of doubled-over relationship between worlds that characterizes the situation of the contemporary virtual. Menard's text, which is completely identical to Cervantes', opens up inside *Don Quijote* an entirely new world, in which Menard's own preoccupations and literary style hold temporary sway. Like virtual property, Menard's *Quixote* relies on the environment provided by an originary framing world, that of the Cervantes novel; and, like virtual property, it cannot be thought of as wholly contained by, or generated through, the primary world upon which it nonetheless depends absolutely for its meaning. In both Pessoa's life and Borges's story, the notion of a total or final adjudication of origins or of the boundaries of the "work" under a purely "self-sufficient system of structures and relations" reveals itself as the greatest fiction of all; what we get instead are worlds inside worlds, worlds with double meanings, worlds that confuse the boundary between the original and the copy, the original and the origin.[39]

---

38. For an account of that conversation and Pessoa's other adventures as Álvaro de Campos, see Sadlier, *Introduction to Fernando Pessoa*, 101–102. Another of Pessoa's heteronyms, Ricardo Reis, is the subject of José Saramago's 1984 novel, *O Ano da morte de Ricardo Reis* (*The Year of the Death of Ricardo Reis*); see Santos, *Atlantic Poets*, 6–16, for a discussion.

39. If these instances differ from Cervantes' *Don Quijote*, it is because the metafictional games that the novel plays return us by its end to a singular and self-sufficient totality in which notions of "true" and "false" correspond entirely to those that govern notions of worldly singularity. There is, for Sancho, no other "Sancho" but Sancho, no world containing a gluttonous Sancho other than a purely modal one. His world recognizes possible worlds but not competing or alternative worlds; for Sancho, there is no multiplicity except the one that he recognizes.

The modernist difference thus lies in the very nature of its fictional worldmaking. "The one world may be taken as many, or the many worlds taken as one; whether one or many depends on the way of taking," Nelson Goodman wrote.[40] The way of taking comes down, in the history of aesthetics, to a question of modality and style, operating not at the level of the sentence but at the level of the worlding, of the worldly imagination. With Borges and Pessoa, we get some sense of what difference a modernist worlding can make, seeing how their work represents (in Borges's case) or exemplifies (in Pessoa's) a strong refusal to assign, within the worldly multiplicity, a primacy or origin that collapses multiplicity into oneness. To be modernist is to treat the multiplicity not as a hierarchy but as a collection. Through this recognition of collectivity, some more complex conception of intellectual property can be virtualized, conceptualized, and made real, since the competing claims of different world systems force a recognition that all property belongs to multiple systems of production and use.

The modernist example points to the limitations of so many of the available solutions to the problem of virtual or intellectual property, which treat property's complexities or ambiguities as a problem to be resolved rather than as a challenge to revise existing epistemological or legal categories, or as a goad to subtlety and play. Edward Castronova's call, for instance, for the "interration" of worlds (he models the word on "incorporation"), dividing them into "open" and "closed" systems that would allow the latter to preserve what he calls humanity's "fundamental right to play" by preventing all commerce across the boundary between worlds, feels both like a solution to the problem of virtual property and like a way of avoiding the problem as such, or a way of deferring judgment and the challenge of complexity in the name of the pragmatic defense of an endangered human possibility.[41] The desire to master complexity—instead of being mastered by or playing with it—belongs in general to the legal mode of thought. Solomon's reputation for wisdom relies on the fact that he had no intention of cutting the contested baby in half. But if one inhabits for a moment the well of loneliness and desire of the story's false mother, it is not clear that there were not other, wiser solutions, including ones that would have, say, adjudicated in a more socially complex way the jealousy that divided the two women, or recognized the complex belonging of both child and women to a multiplicity of competing life worlds and forms of social responsibility, including the responsibility of the community to name and to take ownership of the pain of its members. What would have

---

40. Goodman, *Ways of Worldmaking*, 2.
41. Castronova, "The Right to Play," 202.

happened if both women had called Solomon's bluff, agreeing to or refusing his initial decree? What would that new occasion for wisdom have pushed the king to imagine, or us to believe?

To push for better habits in our thought is not to request a return to some epistemological dreamworld nor to imagine that virtual worlds might become some precapitalist communal utopia.[42] It is rather to suggest that what is happening today in digital virtual worlds presents us with a number of opportunities and challenges: (1) to recognize and research a powerful new form for the enactment, practice, and exemplification of property relations; (2) to locate these new aesthetic and cultural forms within the history of fictional worldmaking and to rewrite the history of the worldmaking aesthetic in light of the now-confirmed possibility of such formations; and (3) to resist, if we can, the modes of logic and habit that will not recognize the virtual worlds' realization of a new kind of property regime and that will, in the name of clarity and efficiency, ignore the novelty of that relation and its challenge to the present. In these tasks, the lessons of modernism are a useful guide. But it may also be the case that our analyses in the field of the virtual return us to a modernism that we did not know, one that writes itself anew before us, even in the same language.

42. Though anyone doing so might wish to investigate the online virtual game world *A Tale in the Desert*, whose property regime is almost entirely communal and whose entire social structure is devoted to the collective production of knowledge, skills, and large-scale building projects.

Appendix
Copyright Protection and Users' Rights: Frequently Asked Questions

This appendix is intended to acquaint scholars, teachers, performers, and adapters of still-protected works with some basic principles and parameters of copyright protection and users' rights. Because of space constraints and in recognition of this book's likeliest readership, it is confined to U.S., EU, UK, Irish, Canadian, and Australian copyright regimes. It should be read as a set of recommendations rather than as legal opinion or advice. The editor and Oxford University Press are not to be held legally responsible for actions undertaken by individuals, groups, companies, or institutions on the basis of the information or opinions contained in this FAQ.[1]

Note: Details about copyright and fair use/fair dealing differ from country to country and are not generalizable from one country to another. Be sure that you are reading the information that is appropriate to the country or countries relevant to you.

What works are in the public domain under which copyright regimes?

United States

Works published in the United States before 1923; works published in the United States between 1923 and 1977, inclusive, without a copyright notice; works published in the United States

---

1. This FAQ is adapted from a document prepared by the members of a Special Panel on Intellectual Property initiated by the International James Joyce Foundation. The panel consisted of Paul K. Saint-Amour (chair), Michael Groden, Carol Loeb Shloss, and Robert Spoo. The original, substantially longer FAQ, "James Joyce: Copyright, Fair Use, and Permissions: Frequently Asked Questions," can be found on the IJJF's website, http://english.osu.edu/research/organizations/ijjf/copyrightfaqs.cfm, and in the *James Joyce Quarterly* 44 (2007): 753–784.

between 1923 and 1963, inclusive, with a copyright notice but whose copyright was not renewed; works published in the United States between January 1, 1978, and March 1, 1989, without a copyright notice and without subsequent registration within five years; all works prepared by an officer or employee of the United States government as part of that person's official duties.

Works published prior to 1923 outside of the United States, and bearing a copyright notice, are now in the public domain in the United States. The situation with respect to works published prior to 1923 outside of the United States without a copyright notice is more complex. According to most commentators and in light of a 1994 change in U.S. copyright law, these works are most likely also in the public domain in the United States. Unfortunately, judicial decisions have not yet dealt with the legislative change in this particular context, and so this cannot be stated with certainty at this point.[2]

European Union (including United Kingdom and Republic of Ireland)

Works published more than seventy years after the calendar year in which the author died.

Canada and Australia

Works published more than fifty years after the calendar year in which the author died.

According to present copyright terms, when do still-copyrighted published works enter the public domain?

United States

For works published between 1923 and the end of 1977, ninety-five years after the year of first publication (provided that, for editions published in the United States, the work was published with a copyright notice and that the copyright in works published between 1923 and the end of 1963 was renewed).

Works created before January 1, 1978, and published between that date and December 31, 2002, will not enter the U.S. public domain before January 1, 2048.

---

2. The legislative change was the adoption of the Uruguay Round Agreements Act (1994), which restored U.S. copyright in foreign-origin works that had fallen into the U.S. public domain prematurely through a failure to comply with U.S. legal formalities. Because the act grants restored copyright for the remainder of the term the work would have enjoyed in the United States, foreign-origin works published prior to 1923 would seem to be affirmatively in the public domain. But the Ninth Circuit's controversial ruling in *Twin Books v. Walt Disney Co.* treats foreign-origin works published between July 1, 1909, and December 31, 1977, as unpublished until their first United-States-compliant publication occurs. As a result, in the Ninth Circuit's jurisdiction (Alaska, Arizona, California, Hawaii, Idaho, Montana, Nevada, Oregon, Washington, Guam, and the Northern Mariana Islands) certain foreign-origin works published between July 1, 1909, and December 31, 1922, may still enjoy copyright if they were not published in the United States and if they lacked a copyright notice recognized by U.S. law of that period. See *Twin Books v. Walt Disney Co.*, 83 F. 3d 1162 (9th Cir. 1996).

A work created on or after January 1, 1978, and published during the author's lifetime enters the public domain seventy years after the calendar year of the author's death.

European Union*

Generally, for works published during the author's lifetime, seventy years after the calendar year of the author's death.

*In Spain, the copyright term for certain older works is the author's life plus eighty years. In France, as a result of special provisions made for artists whose careers were affected by the world wars, copyright is sometimes deemed to last for the duration of the author's life plus more than eighty years. The copyright laws of each country should be separately consulted.

United Kingdom and Republic of Ireland

In the United Kingdom, the copyright in works that had been in the public domain for less than twenty years was "revived" in 1996, pursuant to an EU directive that added twenty years to the term of copyright. These revived copyrights are subject to special provisions that generally favor the public and aspiring users and were adopted to mitigate the reimposition of copyright control on works that had previously been available for common use. The most important of these provisions for most scholars and other users is a "compulsory license" exemption, which provides that "any acts restricted by the [revived] copyright shall be treated as licensed by the copyright owner, subject only to the payment of such reasonable royalty or other remuneration as may be agreed or determined in default of agreement by the Copyright Tribunal" (SI 1995, No. 3297, § 24(1)). Under this provision, any otherwise copyright-restricted use of works with revived copyrights may be undertaken in the United Kingdom without permission, as long as (1) advance notice of the intended use is given by the user to the rights-holder (at least three months' advance notice has been deemed sufficient by a British court), and (2) a reasonable royalty or other remuneration is paid to the rights-holder.

The intended use is treated as licensed under the law as soon as sufficient advance notice has been given; the issue of payment may be dealt with later, if necessary. If no agreement as to a reasonable royalty or other remuneration can be reached between the user and the copyright holder, the United Kingdom's Copyright Tribunal will determine the fee or royalty. There are special provisions explaining how a party may apply to the tribunal for settlement of any disagreement over a reasonable fee or royalty.

The UK compulsory-license provision applies only to *revived* works, not to works whose copyrights were never revived because they had never expired in the United Kingdom.

Note that there is no comparable "compulsory license" for use of revived works in the Republic of Ireland.

In the United Kingdom, works published posthumously enjoy a copyright term of fifty years from the year of first publication. Other EU countries have different terms, however. The Republic of Ireland, for example, appears to subject both lifetime-published and posthumously published works to a term of the author's life plus seventy years.

Canada and Australia

Works published during an author's lifetime enter the public domain fifty years after the calendar year of the author's death.

Posthumously published works enter the public domain fifty years (Canada) or seventy years (Australia) after the end of the calendar year in which they were first published.

In January 2005, a U.S.–Australia free trade agreement extended certain copyright terms in Australia. This extension did not affect works that had entered the Australian public domain prior to January 2005.

What is the copyright status of currently unpublished letters and manuscripts?

United States

Unpublished works are accorded federal copyright protection for the life of the author plus seventy years. In the case of a currently unpublished work created anywhere in the world before January 1, 1978, and not theretofore in the public domain or copyrighted, the work is protected for the author's life plus seventy years or until December 31, 2002, whichever is longer.

United Kingdom

Literary, dramatic, and musical works that were unpublished at the author's death and remained so until August 1, 1989, are protected by copyright in the United Kingdom for fifty years from January 1, 1990, or until December 31, 2039, after which they will enter the UK public domain. Unpublished literary, dramatic, musical, and artistic works created on or after January 1, 1996, enjoy the same copyright term as published works.

Unpublished literary, dramatic, and musical works that are open to inspection in libraries, museums, and other institutions may be photocopied for purposes of research, private study, or with a view to publication, provided one hundred years have elapsed since the end of the calendar year in which the work was created and fifty years have elapsed since the end of the calendar year in which the author died. Note that this provision does not apply to publication.

Canada

The basic rule is that unpublished works are protected for the duration of the author's life plus fifty years. However, if the author died prior to 1949, the copyright in works still unpublished as of 1997 expired at the beginning of 2003.

Australia

It appears that copyright in "undisclosed" literary, dramatic, and musical works can endure perpetually in Australia (though there are provisions that permit the publication of unpublished works found in libraries and archives when the owner of the copyright is not known). A work is "disclosed" if it is published, performed in public, or broadcast, or where records of the work are offered or exposed for sale to the public, whereupon copyright lasts for seventy years from the year of the author's death or from the year of public disclosure.

Note: It is important to understand, with respect to the countries discussed in this section, that photographic reproductions or facsimiles of manuscripts that have been published with the copyright holder's authorization are considered to be *published*, not *unpublished*, works for copyright purposes. Thus, the copyright terms that govern ordinary posthumously published works, and fair use and fair dealing as those doctrines apply to published works, also apply to rights-holder-approved publications of photographically reproduced or facsimile manuscripts. In sum, the same rules apply to such publications as to other published texts.

What are the legal definitions of fair use (United States) and fair dealing (United Kingdom, Republic of Ireland, Canada, and Australia)?

United States

According to § 107 of the U.S. Copyright Act, "fair use," which limits the exclusive rights of the copyright holder, is defined in the following manner:

> The fair use of a copyrighted work, including such use by reproduction in copies or phonorecords or by any other means specified by that section, for purposes such as criticism, comment, news reporting, teaching (including multiple copies for classroom use), scholarship, or research, is not an infringement of copyright. In determining whether the use made of a work in any particular case is a fair use the factors to be considered shall include—
>
> (1) the purpose and character of the use, including whether such use is of a commercial nature or is for nonprofit educational purposes;
> (2) the nature of the copyrighted work;
> (3) the amount and substantiality of the portion used in relation to the copyrighted work as a whole; and
> (4) the effect of the use upon the potential market for or value of the copyrighted work.
>
> The fact that a work is unpublished shall not itself bar a finding of fair use if such a finding is made upon consideration of all the above factors.

Note: Contrary to one of the more persistent myths about copyright law, fair use cannot be reduced to a certain quantity of words or number of lines; it is, rather, a flexible, multi-factor analysis that can be subjective and tends to differ from case to case and court to court. However, some publishers, editors, and organizations have adopted "guidelines" that limit fair use to specific word counts, line counts, or percentages of text. These guidelines sometimes insist that fair use does not apply to certain types of scholarly quotation, such as epigraphs. While these house rules may reflect the comfort level of the publisher or editor, they are not necessarily consistent with the scope of fair use as defined by the law.

It is generally understood that parody may be treated as fair-use criticism or comment in the United States, as long as the parody specifically targets the copyrighted work and does not merely use the work as a springboard for unrelated satire. However, satire might still qualify as a "transformative" fair use, as noted below.

Increasingly, the pivotal consideration under U.S. fair use is whether the purpose and character of the use are "transformative" of, or instead merely "supersede," the copyrighted work. A *transformative use* is one that "adds something new, with a further purpose or different character, altering the first with new expression, meaning, or message" (*Campbell v. Acuff-Rose Music, Inc.*, 510 U.S. 569, 579 (1994)). In the scholarly context, a transformative use would typically be one that subjects a reasonable amount of discontinuously quoted material to critical commentary and analysis, in contrast to a full page or several pages of uninterrupted quoted material that is not treated to substantial analysis or critical commentary by the quoting scholar.

It is important for the scholarly community to understand that, as of 1992, the U.S. Copyright Act was amended so that the privilege of fair use was expressly acknowledged as extending to unpublished as well as published material. While it is clear that fair use may apply to unpublished material, it is also the case that U.S. courts have historically been more reluctant to find fair use in the context of unpublished material. The case law is still developing on this point.

Finally, the fact that one has asked for permission to quote and been denied it by the copyright holder does not, at least in the United States, negate the fair-use privilege if it otherwise applies. Individuals often seek permission, not because they believe that fair use does not apply, but because they wish to avoid litigation or threats of litigation by the copyright holder. Were mere refusal of the copyright holder enough to negate fair use, the law could effectively be overruled by private veto.

United Kingdom

Fair dealing and related exceptions in the United Kingdom include the categories of non-commercial research and private study, criticism and review, and the reporting of current events or official proceedings. Fair dealing requires that the user give sufficient acknowledgment of the author and title of the quoted work. The exemptions for criticism and review apply to works that have already been "made available" to the public, and so do not generally apply to unpublished works.

The UK Intellectual Property Office offers this characterization:

> In certain circumstances, some works may be used if that use is considered to be "fair dealing." There is no strict definition of what this means but it has been interpreted by the courts on a number of occasions by looking at the economic impact on the copyright owner of the use. Where the economic impact is not significant, the use may count as fair dealing.
>
> So, it may be within the scope of "fair dealing" to make single photocopies of short extracts of a copyright[ed] work for non-commercial research or private study, criticism or review, or reporting current events.[3]

In 2008, the Society of Authors offered the following discussion of UK fair dealing:

> It is not possible to give specific guidelines on what constitutes "fair dealing" [for criticism or review]; it is a matter of impression and common sense according to the circumstances. However, it may be relevant to take into account the following:
>
> —the length and importance of the quotation(s)
> —the amount quoted in relation to your commentary

3. In other words, multiple reprographic copies of a protected work made in the course of instruction are *not* fair dealing. See http://www.ipo.gov.uk/c-exception-fairdealing.htm (accessed Nov. 23, 2009).

—the extent to which your work competes with or rivals the work quoted
—the extent to which works quoted are saving you work.

Some years ago The Society of Authors and the Publishers Association stated that they would usually regard as "fair dealing" the use of a single extract of up to 400 words or a series of extracts (of which none exceeds 300 words) to a total of 800 words from a prose work or extracts to a total of 40 lines from a poem, provided that this did not exceed a quarter of the poem.

The words MUST be quoted in the context of "criticism or review."
NOTE: While this statement does not have the force of law, it carried considerable weight with a judge experienced in copyright in a leading infringement case. It does not mean, however, that a quotation "for purposes of criticism or review" in excess of these limits cannot rank as "fair dealing" in some circumstances.[4]

It should be noted that UK fair dealing is less flexible and less broadly construed than the fair-use doctrine in the United States; fair dealing tends to be categorically limited to the various express purposes mentioned above.

Republic of Ireland

Fair dealing under Irish law (for research or private study, criticism, or review) is similar in many ways to fair dealing in the United Kingdom and often draws upon UK judicial decisions. In addition to fair dealing, the Irish copyright statute provides: "The copyright in a work which has been lawfully made available to the public is not infringed by the use of quotations or extracts from the work, where such use does not prejudice the interests of the owner of the copyright in that work and such use is accompanied by a sufficient acknowledgement" (Copyright and Related Rights Act, 2000, § 52(4)). The full significance and application of this provision remain to be explored.

Irish fair dealing requires sufficient acknowledgment of the author and the title of the quoted work.

Canada and Australia

Under Canadian fair-dealing provisions, the following uses do not infringe copyright:

—for the purpose of research or private study
—for the purpose of criticism, review, or news reporting, so long as the source and the name of the author are mentioned
—for purposes of instruction to make a manual reproduction of a work onto a display board or to make a copy of a work to be used on an overhead projector
—live, not-for-profit performance of a work by students at an educational institution before an audience consisting primarily of students and instructors.[5]

4. See http://www.societyofauthors.org/publications/quick_guide_permissions (accessed Aug. 9, 2008).
5. For a more detailed treatment, see http://laws.justice.gc.ca/en/C-42/FullText.html (accessed Nov. 23, 2009).

Australia's fair-dealing provisions are generally similar with respect to research or study, criticism or review, and news reporting. They differ from Canada's in recognizing parody and satire as grounds for fair dealing (see below).

In Canada, a work's being unpublished does not automatically disqualify the person who quotes, copies, or publishes it from the fair-dealing defense, but in general the courts have been reluctant to regard the use of unpublished work as fair dealing. In Australia, a specific exemption permits libraries to provide copies of older unpublished works to patrons for purposes of research or study or with a view to publication.

Factors that may be considered in determining fair dealing in Canada and Australia include the purpose and character of the use, the amount of the use, the alternatives to the use, the nature of the copyrighted work, and the effect of the use on that work. As with UK fair dealing, fair dealing in Canada and Australia is generally less flexible and less broadly construed than the fair-use doctrine in the United States; fair dealing in these countries tends to be categorically limited to the purposes set forth above. Canadian Supreme Court rulings in 2002 and 2004, however, emphasized the danger of excessive copyright protection and described fair dealing as an "integral part" of the Copyright Act—a "user's right"—rather than a limited defense against infringement.[6] The Court's implicit call for a rebalancing of the law has yet to be reflected in statutory reform.

How do I know whether my quotations are within the parameters of fair dealing/fair use?

There are no easy or straightforward answers to this crucial question, as legislation tends to name general categories of permitted use without providing specifics as to proportion, importance, economic impact, etc. In fact, fair-dealing/fair-use guidelines that name specific percentages or numbers of pages generally have no basis in the law and are often circulated by publishers, editors, or organizations with an interest in a narrow construction of fair dealing/fair use.

The UK law makes clear that unless it is for noncommercial criticism or review purposes, it is an infringement of copyright to quote or copy a substantial part of a work in copyright without permission. However, "substantial part" is left undefined; precedent suggests that both the size and the importance of the quotation in relation to the total work are considerations in determining substantiality.

What do I do if my publisher demands that I secure permission to quote an amount of material that seems to me to fall within fair-use/ fair-dealing parameters?

Authors and their estates enjoy rights in works that are in copyright; and performers, adapters, and scholars have privileges as well when they meet the requirements for fair use or fair dealing or fulfill the criteria for another exemption from copyright claims. When a

---

6. See *Théberge v. Galerie d'Art du Petit Champlain Inc.*, 2002 SCC 34, [2002] S.C.R. 336, particularly at paragraph 31; and *CCH Canadian Ltd. v. Law Society of Upper Canada*, [2004] 1 S.C.R. 339, 2004 SCC 13 (CanLII), particularly at paragraph 48.

scholarly work is to be issued, publishers enter the picture, bringing their own interests and their own perspectives on copyright and permissions matters. Scholarly writers and publishers should bring to the transaction a sensible and informed approach to these matters in order to minimize unnecessary problems, while respecting both the scholar's rights and the rights of the subject author or the author's estate.

To this end, publishers should not maintain a blanket policy of requiring all scholarly writers to approach an author or an author's estate whatever the nature and extent of the writer's use of the author's words. If your use of the author's words seems to go beyond fair use/fair dealing or in some other way rules out the privilege of fair use/fair dealing, the publisher may be justified in requiring you to approach the author or estate for permission. But if you reasonably can claim that your use of the author's words meets fair-use/fair-dealing criteria, the publisher should not force you into the possibly protracted, expensive, or even fruitless negotiations that might result from contact with an author or an estate.

In general, it is to be hoped that publishers will, on behalf of their authors, exercise fair use and fair dealing up to the reasonable limits of those doctrines, rather than restrict quotation to the actual or perceived expectations of copyright holders.

As a scholarly writer, you have, on your side, an obligation to know what the fair-use/fair-dealing criteria are for the country or countries that are relevant to your publication, so that you can back up your claim to be exercising fair use/fair dealing if you take that position. And, of course, you should ensure as far as possible that your quotations do indeed meet those criteria.

Be aware that different publishers can have widely varying policies when it comes to approaching literary estates for copyright permissions. These differences can pertain to the size of quotations for which permission is deemed necessary and to the point during the review and publication process by which permissions need to have been secured. It is worth acquainting yourself carefully with the permissions policies of your publisher before you make contact with an author's estate. It would also be in your best interest, early in your communication with a publisher, to ask if it has any policies on fair use/fair dealing and on approaching an author or estate.

Do I need to seek permission from the library or archive that owns a manuscript or letter if I want to quote from the manuscript or letter?

Some libraries and archives expect scholars to seek their permission before quoting from material held in their collections, particularly when the material is unpublished and the scholar gained access to it by visiting the library or archive. This expectation is often contained in an agreement that the scholar is asked to sign before being permitted to view the material on-site or before receiving a photocopy of the material from the library or archive. It is important to bear in mind that this expectation typically reflects the library or archive's desire to be made aware of intended uses of its material and to be cited as the owner of the physical document, and is rarely based in any copyright ownership that the library or archive may claim. Therefore, any permission obtained from the library or archive to use its material will usually not substitute for permission from the copyright holder, if such permission is necessary.

What is *droit moral* (moral right)? Where and for how long is it applicable?

Droit moral traditionally is part of continental (i.e., not Anglo-American) conceptions of authorial rights and descends from natural law regimes such as the French civil code. It confers on authors a semi-sacred reputational right that, in some countries, coexists with and even survives the temporary monopoly created by copyright. The primary moral rights are the right of integrity (i.e., the right against distortion or mutilation of the work) and the right of attribution or paternity (the right to be named as the author of the work and not to be named as the author of a work one did not create). Because *droit moral* protects against distortions and misattributions of an author's work, it is not inconsistent with the privileges of fair use and fair dealing in the ordinary context of accurate, attributed quotations.

In France, where moral rights are perpetual, a parody that intends to harm the original author's work might be held to violate *droit moral* even if it is permissible according to fair-dealing provisions for parody and pastiche. In Spain, *droit moral* empowers the author to restrain "any distortion, modification, or alteration...that is likely to prejudice his legitimate interests or threaten his reputation."

There is no statutory or common-law *droit moral* for writers in the United States, although federal and state statutes there protect creators' moral rights in certain works of visual art. Canadian law (since at least 1988) and Australian law (since 2000) recognize authors' moral rights of integrity and attribution; these rights subsist for the same term as a work's copyright. In the United Kingdom, the right to be identified as the author of a work, the right to object to derogatory treatment of the work, and the right not to have the work falsely attributed have been statutorily protected since at least 1988; these rights also last for the same term as the work's copyright. Since 2001, the Republic of Ireland has protected authors' moral rights by statute; the most prominent moral rights (paternity, integrity, and privacy in photographs and films) subsist there for the same term as copyright.

If I plan to hold a public reading of a protected work, should I seek permission?

United States

Performances or displays of works or portions of works by students or instructors in non-profit educational settings are exempt from copyright claims in the context of (1) face-to-face classroom teaching, or (2) certain course-related digital transmissions.

Outside of the educational context, live, nonprofit, public performances of copyrighted *nondramatic* literary works (novels, stories, poems, and other works that relate events rather than calling for their enactment in dialogue or motion) or *nondramatic* musical works (songs and musical compositions that are not part of a staged performance) are permitted by U.S. law and do not require permission. Note that such performances must not be of dramatic literary works (plays, pantomimes, choreography; scripts for film, television, and radio, etc.) or dramatic musical works (operas, theater musicals, etc.); must not be sponsored for a commercial purpose; must not provide compensation to participants; must not involve a direct or indirect charge for admission; and must not be broadcast over television or radio or streamed over the internet.

A similar exemption applies to live, public performances of copyrighted nondramatic literary works or nondramatic musical works when admission *is* charged, so long as the proceeds, less the reasonable costs of producing the performance, are used exclusively for educational, religious, or charitable purposes and not for private financial gain. Note that the other requirements apply here just as they do in the case of a public performance for which no admission is charged, namely, that the performance be live (not broadcast or streamed), that it not compensate the participants, and that it not be for directly or indirectly commercial purposes.

If admission is charged for the second type of nonprofit public performance, the copyright owner may veto the performance by serving a signed, written notice of objection "at least seven days before the date of the performance," stating "the reasons for the objection" and complying with other requirements established by the Register of Copyrights. (The first type of nonprofit public performance discussed above—the one not involving an admission charge—cannot be vetoed by the copyright owner.)

Note that, for either type of nonprofit performance, there is no limitation in the United States upon the amount of copyrighted material that may be performed. For example, if the above requirements are otherwise satisfied, an individual or group could publicly perform the entirety of a copyrighted edition of *Ulysses* or *Finnegans Wake*, and could incorporate into the performance all of a copyrighted nondramatic Irish song. Comparable public performance exemptions in countries other than the United States are typically not so expansive.

United Kingdom

Performances of copyrighted literary, dramatic, musical, and certain other works in an educational institution for educational purposes do not infringe copyright, so long as the audience consists of teachers, students, and others directly connected with the institution (parents are excluded from this group).

Outside of the educational context, the UK copyright law also contains an exemption for a particular kind of public performance: "The reading or recitation in public by one person of a reasonable extract from a published literary or dramatic work does not infringe copyright in the work if it is accompanied by a sufficient acknowledgement" (CDPA § 59(1)). This exemption would appear to apply to a reading or recitation from any copyrighted literary or dramatic work, so long as the extract is "reasonable" in length and the authorship is "sufficient[ly] acknowledge[d]." "Sufficient acknowledgement" means "an acknowledgement identifying the work in question by its title or other description, and identifying the author" (ibid., § 178).

Republic of Ireland

Ireland has a provision for educational performances that is similar to the United Kingdom's.

Like UK law, the copyright law of the Republic of Ireland has carved out an exemption for certain public performances outside of the educational context: "The reading or recitation in public by one person of any reasonable extract from a literary or dramatic work which has been lawfully made available to the public, where accompanied by a sufficient acknowledgement, shall not infringe the copyright in the work" (CRRA § 90(1)). Like its

UK counterpart, this exemption appears to apply to a reading or recitation from any published, copyrighted literary or dramatic work, as long as the extract is "reasonable" in length and the authorship is "sufficient[ly] acknowledge[d]." "Sufficient acknowledgement" means "an acknowledgement identifying the work concerned by its title or other description and identifying the author" (ibid., § 51(3); see also § 2).

Canada

It is not an infringement of copyright for students to mount a live, nonprofit performance of a copyrighted work at an educational institution before an audience consisting primarily of students and instructors. Note: Canadian law does not exclude "dramatic literary works" from this provision.

Outside of the educational context, the Canadian Copyright Act also contains an exemption for certain public performances of published, copyrighted works: "It is not an infringement of copyright...for any person to read or recite in public a reasonable extract from a published work" (R.S. 1985, c. C-42, § 32.2(1)(d)).

Australia

A teacher's performance of a literary, dramatic, or musical work, or the playing of a record or showing of a film, in the course of educational instruction at a nonprofit place of education is not an infringement of copyright.

Outside of the educational context, Australian copyright law contains a specific exemption for certain public performances of specified published, copyrighted works: "The reading or recitation in public...of an extract of reasonable length from a published literary or dramatic work, or from an adaptation of such a work, does not constitute an infringement of the copyright in the work if a sufficient acknowledgement of the work is made" (Copyright Act of 1968, § 45). "Sufficient acknowledgement" means "an acknowledgement identifying the work by its title or other description and...also identifying the author" (ibid., § 10).

If I plan to quote from protected work in an original musical composition, should I seek permission?

So long as the quotation is from a work in the public domain or is privileged by fair use, fair dealing, or another exemption, permission would not be required. If the work is not in the public domain and if the quotation is extensive or of a nature that would render fair use/fair dealing inapplicable, then permission should be sought.

If I plan to create a visual or sculptural artwork using an author's image, should I seek permission?

United States

Courts have held that the "right of publicity" (a rather irregular body of state-based law that bars people from "appropriat[ing] the commercial value of a person's identity by using without consent the person's name, likeness, or other indicia of identity for purposes of trade") may not prohibit movies, novels, plays, or songs that use people's names or likenesses. However, statuettes, prints, and T-shirts that reproduce a person's likeness for a *commercial* purpose may be found by some state courts to violate the right of publicity. Some courts tend to look more permissively on "transformative" uses of a person's likeness (e.g., works that creatively and expressively alter a likeness or use it as only one among many raw materials, rather than a single realistic or representational image or likeness). And, in some states, the likeness of a deceased person is more broadly usable than that of a living person. The basic rule of thumb: the more transformative and the less commercial the use, the less likely that permission is necessary.

United Kingdom

Although living celebrities have employed UK privacy law to restrict some uses of their likenesses, there is in the United Kingdom no body of law equivalent to the "right of publicity" or "personality rights" in the United States.

Canada

The Canadian tort of "appropriation of personality" is less developed than the U.S. right of publicity law but more developed than UK protections. A deceased celebrity's estate may bring an action under this law for uses of that celebrity's likeness, but the protections appear to be limited to purely and explicitly commercial uses (e.g., celebrity endorsement of a product).

If I plan to create a parody of a protected work, should I seek permission before publishing it?

United States

Although parody is not explicitly mentioned in the U.S. fair-use provision, case law has established that copying aspects of a work for the purpose of parody can be considered a fair use under certain conditions. The chief condition is that the work copied or imitated also be the specific object of the parody. For example, one might not be able lawfully to imitate the melody, chord structure, and lyrics of a Lady Gaga song in order to make a trenchant critique of U.S. foreign policy; a court might consider this to be "satire" and grant no fair-use privilege for it. Gaga's song itself would have to be the target of a parody in order for the imitation to be eligible for the fair-use privilege. However, as noted above, a satire might qualify as a fair use if it is sufficiently transformative of the copyrighted work and satisfies other fair-use requirements under U.S. law.

United Kingdom and Republic of Ireland

A 2001 EU directive permits member states to allow exceptions and limitations to copyright in the cases of caricature, parody, or pastiche. To date, however, neither the United Kingdom nor the Republic of Ireland has formalized any fair-dealing provisions for parody, and UK case law provides no consistent rule of thumb for determining at what point a parody's borrowing from a copyrighted work is substantial enough to be considered an infringement.

Canada

Canadian courts tend not to regard parody as a viable form of fair dealing. Parodists of protected works are advised to seek permission.

Australia

Since 2006, Australian law has recognized a fair dealing provision for purposes of parody and satire. The provision includes literary, dramatic, musical, and artistic works; adaptations thereof; and audio-visual works (films, sound recordings, and broadcasts). Note that the Australian provision does not replicate the distinction that U.S. courts have made between parody and satire.

If I plan to reproduce a photograph of an author or a member of his or her family in my scholarly book or article, should I seek permission from the author or his or her estate before doing so?

In most cases, no. Copyright law with respect to photographs has historically been somewhat complicated, but in most countries, the copyright in a photograph, if any, is initially owned by the "author" of the photograph—typically, the person who snapped the picture. This means that, as a general rule, the subject of a photograph could not have authored it.

An older photograph whose author is unknown—and this is the case with many older photos, especially candid ones—may generally be reproduced without permission, especially if it seems likely that the photo is old enough to be in the public domain. Reproducing a photograph whose author is unknown opens up the possibility—perhaps a remote one, though not out of the question—that the author or his or her descendants might come forward to object. In this situation, your having previously made a good-faith effort to locate the author might help your case, but it would not be a complete defense to an infringement claim.

By contrast, where the photographer's identity is known, efforts should be made to obtain permission from the photographer or his or her estate or representatives, unless the photograph is in the public domain or unless reproducing it would be privileged by fair use/fair dealing or another exemption.

The application of fair use/fair dealing to copyrighted photographs is a subject that is still evolving in the courts. While fair use/fair dealing is never guaranteed, a rule of thumb would be to reproduce a copyrighted photograph without permission only when you are subjecting that image to specific commentary or analysis. At a minimum, such a practice would make your use of the image more likely to qualify as a "transformative" fair use in the United States. In addition, recent judicial decisions in the United States have suggested that reduced, "thumbnail" versions of photographs are more likely to qualify as a fair use than larger, high-resolution images.

The duration of copyrights in photographs often follows the usual rules of copyright, as discussed above. In some countries, however, the duration of photographic copyrights is more complicated. In Germany and Spain, for example, a distinction is drawn between photographic "works" (which satisfy criteria of authorial creativity) and "simple" photographs not constituting "works." These categories are assigned different copyright terms. Many countries do not observe such a distinction, however.

Bibliography

Sources

Ackroyd, Peter. *The Collection: Journalism, Reviews, Essays, Short Stories, Lectures.* London: Random House, 2001.

Adams, John. *The Works of John Adams, Second President of the United States: With a Life of the Author, Notes and Illustrations.* Vol. 1. Edited by Charles Francis Adams. Boston: Little, Brown, 1850–1856.

Adler, Amy. "Against Moral Rights." *California Law Review* 97 (2009): 263–300.

———. "Post-Modern Art and the Death of Obscenity Law." *Yale Law Journal* 99 (1999): 1359–1378.

Adorno, Theodor W. "Chaplin Times Two." Translated by John MacKay. *Yale Journal of Criticism* 9 (1996).

———. *Musikalische Schriften IV.* Frankfurt: Suhrkamp, 2003.

———. "On the Fetish Character in Music and the Regression of Listening." In *Essays on Music,* edited by Richard D. Leppert, translated by Susan H. Gillespie, 288–317. Berkeley: University of California Press, 2002.

———. *Philosophy of Modern Music.* Translated by Anne G. Mitchell and Wesley V. Blomster. New York: Continuum, 2003.

Allen, Jean Thomas. "Copyright and Early Theatre, Vaudeville, and Film Competition." In *Film before Griffith,* edited by John Fell, 176–187. Berkeley: University of California Press, 1983.

Anderson, Benedict. *Imagined Communities.* Rev. ed. London: Verso, 1991.

Appiah, K. Anthony. *In My Father's House: Africa in the Philosophy of Culture.* New York: Oxford University Press, 1992.

Apter, Emily. "What Is Yours, Ours, and Mine: Authorial Ownership and the Creative Commons." *October* 126 (2008): 91–114.

Archer-Shaw, Petrine. *Negrophilia: Avant-Garde Paris and Black Culture in the 1920s.* London: Thames and Hudson, 2000.

Arendt, Hannah. *The Human Condition*. Chicago: University of Chicago Press, 1958.

Arnheim, Rudolf. "Chaplin's Early Films." 1929. Reprinted in "Walter Benjamin and Rudolf Arnheim on Charlie Chaplin," translated by John MacKay. *Yale Journal of Criticism* 9 (1996): 309–314.

Atkin, Jonathan. *A War of Individuals: Bloomsbury Attitudes to the Great War*. Manchester, UK: Manchester University Press, 2002.

Baker, Houston A., Jr. *Modernism and the Harlem Renaissance*. Chicago: University of Chicago Press, 1987.

Baran, Paul A., and Paul M. Sweezy. *Monopoly Capital*. New York: Monthly Review Press, 1966.

Barnes, Julian. "Letter from Paris." *Times Literary Supplement*, Dec. 21, 2001.

Bartle, Richard A. "Pitfalls of Virtual Property." Durham, NC: Themis Group, 2004. http://www.themis-group.com/uploads/Pitfalls%20of%20Virtual%20Property.pdf.

Beach, Sylvia. Sylvia Beach Papers. Princeton University Library.

Becker, Howard S. *Art Worlds*. Berkeley: University of California Press, 1982.

Béja, Morris. "'A Symposium All His Own': The International James Joyce Foundation and Its Symposium." In *Joyce Studies Annual* 2001, edited by Thomas F. Staley. Austin: University of Texas Press, 2001.

Benjamin, Walter. "A Look at Chaplin." 1929. Reprinted in "Walter Benjamin and Rudolf Arnheim on Charlie Chaplin," translated by John MacKay. *Yale Journal of Criticism* 9 (1996): 309–314.

———. "The Work of Art in the Age of Mechanical Reproduction." In *Illuminations: Essays and Reflections*. Edited by Hannah Arendt. Translated by Harry Zohn. New York: Schocken, 1969.

Benkler, Yochai. "Free as the Air to Common Use: First Amendment Constraints on Enclosure of the Public Domain." *NYU Law Review* 74 (1999): 354–446.

———. *The Wealth of Networks: How Social Production Transforms Markets and Freedom*. New Haven, CT: Yale University Press, 2007.

Berman, Marshall. *All That Is Solid Melts into Air: The Experience of Modernity*. New York: Penguin, 1988.

Bloom, Harold. *The Breaking of the Vessels*. Chicago: University of Chicago Press, 1982.

Boling, Patricia. *Privacy and the Politics of Intimate Life*. Ithaca, NY: Cornell University Press, 1996.

Booth, Alison. *How to Make It as a Woman: Collective Biographical History from Victoria to the Present*. Chicago: University of Chicago Press, 2004.

Boris, Eileen. *Art and Labor: Ruskin, Morris, and the Craftsman Ideal in America*. Philadelphia: Temple University Press, 1986.

Borshuk, Michael. *Swinging the Vernacular: Jazz and African American Modernist Literature*. London: Routledge, 2006.

Boscagli, Maurizia, and Enda Duffy. "Joyce's Face." In *Marketing Modernisms: Self-Promotion, Canonization, Rereading*, edited by Kevin J. H. Dettmar and Stephen Myers Watt, 133–162. Ann Arbor: University of Michigan Press, 1996.

Botstein, Leon. "Modernism." *Grove Music Online*. Edited by Laura Macy. http://www.oxfordmusiconline.com/subscriber/article/grove/music/40625 (subscription access).

Bowker, Richard Rogers. *Copyright: Its History and Its Law*. Boston: Houghton Mifflin, 1912.

Boyle, James D. A. *Shamans, Software, and Spleens: Law and the Construction of the Information Society.* Cambridge, MA: Harvard University Press, 1996.

Bracha, Oren. "The Ideology of Authorship Revisited: Authors, Markets and Liberal Values in Early American Copyright." *Yale Law Journal* 118 (2008): 103–163.

———. "Owning Ideas: A History of Anglo-American Intellectual Property." S.J.D. diss., Harvard University, 2005.

Bradbury, Malcolm, and James F. McFarlane. "Movements, Magazines, and Manifestos: The Succession from Naturalism." In *Modernism: 1890–1930*, edited by Malcolm Bradbury and James McFarlane, 192–205. Atlantic Highlands, NJ: Humanities, 1978.

Breyer, Stephen. "The Uneasy Case for Copyright: A Study of Copyright in Books, Photocopies, and Computer Programs." *Harvard Law Review* 84 (1970): 281–351.

Briggs, Asa, and Peter Burke. *A Social History of the Media.* Cambridge: Polity, 2005.

Briggs, Austin. "Chaplin's Charlie and Joyce's Bloom." *Journal of Modern Literature* 20 (1996): 177–186.

Briggs, Julia. *Reading Virginia Woolf.* Edinburgh: Edinburgh University Press, 2006.

Brooks, Cleanth. *The Well Wrought Urn: Studies in the Structure of Poetry.* New York: Houghton Mifflin Harcourt, 1956.

Calabresi, Guido, and A. Douglas Melamed. "Property Rules, Liability Rules and Inalienability: One View of the Cathedral." *Harvard Law Review* 85 (1972): 1089–1128.

Calinescu, Matei. *Five Faces of Modernity: Modernism, Avant-Garde, Decadence, Kitsch, Postmodernism.* Durham, NC: Duke University Press, 1987.

Carpenter, William Boyd. *A Popular History of the Church of England from the Earliest Times to the Present Day.* London: John Murray, 1900.

Casanova, Pascale. *The World Republic of Letters.* Translated by M. B. DeBevoise. Cambridge, MA: Harvard University Press, 2004.

Castronova, Edward. "On Virtual Economies." *Game Studies* 3 (2003). http://www.gamestudies.org/0302/castronova.

———. "The Price of 'Man' and 'Woman': A Hedonic Pricing Model of Avatar Attributes in a Synthetic World." CESifo Working Paper series, no. 957 (2003). http://ssrn.com/abstract=294828.

———. "The Right to Play." *New York Law School Law Review* 49 (2004): 185–210.

———. *Synthetic Worlds: The Business and Culture of Online Games.* Chicago: University of Chicago Press, 2006.

———. "Virtual Worlds: A First-Hand Account of Market and Society on the Cyberian Frontier." CESifo Working Paper series, no. 618 (2001). http://ssrn.com/abstract=415043.

Cavanagh, Clare. "Rereading the Poet's Ending: Mandelstam, Chaplin, and Stalin." *PMLA* 109 (1994): 71–86.

Cervantes, Miguel de. *Don Quijote.* Translated by Burton Raffel. Edited by Diana de Armas Wilson. New York: Norton, 1999.

Césaire, Aimé. *Notebook of a Return to My Native Land/Cahier d'un retour au pays natal.* Translated by Mireille Rosello and Annie Pritchard. Edited by Timothy Mathews and Michael Worton. Newcastle-upon-Tyne: Bloodaxe, 1995.

Chaulet-Achour, Christiane. "Writing as Exploratory Surgery: Yambo Ouologuem's *Bound to Violence.*" In *Yambo Ouologuem: Postcolonial Writer, Islamic Militant*, edited by Christopher Wise, 89–107. Boulder, CO: Rienner, 1999.

Chinitz, David. *T. S. Eliot and the Cultural Divide*. Chicago: University of Chicago Press, 2003.

Chow, Rey. *The Protestant Ethnic and the Spirit of Capitalism*. New York: Columbia University Press, 2002.

Clifford, James. "Negrophilia: 1933, February." In *A New History of French Literature*, edited by Denis Hollier et al., 901–908. Cambridge, MA: Harvard University Press, 1989.

———. "On Ethnographic Allegory." In *Writing Culture: The Poetics and Politics of Ethnography*, edited by James Clifford and George E. Marcus, 98–121. Berkeley: University of California Press, 1986.

———. *The Predicament of Culture: Twentieth-century Ethnography, Literature, and Art*. Cambridge, MA: Harvard University Press, 1988.

Coker, Jerry. *Elements of the Jazz Language for the Developing Improviser*. Miami: Studio 224/Belwin/Warner Bros., 1991.

Coleridge, Samuel Taylor. *Biographia Literaria*. Edited by George Watson. London: Everyman's Library, 1975.

Conant, S. S. "International Copyright: An American View." *Macmillan's Magazine*, May–Oct. 1879.

Coombe, Rosemary J. *The Cultural Life of Intellectual Properties: Authorship, Appropriation, and the Law*. Durham, NC: Duke University Press, 1998.

Corbin, Arthur L. *Cases on the Law of Contracts*. St. Paul, MN: West, 1921.

Cornevin, Robert. "Connaissance des Kabrè Depuis Frobenius." *Le monde non Chrétien* 59–60 (1961): 95–99.

Costigan, George P., Jr. *Cases on the Law of Contracts*. Chicago: Callaghan, 1921.

Cotter, Thomas. "Toward a Functional Definition of Publication in Copyright Law." *Minnesota Law Review* 92 (2008): 1724–1795.

Cottington, David. "What the Papers Say: Politics and Ideology in Picasso's Collages of 1912." *Art Journal* 47 (1988): 350–359.

Coundouriotis, Eleni. *Claiming History: Colonialism, Ethnography, and the Novel*. New York: Columbia University Press, 1999.

Culler, Jonathan D. *Framing the Sign: Criticism and Its Institutions*, vol. 3 of *Oklahoma Project for Discourse and Theory*. Norman: University of Oklahoma Press, 1988.

Current, Richard Nelson, and Marcia Ewing Current. *Loie Fuller: Goddess of Light*. Boston: Northeastern University Press, 1997.

Deenihan, Kevin Edward. "Leave Those Orcs Alone: Property Rights in Virtual Worlds." Working Paper series (2008). http://ssrn.com/abstract=1113402.

Deleuze, Gilles. *The Fold: Leibniz and the Baroque*. Translated by Tom Conley. Minneapolis: University of Minnesota Press, 1993.

Delson, Susan. *Dudley Murphy: Hollywood Wild Card*. Minneapolis: University of Minnesota Press, 2006.

Dettmar, Kevin J. H. "The Illusion of Modernist Allusion and the Politics of Postmodern Plagiarism." In *Perspectives on Plagiarism and Intellectual Property in a Postmodern World*, edited by Lise Buranen and Alice M. Roy, 99–109. Albany: State University of New York Press, 1999.

Dettmar, Kevin J. H., and Stephen Myers Watt, eds. *Marketing Modernisms: Self-Promotion, Canonization, Rereading*. Ann Arbor: University of Michigan Press, 1996.

DeVeaux, Scott. *The Birth of Bebop: A Social and Musical History.* Berkeley: University of California Press, 1997.

———. "'Nice Work if You Can Get It': Thelonious Monk and Popular Song." In *The Thelonious Monk Reader,* edited by Rob van der Bliek, 260–278. New York: Oxford University Press, 2001.

Dickens, Charles. *A Child's History of England.* London: Chapman and Hall, 1870.

———. *The Letters of Charles Dickens, 1842–1843,* vol. 3 of *Letters of Charles Dickens,* edited by Madeline House et al. Oxford: Clarendon, 1974.

Divers, John. *Possible Worlds.* London: Routledge, 2002.

Dolezel, Lubomir. *Heterocosmica: Fiction and Possible Worlds.* Baltimore, MD: Johns Hopkins University Press, 1998.

Dougherty, Candidus. "*Bragg v. Linden:* Virtual Property Rights Litigation." *E-Commerce Law and Policy* 9 (2007). http://papers.ssrn.com/sol3/papers.cfm?abstract_id=1092284.

Dranos, Peter, with John Braithwaite. *Informational Feudalism: Who Owns the Knowledge Economy?* New York: Norton, 2003.

Drone, Eaton S. *A Treatise on the Law of Property in Intellectual Productions in Great Britain and the United States.* Boston: Little, Brown, 1879.

Du Bois, W. E. B. *An Inquiry into the Part Which Africa Has Played in World History.* 8th ed. New York: International Publishers, 1965.

Ducheneaut, Nicolas, and Nicholas Yee. "Avatar Survey: Age." *PlayOn: Exploring the Social Dimensions of Virtual Worlds* (blog). http://blogs.parc.com/playon/archives/2008/07/avatar_survey_a.html.

———. "Avatar Survey: Gender Demographics." *PlayOn: Exploring the Social Dimensions of Virtual Worlds* (blog). http://blogs.parc.com/playon/archives/2008/07/avatar_survey_d.html.

Duerden, Dennis. "The 'Discovery' of the African Mask." *Research in African Literatures* 31 (2000): 29–47.

Duff-Gordon, Lady [Lucile]. *Discretions and Indiscretions.* New York: Stokes, 1932.

Edelman, Lee. *No Future: Queer Theory and the Death Drive.* Durham, NC: Duke University Press, 2004.

Edison, Thomas A. *Thomas A. Edison Papers: A Microfilm Edition.* Frederick, MD: University Publications of America, 1987–.

Edwards, Brent Hayes. *The Practice of Diaspora: Literature, Translation, and the Rise of Black Internationalism.* Cambridge, MA: Harvard University Press, 2003.

Eidelberg, Martin, and Nina Gray. *A New Light on Tiffany: Clara Driscoll and the Tiffany Girls.* New York: New-York Historical Society, 2007.

Eilenberg, Susan. "Mortal Pages: Wordsworth and the Reform of Copyright." *English Literary History* 56 (1989): 351–374.

Eliot, T. S. *Collected Poems: 1909–1962.* New York: Harcourt, Brace and World, 1963.

———. "Tradition and the Individual Talent." 1919. Reprinted in *Selected Prose of T. S. Eliot,* edited by Frank Kermode, 37–44. New York: Harcourt Brace Jovanovich, 1975.

———. [Apteryx, pseud.] "Verse Pleasant and Unpleasant." *Egoist* 5 (1918): 43.

Ellmann, Richard. Richard Ellmann Papers. McFarlin Library, University of Tulsa.

Errington, Shelly. *The Death of Authentic Primitive Art and Other Tales of Progress.* Berkeley: University of California Press, 1998.

———. "What Became Authentic Primitive Art?" *Cultural Anthropology* 9 (1994): 201–226.

Etherington-Smith, Meredith, and Jeremy Pilcher. *The "It" Girls.* New York: Harcourt Brace Jovanovich, 1986.

Feather, John. *Publishing, Piracy, and Politics: An Historical Study of Copyright in Britain.* London: Mansell, 1994.

Feltes, N. N. "International Copyright: Structuring 'the Condition of Modernity' in British Publishing." *Cardozo Arts and Entertainment Law Journal* 10 (1991–1992): 535–544.

Finkelstein, Haim. "Dalí and *Un Chien andalou:* The Nature of a Collaboration." In *Dada and Surrealist Film,* edited by Rudolf E. Kuenzli, 128–142. New York: Willis Locker and Owens, 1987.

Fisk, Catherine L. "Credit Where It's Due: The Law and Norms of Attribution." *Georgetown Law Journal* 95 (2006): 49–117.

———. "The Origin of the Work for Hire Doctrine." *Yale Journal of Law and the Humanities* 15 (2003): 1–70.

———. *Working Knowledge: Employee Innovation and the Rise of Corporate Intellectual Property, 1800–1930.* Chapel Hill: University of North Carolina Press, 2009.

Forrest, Jennifer. "The 'Personal' Touch: The Original, the Remake, and the Dupe in Early Cinema." In *Dead Ringers: The Remake in Theory and Practice,* edited by Jennifer Forrest and Leonard R. Koos, 89–126. Albany: State University of New York Press, 2001.

Foucault, Michel. *The History of Sexuality,* vol. 1: *An Introduction.* Translated by Robert Hurley. New York: Vintage, 1990.

———. *"Society Must Be Defended": Lectures at the Collège de France, 1975–1976.* Edited by Mauro Bertani and Alessandro Fontana. Translated by David Macey. New York: Picador, 2003.

———. "What Is an Author?" Translated by Josué V. Harari. In *The Foucault Reader.* Edited by Paul Rabinow. New York: Pantheon, 1984.

Friedman, Lawrence M. *Guarding Life's Dark Secrets: Legal and Social Controls over Reputation, Propriety, and Privacy.* Stanford, CA: Stanford University Press, 2007.

Friedman, Susan Stanford. "Migration, Encounter, and Indigenisation: New Ways of Thinking about Intertextuality in Women's Writing." In *European Intertexts: Women's Writing in English in a European Context,* edited by Angela Leighton, Ana María Sánchez-Arce, and Patsy Stoneman, 215–271. Oxford: Lang, 2005.

Frobenius, Leo. *Histoire de la civilisation Africaine.* 4th ed. Translated by H. Back and E. Ermont. Paris: Gallimard, 1936.

———. *The Voice of Africa.* 2 vols. Translated by Rudolf Blind. London: Hutchinson, 1913.

Frobenius, Leo, and A. H. Keane. *The Childhood of Man: A Popular Account of the Lives, Customs and Thoughts of the Primitive Races.* London: Seeley, 1909.

Froula, Christine. *Virginia Woolf and the Bloomsbury Avant-Garde: War, Civilization, Modernity.* New York: Columbia University Press, 2005.

Fuller, Loie. *Fifteen Years of a Dancer's Life.* Boston: Small, Maynard, 1913.

Gaines, Jane. *Contested Culture: The Image, the Voice, and the Law.* Chapel Hill: University of North Carolina Press, 1991.

Gallagher, Catherine. "Undoing." In *Time and the Literary,* edited by Karen Newman, Jay Clayton, and Marianne Hirsch, 11–29. New York: Routledge, 2002.

Gallup, Donald Clifford. *Pigeons on the Granite: Memoirs of a Yale Librarian.* New Haven, CT: Yale University Press, 1998.

Gan, Wendy. *Women, Privacy and Modernity in Early Twentieth-century British Writing.* New York: Palgrave Macmillan, 2009.

Garber, Frederick. "Fabulating Jazz." In *Representing Jazz*, edited by Krin Gabbard, 70–103. Durham, NC: Duke University Press, 1995.

Gasaway, Laura N. "When Works Pass into the Public Domain." http://www.unc.edu/~unclng/public-d.htm.

Gates, Henry Louis, Jr. *The Signifying Monkey: A Theory of Afro-American Literary Criticism.* New York: Oxford University Press, 1988.

Gendron, Bernard. "Fetishes and Motorcars: Negrophilia in French Modernism." *Cultural Studies* 4 (1990): 141–155.

Genette, Gérard. *Paratexts: Thresholds of Interpretation.* Translated by Jane E. Lewin. Cambridge: Cambridge University Press, 1997.

Gertzman, Jay A. *Bookleggers and Smuthounds: The Trade in Erotica, 1920–1940.* Philadelphia: University of Pennsylvania Press, 1999.

Gikandi, Simon. "Picasso, Africa, and the Schemata of Difference." *Modernism/Modernity* 10 (2003): 455–480.

Gilbert, Steven E. *The Music of Gershwin.* New Haven, CT: Yale University Press, 1995.

Gillespie, Dizzy, with Al Fraser. *To Be, or Not… to Bop: Memoirs.* Garden City, NY: Doubleday, 1979.

Goehr, Lydia. *The Imaginary Museum of Musical Works: An Essay in the Philosophy of Music.* Rev. ed. New York: Oxford University Press, 2007.

Goldberg, Victor. *Framing Contract Law: An Economic Perspective.* Cambridge, MA: Harvard University Press, 2006.

Goodman, Nelson. *Ways of Worldmaking.* Indianapolis, IN: Hackett, 1978.

Gordon, Wendy J. "A Property Right in Self-Expression: Equality and Individualism in the Natural Law of Intellectual Property." *Yale Law Journal* 102 (1993): 1533–1609.

Goux, Jean-Joseph. *Symbolic Economies.* Translated by Jennifer Curtiss Gage. Ithaca, NY: Cornell University Press, 1990.

Graeber, David. *Toward an Anthropological Theory of Value.* New York: Palgrave, 2001.

Greenberg, Clement. "Avant-Garde and Kitsch." *Partisan Review* 6 (1939): 34–49.

———. "Modernist Painting." In *Modern Art and Modernism: A Critical Anthology*, edited by Francis Frascina and Charles Harrison, 5–10. London: Harper and Row, 1982.

Greenman, Ben. "Silence Is Beholden." *New Yorker*, Sept. 30, 2002.

Grossman, Lev. "*Time*'s Person of the Year: You." *Time*, Dec. 13, 2006.

Guillaume, Paul, and Thomas Munro. *Primitive Negro Sculpture.* New York: Harcourt Brace, 1926.

Guillory, John. "The Memo and Modernity." *Critical Inquiry* 31 (2004): 108–132.

Gunning, Tom. "Heard over the Phone: *The Lonely Villa* and the de Lorde Tradition of the Terrors of Technology." *Screen* 32 (1991): 184–196.

Haden-Guest, Anthony. "The Talk of the Town: Picasso Pic Has Heirs Seeing Red!" *New Yorker*, Aug. 21, 1995.

Hamilton, Ian. *In Search of J. D. Salinger.* New York: Random House, 1988.

———. *Keepers of the Flame: Literary Estates and the Rise of Biography.* London: Pimlico, 1993.

Hammarskjöld, Dag. "The World of Modern Art." *Bulletin of the Museum of Modern Art* 22 (1954): 9.

Hammond, Paul, ed. *The Shadow and Its Shadow: Surrealist Writings on the Cinema.* 3rd ed. San Francisco: City Lights, 2000.

Hardt, Michael, and Antonio Negri. *Multitude: War and Democracy in the Age of Empire.* New York: Penguin, 2004.

Hardwick, Elizabeth. *Sight Readings: American Fictions.* New York: Random House, 1998.

Harvey, Mark S. "Jazz and Modernism: Changing Conceptions of Innovation and Tradition." In *Jazz in Mind: Essays in the History and Meaning of Jazz,* edited by Reginald T. Buckner and Steven Weiland, 128–147. Detroit, MI: Wayne State University Press, 1991.

Hayot, Eric, and Edward Wesp. "Reading Game/Text: *EverQuest,* Alienation, and Digital Communities." *Postmodern Culture* 14 (2004). http://pmc.iath.virginia.edu/text-only/issue.104/14.2hayot_wesp.txt.

Henderson, Amy. "Media and the Rise of Celebrity Culture." *Organization of American Historians Magazine of History* 6 (1992): 49–54.

Hollstrom, Katie. "Legal Conceptions of Virtual Property: Should Virtual Property Be Afforded the Same Rights as Its Real-World Counter-Part?" *Law and Society Journal at the University of California, Santa Barbara* 7 (2007–2008): 59–68.

Hood, Thomas. "Copyright and Copywrong, Letter II." *Prose and Verse.* Vol. 2. New York: Wiley and Putnam, 1845.

Horkheimer, Max, and Theodor W. Adorno. *Dialectic of Enlightenment.* Translated by John Cumming. New York: Continuum, 1993.

Hornby, Nick. *The Polysyllabic Spree.* San Francisco: McSweeney's Believer Books, 2004.

Horncastle, F. W. "Plagiarism." *Quarterly Musical Magazine and Review* 4 (1822): 141–157.

Horowitz, Steven J. "Competing Lockean Claims to Virtual Property." *Harvard Journal of Law and Technology* 20 (2007): 443–458.

Huff, Theodore. *Charlie Chaplin.* New York: Arno, 1972.

Huggan, Graham. "Anthropologists and Other Frauds." *Comparative Literature* 46 (1994): 113–128.

Hughes, Langston. *Montage of a Dream Deferred.* 1951. Reprinted in *The Collected Poems of Langston Hughes,* edited by Arnold Rampersad, 387–429. New York: Vintage, 1994.

Hussey, Mark. *Virginia Woolf A–Z.* Oxford: Oxford University Press, 1995.

Hutcheon, Linda. "Literary Borrowing... and Stealing: Plagiarism, Sources, Influences, and Intertexts." *English Studies in Canada* 12 (1986): 229–239.

Huyssen, Andreas. *After the Great Divide: Modernism, Mass Culture, Postmodernism.* Bloomington: Indiana University Press, 1986.

Hyland, William G. *George Gershwin: A New Biography.* Westport, CT: Praeger, 2003.

Ibsen, Henrik. *Hedda Gabler.* 1890. Reprinted in *Ibsen: The Complete Major Prose Plays,* translated by Rolf Fjelde, 689–778. New York: Farrar, Straus and Giroux, 1978.

Irele, Abiola. "A New Mood in the African Novel." *West Africa* (Sept. 20, 1969): 1113–1115.

Irving, Washington. *Letters.* Vol. 1. Edited by Ralph M. Aderman et al. Boston: Twayne, 1978.

Ita, J. M. "Frobenius in West African History." *Journal of African History* 13 (1972): 673–688.

Jackson, Kathy Merlock. "Mickey and the Tramp: Walt Disney's Debt to Charlie Chaplin." *Journal of American Culture* 26 (2003): 439–444.

Jaffe, Aaron. *Modernism and the Culture of Celebrity.* Cambridge: Cambridge University Press, 2005.

Jahn, Janheinz. *Leo Frobenius: The Demonic Child.* Translated by Reinhard Sander. Austin: African and Afro-American Studies and Research Center, University of Texas, 1974.

James, Henry. "An Animated Conversation." 1889. Reprinted in Henry James, *Essays in London and Elsewhere*, 280–285. New York: Harper, 1893.

———. *The Notebooks of Henry James.* Edited by F. O. Matthiessen and Kenneth B. Murdock. New York: Oxford University Press, 1961.

Jameson, Fredric. *Archaeologies of the Future: The Desire Called Utopia and Other Science Fictions.* London: Verso, 2005.

———. "Postmodernism and Consumer Society." In *The Anti-Aesthetic: Essays on Postmodern Culture*, edited by Hal Foster, 111–125. Port Townsend, WA: Bay, 1983.

Jarrett, Michael. "Four Choruses on the Tropes of Jazz Writing." *American Literary History* 6 (1994): 336–353.

Jaszi, Peter. "Caught in the Net of Copyright." *Oregon Law Review* 75 (1998): 303.

———. "On the Author Effect: Contemporary Copyright and Collective Creativity." In *The Construction of Authorship: Textual Appropriation in Law and Literature*, edited by Martha Woodmansee and Peter Jaszi, 29–56. Durham, NC: Duke University Press, 1994.

———. "Toward a Theory of Copyright: The Metamorphoses of 'Authorship.'" *Duke Law Journal* (1991): 455–502.

"Jazz Has Got Copyright Law and That Ain't Good." Note. *Harvard Law Review* 118 (2005): 1940–1961.

Jefferson, Thomas. *The Writings of Thomas Jefferson: Memorial Edition.* Vol. 7. Washington, DC: Thomas Jefferson Memorial Association of the United States, 1903.

Jenkins, Henry. *Convergence Culture: Where Old and New Media Collide.* New York: New York University Press, 2006.

Jensen, Robert. *Marketing Modernism in Fin-de-Siècle Europe.* Princeton, NJ: Princeton University Press, 1994.

Johnson, Patricia. *Real Fantasies: Edward Steichen's Advertising Photography.* Berkeley: University of California Press, 1997.

Johnson, Paul E. *Sam Patch, the Famous Jumper.* New York: Hill and Wang, 2003.

Johnston, Georgia. "Women's Voice: *Three Guineas* as Autobiography." In *Virginia Woolf: Themes and Variations*, edited by Vara Neverow-Turk and Mark Hussey, 322–328. New York: Pace University Press, 1993.

Jones, Caroline A. *Machine in the Studio: Constructing the Postwar American Artist.* Chicago: University of Chicago Press, 1996.

Joyce, James. *Letters of James Joyce.* 3 vols. Edited by Stuart Gilbert and Richard Ellmann. New York: Viking, 1957–1966.

———. *Selected Letters of James Joyce.* Edited by Richard Ellmann. New York: Viking, 1975.

J. Walter Thompson Company Collection. Perkins Library, Duke University.

Kadir, Djelal. "To World, to Globalize: Comparative Literature's Crossroads." *Comparative Literature Studies* 41 (2004): 1–9.

Kaplan, David. "The End of History." *Newsweek*, Dec. 25, 1989, 80.

Katz, Daniel. *American Modernism's Expatriate Scene: The Labour of Translation.* Edinburgh: Edinburgh University Press, 2007.

Kerman, Joseph. *Musicology.* London: Fontana, 1985.

Knowlson, James. *Damned to Fame: The Life of Samuel Beckett.* London: Bloomsbury, 1996.

Komara, Edward. "The Dial Recordings of Charlie Parker." In *The Bebop Revolution in Words and Music,* edited by Dave Oliphant, 79–103. Austin, TX: Harry Ransom Humanities Research Center, 1994.

Kracauer, Siegfried. "Two Chaplin Sketches." Translated by John MacKay. *Yale Journal of Criticism* 10 (1997): 115–120.

Kristeva, Julia. *Revolution in Poetic Language.* Translated by Margaret Waller. New York: Columbia University Press, 1984.

Kurzon, Dennis. "*Peters Edition v. Batt:* The Intertextuality of Silence." *International Journal for the Semiotics of Law* 20 (2007): 285–303.

Landes, William M., and Richard A. Posner. *The Economic Structure of Intellectual Property Law.* Cambridge, MA: Belknap, 2003.

Larson, Charles R. *The Novel in the Third World.* Washington, DC: INSCAPE, 1976.

Lastowka, Greg, and Dan Hunter. "The Laws of Virtual Worlds." *California Law Review* 92 (2004): 1–73.

Lears, Jackson. *Fables of Abundance: A Cultural History of Advertising in America.* New York: Basic, 1994.

Legislative History of the 1909 *Copyright Act.* Vol. 5. Edited by E. Fulton Brylawski and Abe A. Goldman. South Hackensack, NJ: Rothman, 1976.

Lemke, Sieglinde. *Primitivist Modernism: Black Culture and the Origins of Transatlantic Modernism.* Oxford: Oxford University Press, 1998.

Lessig, Lawrence. *Remix: Making Art and Commerce Thrive in the Hybrid Economy.* New York: Penguin, 2008.

Leval, Pierre N. "Toward a Fair Use Standard." *Harvard Law Review* 103 (1990): 1105–1161.

Levine, Jennifer Schiffer. "Originality and Repetition in *Finnegans Wake* and *Ulysses.*" *PMLA* 94 (1979): 106–120.

Levine, Lawrence W. *Highbrow/Lowbrow: The Emergence of Cultural Hierarchy in America.* Cambridge, MA: Harvard University Press, 1988.

———. "Jazz and American Culture." In *The Jazz Cadence of American Culture,* edited by Robert G. O'Meally, 431–447. New York: Columbia University Press, 1998.

Leyda, Jay. "A Note on Progress." *Film Quarterly* 21 (1968): 28–33.

———. "Waiting Jobs." *Film Quarterly* 16 (1962–1963): 29–33.

Lidderdale, Jane, and Mary Nicholson. *Dear Miss Weaver: Harriet Shaw Weaver, 1876–1961.* London: Faber and Faber, 1970.

Light, Alison. *Mrs. Woolf and the Servants: An Intimate History of Domestic Life in Bloomsbury.* New York: Bloomsbury Press, 2008.

Litman, Jessica. "Lawful Personal Use." *Texas Law Review* 85 (2007): 1871–1920.

Lott, Eric. "Double V, Double-Time: Bebop's Politics of Style." *Callaloo* 36 (1988): 597–605.

Lowe, Melanie. "Claiming Amadeus: Classical Feedback in American Media." *American Music* 20 (2002): 102–119.

Lukács, Georg. *"Writer and Critic" and Other Essays.* Translated by Arthur D. Kahn. New York: Grosset and Dunlap, 1978.

Machacek, Gregory. "Allusion." *PMLA* 122 (2007): 522–536.

Mackintosh, Sir James. "A Discourse on the Law of Nature and Nations." 1799. Reprinted in *The Miscellaneous Works of the Right Honourable Sir James Mackintosh.* Vol. 1. London: Longman, Brown, Green, and Longmans, 1846.

Maddox, Brenda. *Nora: The Real Life of Molly Bloom.* Boston: Houghton Mifflin, 1988.

Maland, Charles. *Chaplin and American Culture: The Evolution of a Star Image.* Princeton, NJ: Princeton University Press, 1989.

Malraux, André. *Picasso's Mask.* Translated by June Guicharnaud and Jacques Guicharnaud. New York: Da Capo, 1995.

Mao, Douglas, and Rebecca L. Walkowitz. "The New Modernist Studies." *PMLA* 123 (2008): 737–748.

Marchand, Roland. *Advertising the American Dream: Making Way for Modernity, 1920–1940.* Berkeley: University of California Press, 1986.

Marchand, Suzanne. "Leo Frobenius and the Revolt against the West." *Journal of Contemporary History* 32 (1997): 153–170.

Mason, Alpheus Thomas. *Brandeis: A Free Man's Life.* New York: Viking, 1946.

Max, D. T. "The Injustice Collector: Is James Joyce's Grandson Suppressing Scholarship?" *New Yorker,* June 19, 2006.

Mazzeo, Tilar J. *Plagiarism and Literary Property in the Romantic Period.* Philadelphia: University of Pennsylvania Press, 2006.

McCabe, John. *Charlie Chaplin.* Garden City, NY: Doubleday, 1978.

McCabe, Susan. "'Delight in Dislocation': The Cinematic Modernism of Stein, Chaplin, and Man Ray." *Modernism/Modernity* 8 (2001): 429–452.

McCarthy, J. Thomas. *The Rights of Publicity and Privacy.* 2nd ed. Eagan, MN: Thomson Reuters, 2009.

McDonald, Robert. "*Bound to Violence:* A Case of Plagiarism." *Transition* 41 (1972): 64–68.

McHard, James. *The Future of Modern Music: A Philosophical Exploration of Modernist Music in the Twentieth Century and Beyond.* Livonia, MI: Iconic, 2008.

McMurry, Frank M., and A. E. Parkins. *Advanced Geography.* New York: Macmillan, 1921.

Meadows, Eddie S. *Bebop to Cool: Context, Ideology and Musical Identity.* Westport, CT: Praeger, 2003.

Meisel, Perry. *The Myth of the Modern: A Study in British Literature and Criticism after 1850.* New Haven, CT: Yale University Press, 1987.

Menger, Pierre-Michel. "Artistic Labor Markets and Careers." *Annual Review of Sociology* 25 (1999): 541–574.

Merman, Ethel, as told to Pete Martin. *Who Could Ask for Anything More?* Garden City, NY: Doubleday, 1955.

Miller, Christopher L. *Blank Darkness: Africanist Discourse in French.* Chicago: University of Chicago Press, 1985.

Milton, Joyce. *Tramp: The Life of Charles Chaplin.* New York: Da Capo, 1998.

Monnet, Pierre. *Dictionnaire pratique de propriété littéraire.* Paris: Cercle de la Librairie, 1962.

Monson, Ingrid T. *Saying Something: Jazz Improvisation and Interaction.* Chicago: University of Chicago Press, 1996.

Montgomery, David. *The Fall of the House of Labor.* New York: Cambridge University Press, 1983.

Moore, Marianne. *The Poems of Marianne Moore.* Edited by Grace Schulman. New York: Viking, 2003.

Mouralis, Bernard. "Un Carrefour D'Écritures: *Le Devoir de Violence* de Yambo Ouologuem." *Nouvelles du Sud* 5 (1986): 63–74.

Mpiku, J. Mbelolo ya. "From One Mystification to Another: 'Négritude' and 'Négraille' in *Le Devoir de Violence.*" In *Yambo Ouologuem: Postcolonial Writer, Islamic Militant*, edited by Christopher Wise, 23–38. Boulder, CO: Rienner, 1999.

Murphy, Peter, ed. *Evidence, Proof, and Facts: A Book of Sources.* New York: Oxford University Press, 2003.

Musser, Charles. *Before the Nickelodeon: Edwin S. Porter and the Edison Manufacturing Company.* Berkeley: University of California Press, 1991.

Nancy, Jean-Luc. *The Creation of the World; or, Globalization.* Translated by François Raffoule and David Pettigrew. Albany: State University of New York Press, 2007.

Neill, Elizabeth. *Rights of Privacy and the Privacy Trade: On the Limits of Protection for the Self.* London: McGill-Queen's University Press, 1984.

Netanel, Neil Weinstock. *Copyright's Paradox.* New York: Oxford University Press, 2008.

Newman, Hilary. "*Three Guineas* and *The Life of Sophia Jex-Blake.*" *Virginia Woolf Bulletin* 25 (2007): 23–31.

Nietzsche, Friedrich. "David Strauss: Writer and Confessor," translated by Herbert Golder. In *Unmodern Observations*, edited by William Arrowsmith, 1–72. New Haven, CT: Yale University Press, 1990.

Norris, Frank. *McTeague: A Story of San Francisco.* New York: Doubleday, Page, 1914.

Ogren, Kathy. *The Jazz Revolution: Twenties America and the Meaning of Jazz.* New York: Oxford University Press, 1989.

Oliar, Dotan, and Christopher Sprigman. "There's No Free Laugh (Anymore): The Emergence of Intellectual Property Norms and the Transformation of Stand-Up Comedy." *Virginia Law Review* 94 (2008): 1787–1867.

Oliphant, Dave, ed. *The Bebop Revolution in Word and Music.* Austin, TX: Harry Ransom Humanities Research Center, 1994.

Olney, James. *Tell Me Africa: An Approach to African Literature.* Princeton, NJ: Princeton University Press, 1973.

O'Meally, Robert G., ed. *The Jazz Cadence of American Culture.* New York: Columbia University Press, 1998.

O'Neill, Alistair. "Lucile." In *Encyclopedia of Clothing and Fashion*, edited by Valerie Steele, vol. 2, 364–365. Farmington Hills, MI: Scribner's, 2005.

O'Shea, Michael Vincent, et al., eds. *The World Book: Organized Knowledge in Story and Picture.* Chicago: World Book, 1918.

Osteen, Mark. "Introduction: Blue Notes toward a New Jazz Discourse." *Genre: Forms of Discourse and Culture* 37 (2004): 1–46.

Osterberg, Robert C., and Eric C. Osterberg. *Substantial Similarity in Copyright Law.* New York: Practicing Law Institute, 2004.

Ouologuem, Yambo. *Bound to Violence.* Translated by Ralph Manheim. London: Heinemann, 1971.

———. *Le Devoir de violence: Roman.* Paris: Seuil, 1968.

———. "The Duty of Violence." In *The Yambo Ouologuem Reader*, edited by Christopher Wise. Trenton, NJ: Africa World Press, 2008.

———. "An Interview with Yambo Ouologuem." *Journal of the New African Literature and the Arts* 9–10 (1971): 134–138.

———. *Lettre à la France nègre.* Edited by Pierre Bisiou. Paris: Serpent à Plumes, 2003.

———. [Utto Rodolph, pseud.] *Les Milles et une bibles du sexe.* Paris: Dauphin, 1969.

Paddison, Max. *Adorno's Aesthetics of Music.* Cambridge: Cambridge University Press, 1993.

Paraskeva, Anthony. "Wyndham Lewis v. Charlie Chaplin." *Forum for Modern Language Studies* 43 (2007): 223–234.

Parker, Douglass. "'Donna Lee' and the Ironies of Bebop." In *The Bebop Revolution in Words and Music,* edited by Dave Oliphant, 161–201. Austin, TX: Harry Ransom Humanities Research Center, 1994.

Parrinder, Patrick, and Warren Chernaik, eds. *Textual Monopolies: Literary Copyright and the Public Domain.* London: Office for Humanities Communication, 1997.

Pasco, Allan H. *Allusion: A Literary Graft.* Charlottesville, VA: Rookwood, 2002.

Passerin d'Entrèves, Maurizio, and Ursula Vogel, eds. *Public and Private: Legal, Political and Philosophical Perspectives.* London: Routledge, 2000.

Patrick, James. "Charlie Parker and the Harmonic Sources of Bebop Composition: Thoughts on the Repertory of New Jazz in the 1940s." *Journal of Jazz Studies* 2 (1975): 3–23.

Patry, William F. *Copyright Law and Practice.* Washington, DC: Bureau of National Affairs, 1994. http://digital-law-online.info/patry/index.html.

———. *The Fair Use Privilege in Copyright Law.* Washington, DC: Bureau of National Affairs, 1985.

Patry, William F., and Richard A. Posner. "Fair Use and Statutory Reform in the Wake of *Eldred.*" *California Law Review* 92 (2004): 1639–1661.

Patterson, L. Ray. "Free Speech, Copyright, and Fair Use." *Vanderbilt Law Review* 40 (1987): 1–66.

Patterson, L. Ray, and Stanley W. Lindberg. *The Nature of Copyright: A Law of Users' Rights.* Athens: University of Georgia Press, 1991.

Pessoa, Fernando. *The Selected Prose of Fernando Pessoa.* Translated and edited by Richard Zenith. New York: Grove, 2001.

Pound, Ezra. *The Cantos.* New York: New Directions, 1995.

———. *Confucius, Digest of the Analects.* Milan: Giovanni Scheiwiller, private printing, 1937.

———. "Copyright and Tariff." *New Age* 23 (Oct. 3, 1918): 363.

———. *Ezra and Dorothy Pound: Letters in Captivity, 1945–1946.* Edited by Omar Pound and Robert Spoo. New York: Oxford University Press, 1999.

———. Ezra Pound Collection. Beinecke Library, Yale University.

———. *Ezra Pound's Poetry and Prose: Contributions to Periodicals.* 11 vols. Edited by Lea Baechler et al. New York: Garland, 1991.

———. *Ezra Pound Speaking: Radio Speeches of World War II.* Edited by Leonard W. Doob. Westport, CT: Greenwood, 1978.

———. *Guide to Kulchur.* Norfolk, CT: New Directions, 1952.

———. *I Cantos.* Translated and with notes by Mary de Rachewiltz. Milan: Mondadori, 1985.

———. *"If This Be Treason…."* Siena, Italy: printed for Olga Rudge by Tip. Nuova, 1948.

———. "In Explanation." *Little Review* 4 (1918): 5.

———. Interview by Vanni Ronsisvalle and Pier Paolo Pasolini, 1968. Translated by David Anderson. *Paideuma* 10 (1981): 331–345.

———. *Lavoro e Usura.* Milan: All'insegna del pesce d'oro, 1954.

———. *Pound/Joyce: The Letters of Ezra Pound to James Joyce, with Pound's Essays on Joyce.* Edited by Forrest Read. New York: New Directions, 1967.

———. *Profile: An Anthology.* Milan: John Scheiwiller, private printing, 1932.

———. *Selected Letters of Ezra Pound: 1907–1941.* Edited by D. D. Paige. New York: New Directions, 1970.

———. *Selected Prose: 1909–1965.* Edited by William Cookson. New York: New Directions, 1973.

———. *The Spirit of Romance.* Rev. ed. New York: New Directions, 1968.

———. "Tariff and Copyright." *New Age* 23 (Sept. 26, 1918): 348.

Pratt, Walter F., Jr. "American Contract Law at the Turn of the Century." *South Carolina Law Review* 39 (1987–1988): 415–464.

Prost, Antoine. "Public and Private Spheres in France." In *A History of Private Life: Riddles of Identity in Modern Times*, edited by Antoine Prost and Gérard Vincent. Translated by Arthur Goldhammer. Cambridge, MA: Harvard University Press, 1991.

Prost, Antoine, and Gérard Vincent, eds. *A History of Private Life: Riddles of Identity in Modern Times.* Translated by Arthur Goldhammer. Cambridge, MA: Harvard University Press, 1991.

Puchner, Martin. *Poetry of the Revolution.* Princeton, NJ: Princeton University Press, 2006.

Quiller-Couch, Arthur. *On the Art of Writing: Lectures Delivered in the University of Cambridge, 1913–1914.* Cambridge: Cambridge University Press, 1916.

Rachewiltz, Mary de. *Discretions.* Boston: Little, Brown, 1971.

Radin, Margaret Jane. *Reinterpreting Property.* Chicago: University of Chicago Press, 1993.

Rainey, Lawrence. *Institutions of Modernism: Literary Elites and Public Culture.* New Haven, CT: Yale University Press, 1998.

Ramsaye, Terry. *A Million and One Nights: A History of the Motion Picture through 1925.* New York: Simon and Schuster, 1926.

Randall, Marilyn. *Pragmatic Plagiarism: Authorship, Profit, and Power.* Toronto: University of Toronto Press, 2001.

Ransom, John Crowe. "Criticism, Inc." In *Praising It New: The Best of the New Criticism*, edited by Garrick Davis and William Logan, 49–61. Athens: Ohio University Press, 2008.

Reynard, Clive. "The Impact of the European Directive on Inexpensive Reprint Editions." In *Textual Monopolies: Literary Copyright and the Public Domain*, edited by Patrick Parrinder and Warren Chernaik, 45–54. London: Office for Humanities Communication, 1997.

Ricketson, Samuel. *The Berne Convention for the Protection of Literary and Artistic Works: 1886–1986.* London: Centre for Commercial Law Studies, Queen Mary College and Kluwer, 1987.

Rimmer, Matthew. "Damned to Fame: The Moral Rights of the Beckett Estate." *Australian Library and Information Association* 24 (2003). http://www.alia.org.au/publishing/incite/2003/05/beckett.html.

Robinson, David. *From Peep Show to Palace: The Birth of American Film.* New York: Columbia University Press, 1996.

Robinson, J. Bradford. "The Jazz Essays of Theodor Adorno: Some Thoughts on Jazz Reception in Weimar Germany." *Popular Music* 13 (1994): 1–25.

Rodgers, Edward S. "Copyright and Morals." *Michigan Law Review* 18 (1920): 390–404.

Ronen, Ruth. *Possible Worlds in Literary Theory.* Cambridge: Cambridge University Press, 1994.

Rose, Carol M. "Canons of Property Talk; or, Blackstone's Anxiety." *Yale Law Journal* 108 (1998): 601–632.

Rose, Mark. *Authors and Owners: The Invention of Copyright.* Cambridge, MA: Harvard University Press, 1993.

Rosenberg, Deena. *Fascinating Rhythm: The Collaboration of George and Ira Gershwin.* New York: Dutton, 1991.

Rosner, Victoria. *Modernism and the Architecture of Private Life.* New York: Columbia University Press, 2005.

Rossler, Beate, ed. *Privacies: Philosophical Evaluations.* Stanford, CA: Stanford University Press, 2004.

Roy, William G. *Socializing Capital.* Princeton, NJ: Princeton University Press, 1997.

Ruedel, Ulrich. "Send in the Clones." *BFI Charles Chaplin Symposium*, July 2005. http://chaplin.bfi.org.uk/programme/conference/pdf/ulrich-ruedel.pdf.

Russell, Ross. *Bird Lives: The High Life and Hard Times of Charlie (Yardbird) Parker.* New York: Da Capo Press, 1996.

Sadlier, Darlene J. *An Introduction to Fernando Pessoa: Modernism and the Paradoxes of Authorship.* Gainesville: University of Florida Press, 1998.

Saint-Amour, Paul K. *The Copywrights: Intellectual Property and the Literary Imagination.* Ithaca, NY: Cornell University Press, 2003.

———. "Soliloquy of Samuel Roth: A Paranormal Defense." *James Joyce Quarterly* 37 (2000): 459–477.

Saint-Amour, Paul K., Michael Groden, Carol Shloss, and Robert Spoo. "James Joyce: Copyright, Fair Use, and Permission: Frequently Asked Questions." *James Joyce Quarterly* 44 (2007): 753–784.

Salmon, Richard. *Henry James and the Culture of Publicity.* New York: Cambridge University Press, 1997.

Samuelson, Pamela. "Preliminary Thoughts on Copyright Reform." *Utah Law Review* 3 (2007): 551–571.

Santos, Irene Ramalho. *Atlantic Poets: Fernando Pessoa's Turn in Anglo-American Modernism.* Hanover, NH: University Press of New England, 2003.

Saunders, David. *Authorship and Copyright.* London: Routledge, 1992.

Schickel, Richard, ed. *The Essential Chaplin: Perspectives on the Life and Art of the Great Comedian.* Chicago: Dee, 2006.

Schneiderman, Davis. "Everybody's Got Something to Hide Except for Me and My Lawsuit: William S. Burroughs, DJ Danger Mouse, and the Politics of 'Grey Tuesday.'" *Plagiary* 1 (2006): 191–206.

Schoenberg, Arnold. "Brahms the Progressive." In *Style and Idea.* Edited by Leonard Stein. Translated by Leo Black. Berkeley: University of California Press, 1975.

Schreiner, Olive. *From Man to Man or Perhaps Only…1926.* London: Virago, 1982.

Schwarz-Bart, André. *The Last of the Just.* Translated by Stephen Becker. New York: Atheneum, 1960.

Schweitzer, Marlis. "The Mad Search for Beauty: Actresses' Testimonials, the Cosmetics Industry, and the Democratization of Beauty." *Journal of the Gilded Age and Progressive Era* 4 (2005): 255–292.

Scott, Gini Graham. *Mind Your Own Business: The Battle for Personal Privacy.* New York: Insight, 1995.

Scott, Hugh Arthur. "Indebtedness in Music." *Musical Quarterly* 13 (1927): 497–509.

Scrutton, Thomas. *The Laws of Copyright: An Examination into the Principles Which Should Regulate Literary and Artistic Property in England and Other Countries.* London: John Murray, 1883.

Segrave, Kerry. *Piracy in the Motion Picture Industry.* Jefferson, NC: McFarland, 2003.

Seldes, Gilbert. *The Seven Lively Arts.* New York: Harper, 1924.

Sellin, Eric. "Ouologuem's Blueprint for *Le Devoir de Violence.*" *Research in African Literatures* 2 (1971): 117–120.

———. "The Unknown Voice of Yambo Ouologuem." *Yale French Studies* 53 (1976): 137–162.

Senghor, Léopold Sédar. "The Lessons of Leo Frobenius." In *Leo Frobenius: An Anthology,* edited by Eike Haberland, vii–xiii. Wiesbaden, Germany: Steiner, 1973.

Serrano, Richard. *Against the Postcolonial: "Francophone" Writers at the Ends of French Empire: After the Empire.* Lanham, MD: Lexington, 2005.

Seville, Catherine. "Authors as Copyright Campaigners: Mark Twain's Legacy." *Journal of the Copyright Society U.S.A.* 55 (2008): 283–359.

Shell, Marc. *Money, Language and Thought.* Baltimore, MD: Johns Hopkins University Press, 1982.

Sheppard, R. Z., Helen Gibson, and Raji Samghabadi. "Trespassers Will Be Prosecuted: In Search of J. D. Salinger." *Time,* May 23, 1988.

Sherman, Brad, and Lionel Bently. "Balance and Harmony in the Duration of Copyright: The European Directive and Its Consequences." In *Textual Monopolies: Literary Copyright and the Public Domain,* edited by Patrick Parrinder and Warren Chernaik, 15–37. London: Office for Humanities Publication, 1997.

———. *The Making of Intellectual Property Law: The British Experience, 1760–1911.* Cambridge: Cambridge University Press, 1999.

Shloss, Carol Loeb. "*Lucia Joyce:* Supplementary Material." http://www.lucia-the-authors-cut.info.

———. *Lucia Joyce: To Dance in the Wake.* New York: Farrar, Straus and Giroux, 2003.

Silver, Brenda R. *Virginia Woolf, Icon.* Chicago: University of Chicago Press, 1999.

———. *Virginia Woolf's Reading Notebooks.* Princeton, NJ: Princeton University Press, 1983.

Simon, George. "Bop's Dixie to Monk." In *The Thelonious Monk Reader,* edited by Rob van der Bliek, 53–56. New York: Oxford University Press, 2001.

"Something *New* out of Africa?" *TLS: Times Literary Supplement,* May 5, 1972.

Soyinka, Wole. *Myth, Literature and the African World.* Cambridge: Cambridge University Press, 1976.

———. *You Must Set Forth at Dawn: A Memoir.* New York: Random House, 2006.

Spoo, Robert. "Archival Foreclosure: A Scholar's Lawsuit against the Estate of James Joyce." *American Archivist* 71 (2008): 544–551.

———. "Copyright Protectionism and Its Discontents: The Case of James Joyce's *Ulysses* in America." *Yale Law Journal* 108 (1998): 633–667.

———. "Copyrights and 'Design-Around' Scholarship." *James Joyce Quarterly* 44 (2007): 563–585.

———. "Fair Use of Copyrighted Works in the Digital Age." *California Business Law Practitioner* 23 (2008): 37–47.

———. "'For God's Sake, Publish; Only Be Sure of Your Rights': Virginia Woolf, Copyright, and Scholarship." In *Woolf Editing/Editing Woolf*, edited by Eleanor McNees and Sara Veglahn. Clemson, SC: Clemson University Digital Press, 2009.

———. "Litigating the Right to Be a Scholar." In *Joyce Studies Annual* 2008. Edited by Philip Sicker and Moshe Gold. Bronx, NY: Fordham University Press, 2008.

Stahl, Matthew. "Authentic Boy Bands on TV? Performers and Impresarios in *The Monkees* and *Making the Band*." *Popular Music* 21 (2002): 307–329.

Strauss, William S. *Protection of Unpublished Works*. 1957. Reprinted in Senate Committee on the Judiciary, 86th Cong., study no. 29, *Copyright Law Revision* (Washington, DC: Committee Print, 1961).

Stravinsky, Igor. *Stravinsky: Selected Correspondence*. Edited by Robert Craft. New York: Knopf, 1984.

Surowiecki, James. "The Permission Problem." *New Yorker*, Aug. 11, 2008.

Szendy, Peter. *Listen: A History of Our Ears*. Translated by Charlotte Mandell. Bronx, NY: Fordham University Press, 2008.

Tarr, Ralph S., and Frank M. McMurry. *World Geographies*. 2nd book. Rev. ed. New York: Macmillan, 1919.

Taylor, Richard. "Editing the Variorum *Cantos*: Process and Policy." *Paideuma* 31 (2002): 311–334.

Tebbel, John. *A History of Book Publishing in the United States*. 2 vols. New York: Bowker, 1972.

Thomas, Lorenzo. "The Bop Aesthetic and the Black Intellectual Tradition." In *The Bebop Revolution in Words and Music*, edited by Dave Oliphant, 105–117. Austin, TX: Harry Ransom Humanities Research Center, 1994.

Thomas, Michael Tilson. "Igor Stravinsky's Copyright Blues." In *The MTT Files*, produced by American Public Radio and the San Francisco Symphony. http://americanpublicmedia.publicradio.org/programs/mtt_files/mtt_04.shtml.

Thompson, E. P. *The Making of the English Working Class*. New York: Vintage, 1963.

Thomson, Ellen Mazur. "Alms for Oblivion: The History of Women in Early American Graphic Design." *Design Issues* 10 (1994): 27–48.

Todd, Margaret. *The Life of Sophia Jex-Blake*. London: Macmillan, 1918.

Trachtenberg, Alan. *The Incorporation of America*. New York: Hill and Wang, 1982.

Tratner, Michael. *Modernism and Mass Politics: Joyce, Woolf, Eliot, Yeats*. Stanford, CA: Stanford University Press, 1995.

Turner, Catherine. *Marketing Modernism between the Two World Wars*. Amherst: University of Massachusetts Press, 2003.

U.S. Central Intelligence Agency. *The World Factbook* 2009. https://www.cia.gov/library/publications/the-world-factbook/fields/2102.html.

U.S. Copyright Office. "Copyright Registration for Derivative Works." http://www.copyright.gov/circs/circ14.pdf.

Vaidhyanathan, Siva. *Copyrights and Copywrongs: The Rise of Intellectual Property and How It Threatens Creativity*. New York: New York University Press, 2001.

Valéry, Paul. *Aesthetics*. Translated by Ralph Manheim. New York: Pantheon, 1964.

van der Bliek, Rob, ed. *The Thelonious Monk Reader*. New York: Oxford University Press,

Veblen, Thorstein. *The Theory of the Leisure Class.* 1899. Edited by Martha Banta. New York: Oxford University Press, 2007.

Venuti, Lawrence. *The Scandals of Translation: Towards an Ethics of Difference.* New York: Routledge, 1998.

Von Sternberg, Constantin. "On Plagiarism." *Musical Quarterly* 5 (1919): 390–397.

Walkiewicz, E. P., and High Witemeyer, eds. *Ezra Pound and Senator Bronson Cutting: A Political Correspondence, 1930–1935.* Albuquerque: University of New Mexico Press, 1995.

Warren, Samuel D., and Louis D. Brandeis. "The Right to Privacy." *Harvard Law Review* 4 (1890): 193–220.

Watkins, Glenn. *Soundings: Music in the Twentieth Century.* New York: Schirmer, 1988.

Weintraub, Jeff, and Krishan Kumar, eds. *Public and Private in Thought and Practice: Perspectives on a Grand Dichotomy.* Chicago: University of Chicago Press, 1997.

Wexler, Joyce Piell. *Who Paid for Modernism? Art, Money, and the Fiction of Conrad, Joyce, and Lawrence.* Fayetteville: University of Arkansas Press, 1997.

W[hiteman], K[aye]. "In Defence of Yambo Ouologuem." *West Africa* (July 21, 1972): 939–940.

Whitman, Walt. *The Complete Poetry and Prose of Walt Whitman.* Vol. 2. Edited by Malcolm Cowley. New York: Pellegrini and Cudahy, 1948.

Wicke, Jennifer A. *Advertising Fictions: Literature, Advertising, and Social Reading.* New York: Columbia University Press, 1988.

Wilentz, Sean. *Chants Democratic.* New York: Oxford University Press, 1984.

Willey, Ann Elizabeth. "Pornography, or the Politics of Misbehaving? A Feminist Reading of the Voices of Yambo Ouologuem." In *Yambo Ouologuem: Postcolonial Writer, Islamic Militant,* edited by Christopher Wise, 139–151. Boulder, CO: Rienner, 1999.

Williams, Raymond. *The Politics of Modernism: Against the New Conformists.* New York: Verso, 1989.

———. "When Was Modernism?" *New Left Review* 175 (1989): 48–52.

Wise, Christopher, ed. *Yambo Ouologuem: Postcolonial Writer, Islamic Militant.* Boulder, CO: Rienner, 1999.

Witkovsky, Matthew S. "Surrealism in the Plural: Guillaume Apollinaire, Ivan Goll and Devětsil in the 1920s." *Papers of Surrealism* 2 (2004): 1–14.

Woodmansee, Martha. "The Genius and the Copyright: Economic and Legal Conditions of the Emergence of the 'Author.'" *Eighteenth-century Studies* 17 (1984): 425–448.

Woodmansee, Martha, and Peter Jaszi, eds. *The Construction of Authorship: Textual Appropriation in Law and Literature.* Durham, NC: Duke University Press, 1994.

Woolf, Leonard. *Downhill All the Way: An Autobiography of the Years 1919 to 1939.* New York: Harcourt Brace Jovanovich, 1967.

Woolf, Virginia. *Collected Essays.* Vol. 1. Edited by Leonard Woolf. London: Hogarth, 1966.

———. *The Diary of Virginia Woolf.* 5 vols. Edited by Anne Olivier Bell and Andrew McNeillie. New York: Harcourt Brace Jovanovich, 1977–1984.

———. "A Letter from Virginia." Edited by Stephen Barkway. *Virginia Woolf Bulletin* 17 (2004): 13–16.

———. *The Letters of Virginia Woolf.* 6 vols. Edited by Nigel Nicolson and Joann Trautmann. New York: Harcourt Brace Jovanovich, 1975–1980.

———. *A Room of One's Own.* 1929. New York: Harcourt Brace Jovanovich, 1981.

————. *Three Guineas*. 1938. New York: Harcourt Brace Jovanovich, 1966.

————. *Women and Fiction: The Manuscript Versions of "A Room of One's Own."* Edited by S. P. Rosenbaum. Oxford: Blackwell, 1992.

Wrenn, Gregory J. "Comment: Federal Intellectual Property Protection for Computer Software Audio-Visual Look and Feel: The Lanham, Copyright and Patent Acts." *High Tech Law Journal* 4 (1989): 279.

Yankwich, Leon R. "Legal Protection of Ideas: A Judge's Approach." *Virginia Law Review* 43 (1957): 375–395.

Yasusada, Araki [Kent Johnson]. *Doubled Flowering: From the Notebooks of Araki Yasusada.* New York: Roof, 1997.

Yee, Nicholas. "The Blurring of Work and Play." *Daedalus Project* (July 9, 2004). http://www.nickyee.com/daedalus/archives/000819.php.

————. "The Demographics, Motivations and Derived Experiences of Users of Massively-Multiuser Online Graphical Environments." *Presence: Teleoperators and Virtual Environments* 15 (2006): 309–329.

————. "The Labor of Fun: How Video Games Blur the Boundaries of Work and Play." *Games and Culture* 1 (2006): 68–71.

Zimmerman, Diane. "Is There a Right to Have Something to Say?" *Fordham Law Review* 73 (2004): 297–375.

Zukofsky, Paul. "Copyright Notice by PZ." *Z-site: A Companion to the Works of Louis Zukofsky.* http://www.z-site.net/copyright-notice-by-pz.

Legal Cases

American Mutoscope & Biograph v. Edison, 137 F. 262 (C.C.D.N.J. 1905).

Barnes v. Miner, 122 F. 480 (C.C.S.D.N.Y. 1903).

Barsha v. Metro-Goldwyn-Mayer, 32 Cal. App. 2d 556, 90 P.2d 371 (1939).

Bobbs-Merrill Co. v. Straus, 147 F. 15, 19 (2d Cir. 1906), *aff'd*, 210 U.S. 339, 28 S. Ct. 722 (1908).

Broder v. Zeno, 88 F. 74 (C.C.N.D. Cal. 1898).

Burke v. National Broadcasting Co., 598 F.2d 688 (1st Cir. 1979).

CCH Canadian Ltd. v. Law Society of Upper Canada, [2004] 1 S.C.R. 339, 2004 SCC 13 (CanLII).

Chaplin v. Amador, 93 Cal. App. 358, 69 P. 544 (1928).

Chaplin v. Western Feature Prods., No. 103571 (Cal. Super. Ct. July 11, 1925).

Clancy v. Metro-Goldwyn Pictures, 37 U.S.P.Q. (BNA) 406 (S.D.N.Y. 1938).

Daly v. Palmer, 6 F. Cas. 1132 (C.C.S.D.N.Y. 1868).

Edison v. Edison Polyform Co., 67 A. 394 (N.J. Ch. 1907).

Eldred v. Ashcroft, 537 U.S. 186 (2003) 239 F.3d 372, *aff'd*.

Feist Publications v. Rural Telephone Co., 499 U.S. 340 (1991).

Fuller v. Bemis, 50 F. 926 (C.C.S.D.N.Y. 1892).

Golan v. Gonzales, 501 F.3d 1179, 1184 (10th Cir. 2007).

Golan v. Holder, 611 F. Supp. 2d 1165 (D. Colo. 2009).

Gottsberger v. Aldine Book Publishing Co., 33 F. 381 (C.C.D. Mass. 1887).

Grigsby v. Breckinridge, 2 Bush 480, 1867 WL 4043 (Ky. App. 1867).

Haelan Laboratories v. Topps Chewing Gum, 202 F.2d 868 (2d Cir. 1953).

Harper & Row v. Nation Enterprises, 723 F.2d 195 (2d Cir. 1983), *rev'd*, 471 U.S. 539 (1985).

Hayes v. Rule, 2005 WL 2136946 (M.D. N.C. 2005).

Hein v. Harris, 175 F. 875 (C.C.S.D.N.Y. 1910), *aff'd*, 183 Fed. 107 (2d Cir. 1923).

International News Service v. Associated Press, 248 U.S. 215 (1918).

Joyce v. Roth (N.Y. Sup. Ct. 1928).

Kramer v. Newman, 749 F. Supp. 542 (S.D.N.Y. 1990).

Kustoff v. Chaplin, 120 F.2d 551 (9th Cir. 1941).

Lahr v. Adell Chemical, 300 F.2d 256 (1st Cir. 1962).

The Letter Edged in Black Press, Inc. v. Public Building Commission of Chicago, 320 F. Supp. 1303 (1970).

Lone Ranger v. Cox, 124 F.2d 650 (4th Cir. 1942).

Lugosi v. Universal Pictures, 25 Cal. 3d 813, 603 P.2d 431 (1979).

Mackenzie v. Soden Mineral Springs Co., 18 N.Y.S. 240 (N.Y. Sup. Ct. 1891).

Manola v. Stevens & Myers, N.Y. Times, June 21, 1890, at 2 (N.Y. Sup. Ct. June 20, 1890).

Marks v. Jaffa, 26 N.Y.S. 908 (N.Y. City Super. Ct. 1893).

Martinetti v. Maguire, 16 F. Cas. 920 (C.C. Cal. 1867).

Marx Bros. v. United States, 96 F.2d 204 (9th Cir. 1938).

Midler v. Ford Motor Co., 849 F.2d 460 (9th Cir. 1988).

Milliken v. Bradley, 418 U.S. 717, 746 (1974).

Milliken v. Bradley, 433 U.S. 267, 280 (1977).

New Era Publications International, ApS v. Henry Holt and Company, Inc., 695 F. Supp. 1493 (S.D.N.Y. 1988), *aff'd*, 873 F.2d 576 (2d Cir. 1989), *cert. denied*, 493 U.S. 1094 (1990).

Newton v. Diamond, 204 F. Supp. 2d 1244 (C.D. Cal. 2002), *aff'd*, 349 F.3d 591 (9th Cir. 2003).

Northern Music Corp. v. King Record Distributing Co., et al. 105 F. Supp. 393 (S.D.N.Y. 1952).

Olmstead et al. v. United States, 277 U.S. 438, 471 (1928).

Pollard v. Photographic Co., 40 Ch. Div. 345 (Ch. Div. 1888).

Roberson v. Rochester Folding Box Company, 65 N.Y.S 1110 (N.Y. 1900).

Roy Export Co. v. Columbia Broadcasting System, 672 F.2d 1095 (2nd Cir. 1982).

Salinger v. Random House, Inc., and Ian Hamilton, 650 F. Supp. 413 (S.D.N.Y. 1986), *rev'd*, 811 F.2d 90, 96 (2d Cir. 1987), *cert. denied*, 484 U.S. 890 (1987).

Shloss v. Sweeney and the Estate of James Joyce, 515 F. Supp. 2d 1068, 1083, 1086 (N.D. Cal. 2007).

Supreme Records, Inc. v. Decca Records, Inc., 90 F. Supp. 90 (S.D. Cal. 1950).

Tempo Music v. Famous Music, 838 F. Supp. 162 (S.D.N.Y. 1993).

Théberge v. Galerie d'Art du Petit Champlain Inc., 2002 SCC 34, [2002] S.C.R. 336.

Tisi v. Patrick, 97 F. Supp. 2d 539 (S.D.N.Y. 2000).

Twin Books v. Walt Disney Co., 83 F. 3d 1162 (9th Cir. 1996).

Werckmeister v. American Lithographic Co., 134 F. 321, 325 (2d Cir. 1904).

White v. Kimmell, 193 F.2d 744, 746–747 (9th Cir. 1952).

White v. Samsung Electronics America, Inc., 971 F.2d 1395 (9th Cir. 1992).

Wood v. Lucy, Lady Duff-Gordon, 118 N.E. 214 (N.Y. 1917).

Wright v. Warner Books, Inc., 748 F. Supp. 105 (S.D.N.Y. 1990), *aff'd*, 953 F.2d 731 (2d Cir. 1991).

Contributors

Peter Decherney is an associate professor of cinema studies and English at the University of Pennsylvania. He is the author of *Hollywood and the Culture Elite: How the Movies Became American* and many articles on the Hollywood film industry, the history of media regulation, and fair use and academia, among other topics. In 2006, he and two colleagues successfully petitioned for an exemption to the Digital Millennium Copyright Act for media professors creating clips for teaching. He recently completed a new book on the history and future of Hollywood and copyright law.

Joanna Demers is an associate professor of musicology at the University of Southern California's Thornton School of Music. Her book *Steal This Music: How Intellectual Property Law Affects Musical Creativity* won the 2006 Book of the Year award from the Popular Culture Association. Her *Listening through the Noise: The Aesthetics of Experimental Electronic Music* was published by Oxford University Press in 2010. Demers also freelances as a forensic musicologist, assessing the legal dimensions of clients' musical borrowings and appropriations.

Catherine L. Fisk is the Chancellor's Professor of Law at the School of Law, University of California, Irvine. Fisk is the author of *Working Knowledge: Employee Innovation and the Rise of Corporate Intellectual Property, 1800–1930*. She is working on a book on attribution, human capital, and intellectual property in the twentieth-century employment relationship, an early installment of which was published in the *Georgetown Law Journal*. Fisk was previously on the faculties of Duke University and the University of Southern California.

Mark A. Fowler is a partner at Satterlee Stephens Burke & Burke LLP, where he represents publishers, broadcasters, cablecasters, digital media clients, and advertising agencies in defamation, intellectual property, antitrust, and reporters' rights matters. In addition to his litigation practice, he counsels media clients on a variety of issues and assists them with intellectual property transactions. Formerly a professional editor and writer, he has appeared on TV and radio talk shows in connection with his nonfiction books for general audiences.

He frequently lectures on copyright law, the First Amendment, and new legal issues affecting digital media.

Stanford G. Gann Jr. is the literary executor of the estate of Gertrude Stein. A native of Baltimore, he is a principal with the law firm of Levin & Gann, P.A., where he primarily handles and litigates construction, collection, property boundary, and bankruptcy matters. Gann represents a wide range of clients, including financial institutions, developers, local corporations, and individuals, and has lectured on mechanic's liens, collections, real estate, and many other subjects.

Elizabeth Townsend Gard is an associate professor, the co-director of the Tulane Center for Intellectual Property Law and Culture, and the director of the Usable Past Copyright Project at Tulane University Law School. Her research areas include podcasting the traditional classroom; *Second Life* and virtual property; and unpublished works and the public domain. She is currently developing the Durationator software to assist users in determining the copyright status of any given work across multiple national legal regimes. She is also completing work on a book, *The Making of the Great War Generation: A Comparative Biography*.

W. Ron Gard teaches American literature, theory, and writing at the University of New Orleans and is the associate director for legal and cultural theory on the Usable Past Copyright Project at Tulane Law School. His dissertation, "Bodies of Capital: Spatial Subjectivity in Twentieth-century U.S. Fiction," provides a theory of how subjectivity arises at the intersection of physical bodies and material space, a performative negotiation bound up with the economic forces shaping the sociospatial environment. He is currently exploring the racial implications of this theory through a reading of Colson Whitehead's novel *Apex Hides the Hurt*.

Oliver Gerland is an associate professor of theater at the University of Colorado, Boulder. After writing *A Freudian Poetics for Ibsen's Theatre: Repetition, Recollection and Paradox*, he became interested in copyright during a sabbatical year in Oxford and is currently at work on a systematic account of Anglo-American theater and copyright law. His work has appeared in *Theatre Journal, Modern Drama*, and *Mosaic: A Journal for the Interdisciplinary Study of Literature*.

Eric Hayot is a professor of comparative literature and the director of Asian studies at the Pennsylvania State University. He is the author of *Chinese Dreams: Pound, Brecht, Tel Quel* and *The Hypothetical Mandarin: Sympathy, Modernity, and Chinese Pain*. He and his co-author, Edward Wesp, have published essays about online virtual worlds in *Postmodern Culture, Comparative Literature Studies*, and *Game Studies*. His new project is on worldedness and modern literary history.

Celia Marshik is an associate professor of English at the State University of New York, Stony Brook. Marshik is the author of *British Modernism and Censorship;* her articles on G. B. Shaw, Virginia Woolf, Radclyffe Hall, and others have appeared in *Victorian Literature and Culture, Journal of Modern Literature, Modern Fiction Studies*, and *Yale Journal of Criticism*. Her present work focuses on clothing in the literature and culture of the 1920s, but her abiding interest remains the intersection between literature and the governing bodies responsible for forming and enforcing the law. She has been an officer of the International Virginia Woolf Society since 2006.

Mark Osteen, a professor of English and the director of film studies at Loyola University, Maryland, is the author of *The Economy of* Ulysses: *Making Both Ends Meet* and *American Magic and Dread: Don DeLillo's Dialogue with Culture.* He has edited two essay collections— *The New Economic Criticism* (with Martha Woodmansee) and *The Question of the Gift*— and has written several essays exploring the intersections between capitalism and originality. A veteran jazz musician, he has also edited a special double issue of *Genre* called *Blue Notes: Toward a New Jazz Discourse.*

Mary de Rachewiltz has been for over twenty years the curator of the Ezra Pound Archive in the Collection of American Literature at Yale University's Beinecke Rare Book and Manuscript Library. She has translated Pound's *Cantos* into Italian as well as *The Noh Plays, The Chinese Written Character,* and *Elektra.* The author of several volumes of original poetry and of the memoir *Discretions: Ezra Pound, Father and Teacher,* she continues to read and reread Pound and his sources.

Paul K. Saint-Amour is an associate professor of English at the University of Pennsylvania and has been a fellow at the Stanford Humanities Center, the Society for the Humanities at Cornell, and the National Humanities Center. His book *The Copywrights: Intellectual Property and the Literary Imagination* won the MLA prize for a first book. From 2004 to 2006, Saint-Amour chaired an International James Joyce Foundation fact-finding panel about the permissions history and criteria of the estate of James Joyce. He is currently at work on a book-length project entitled *Archive, Bomb, Civilian: Modernism in the Shadow of Total War.*

Carol Loeb Shloss, a professor of English at Stanford University, is the author of five books, most recently *Lucia Joyce: To Dance in the Wake.* She spent the 2007–2008 academic year as the Ellen Andrews Wright Senior Fellow at the Stanford Humanities Center, where she was also awarded a collaborative research grant to do further work on the unpublished letters of James Joyce. Shloss is currently writing the second volume of a trilogy entitled *Modernism's Daughters,* which explores the lives of Lucia Joyce, Mary de Rachewiltz, and Anna Freud alongside the problems of inheritance that modernism poses to succeeding generations.

Joseph R. Slaughter is an associate professor of English and comparative literature at Columbia University, where he teaches courses on modern African, Latin American, and Caribbean literatures, human rights, critical theory, and plagiarism. He is the author of the René Wellek Prize–winning book *Human Rights, Inc.: The World Novel, Narrative Form, and International Law,* which explores the formal and ideological relations between the bildungsroman's rise and the consolidation of human rights law. He is currently at work on *New Word Orders,* a study of the role of plagiarism and other forms of intellectual property theft in the development and globalization of the novel.

Robert Spoo is an associate professor of law at the University of Tulsa College of Law and has represented authors, scholars, documentary filmmakers, record companies, and other creators and users of intellectual property. Co-chair of the Modernist Studies Association Task Force on Fair Use, he acts as general counsel for the International James Joyce

Foundation. Prior to his legal career, Spoo taught in the English Department at the University of Tulsa, where he was the editor of *James Joyce Quarterly*. He has published numerous books and articles on James Joyce, Ezra Pound, and other modern literary figures and is currently working at the intersection of intellectual property, modernism, and the copyright-related needs of scholars.

Edward Wesp is an assistant professor of English at Western New England College. A scholar of narrative form in nineteenth-century American literature, he is currently at work on a study of the development of Hawthorne's literary aesthetics and has most recently contributed to the MLA collection *Approaches to Teaching Poe's Prose and Poetry*. Wesp's work with Eric Hayot on digital media has appeared in *Postmodern Culture, Comparative Literature Studies*, and *Game Studies*.

Index